SEVENTH EDITION

Thinking for Yourself

Developing Critical Thinking Skills
Through Reading and Writing

Marlys Mayfield

College of Alameda

THOMSON
™
WADSWORTH

Australia • Brazil • Canada • Mexico • Singapore • Spain
United Kingdom • United States

Thinking for Yourself:
Developing Critical Thinking Skills Through Reading and Writing, Seventh Edition
Marlys Mayfield

Publisher: *Michael Rosenberg*
Acquisitions Editor: *Stephen Dalphin*
Development Editor: *Cathlynn Richard Dodson*
Assistant Editor: *Cheryl Forman*
Technology Project Manager: *Joe Gallagher*
Managing Marketing Manager: *Mandee Eckersley*
Marketing Assistant: *Dawn Giovanniello*
Advertising Project Manager: *Patrick Rooney*
Associate Project Manager, Editorial Production: *Karen Stocz*

Senior Art Director: *Bruce Bond*
Print Buyer: *Betsy Donaghey*
Senior Permissions Editor: *Isabel Alves*
Text Designer: *Denise Hoffman*
Photo Manager: *Sheri Blaney*
Cover Designer: *Diane Levy*
Cover Printer: *Phoenix Color Corp.*
Compositor: *International Typesetting and Composition*
Printer: *Courier Westford*
Cover Art: *© Randy Lincks/Masterfile*

Library of Congress Control Number:
2006920847

Student Edition: ISBN 1-4130-1772-X

Thomson Higher Education
25 Thomson Place
Boston, MA 02210-1202

For more information about our products, contact us at:
Thomson Learning Academic Resource Center
1-800-423-0563

For permission to use material from this text or product, submit a request online at **http://www.thomsonrights.com**
Any additional questions about permissions can be submitted by e-mail to
thomsonrights@thomson.com

Credits appear on pages 406–408, which constitute a continuation of the copyright page.

BRIEF CONTENTS

CONTENTS

THE FAR SIDE® BY GARY LARSON

"Wait! Wait! Listen to me! ... We don't *have* to be just sheep!"

For over 20 years and through seven editions, this Gary Larson cartoon has appeared at the bow of the ship. For me this cartoon best explains critical thinking as a universal experience, a sudden awakening from passive collective trance into mental clarity, a sudden recognition of one's own choices and one's own power. Universal is also the yearning to rely on our own thinking and to find its assured, coherent, clear and convincing expression. The promise of *Thinking for Yourself* is all about this.

About the Text

This book originated in 1980 through some acts of waking up. I began to focus on the nagging dissatisfaction I had felt over fifteen years about teaching English composition. I could help my students edit their writing, but I could not help them improve what generated their writing: their thinking and perceiving. Nor, for that matter, did I know how to do that for myself.

As I set out to investigate this problem, I learned that other educators were beginning to talk about the possibility of teaching thinking; some were saying that thinking was a trainable skill, just like reading and writing. At that time we did not realize that we were on the edge of a high-spirited educational reform movement, one that would generate multiple conferences, academic debates, manifold research, new teacher training programs, new educational requirements, courses and textbooks.

In 1982 I started teaching a Critical Thinking/Composition course at the College of Alameda undeterred by the lack of suitable texts then available for this purpose. I prepared handouts of exercises and assignments, kept a class log, and wrote new materials each week in answer to student questions. My students' problems surprised me: they could not write argumentation because they did not know the differences between facts and inferences, between facts and opinions, facts and evaluations, reasons and conclusions. I discovered, moreover, that they had real difficulties understanding assumptions and could not identify political viewpoints. Gradually a text evolved based on what my students wanted and needed to know rather than on my own preconceptions about what they should already know. It took three years of writing, field-testing, and revising for me to produce the first edition that was released in 1986. The text was unique in that it served two purposes:

- To teach English composition by focusing on the perceiving-thinking process.
- To teach critical thinking through exercises in writing.

Twenty years later this book continues to flourish and evolve. My enthusiasm for this work has not diminished although the time required for growing each new edition can feel as burdensome as a mother elephant's pregnancy. Aside from writing, I do all of my own research in order to update the text, a job that requires following the news several hours a day. Three years ago this habit led me to think more about the importance of public media literacy, then design a new course called "On Being Well-Informed" for the College of Marin. The core content of this course appears in this edition as Appendix Two.

One complex challenge met in preparing each edition has been that of intuiting what topics and examples would remain timely over the next four years. Yet today, with the advent of Internet, a composition/reading text need not serve as a student's sole resource on current and controversial topics. Wadsworth, for instance, provides direct access to both InfoTrac College

Edition and Opposing Viewpoints. Nevertheless, it must be said that I share with my colleagues the worry that for many students, exposure to too many serious controversial topics can be overwhelming. Some days it may even appear that we are facing social, political, and environmental crises that have exceeded our capacities for understanding and coping. Our nation remains bitterly divided on approaches and solutions, with factions struggling for validation of their own values and priorities, their own familiar frames of reference. Yet for this very reason, if we would heal our divisions and work together toward common survival, we would seem to need critical thinking education more than ever. More than ever we need a common reference to the arbiter of critical thinking standards.

New to This Edition

For this edition eleven new readings were selected, eight new cartoons, eight new enigmatic photographs, and thirteen Internet research exercises. Some readings were chosen for their timeliness, others for their timelessness; each illustrates a chapter concept and each provides another step on a gradient of intellectual/ethical/motivational learning. In addition, the chapters on Assumptions, Argument, and Viewpoints have been revised and expanded to make them easier to teach and understand.

Entirely new to this edition is Appendix Two: Media Literacy, a short mini-chapter that can be integrated into the study of other chapters or left as an optional student reading. This section is about how to read the news, how to assess sources and information for reliability, and accomplish this all more efficiently. A second major innovation is a new Student Self-Study Website that contains multiple resources such as chapter overviews, self-grading chapter multiple-choice quizzes, a glossary of definitions, and web links. This website will continue to grow over time with the addition of other materials.

Text Use

This text is intended chiefly for use in the first, second, or third semester English composition university transfer courses. It also serves philosophy, social studies, and business instructors, as well as corporate trainers. More recently it has proved useful in providing a humanities component for students in two-year technical colleges.

Each edition seeks to offer more flexibility and teaching options. While the whole contains enough material for a two-quarter or two-semester course, instructors can tailor the material to fit the requirements of a one-quarter or one-semester course. Those instructors who need to emphasize composition can select from 58 assignments in this text. Those who want to emphasize critical reading have 40 selections to choose from, selections that also suggest additional writing assignments. Those planning to assign research papers will find detailed student guidance in Appendix One.

Approach and Coverage

1. The text offers the simplicity of an organization based on concepts, concepts which are familiar, yet often misunderstood, concepts which, when correctly understood, make critical thinking possible.

2. This text teaches both critical thinking and composition by emphasizing awareness of the personal thinking process. From the training of personal awareness, it moves to the more advanced stages of analyzing the thinking of others.

3. This book begins on a more fundamental level than most other critical thinking books, yet proceeds to a more advanced level than most, leading students to develop some highly sophisticated analytical skills applied to reading and writing.

4. The first half of the text works extensively with critical thinking in non–verbal problems, using photographs, cartoons, descriptive assignments, and report assignments. The second half moves into more traditional applications of critical thinking through verbal problems, analyses, and arguments.

5. The text constantly provokes its readers to think; indeed, they are obliged to think in order to work their way through the materials. Its problem and writing assignments require personal confrontations with thinking habits that might otherwise remain elusive.

6. In its style and pedagogy, the text shows consistent concern for the interaction of the cognitive and affective domains of learning. It also addresses directly the problems of distinguishing between feelings that clarify thinking and those that hinder thinking.

7. The text uses practical, everyday examples, connecting the concepts learned about thinking to everyday problems. Direct quotations concerning current political and social issues are used extensively to illustrate the ubiquity and influence of arguments in our lives. They also show our need for standards by which to judge them.

8. The text uses every means possible to assure student success. Discovery exercises encourage students to assess their own knowledge and discover key principles for themselves. The learning of new concepts is continuously reinforced through the use of summaries, quizzes,

and application assignments. Directions for writing assignments are designed to prevent confusion, while the scoring boxes clarify expectations and standards for grading.

Special Features

1. A study of the table of contents shows that Parts I and II cover basic material not usually presented in such depth in critical thinking texts, whereas Part III offers extensive treatment of the more traditional topics of critical thinking, such as argument, fallacies, inductive reasoning, and deductive reasoning.

2. Multiple tools for evaluating student progress appear in this edition. Each chapter ends with a summary and true-false chapter quiz for the purposes of oral review or written exams. Reviews of Learning Objectives appear at the end of each major section, and scoring boxes provide an opportunity for peer scoring of most composition assignments. The *Instructor's Manual* contains tests for Parts I and II; it also includes content questions and essay questions for each chapter; tests on dictionary skills; additional tests on fallacies, reasons, and conclusions; a model research take-home final; additional in-class final exams; a list of media resources, and a bibliography on teaching thinking skills. This manual is now available both in print and online.

3. This text offers three types of composition assignments. *The Composition Writing Applications* follow a progression of rhetorical complexity from description and narration through the longer research papers. *The Core Discovery Writing Applications* offer experiential understanding of the concepts and skills taught through the text. Each core application is designed to mirror thinking through the writing process, heighten self-awareness, and bring skill deficiencies to the surface. English instructors will want to focus on the core discovery applications as well as draw from the composition series and advanced composition assignments; those using this text for a critical thinking course may want to only use the core discovery applications. *The Advanced Composition Series* are designed for students who may need more challenging assignments. Writing assignments also may be selected from the questions that follow readings and Internet research exercises.

4. Multicultural viewpoints appear in the text's essays, short stories, and the boxed series on argument. Each reading selection expands on the concepts introduced in each chapter. Whether they appear in the form of fiction or essays, all are designed to stimulate thinking.

5. Internet research exercises are intended for a new generation of students comfortable with this medium; they allow the text to expand beyond its borders of space and time. The same may be said of the new Student Self-Study Website.

6. Argument building and analysis are the most complex skills taught in the text. For this reason, they are introduced through the Building Arguments series in each chapter, both preceding and following Chapter 9 Arguments. The first assignment requiring the writing of a short argument appears in Chapter 6 Opinions. The culmination of the whole series appears in Appendix One with two optional research assignments.

7. Appendix Two: Media Literacy may be assigned at any time during the course or left for optional student reading. The information that it provides on source evaluation can also be used to supplement Chapter 8 Viewpoints or in the preparation for writing research papers.

Acknowledgments

From all those who contributed to this new edition as it grew from 2004 to 2006, I wish to thank and dedicate this book to my students at the College of Marin and the National Center for Teaching Thinking.

Among individuals, my greatest appreciation goes to Stephen Dalphin, Acquisitions Editor at Thomson Wadsworth who also was shepherd for the text's fifth and sixth editions as published through Harcourt and Heinle; next I want to thank Cate R. Dodson, Developmental Editor, for her daily encouraging assistance. Above all I feel truly grateful to those colleagues and text adopters who gave me direct feedback during the last two years. They include Don Hongisto of *Merritt College*, Lillian Vallee of *Modesto Junior College*, Judy Wood of the *High Tech Institute* in Phoenix, Lee Cerling of the *University of Southern California*, Kathy Thompson of *Alverno College* and my colleagues at the *National Center for Teaching Thinking:* Robert Swartz, Barry Beyer, Robert Ennis, and Rita Hagevik. This book continues to draw from a collaboration of minds.

Thank you to the reviewers of the seventh edition: Deborah Jones, *High-Tech Institute, Phoenix, AZ;* Carmen Seppa, *Mesabi Community College, Virginia, MN;* Jerry Herman, *Laney College, Oakland, CA;* Alice Adams, *Glendale Community College, Glendale, AZ;* Cisley Stewart, *SUNY, Suffolk, NY;* and Joe McGarrity, *Corsicana College, Hammonton, NJ.*

The years spent writing these seven editions have brought me many devoted helpers and illuminating advisors. I would also like to thank the reviewers of the first three editions. They include Gary Christensen, *Macomb County Community College;* Robert Dees, *Orange Coast College;* Yvonne Frye,

Community College of Denver; Helen Gordon, *Bakersfield College*; Patricia Grignon, *Saddleback College*; Elizabeth Hanson-Smith, *California State University, Sacramento*; Ralph Jenkins, *Temple University*; Shelby Kipplen, *Michael J. Owens Technical College*; Eileen Lundy, *University of Texas, San Antonio*; Daniel Lynch, *La Guardia Community College*; L. J. McDoniel, *St. Louis Community College, Meramec*; Paul Olubas, *Southern Ohio College*; Sue Sixberry, *Mesabi Community College*; Patricia Smittle, *Santa Fe Community College*; Fran Bahr, *North Idaho College*; Charlene Doyon, *University of Lowell*; Carol Enns, *College of the Sequoias*; Jon Ford, *College of Alameda*; Nancy Glock, *California Community Colleges*; James Haule, *University of Texas, Pan American*; Jerry Herman, *Laney College*; Becky Patterson, *University of Alaska*; Suzette Schlapkohl, *Scottsdale Community College*; Pamela Spoto, *Shasta College*; and Mark Weinstein, *Montclair State College*.

Reviewers I wish to thank for the fourth edition include C. George Fry, *Lutheran College of Health Professions*; Adrienne Gosselin, *Cleveland State University*; Marilyn Hill, *American River College*; Susan A. Injejikian, *Glendale Community College*; Henry Nardone, *King's College*; Ronn Talbot Pelley, *City University*; and Edith Wollin, *North Seattle Community College*.

Reviewers for the fifth edition included Sandra G. Brown, *Ocean County College, Tom's River, New Jersey*; Dan Clurman, *Golden Gate University, San Francisco*; Maureen Girard, *Monterey Peninsula College, Monterey*; Elizabeth Nelson, *Tidewater Community College, Chesapeake*; Alice K. Perrey, *St. Charles County Community College, St. Peters, Missouri*; Jim Wallace, *King's College, Northeastern Pennsylvania*.

Reviewers for the sixth edition included Michael Berberich, *Galveston College*; Sandra Blakeman, *Hood College*; Maureen Girard, *Monterey Peninsula College*; David Lambert, *City College*, Kerri Morris, *University of Alaska, Anchorage*; Bruce Suttle, *Parkland College*.

I extend my gratitude to the staff of Thomson Wadsworth who gave so much devotion to the production of this project. Those with whom I had the most frequent contact over many months included Karen Stocz, Production Editor and Ben Kolstad, Editorial Services Manager of ITC. I wish also to extend special appreciation to my copy editor, Peggy Tropp, as well as the designer of this edition, Denise Hoffman.

Finally, I wish to thank my own personal assistant and former student, Patricia Leslie.

Marlys Mayfield

Introduction to Critical Thinking

NOTHING MUCH ON THE TUBE....
OH WELL, STILL BEATS THINKING.

Used with permission of John Grimes.

JOHN GRIMES

Learning How You Think

This is a book about thinking that will constantly require you to think. Sometimes you will be asked to think out problems for yourself before they are discussed either in the text or in class. In addition, you will always be asked to *observe the way you think* as you go. Discovery Exercises that introduce each chapter in this text will show you *how* you think. They will also help you discover some principles about thinking on your own.

Even this Introduction will begin with a Discovery Exercise. All students should complete it at the same time together in class before continuing to read in this book. After the whole class shares and discusses this exercise, you might each better appreciate the remainder of this Introduction, which discusses the attitudes needed to study critical thinking, a definition of critical thinking, and the habits and values of a critical thinker.

DISCOVERY EXERCISE

■ Experiencing How We Actually Think: An Exercise for the Whole Class to Complete Together

This is an exercise designed for thinking in two stages: first quietly alone and then only afterwards with others. Look at the photograph. Based on what you see there, rate each of the following statements as either *true*, *false*, or *can't answer*. Write your answers without discussing either the questions or your replies with anyone else.

_____ 1. This is graduation day for the Johnson family.
_____ 2. The parents are proud of their daughter.
_____ 3. The little brother is also proud.

_____ 4. This is a prosperous family.

_____ 5. This photo was taken on campus right after the ceremony.

When you have finished this quiz, wait, without talking to anyone else about your choices. Sharing too soon could spoil the results of this experiment. When all have finished, the instructor will poll your answers to each statement. Then you will be asked to break up into two or more groups to defend your answers. Each group will try to arrive at a consensus, functioning somewhat like a jury.

▪ *After the Discussion*

Review the following questions through discussion or writing. You will notice that some of these questions will already have been raised in your groups.

1. What are your definitions of the following terms?
   True   False   Can't Answer
2. Can a statement be rated *true* if it contains an assumption?
3. Is it possible to determine whether a written statement is *true* if it contains ambiguous words or phrases?
4. Should a statement be rated *true* if it is highly probable?
5. What makes a statement *true* or *false?*
6. Did you find yourself reluctant to choose the option of *can't answer?* Why or why not?
7. How can we know whether or not something is *true?*
8. What did this exercise teach you?

Learning from Sharing How We Think

A surprise can lead us to more learning.

Your work on this last assignment took you from thinking alone to thinking with others. You may have been surprised to discover that there were such different perceptions of a simple photograph.

If your discussion moved your thinking from certainty into uncertainty, you may feel somewhat confused or unsettled at this time. The term we will use for this unsettled state is *disequilibrium.* We feel this kind of discomfort when we need more time to integrate something unfamiliar. Moreover, we feel vulnerable when our thinking is exposed. Even in school, where we are committed to learning, it is not always easy to say "I don't know," "I am confused," or "I was wrong." We have to ascertain first if it is safe to be so honest.

Yet if we want to learn new skills, we have to be willing to feel awkward at times. We have to expose our thinking before we can review it. Such a process requires humility, sensitivity, kindness, and humor from everyone involved—from instructors as well as from students. Indeed, if we are not feeling awkward, we may not be really learning.

In review, this assignment was meant to remind you

- What occurs when you think on your own
- How we can further our thinking together in groups
- How such a process can teach us more about thinking

What Is Critical Thinking?

Critical thinking brings conscious awareness, skills, and standards to the process of observing, analyzing, reasoning, evaluating, reading, and communicating.

Thinking is purposeful mental activity.

Critical means to take something apart and analyze it on the basis of standards. The word *critical* comes from *skeri* (Anglo-Saxon) = to cut, separate, sift; and *kriterion* (Greek) = a standard for judging.

Standards of Critical Thinking

Clarity	Precision	Accuracy	Relevance
Completeness	Soundness	Reliability	Fairness

When we look up the word *thinking* in a dictionary, we find it covers nineteen different mental operations. These range from reasoning to solving problems, to conceiving and discovering ideas, to remembering, to daydreaming. Some of these forms are conscious and directed, whereas others seem to operate on their own without control or awareness. When we need to solve a math problem, we focus and concentrate. When we relax, thoughts and fantasies can come and go without direction. In this book, we will be using the word *thinking* in the sense of *purposeful mental activity*.

What, then, is critical thinking? Most of us associate the word *critical* with negativity or habitual fault-finding. Yet if we look at the history of the word, we can see that connotation was not in its original meaning.

The root of *critical* comes from *skeri,* which means to cut, separate, or sift; thus, its original idea was to take something apart or to analyze it. Moreover, *critical* is also related to the Greek word *kriterion,* which means a standard for judging. Putting together these two original ideas, we see that the word *critical* means *analyzing on the basis of a standard.* When we are negative and fault-finding, our standards are not clear, and our purpose is not that of developing reliable knowledge.

Dictionaries do not, as yet, define critical thinking, nor is there one definition that all teachers in this field can agree upon; today there are as many definitions of critical thinking as there are writers on the subject. But all would agree that critical thinking is a purposeful form of mental activity; many would agree that it involves learning conscious awareness of the thinking process itself. Finally, all agree that it is one guided by clear **standards.**

Now, what are the standards of critical thinking? They are the same intellectual standards scientists and scholars have used for centuries to evaluate the reliability of reasoning and information. They include clarity, accuracy, precision, consistency, relevance, reliability, soundness, completeness, and fairness. All these standards help us to aim for truth or to come as close to truth as we can.

When we study critical thinking, we gain **knowledge** of norms and rules for clear and effective thinking. The **norms** embody the standards; the **rules** help us measure them. Each chapter of this text explains norms through rules and examples that compare skilled to unskilled forms of thinking.

What is most difficult about learning critical thinking, however, is that it cannot be mastered through knowledge of norms and rules alone. Critical thinking is an active skill-building process, not a subject for passive academic study. We need to learn how to apply these standards to our own thinking and help others do the same. And when we accept the challenge of such learning, we go through a process of *unlearning* old habits while also acquiring better ones. Then gradually as we develop these new skills and habits, our knowledge of critical thinking becomes integrated into our lives.

As we work our way through this text, we will be learning both knowledge and skills in spirals of repetition and expansion. What we learn about knowledge and standards will better help us understand the skills required. And developing these skills will help us better appreciate the knowledge and standards required. Thus, we will progress through this text not like mountain climbers, but more like surfers. We will move forward by sometimes rising with the waves, sometimes falling, and sometimes balancing in wondrous new spirals.

> Critical thinking brings conscious awareness, skills, and standards to the process of observing, analyzing, reasoning, evaluating, reading, and communicating.

Relationship to Creative Thinking

> Critical thinking analyzes and evaluates given material; creative thinking invents something new.

It is beyond the scope of this book to teach creative thinking, but a brief comparison can help us understand critical thinking better. In brief, whereas critical thinking analyzes and evaluates ideas, creative thinking invents new ideas. To engage in critical thinking, we depend more on the brain's verbal, linear, logical, and analytical functions. Creative thinking also includes these functions but can rely even more on our intuitive-holistic-visual ways of knowing. In the past, these different functions were described as stemming from either the left or right hemispheres of the brain. Recent discoveries in neuroscience have called the simplicity of this distinction into question. Nonetheless, no matter how complex our brains may be, most of us would agree that we experience very different mental states when playing tennis, singing a song, writing a letter, or doing math. Moreover, some of us learn how to enhance our performance in these different activities through **heuristics**, or techniques that help us access the appropriate mental state.

In writing, for instance, we can draw from hidden reserves of creativity by using free writing or clustering. In order to do this, we need to maintain a more relaxed, nonjudgmental state of mind willing to *receive* whatever feelings, symbols, memories, or images may emerge. As we relate to this material, new patterns and insights may arise that would not have resulted from many hours of "hard thinking."

We think critically when we organize, edit, or outline the raw material gained from such a process. Yet we may need to return to a more creative mode of thinking, called **imagination**, should we sense the need to develop new ideas, spot assumptions, assume unfamiliar points of view, formulate multiple inferences, make predictions, and see consequences and implications. Afterwards we may return to analytical thinking again. Bit by bit through such a process, a final work may emerge from this synthesis of critical and creative thinking skills.

We learn to make more conscious use of our critical and creative thinking abilities as we respect their different ways of functioning. If we need to analyze a situation, we sit down in the posture of Rodin's statue *The Thinker,* remain still, and concentrate. When we need to think creatively, we maintain a quality of concentration while also listening to, and following, impulses from within ourselves that we might otherwise censor. Even when we stop concentrating—in deep sleep or while taking a walk—our minds can continue to work creatively on a problem. Once the process is complete, a fresh solution to a complex problem can occur in a sudden flash of insight; it can surprise us while we are doing something entirely mundane and unrelated, such as washing the car, patting a dog, or opening the refrigerator door.

While working with our creative and critical abilities, we need to remember that different standards apply. Critical thinking is concerned mainly with truth, while creative thinking also loves beauty; it wants its designs, ideas, or solutions to be not just adequate, but elegant. Albert Einstein was the model of a scientist who worked quite consciously with his capacities for both creative and critical thinking. He conceived theorems with a simplicity that proved to be both practical and beautiful. Einstein himself valued the creative process so highly that he once said, "Imagination is more important than knowledge."

If you are interested in learning more about the traits and skills of creative thinking, many good books are available such as *A Whack on the Side of the Head* by Roger Van Oech, *Creating Minds* by Howard Gardner, *Sparks of Genius* by Robert and Michele Root-Bernstein, and *Uncommon Genius* by Denise Shekerjian. In addition, Edward de Bono (whom you will meet in Chapter 5) has written dozens of books about creative thinking.

In this text you will also meet a number of authors who demonstrate well-integrated critical and creative thinking abilities. Such authors are able to develop original and complex ideas, yet present them with a simplicity that results from many hours of thinking and writing; such work can inspire their readers to think more deeply as well. Finally, most illustrate the virtues, values, and habits of critical thinkers as listed on the last page of this Introduction.

Why Learn Critical Thinking?

We already know how to do many complex kinds of thinking, for many purposes. All of us have developed our own way of solving problems, using "street smarts" and common sense or even trial and error. Yet what we already know can be substantially strengthened by conscious attention, just as those who already know how to walk or fight can greatly improve their abilities by studying dance or karate. This improvement comes from paying closer attention to what we already do, finding the right labels, and finding ways to do it better.

Critical thinking isn't the only form of clear thinking, nor is it always appropriate. If you are just hanging out, swapping stories, sharing feelings, speculating, the killjoy who demands that every term be defined, every fact be supported, every speculation be qualified is completely out of place. You don't use an electric saw to slice a roast, but when you do need an electric saw, it is invaluable.

Critical thinking skills are powerful tools. They can empower those who use them more than anything else you learn in college. They can't be picked up on the run; they require careful, disciplined, systematic study. But such study will pay off not only in the short run by improving performance in every single course, but also in the long run by

- Providing protection from manipulation and propaganda
- Helping you exercise more awareness and self-control
- Lessening the likelihood of making serious mistakes
- Helping you make better decisions
- Contributing to better decision making in groups

Although the study of critical thinking leads to mental independence, it is also a path to more productive work with others. It helps people to openly share the workings of their minds: to recognize and direct inner processes for understanding issues, to express ideas and beliefs, to make decisions, and to analyze and solve problems. Critical thinking allows us to welcome life's problems as challenges to be solved. And it gives us the confidence that we can make sense and harmony out of a confusing world.

The Habits of a Critical Thinker

Many of the habits depicted in the accompanying chart may already be part of your life; others may be as yet undeveloped. Because this book is about learning through your own discoveries, these habits will not be fully explained at this time. As you grow in your ability to recognize, monitor,

TABLE 1.1 Habits of a Critical Thinker

Awareness	Self-Control	Skills
• Observes self and others in the process of perceiving, thinking, and feeling • Observes and monitors own level of concentration and relative states of confusion or clarity	**Restrains impulses** • To stereotype, to jump to premature judgments and conclusions • To glance instead of observe • To hurry rather than stay present to what is needed • To not ask questions, take too much for granted, not verify information • To cover up mistakes and avoid what can feel difficult to confront **Stands by values** • To discover and express what is true • To be fair, reliable, respectful, and responsible • To seek truth before rightness • To be willing to admit mistakes • To be willing to concede to a better argument • To exercise courage	• Suspends judgment when appropriate • Listens and observes • Uses writing to improve thinking and get ideas across • Reads critically • Persists in gathering and understanding information, getting ideas across, and solving problems • Methodically separates facts from inferences, opinions, and evaluations • Checks for evidence and valid reasoning • Recognizes assumptions • Views content and viewpoint in terms of frame of reference • Uses words with precision and sensitivity to word definitions, connotations, slant, ambiguity • Can prepare a persuasive argument based on sound reasoning • Recognizes fallacies of reasoning • Recognizes unfair persuasion and propaganda

and reshape your own critical thinking habits, you will begin to assimilate your own list. Once you have finished studying this book, you might return to the habits listed here in order to see how far you have come.

The goal is now clear; the time has come to start down its path.

PART I

Basics of
Critical Thinking

CHAPTER 1

Observation Skills:

What's Out There?

"I was going so fast I figured it was better to keep my eyes on the road instead of the speedometer.

ANDERSON

Used with permission of Mark Anderson.

If we base our thinking on poor observations, then no matter how many strategies we devise, or how well we reason, that thinking will be faulty. A wise saying puts it more simply: "You don't have to stay awake at night to get ahead. All you have to do is stay awake in the daytime." This chapter consists mainly of exercises that require observing. The opening Discovery Exercises are designed to show you how *you* observe and how that may be different from the way others observe. Additional exercises are intended to help improve your ability to observe.

DISCOVERY EXERCISES

■ *Comparing Our Perceptions*

In class, write a one-paragraph description of the photograph below. Try to describe what you see in such a way that your readers will be able to visualize it without having the picture before them. Do not discuss your work with anyone else in class while you observe and write.

When you have finished, form small groups to read your descriptions aloud to one another. As you listen, notice in what details your descriptions are similar or different. When your group has finished, signal to the instructor that you are ready for a full class discussion of the following questions.

1. How can our differences be explained?
2. How can we know what is correct and what is not?

In completing this exercise, you may have discovered that what we first see from a glance can be quite different from what we discover when we actually *see*. You may have also discovered that we look for what is familiar, and if we can't find the familiar, we can even distort the unfamiliar to make it seem familiar. Thus, some telling details deemed irrelevant by some will seem highly relevant to others.

■ What Is Observing?

> To **observe** means to hold something in front of us.
> *ob* (Latin prefix) = in front of
> *servare* (Latin) = to keep, hold, watch, pay attention
>
> To **watch** is to stay awake.
> *waeccan* (Old English derived from Indo-European *weg*, meaning to stay strong) When we watch, therefore, we stay strong and awake.

The word **observe**, like other words that are the subjects of future chapters, is one that we hear and use every day. Therefore you might wonder why it needs defining at all. Let's hold that question until the following exercises are completed.

■ Observing a Cube

In this exercise, look at Figure 1.1. Observe the cube by watching it, looking at it intently, and staying "strong and awake" in your concentration. Then write down your answers to the following questions:

1. What happens to the cube as you observe it?
2. How does observing feel as you do it?

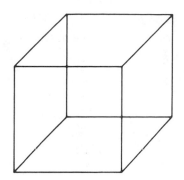

FIGURE 1.1 Observing a Cube

■ *Observation and Insight*

Carefully study the cartoons that appear in this chapter. For each one, notice and write down (1) what you have to notice in order to decode its meaning; (2) how you react when you "get it"; and (3) how you feel when you can't be sure what it is about.

Sidewalk Bubblegum ©1996 Clay Butler

Using Observation Skills to Develop New Knowledge

The beginning of science is the ability to be amazed by apparently simple things. (Noam Chomsky)

It is more convenient to assume that reality is similar to our preconceived ideas than to freshly observe what we have before our eyes. (Robert Fritz)

Those of you who discovered something new from these exercises learned because you observed in the true sense of staying awake and being closely attentive. Therefore you became aware of details, which a sweeping glance would have missed, that revealed significance about the whole. The following reading illustrates this process of learning. It is the story of a trial that a student went through that tested his capacity to do graduate research in science. Samuel H. Scudder (1837–1911) was an American naturalist who attended Lawrence Scientific School at Harvard, where he

Used with permission of Johr Heine.

studied under the great biologist (then called a naturalist) Professor Jean Louis R. Agassiz. Read carefully, for at the end you will be asked some questions followed by a writing exercise.

● R E A D I N G ●

Look at Your Fish

Samuel H. Scudder

It was more than fifteen years ago that I entered the laboratory of Professor Agassiz and told him I had enrolled my name in the Scientific School as a student of natural history. He asked me a few questions about my object in coming, my antecedents generally, the mode in which I afterwards proposed to use the knowledge I might acquire, and, finally, whether I wished to study any special branch. To the latter I replied that, while I wished to be well grounded in all departments of zoology, I purposed to devote myself specially to insects.

"When do you wish to begin?" he asked.

"Now," I replied.

This seemed to please him, and with an energetic "Very well!" he reached from a shelf a huge jar of specimens in yellow alcohol. "Take this fish," he said, "and look at it; we call it a haemulon; by and by I will ask what you have seen."

5　　　With that he left me, but in a moment returned with explicit instructions as to the care of the object entrusted to me.

"No man is fit to be a naturalist," he said, "who does not know how to take care of specimens."

I was to keep the fish before me in a tin tray and occasionally moisten the surface with alcohol from the jar, always taking care to replace the stopper tightly. These were not the days of ground-glass stoppers and elegantly shaped exhibition jars; all the old students will recall the huge neckless glass bottles with their leaky, wax-besmeared corks, half-eaten by insects and begrimed with cellar dust. Entomology was a cleaner science than ichthyology, but the example of the Professor, who had unhesitatingly plunged to the bottom of the jar to produce the fish, was infectious, and though this alcohol had a "very ancient and fishlike smell," I really dared not to show any aversion within these sacred precincts and treated the alcohol as though it were pure water. Still I was conscious of a passing feeling of disappointment, for gazing at a fish did not commend itself to an ardent entomologist. My friends at home, too, were annoyed when they discovered that no amount of eau-de-Cologne would drown the perfume that haunted me like a shadow.

In ten minutes I had seen all that could be seen in that fish, and started in search of the Professor—who had, however, left the Museum; and when I returned, after lingering over some of the odd animals stored in the upper apartment, my specimen was dry all over. I dashed the fluid over the fish as if to resuscitate the beast from a fainting fit and looked with anxiety for a return of the normal sloppy appearance. This little excitement over, nothing was to be done but to return to a steadfast gaze at my mute companion. Half an hour passed—an hour—another hour; the fish began to look loathsome. I turned it over and around, looked it in the face—ghastly; from behind, beneath, above, sideways, at a three-quarters' view—just as ghastly. I was in despair; at an early hour I concluded that lunch was necessary; so, with infinite relief, the fish was carefully replaced in the jar, and for an hour I was free.

On my return, I learned that Professor Agassiz had been at the Museum but had gone and would not return for several hours. My fellow students were too busy to be disturbed by continued conversation. Slowly I drew forth that hideous fish, and with a feeling of desperation again looked at it. I might not use a magnifying glass; instruments of all kinds were interdicted. My two hands, my two eyes, and the fish: it seemed a most limited field. I pushed my finger down its throat to feel how sharp the teeth were. I began to count the scales in the different rows, until I was convinced that that was nonsense. At last a happy thought struck me—I would draw the fish; and now with surprise I began to discover new features in the creature. Just then the Professor returned.

10   "That is right," said he; "a pencil is one of the best of eyes. I am glad to notice, too, that you keep your specimen wet and your bottle corked."

With these encouraging words, he added:

"Well, what is it like?"

He listened attentively to my brief rehearsal of the structure of parts whose names were still unknown to me; the fringed gill-arches and movable operculum; the pores of the head, fleshy lips and lidless eyes; the lateral line, the spinous fins and forked tail; the compressed and arched body. When I finished, he waited as if expecting more, and then, with an air of disappointment:

"You have not looked very carefully; why," he continued more earnestly, "you haven't even seen one of the most conspicuous features of the animal, which is as plainly before your eyes as the fish itself; look again, look again!" and he left me to my misery.

15   I was piqued; I was mortified. Still more of that wretched fish! But now I set myself to my task with a will and discovered one new thing after another, until I saw how just the Professor's criticism had been. The afternoon passed quickly; and when, toward its close, the Professor inquired:

"Do you see it yet?"

"No," I replied, "I am certain I do not, but I see how little I saw before."

"That is next best," said he, earnestly, "but I won't hear you now; put away your fish and go home; perhaps you will be ready with a better answer in the morning. I will examine you before you look at the fish."

This was disconcerting. Not only must I think of my fish all night, studying, without the object before me, what this unknown but most visible feature might be; but also, without reviewing my discoveries, I must give an exact account of them the next day. I had a bad memory; so I walked home by the Charles River in a distracted state, with my two perplexities.

20   The cordial greeting from the Professor the next morning was reassuring; here was a man who seemed to be quite as anxious as I that I should see for myself what he saw.

"Do you perhaps mean," I asked, "that the fish has symmetrical sides with paired organs?"

His thoroughly pleased "Of course! of course!" repaid the wakeful hours of the previous night. After he had discoursed most happily and enthusiastically—as he always did—upon the importance of this point, I ventured to ask what I should do next.

"Oh, look at your fish!" he said, and left me again to my own devices. In a little more than an hour he returned and heard my new catalogue.

"That is good, that is good," he repeated; "but that is not all; go on"; and so for three long days he placed that fish before my eyes, forbidding me to look at anything else, or to use any artificial aid. "Look, look, look," was his repeated injunction.

25   This was the best entomological lesson I ever had—a lesson whose influence has extended to the details of every subsequent study; a legacy the Professor had left to me, as he has left it to many others, of inestimable value, which we could not buy, with which we cannot part.

A year afterward, some of us were amusing ourselves with chalking outlandish beasts on the Museum blackboard. We drew prancing starfishes; frogs in mortal combat; hydra-headed worms; stately crawfishes, standing on their tails and bearing aloft umbrellas; and grotesque fishes with gaping mouths and staring eyes. The Professor came in shortly after and was as amused as any at our experiments. He looked at the fishes.

"Haemulons, every one of them," he said; "Mr. _____ drew them."

True; and to this day, if I attempt a fish, I can draw nothing but haemulons.

The fourth day, a second fish of the same group was placed beside the first, and I was bidden to point out the resemblances and differences between the two; another and another followed, until the entire family lay before me, and a whole legion of jars covered the table and surrounding shelves; the odor had become a pleasant perfume; and even now, the sight of an old, six-inch, worm-eaten cork brings fragrant memories.

30   The whole group of haemulons was thus brought in review; and whether engaged upon the dissection of the internal organs, the preparation and examination of the bony framework, or the description of the various parts, Agassiz's training in the method of observing facts and their orderly arrangement was ever accompanied by the urgent exhortation not to be content with them.

"Facts are stupid things," he would say, "until brought into connection with some general law."

At the end of eight months, it was almost with reluctance that I left these friends and turned to insects; but what I had gained by this outside experience has been of greater value than years of later investigation in my favorite groups.

●   ●   ●

Study/Writing/Discussion Questions

1. Why did Agassiz keep saying "Look at your fish!"? What was he trying to teach Scudder?

2. How would you describe the stages in Scudder's process of looking? What happened at each stage?

3. How did Scudder change personally in the course of his "trial"?

4. Explain why you think Agassiz's method of teaching was either effective or wasteful.

Core Discovery Writing Application

Creativity is piercing the mundane to find the marvelous. (Bill Moyers)

■ Observing the Familiar: Vegetable or Fruit

This is a demanding assignment; once you have finished, you might realize it provided an initiation experience comparable to that described by Scudder. If you are willing to commit to the task laid out in the following instructions, it can bring some surprising rewards. It will test your ability to "hang in there" despite cycles of discomfort. The only necessary prerequisite is a willingness to stretch your limits by spending *at least one hour in the process of observing and recording.*

You might have sufficient time to complete this assignment in class. However, it is more likely that your instructor will make this a home assignment. If that is the case, be sure to set up a place to work at home where you will not be distracted or interrupted.

■ Assignment Directions

1. First of all, set up your note sheets by drawing a line down the center of several pages to create two columns with these two headings:

Physical Details (what I observe and discover about the object)	Inner Process Details (what I observe and discover happening within myself as I work: my moods, reactions, associations, and thoughts)

2. Select as your subject one vegetable or fruit that you have seen and handled many times such as a sweet potato, an onion, a tomato, or an apple. Whatever you can find in your neighborhood grocery store or home refrigerator will do. It does not have to be an exotic mango or persimmon. Consider your selection to be your specimen for study just as Scudder worked with one fish.

3. Set up your workplace on your desk or a kitchen table. Perhaps you will want to have a knife and cutting board handy as well as some drawing paper for sketching.

4. Begin by really taking your time to explore this object. Let yourself become absorbed in the task like either a curious child or a dedicated scientist. As your mind slows down, your sensations will tell you more, and you will make more and more discoveries. Remember to

notice not only parts but also wholes, not only see but also touch, hear, smell, and taste. Whenever you become aware of a characteristic that you can articulate, write that down in the left column under "Physical Details."

5. Do not forget to use the right column for noting your personal reactions as you work. At what points did you become bored? Excited? Angry? Impatient? Lost in daydreams? Acknowledge these distractions by writing them down as you bring your attention back to the task of observing your object.

6. See how many times you need to renew your commitment to keep observing. Note all the stages of interest and concentration that you pass through: the plateaus, valleys, and peaks.

7. When you know for certain that you have finished, assemble your notes and prepare to write up a complete description of your fruit or vegetable.

8. Your final description may take one of two forms: (1) a report that describes the object completely with the addition of a final paragraph describing your own inner personal process, or (2) a narrative—or story of your observing process—that describes your object, the stages you went through, the progression of your discoveries, insights, and reactions.

9. Type up your final draft as a double-spaced paper. Suggested length is *at least two pages.*

● STUDENT WRITING EXAMPLE

This example is not offered as a model for you to imitate like a recipe. Rather, it is meant to demonstrate how one student became absorbed in his work and solved the problem of staying sensitive to his subject and himself at the same time. Read it as a reminder of what the assignment is asking you to do, then forget it and create your own paper by being true to your own experience. Remember that one purpose of this exercise is to help you discover your own observation style and biases.

MY PINK LADY

Noam Manor

It was late at night, and I was lying in bed trying to make up my mind about this assignment. It intimidated me. I felt that I was not creative enough, that my description skills were insufficient. I thought of my recent journey through the tropical countries of Central America where I could walk through produce markets where each booth was a work of art. I wish I could go back now and search for my chosen fruit; perhaps I would select a remarkable pineapple from the Mercado in Antigua or a lush mango from San Cristobal de la Casas. In an attempt to compensate for my frustration, I got out of bed hoping to accommodate an unexpected appetite. Without thinking too much, I picked up an apple from the produce bin and went back to bed. When I was getting ready to bite into it, I unpredictably halted. I looked at it very closely. I realized that the assignment was not about finding an impressive, striking piece of fruit, but about being able to slow down and patiently spend some time with it. The goal, as I saw it, was to communicate my discoveries and impressions.

The more time I spent with it, the more there was to see. I was intrigued. The apple was no longer an ordinary piece of fruit, but a whole world, an entire universe. I held it between my palms stroking it gently. I was flushed with a streaming feeling of comfort. I rolled the apple in my hand, rubbing it first against my face and then continued along my neck. It felt like smooth gold warmed by my body heat. It was slippery, almost like an ice cube threatening to melt away in between my fingers. I held it in my hand again, away from my body. It was warmer now. Its shape, temperature, size, and blood red color made me feel that I was holding a human heart. I set it on the bed and stepped back. Standing a few feet away, it looked perfectly round, the size of a baseball. It appeared as if two fingers indented a sphere on both ends. The two indentations were not identical; they reminded me of bellybuttons. I wrapped my left hand around it, and with my right hand, I rolled the apple back and forth. It made the sound of two bodies rubbing against each other, somewhere in between the sound of sandpaper working its way through a piece of wood and the sound of two large hands giving a massage. I tapped on it. Its skin rejected my plunk, generating the sound of a single handclap. I tapped on it once again, this time not stopping after hearing the sound of the handclap. It was possible to play rhythms on it as different parts of the apple produced different sounds. The thought of an innovative musician playing the "alto-apple" on a stage brought a smile to my face. The apple's color varied from light red grapefruit pink to scarlet. As I looked at it, I imagined the apple being picked from the tree by a highly skilled artist, who infused it using the full range of reds on her pallet. It had two yellowish green scars opposite each other and a couple of rotten brown bruises. I brought the apple very close to my face trying to get a better sense of its hues. Immeasurably small dots covered its entire surface. It made me think that I was looking through a microscope at a bright red strawberry, or at blood cells flowing through my veins. The apple's outer boundary was glossy, and the light coming from the corner of the room reflected in it. I started stroking the apple again. It had lost some of its warmth. Its texture suddenly felt unnatural, for it was covered with a generous layer of wax, which made my friend for the evening somewhat sticky. I closed my eyes and let the apple lay in my palm. It quickly equaled my body heat, and as the wax coating got warmer, the apple felt even stickier. I brought the apple close to my nose, so I could smell it. Its fragrance was clean and pure. It opened my airways. It reminded me of the scent of honeydew early in the morning in an ancient Redwood forest and the odor of bees producing honey in an apiary. When I licked its skin, I discovered that it was almost tasteless with a hint of sweetness.

The moment I dreaded had arrived. I hesitated to taste it because I had become attached. I could identify with the temptation Adam and Eve failed to resist. I closed my eyes and bit into it. Its flesh clung to my teeth while cool juice dripped into my mouth and sprayed my cheeks and my palm. It tasted like what an apple would taste like in Plato's World of Ideas. I felt that it was designed to represent the core and essence of its species. The juice was reminiscent of sweet alcoholic cider. When I was chewing it, it tried to resist my teeth. I could hear in my ears the sound of a boot stepping on thick snow covered with a thin layer of ice. I had to swallow it as the experience overwhelmed my senses. The flesh was now exposed. I felt it with my fingers and rubbed it against my bare bottom lip. It had the texture of soft sandpaper or a potato. I scraped off an ultrathin layer of the skin with my teeth. It barely had any flavor, and it had the texture of a leaf or a utilities bill. I realized that the skin was there only to protect the flesh, where the personality of the apple lies. I took another bite. The sweet-sour juice poured into my mouth. The recognizable harsh consistency of the skin was juxtaposed against the spongy flesh to create the unique flavor. Its reaction when I was chewing it made me feel that it was alive, that it was trying to resist me. The contrast between the bright colors of its skin and the yellowish-white flesh made it look naked to me. I kept eating the apple until its "skeleton" was entirely exposed. The remains of its flesh turned brown. The apple, which minutes earlier was beautiful, prideful, and appealing, seemed to be out of balance. It looked damaged, incomplete. As time passed, it became browner. The apple had small, tear-shaped, dark brown seeds hiding behind its ribs. They were stored in tiny, shallow cups. I once again looked at the remains of the apple. There was not much left but the indentations of my teeth.

I feel that this observation exercise helped me to achieve a breakthrough in my writing. I learned that there is always more to see and more to say. It taught me that the use of a dictionary and a thesaurus is extremely helpful. I was satisfied with the fact that I let emotions and spontaneous associations be part of my expression. I experienced the opening of some channels in my mind that had always been blocked. At no point during the observation process was I bored or fed up with it. On the contrary, it made me excited and jubilant that I could see things that I felt were beyond me.

Used with permission of Noam Manor.

Evaluating Your Work by Using the Scoring Boxes

The scoring box offers a simple, consistent checklist for reviewing the assignment's objectives, for understanding its priorities, and for clarifying standards for peer feedback, draft revision, and quite possibly, instructor grading.

A scoring box, like the one on the following page, follows each Writing Application Assignment in this book. The scoring box is intended to remind you of what thinking skills the assignment is intended to foster. For instance, you will notice that you are given 20 points for completing at least two full typed pages for this first assignment. In other words, if you only skim through this assignment, you will not have much to say, certainly not enough to fill two typed pages. Thus, these 20 points represent a reward for persevering in your observing long enough to produce that much material; it shows to what extent you stretched your capacities to observe.

If your typed draft comes to less than two pages, this could mean that you will need to return to your subject for another round of observing with note taking. Or it could mean that you only need to go over your notes again and reconsider what you discovered but did not fully explain.

Thus, the scoring boxes can serve first as a checklist to help you determine the strengths and weaknesses of your first draft. Second, they can be used in class to guide you and your classmates in assessing one another's work. If your peers give you some useful feedback in the form of low ratings in some areas, and if your instructor agrees, then you might want to give your draft another revision before submitting it for a grade. Finally, if your instructor so chooses, the boxes may serve as standards for the final grading of your paper. In summary, the scoring boxes have the following purposes:

1. To clarify each assignment's skill-building components
2. To clarify priorities and criteria
3. To clarify standards for a peer critical analysis that will take place in class
4. To enable you to turn in your best work for a grade

It needs to be emphasized that this evaluation technique is not intended to set up an arbitrary point grading system. Its most important purpose is to take more of the stress out of writing—for both students and instructors. The scoring boxes accomplish this by

1. Reminding you of the instructions' components
2. Keeping your attention on all of the instructions
3. Preventing wasted time from going off on the wrong track
4. Clarifying what priorities and standards you are expected to meet
5. Making it easy for your peers and instructor to judge your work with focus and fairness

Scoring for Description of Fruit or Vegetable
1. Minimum of two full pages. *20 points*
2. All senses used. *24 points* (3 points each)
Touch/texture	*Sound*
Taste	*Color*
Smell	*Shape*
Temperature	*Changes that occur during description*
3. Physical description at least 2/3 of paper. *10 points*
4. Language accuracy. *10 points*
5. Crucial aspects not omitted (skin, seeds, interior aspects, and design). *10 points*
6. Inner process described. *10 points*
7. No distracting errors of spelling, punctuation, or sentence structure. *16 points*

Alternate Core Discovery Writing Application

■ *Observing the Unfamiliar: A Tool*

Bring to class some household tool whose function may be unfamiliar or difficult for most people to identify. This could be a cooking implement, a highly specialized tool for some craft, a cosmetic tool, or any interesting item from your kitchen drawer or tool chest. Do not select anything that has sharp points or blades. Carry this object to class in a paper sack so that no one else can see it. Do not discuss what you have brought with anyone else.

Step 1　The instructor will ask you to exchange your bag with someone else. Sitting at your desk with your eyes closed, put the bag on your lap under your desk and take the object out of the bag quietly. Spend at least fifteen minutes exploring your subject with your hands, getting to know its shape and texture by touch. Set aside your concerns about how to label it. Your perceiving mind will want to categorize it immediately according to some mental stereotype. "Oh," it will say, "that is just a can opener. All can openers are the same. I know what this looks like already." When this happens, just notice what your mind is doing and go on exploring the object as though you were a child, enjoying its touch, its smell, temperature, and taste (if you dare!). *Remember, this is not a guessing game whose purpose is to label an object, but an exercise in gaining information about an object through your senses.* Get all the data you can without looking. Try to guess its color. Take notes as you go along.

Step 2 When the instructor gives the signal, put the tool on top of your desk and open your eyes. Notice and write down your first reaction. Now spend at least fifteen minutes observing the visual details of your object and taking more notes. Gather all the information you can now from seeing.

Step 3 After class, put all your information together and write at least a one-page typed description that enables readers to imagine the object. (You can also provide a drawing.) Organize your information so that the reader can follow your process of exploration. In a final paragraph, or as you go along, describe what it felt like for you as you worked. Were there different stages in your process? Did you feel frustrated and anxious if you couldn't label your object?

Scoring for the Tool Exercise

1. One full page minimum. *15 points*
2. Exploration of the following elements. *40 points* (5 points each)
   Temperature
   Texture
   Weight
   Smell
   General shape and parts
   Colors
   Sounds
   Visual design elements such as scratches, trademarks, thumbprints
3. Inferences or guesses regarding its function. *15 points*
4. Physical description complete. *10 points*
5. No distracting errors of spelling, punctuation, sentence structure. *10 points*
6. Personal process described. *10 points*

● STUDENT WRITING EXAMPLE

UNDERCOVER TOOL
Kenneth Wong

My partner handed me the brown paper bag that contained some unidentified tool. I placed the bag under my desk and reached inside, took it out, and dropped the bag to the floor. I immediately knew that what I was holding was a plastic disposable spoon. I was extremely disappointed that my partner did not take the time and effort to look for something more challenging. In my mind I imagined that she forgot to bring her tool and ran down to the cafeteria to see what she could scrounge up. Although I was displeased with my object, I decided to make the best of the situation. I began my investigation through touch. My first observation was that the tool felt smooth and concave. I thought it resembled the shape of a half lemon without all the pulp. Judging from the smoothness of the object, I imagined it to be as clean and glossy as glass. As I felt my way up the object, I noticed it had a stem extending from its head. The extension was also relatively smooth except for what appeared to be a border about 2 mm thick along its edges. I could also feel a rough surface on the hind side of the stem. I assumed it was an imprint of the manufacturer's name. I identified a "D" in the writing and continued to survey the rest of this new terrain. In a valiant attempt to entertain myself, I attempted to decipher the rest of the writing. However, I failed miserably. After exploring the head and stem, my mind went blank. I assumed that was all there was to know about this typical plastic spoon.

After sitting still for about a minute, I decided to continue my investigation. I began examining the object with greater precision and concentration. I tried flicking the object and noticed it made a peculiar "click." Then I tried flicking it harder and harder. The noise would get louder but the tone and pitch of the click remained constant. My action of flicking the spoon then made me notice its flexibility, which led me to conclude that it was definitely not made of metal. I also began feeling for warmth. The object wasn't cold; however, it wasn't exactly warm either. I knew then for sure that the object was made of flexible plastic.

My mind went numb again until I had another great idea. I began playing catch with the tool, still keeping it under the table, of course. I realized it was very light in weight, almost weightless. It had a very airy sensation. The tool landed in my palms gently and with great ease. Then I tried bending the object and realized it was not as flexible as I first had imagined. After a certain point the object felt suddenly stiffer as though it were about to snap: so I let go. I realized that this spoon was not as flexible as ones I had used before. It was much stronger and more solid. However, the longer I played with it, the more flexible it became. It also seemed to get warmer. I placed my thumb in the concave head of the spoon and left it there while I continued to examine the object with my other hand. When I released my thumb, I could feel that the tool was much warmer in that area. Then I remembered to smell the tool. I couldn't detect any scent I could describe, either of plastic or of food.

The fifteen-minute examination time was finally over, thank God. I was about to go out of my mind with boredom. I brought my spoon up to my eyes and immediately a rush of images flooded my head. Though I wasn't exactly surprised by the identity of my object, little things like the reflection that came off the shine of the spoon captured my attention. I was stunned by the piercing glow of its white plastic: its shimmering whiteness resembled strong sunlight reflecting off fresh snow. I now also saw small dents and scratches that my fingertips had not detected. The curves of the spoon were also more detailed than I had pictured. Next I flipped the spoon on its backside to see what had been written there. I read "DIXIE."

5   I took the object home for a closer examination, but I didn't notice any other features I had overlooked. However, I did use the plastic spoon to shoot roasted peanuts at my brother. The spoon later snapped when I tried shooting a peanut across my living room.

I realized afterwards that even though I didn't need my vision to discover the identity of my object, there was a lot in that tool that I would have overlooked if I had used my vision first. After spending so much time first depending on touch, the final use of my vision brought me into a heightened relationship to the tool. Truly then I was seeing the tool with my own eyes.

Reprinted with permission of Kenneth Wong.

The Observation Process: Sensing, Perceiving, Thinking

> When you can slow down sufficiently to experience the operation of your own sensing, perceiving, and thinking, then you can begin to use each faculty with more skill.

When you worked with your fruit, vegetable, or tool, you went through a process of collecting data, seeing patterns, and drawing conclusions. You used a process called **inductive reasoning.** If you observed your own mental processes as you proceeded in this simple task, you might have noticed that you went through different stages, using different skills.

So what are the parts of this process? When we take in data without preconceptions we are **sensing;** when we focus on particular sensations and categorize them according to our memory system, we are **perceiving;** and when we draw conclusions about their patterns and meaning, we are **thinking.**

Thinking

Thinking comes from the root Indo-European word *thong*, a word related to *thing*. When we think, we *thing-a-fy;* we make "things" of nature and events from our perceptions of them.

Perceive comes from the Latin word *percipere—per*, meaning thoroughly, and *capere*, meaning to catch, seize, or hold. When we perceive something, we catch and hold it in consciousness until we recognize patterns and find meaning.

Sensing comes from the Latin *sentire*, to feel.

Sensing occurs through sense organs such as the eyes and skin. When our sense organs become activated by stimuli—such as by a bright, warm light—they send this information through the nervous system to the brain. When we sense something, we *feel* it; we feel certain about the presence of something. As we sense, we may not yet have the words to identify or explain what is happening, because in order to find words, we have to think. *Yet, when we begin to think, we risk cutting ourselves off from our sensations.* We cannot fully sense and think at the same time. If we open the front door in the morning to sense how warm the day is, we have to stop thinking in order to sense the temperature of air on face and skin. If we want to truly hear music, we can't be absorbed in our thoughts.

In everyday speech, the word *perceiving* is often used loosely as a synonym for sensing, although there are distinct differences. Perception is both passive and active; it holds sensations in consciousness long enough to interpret them. This holding allows the time needed to find patterns, to organize, and to interpret the sensations. A study of Figure 1.2 will show you how your own perception operates to interpret space, dimension, and shape.

Perception helps us move through the physical world. When we are walking, we use perception to tell us the level of the surface below our feet; without perception, we would fall over curbs. Perception also helps us detect dimensions, telling us the difference between a lamp and its shadow. It enables us to identify sounds and estimate their location.

All of us sense, perceive, and think continually. But what is *thinking?* Philosopher Alan Watts uses the etymology of the word to show us how the earlier peoples (who gave us our language) explained thinking. The root word *thong* tells us that thinking is used to make "things" of nature and of events. We give a name to what we perceive, thus making it into a thing we can move around in our heads. A psychologist, Jean Piaget, defined thinking as "an active process whereby people organize their

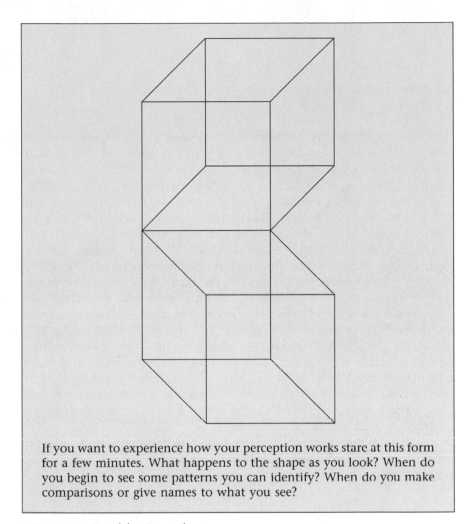

If you want to experience how your perception works stare at this form for a few minutes. What happens to the shape as you look? When do you begin to see some patterns you can identify? When do you make comparisons or give names to what you see?

FIGURE 1.2 Perceiving Perception

perceptions of the world." Both these definitions explain thinking in terms of what people do with their perceptions.

Our intention in studying these definitions has been to help us become more aware of the observing process. When we can match precise words to inner experience, we can better observe and think about that experience. We can monitor and direct what was previously unidentified and invisible. Its stages can be consciously directed as we

- Take in data (sensing)
- Interpret the data (perceiving)
- Draw conclusions and communicate (thinking)

Barriers to Observation

The barriers lie inside us.

Thinking is an active process whereby people organize their perceptions of the world. (Jean Piaget)

We can well empathize with Scudder's experience in learning how to observe. His first mistake was to hurry. ("In ten minutes I had seen all that could be seen in that fish.") All of us know how difficult it can be to slow down, especially when we value striving for speed and efficiency. Yet our senses require a much slower speed than our thinking in order to process information. Therefore the need to shift down can feel highly uncomfortable at first. It might even make us feel impatient, anxious, or irritable. Yet if we stay on task and simply observe our feelings, we may soon become absorbed in deep concentration. *One explanation for this phenomenon is that we have moved from left brain over into right brain dominance.* Here concern about time is lost; words are lost; there is just silence and presence. And at this point, we begin to make discoveries. Yet typically this exciting interval will continue for only about six minutes. Then we reach a plateau where nothing new emerges. Again we will feel restless. However, if we just hang in there or take a short break, a new cycle of interest will begin again, leading to new discoveries—until we reach another plateau. Yet as Scudder discovered, each time he returned to observing, a new cycle would begin, leading to additional understandings.

Like Scudder, our experiencing—even suffering through—such a process can teach us that we have a far greater capacity to discover than we knew; it can show us that we *can* rely more on ourselves.

Short Break Study Questions

1. Did you ever feel uncomfortable while working on either or both of these assignments? How did you handle your discomfort?
2. Discuss other examples taken from your own life, or those of others, where persistence in overcoming inner obstacles led to breakthroughs.

How Discomfort Leads Us to Think

In our daily lives, when we are presented with a problem, our first reaction may be one of denial and inertia. We may try first to explain this situation in a way that will not require any change or effort from us. Let's take the case of a young man who tries one job after another, only to always find himself bored or fired. He attributes his problem to bad luck.

As time goes by, if he continues to fail, he may begin to review his situation all over again. In short, he may really begin to think about it. Perhaps he might consider that more training or college would get him a better job. Should returning to school work for him, he will find himself feeling better. His thinking will have taken him out of a problem that was causing him more and more discomfort.

Let's look again at Jean Piaget's definition of thinking as "an active process whereby people organize their perceptions of the world." At one point, Piaget described this process as involving both **assimilation** (or easily inserting new data into an existing mental folder) and **accommodation** (or having to create a new folder). When we cannot grasp a new idea or make it fit with what we already know, we feel discomfort, or what Piaget called "disequilibrium." We may not even realize that this discomfort stems from our inability to assimilate that new idea. Indeed, we may blame something or someone else for our discomfort. But if we can create a new file drawer to rightly accommodate this new idea, we will then feel immediately better. Our equilibrium has been restored.

Should we run away from the problem, our discomfort will still remain there on a suppressed level. Basically, we human beings feel good when we can make sense of things, but uncomfortable when we don't (see Figure 1.3). And that discomfort can push us to think.

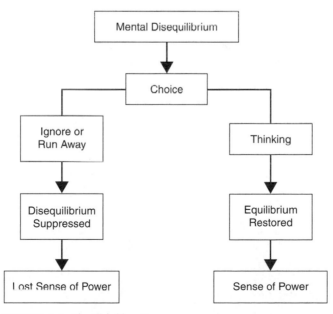

FIGURE 1.3 The Thinking Process

Building Arguments
Observation Skills

This is the first of a series called Building Arguments that runs through each chapter. Each is designed to show you how that chapter's concept applies to the construction of an argument. This chapter will help prepare you for Chapter 9 when you will need to integrate all you have learned from each chapter into the analysis and writing of arguments.

Here are some key terms related to arguments that you will need to understand:

Parts of an argument—An argument consists of two parts: a *principal claim* (also called a conclusion) and *reasons* that justify the claim or conclusion.

Principal claim is the thesis of an argument. It is the conclusion that the argument wants you to accept.

Reasons support or justify the principal claim through evidence or other claims. Observation skills furnish us with one form of evidence. (Other forms include records, testimony, and statistics.)

Hypotheses—When we observe, we collect data and form tentative ideas or *hypotheses* about the data's meaning. Notice how Christopher Columbus draws hypotheses from his journal observations made below.

> They came swimming to the ships' boats, where we were, and brought us parrots and cotton thread in balls, and spears and many other things. They all go naked as their mothers bore them . . . they were very well built, with very handsome bodies and very good faces. Their hair is coarse almost like the hairs of a horse's tail and short; they wear their hair down over their eyebrows, except for a few strands behind, which they wear long and never cut. Some of them are painted black, and they are the colour of the people of the Canaries, neither black nor white, and some of them are painted white and some red and some in any colour they can find. . . . They do not bear arms or know them, for I showed to them swords and they took them by the blade and cut themselves through ignorance. (So far all these sentences are claims presented as evidence gained from observation.) They should be good servants and of quick intelligence, since I see that they very soon say all that is said to them, and I believe that they would easily be made Christians, for it appeared to me that they had no creed (summary conclusions/ hypotheses).

From the *Journal of Christopher Columbus,* October 12, 1492.

Exercise

1. Give your reaction to Columbus's conclusion. What were the historical consequences?
2. What other possible hypotheses would have taken history in a totally different direction?

The Rewards of Skilled Observation

Sensitive, accurate observing is an essential skill of both scientists and artists. The following reading, "The Innocent Eye," is taken from a book on art design. This book consists of exercises for developing design perception and control. Dorr Bothwell, the painter who wrote this essay, was still exhibiting her works and winning national awards, until her death at the age of 98. Her essay serves as a reminder of what you may have already discovered—that although observing may require self-control and patience, it nevertheless can lead to the rapture, power, and wonder we feel when immersed in the creative process.

● R E A D I N G ●

The Innocent Eye

Dorr Bothwell

Creative observation of our surroundings revives in us a sense of the wonder of life. Much of this discovery involves the recovery of something that we all once had in childhood. When we were very young we were all artists. We all came into this world with the doors of perception wide open. Everything was a delightful surprise. Everything, at first, required the slow, loving touch of our tongues and our hands. Long before we could speak we knew the comfort of our mother's warm body, the delightful feel of a furry toy. Smooth and rough surfaces, things cold and hot, surprised and enchanted us. Touch by touch we built up our store of tactile impressions, keenly sensed in minute detail.

Later on, this tactile sensing was transferred to our eyes, and we were able to "feel" through the sense of vision things beyond the grasp of our hands. This kind of seeing was not the rapid sophisticated eye sweep of the well informed. This kind of seeing was a slow, uncritical examination in depth. The more we looked the more lovely and surprising things appeared, until we were pervaded by that wordless thrill which is the sense of wonder.

None of us has lost our store of tactile memories. Nor have we lost our sense of wonder. All that has happened is that we have substituted identifying and labeling, which can be done very rapidly, for the tactile sort of feel-seeing which requires much more time and concentration. For example, if you were asked to look at the edge of your desk and estimate its length, it would only take you a few seconds to flick your eyes back and forth and say it is so many inches long. But suppose you were asked to run the tip of your finger along the edge of the desk and count every tiny nick? You would press your finger along the edge and move it very, very slowly, and your eye would move no faster than your finger. This slow, concentrated way of feeling and seeing is the first step towards regaining our sense of wonder.

There was a time when man moved no faster than his feet or the feet of some animal that could carry him. During that period the artistic or creative spirit seemed to have free expression. Today, in order to be creative and yet move smoothly and efficiently through our fast-paced world, we must be able to function on two different speed levels. The mistake we have made, often with tragic results, is to try to do *all* our living at the speed our machines have imposed upon us.

5   In order to live at this speed we must scan the surface of things, pick out salient aspects, disregard secondary features; and there is certainly nothing wrong in this if we are driving on a busy freeway. But when we allow this pressure to invade every aspect of our life, we begin to "lose touch," to have a feeling that we are missing something, and we are hungry for we don't know what. When that happens, we have begun to suffer from aesthetic malnutrition. Fortunately, the cure for this condition is very pleasant, and although it takes a little self-discipline at the beginning, the results are worth the effort.

When we see as design artists, we become especially aware of the interaction between positive and negative space. In architecture we are suddenly aware of the spaces between the windows, at the ballet we notice how the spaces between the dancers open and close, and in music we realize that rhythm is made by the shapes of silence between the notes.

Everywhere we look we see this principle in action. Trees are not silhouetted against blank air, but hold blue spangles between their leaves while branches frame living shapes of sky. Space seems to be pulled between the leaves of a fern. We delight in the openings between the petals of a flower or the spokes of a wheel. This endless exchange between form and space excites us. Once more we feel in touch with our world; our aesthetic sense is being fed and we are comforted.

We may have been taught that butterflies are lovely and toads are ugly, so we admire the butterfly and shrink away from the toad without really examining it to find out if what we had been taught is true. Or we are taught that flowers are good and weeds are bad, so we pull up the latter without a glance. To the artist's eye there is no good or bad. There is just the inappropriate. In the garden, weeds are not appropriate, but in the vacant lot they offer a world of enchantment. And after we have learned to see the beauty in weeds, even though we have to pull them out of the garden, we can first admire their design.

When no preconceived ideas keep us from looking and we take all the time we need to really "feel" what we see—when we are able to do that—the universe opens up and we catch our breath in awe at the incredible complexity of design in the humblest things. It is only when this happens that we regain our sense of wonder.

From Dorr Bothwell and Marlys Mayfield, *Notan: The Dark Light Principle of Design*. New York: Dover, 1991. Used with permission of Dorr Bothwell.

● ● ●

FIGURE 1.4 Can you see in this design the interaction between positive and negative space described in "The Innocent Eye"? Is either less important than the other?

Study/Writing/Discussion Questions

1. Explain the statement, "When we were very young we were all artists."

2. Explain what the author means by the expression "aesthetic malnutrition" that comes from high-speed living.

3. Describe what is meant by the "interaction of positive and negative space." (See Figure 1.4.)

4. Explain what is meant by the statement, "To the artist's eye there is no good or bad. There is just the inappropriate." When you were writing your descriptions of objects, was there a feeling of dislike for the object that kept you from making contact with it fully? Did your attitude change as you continued to work?

Chapter Summary

1. If we want to develop more conscious thinking habits, we have to first observe our own thinking processes so we can recognize our strengths and weaknesses.

2. Careful observation can help us see details that contain the key to unlocking problems or arriving at insights. It can also help us discover new knowledge.

3. Observation is a process of sensing, perceiving, and thinking. Sensing is collecting data through the sense organs. Perceiving is holding sense data in consciousness until we can categorize and interpret it. Thinking organizes our perceptions.

4. Careful observation requires us to stay awake, take our time, give full attention, and suspend thinking in an attitude of listening.

5. The rewards of cultivating observation skills are self-understanding, creativity, rapture, power, and wonder.

Chapter Quiz

Rate each of the following statements as *true* or *false*. Justify your answer with an example or explanation to prove and illustrate your understanding. *Do not omit this part of the test.* True/false answers can be guessed. But when you defend your answer by example or explanation, you demonstrate not only your memory and understanding but also that you can apply what you have learned. The first question is answered for you.

FALSE   1. Observation skills are learned mainly through book learning. *Support for Answer:* On the contrary, observation is learned from participation, which is more active and spontaneous than reading. Samuel Scudder learned observing through the active coaching of his teacher Agassiz as well as from his own efforts, curiosity, and persistence in studying his fish.

_____   2. The standard academic study of all the physical sciences requires observation skills, whether in the field or laboratory.

_____   3. In thinking, the correctness of our conclusions usually depends on the clarity of our perceptions.

_____   4. Observation skills can be extended to observing how you observe.

_____   5. An insight is an experience of understanding that can occur spontaneously after we observe something intently for a while. One illustration of this experience is the story of Archimedes, who, while in his bath, discovered the means of measuring the volume of an irregular solid by the displacement of water.

_____   6. Agassiz was simply too busy to give his student all the assistance he needed.

_____   7. *Perception* and *sensation* are synonyms.

_____   8. It is difficult to feel sensation and to think at the same time. If we want to feel whether a pair of new shoes fits properly, we have to pay attention.

_____   9. *Assimilation,* according to Piaget, is an experience of easily understanding something that readily fits into our preexisting schemes or worldview.

_____ 10. The word *thinking,* according to the dictionary, has only one meaning.

Composition Writing Application

■ *Survival as a Result of Observing: A Descriptive Narrative Essay*

Describe an experience in which your safety, welfare, comfort, or survival depended upon your ability to observe a situation or problem clearly. This could involve a danger in city life, in camping, or in sports, or perhaps a life decision where observation skills were crucial. Write from three to five pages, telling your story as a narrative. Remember that the theme that should tie your story together is the theme of observation. Be sure to emphasize in your story where you observed and where you did not and what the consequences were.

▪ Review of Assignment Guidelines

1. *Form:* A story or narrative
2. *Theme:* How observation skills helped you survive
3. *Length:* Three to five typed pages or until you feel the story is complete

Scoring for Narrative Essay

1. Minimum of three typed pages. *20 points*
2. Story offers enough specifics to enable the reader to go through the experience. *20 points*
3. Story flows; the reader can follow it without difficulty. *10 points*
4. The language is accurate, appropriate, and appears carefully chosen. *10 points*
5. The use of observation skills is clearly a theme in the story. *25 points*
6. Free of errors in spelling, sentence structure, and punctuation. *15 points*

● R E A D I N G ●

Desert Solitaire

Edward Abbey (1925–1989)

This excerpt is taken from a chapter called "The Serpents of Paradise" in Desert Solitaire: A Season in the Wilderness, written in 1968, about the author's experience working as a park ranger in Arches National Monument in southeast Utah. About his work he said, "This is not primarily a book about the desert. I have striven above all for accuracy, since I believe that there is a kind of poetry, even a kind of truth, in simple fact." Note as you read how he uses his observation skills to record simple details and simple actions that evoke the world in which he lived.

As mentioned before, I share the housetrailer with a number of mice. I don't know how many but apparently only a few, perhaps a single family. They don't disturb me and are welcome to my crumbs and leavings. Where they came from, how they got into the trailer, how they survived before my arrival (for the trailer had been locked up for six months), these are puzzling matters I am not prepared to resolve. My only reservation concerning the mice is that they do attract rattlesnakes.

I'm sitting on my doorstep early one morning, facing the sun as usual, drinking coffee, when I happen to look down and see almost between my bare feet, only a couple of inches to the rear of my heels, the very thing I had in mind. No mistaking that wedgelike head, that tip of horny segmented tail peeping out of the coils. He's under the doorstep and in the shade where the ground and air remain very cold. In his sluggish condition he's not likely to strike unless I rouse him by some careless move of my own.

There's a revolver inside the trailer, a huge British Webley .45, loaded, but it's out of reach. Even if I had it in my hands I'd hesitate to blast a fellow creature at such close range, shooting between my own legs at a living target flat on solid rock thirty inches away. It would be like murder; and where would I set my coffee? My cherry-wood walking stick leans against the trailerhouse wall only a few feet away but I'm afraid that in leaning over for it I might stir up the rattler or spill some hot coffee on his scales.

Other considerations come to mind. Arches National Monument is meant to be among other things a sanctuary for wildlife—for all forms of wildlife. It is my duty as a park ranger to protect, preserve and defend all living things within the park boundaries, making no exceptions. Even if this were not the case, I have personal convictions to uphold. Ideals, you might say. I prefer not to kill animals. I'm a humanist; I'd rather kill a *man* than a snake.

5   What to do. I drink some more coffee and study the dormant reptile at my heels. It is not after all the mighty diamondback, *Crotalus atrox*, I'm confronted with but a smaller species known locally as the horny rattler or more precisely as the Faded Midget. An insulting name for a rattlesnake, which may explain the Faded Midget's alleged bad temper. But the name is apt: he is small and dusty-looking, with a little knob above each eye—the horns. His bite, though temporarily disabling, would not likely kill a full-grown man in normal health. Even so I don't really want him around. Am I to be compelled to put on boots or shoes every time I wish to step outside? The scorpions, tarantulas, centipedes, and black widows are nuisance enough.

I finish my coffee, lean back and swing my feet up and inside the doorway of the trailer. At once there is a buzzing sound from below and the rattler lifts his head from his coils, eyes brightening, and extends his narrow black tongue to test the air.

After thawing out my boots over the gas flame I pull them on and come back to the doorway. My visitor is still waiting beneath the doorstep, basking in the sun, fully alert. The trailerhouse has two doors. I leave by the other and get a long-handled spade out of the bed of the government pickup. With this tool I scoop the snake into the open. He strikes; I can hear the click of the fangs against steel, see the strain of venom. He wants to stand and fight, but I am patient; I insist on herding him well away from the trailer. On guard, head aloft—that evil slit-eyed weaving head shaped like the ace of spades—tail whirring, the rattler slithers sideways, retreating slowly before me until he reaches the shelter of a sandstone slab. He backs under it.

You better stay there, cousin, I warn him; if I catch you around the trailer again I'll chop your head off.

A week later he comes back. If not him, his twin brother. I spot him one morning under the trailer near the kitchen drain, waiting for a mouse. I have to keep my promise.

10　　This won't do. If there are midget rattlers in the area there may be diamondbacks too—five, six or seven feet long, thick as a man's wrist, dangerous. I don't want *them* camping under my home. It looks as though I'll have to trap the mice.

However, before being forced to take that step I am lucky enough to capture a gopher snake. Burning garbage one morning at the park dump, I see a long slender yellow-brown snake emerge from a mound of old tin cans and plastic picnic plates and take off down the sandy bed of a gulch. There is a burlap sack in the cab of the truck which I carry when plucking Kleenex flowers from the brush and cactus along the road; I grab that and my stick, run after the snake and corner it beneath the exposed roots of a bush. Making sure it's a gopher snake and not something less useful, I open the neck of the sack and with a great deal of coaxing and prodding get the snake into it. The gopher snake, *Drymarchon corais couperi,* or bull snake, has a reputation as the enemy of rattlesnakes, destroying or driving them away whenever encountered.

Hoping to domesticate this sleek, handsome and docile reptile, I release him inside the trailerhouse and keep him there for several days. Should I attempt to feed him? I decide against it—let him eat mice. What little water he may need can also be extracted from the flesh of his prey.

The gopher snake and I get along nicely. During the day he curls up like a cat in the warm corner behind the heater and at night he goes about his business. The mice, singularly quiet for a change, make themselves scarce. The snake is passive, apparently contented, and makes no resistance when I pick him up with my hands and drape him over an arm or around my neck. When I take him outside into the wind and sunshine his favorite place seems to be inside my shirt, where he wraps himself around my waist and rests on my belt. In this position he sometimes sticks his head out between shirt buttons for a survey of the weather, astonishing and delighting any tourists who may happen to be with me at the time. The scales of a snake are dry and smooth, quite pleasant to the touch. Being a cold-blooded creature, of course, he takes his temperature from that of the immediate environment—in this case my body.

We are compatible. From my point of view, friends. After a week of close association I turn him loose on the warm sandstone at my doorstep and leave for patrol of the park. At noon when I return he is gone. I search everywhere beneath, nearby and inside the trailerhouse, but my companion has disappeared. Has he left the area entirely or is he hiding somewhere close by? At any rate I am troubled no more by rattlesnakes under the door.

● ● ●

Study/Writing/Discussion Questions

1. How do observation skills protect the writer in this situation?
2. How does he combine his knowledge of animals together with his observation skills to anticipate future problems?
3. How does he use his observation and imagination together in order to find an unusual solution to his problem?
4. Why do you suppose he does not consider poisoning and trapping the mice or shooting the rattlesnakes one by one?
5. What values does he hold—and what aversions does he lack—that would enable him to enjoy this solution?

Optional Internet Research Assignment

1. Using a search engine such as Google, what more can you learn about the life and works of Edward Abbey?
2. Andy Goldsworthy is a British artist who produces ephemeral outdoor sculptures using natural materials such as snow, ice, leaves, bark, rock, clay, stones, feathers, fur, twigs, and petals. He describes his work as "collaborations with nature." By putting in a search under "Andy Goldsworthy" you can study his photographs of his sculptures that will enable you to see nature through this artist's eyes in a new way. You may also want to catch the film called *Rivers and Tides,* which demonstrates how Goldsworthy creates by continually observing.
3. Suppose you were promoted to become the manager of a retail clothing store. Make a list of all the things you would need to observe in order to do your job better. Consider your salespeople, your customers, the layout of the store, and other factors. After you have made your list, see if you can find additional tips by putting in an Internet search under "Observation Skills in Business". Report back your findings.

CHAPTER 2

Word Precision:
How Do I Describe It?

" *I liked it because you can read it with both the TV and the radio on.*"

Used with permission of Richard Guindon.

In order to share our experiences with others through writing, we need to give much thought to our choice of words. This chapter takes a close look at that process of translation. It will describe how

- Words interconnect with thinking and perceiving
- A good dictionary helps thinking

- Words are defined
- Words convey feelings
- Concepts abstract thought
- Critical reading works

This chapter cannot cover everything a college student needs to know about words. But when you have finished this chapter, you should know more about how well you actually work with words, how word confusion and word clarity affect your thinking, and how word precision can satisfy the spirit.

On Finding the Right Word

The search to find the right match between words and experience can lead to the learning of new words. Moreover, each new word that we master enables us to see even more of the world.

Looking back at your descriptive writing in the last chapter, you may have noticed that there were also different stages involved in your word search. The first was probably one of silent absorption. If words came to you at that time, they could have interfered with your sensing process. Nevertheless— once you were ready to write down your experiences—you may have been surprised to find yourself at a loss for words. You knew what you had seen or touched or felt, but you also realized that any word choices were only *translations* into another medium that might never fully duplicate your silent experience. It took persistence to continue searching for the words that would make your translation as true as possible to your experience. If you were describing an orange, you might have found that although you had held hundreds of oranges, you still could not describe its color, texture, smell, and taste. For instance, if you wrote down, "It tastes like an orange," you knew already that the word *orange* was inadequate. To erase this and write down "citrus flavor" would have been still more abstract, including the taste of lemons, grapefruit, and tangerines. You could have picked up the orange to taste it again, giving more studied awareness to your senses. This round of savoring could have summoned up such words as *sticky-sweet, tangy-flesh, spicy-warm*. If you still were not satisfied, you could have gone to *Random House Word Menu* or *Roget's International Thesaurus* and looked under the lists of words for *sweetness* and *sourness*, finding choices like *pungent, acidic,* and *fermented*. Here you would have also discovered more words to describe the colors in the orange's rind: *reddish-yellow, ocher, pumpkin, gold, apricot, carrot, yellow-orange, gilt, canary, beige, saffron, topaz-yellow, green, emerald, olive, chartreuse, nut-brown, fawn, rusty, bronze,* and *chestnut*.

Keeping an experience in mind as a constant, while searching both through word memory and thesaurus to find appropriate word correspondences, is a complex mental operation. Writing challenges you to stretch your abilities to use the words you know and to find new ones. Through this process you will move in time toward greater word mastery. Nevertheless, learning more words enables you to actually *see* more. To learn the words for things, you have to pay more attention to them. And once you recognize by name a Washington navel orange and a Valencia orange, you also perceive more of their details: the navels' shapes, the rinds' different textures, the subtleties of their shades of color. When someone offers you an orange, you enjoy appreciating its characteristics and talking about them, for your perception, together with your vocabulary, has enabled you to make finer differentiations. *The advantage of having a precise vocabulary to describe your experience is that it enables you to learn and experience even more.*

DISCOVERY EXERCISE

■ Taking an Interest in Dictionaries

Rate each of the following statements as *true* or *false*. Be prepared to defend your answers in writing or in a class discussion.

1. Dictionaries are like phone books; basically, they all offer the same information.
2. If a dictionary is named Webster's, that means it is one of the best.
3. Experts who decide how we should speak English write dictionaries.
4. Small, pocket dictionaries are the best kind to use for in-depth word study because they eliminate unnecessary, confusing information and make understanding easier.
5. Because a dictionary can confuse us with so many definitions for any single word, it is better to try to figure out a word's meaning from its context or ask someone else.
6. Dictionaries are like cookbooks; a family needs to buy only one for the family's lifetime.
7. Dictionaries give us information about spelling and definitions, but that is about all they offer.
8. An online dictionary is just as good for understanding and using a new word as a printed dictionary.

Here is a discussion of the correct answers. Read this only *after* you've completed the quiz.

1. *False.* A comparative study of several dictionaries—for instance, *The American Heritage Dictionary, Webster's Collegiate,* and *Webster's New World Dictionary*—will make this apparent.

2. *False*. Noah Webster was a nineteenth-century American lexicographer. The Merriam Company purchased the rights to his book and has continued, under the name Merriam-Webster, to publish and revise the large *Webster's New International Dictionary*. However, because the name Webster's is not protected by a copyright, many other companies have used it to put out both excellent and inferior products. The most prestigious and scientifically researched dictionary is the *Oxford English Dictionary*, bound in versions that range from two to twenty volumes.

3. *False*. Dictionaries serve as authoritative reference sources; however, they are not authoritative in the sense of being infallible but in the sense of offering reliable historical information about words and their use. In the case of *The American Heritage Dictionary*, this information is based on the opinions of a panel of lexicographers, linguists, writers, and scientists. Dictionaries are not written to dictate dogma but only to reflect agreements and standards about how people use their language, in both popular speech and formal writing.

4. *False*. Pocket dictionaries may be more convenient to carry and use for understanding simpler words or spellings, but they are too condensed for use in the more serious study of word ideas, concepts, and usage. Moreover, their definitions can sometimes be oversimplified to the point of being misleading. Finally, and more obviously, a pocket dictionary containing 30,000 words cannot offer you as much as an unabridged dictionary with 600,000 words or a college desk-sized one with 60,000 words.

5. *False*. Although most study skill texts suggest this, and most English composition-reading texts select the vocabulary for you, a guess based on your view of the context may be mistaken, and your friend may be even more confused than you. The result may be the need to "unlearn" a misunderstood word later. If you are skilled in dictionary use, it is not a chore to confirm a guess or a friend's definition by consulting the dictionary. Furthermore, certainty about a word's meaning can enable you to cement it more confidently into your memory.

6. *False*. If your dictionary is more than fifteen years old, it is time to buy a new one. The English language acquires or invents thousands of new words each year, and our customs about word usage change also.

7. *False*. It's worth spending a little time just browsing through your dictionary to find out all it has to offer. You'll find a concise history of the English language, for one thing.

8. *True and False*. Some online dictionaries have all the limitations of pocket dictionaries. For completeness, *Merriam-Webster Online* is one of the best; it even includes etymological information. One drawback to online dictionaries is that because you can only search for one word at a time, you cannot learn from browsing.

How Well Do You Use Your Dictionary?

Bring to class a college desk-sized dictionary. If you need to buy one, the following are recommended. These are comprehensive, hardcover, up-to-date dictionaries that will help you through all your college courses.

- *The American Heritage College Dictionary*, Fourth Edition (Houghton Mifflin, 2002)
- *Webster's New World College Dictionary*, Fourth Edition (John Wiley & Sons, 1999)

Working with a partner, take turns finding three random entries to discuss. Explain to your partner every piece of information that you find there, including every symbol and every abbreviation. If you do not understand something, take the time to look it up. (If, for instance, you do not understand what is meant by the abbreviation *OF,* find out where your dictionary explains its abbreviations.) Work together to understand *all* the information given, and do not let one another off the hook until you sense everything interpreted is fully understood.

Finally, one of you should write down your answers to the following questions:

1. State the name of the dictionary you own and its date of publication. How many pages does it have? How many entries are there? Is it a desk-sized dictionary?

2. Test your knowledge of the history of the English language by explaining what your dictionary means when it refers to a word as *Anglo-Saxon* or *Middle English, Late Latin,* and *Indo-European.*

3. Look up *Pago Pago.* Write down how it is pronounced. Pronounce it for your partner.

4. Have you ever discovered that you had misunderstood a familiar word and were misusing it? Give an example and explain how you found out.

5. How does the word *plan* differ from the words *design, project,* and *scheme?* The *Webster's New World Dictionary* will explain how they differ in connotation. What are word connotations, and why are they important to consider when you make your selection?

6. Describe the mental signals that show you, in dictionary study, that you have fully understood a new word. Do you usually persist in word study until you have these signals?

7. If you can't find a word or clear definition of a word in one dictionary, do you usually consult another dictionary? Explain why or why not.

8. Describe situations in which you might use a thesaurus.

9. Compare the advantages of using an electronic handheld dictionary to a pocket print dictionary. What are the advantages of online dictionaries? Explain why you might prefer electronic to print media, or vice versa.

Clear Thinking Depends on Clear Word Definitions

Confusion about words affects not only our communications but also our alertness and consciousness. We can be confused about not only unfamiliar words but also familiar ones.

Clear thinking and expression depend on clear word understanding. Yet, as obvious as this idea may seem, word clarity is not necessarily common. It takes dedication and some effort to truly understand all the words that pass through your day. Yet the effort need not be so great if you can establish two simple habits:

1. Pay attention to the inner discomfort that indicates you have not fully understood a word.

2. Take the time to clear things up.

Word confusion stands out more in conversation than in reading. If a friend were to say you were *contumacious,* you would have to ask what that word meant before you could respond. However, in reading it can be easier to ride over word confusion, just as it is in listening to radio or television. Moreover, a person can be just as confused about familiar words as unfamiliar ones. Unfamiliar words are easier to recognize, such as when we first hear the word *factoid;* however, we may not realize that there's more to learn about the meaning of the word *fact.* This text is organized, in terms of its chapter headings, around words that describe the thinking process; although these are ordinary words, they are, nevertheless, subject to much confusion. In the previous chapter much attention was given to defining such words as *observing, perceiving, sensing,* and *thinking.*

Dictionaries are your most reliable resources for the study of words. Yet the habit of using them needs to be cultivated. Of course it can feel like an annoying interruption to stop your reading and look up a word. You might tell yourself that if you keep going, you would eventually understand it from the context. Indeed, reading study guides often advise just that. However, should understanding not occur, you will find yourself soon becoming drowsy. Often it's not the need for sleep that is occurring but a gradual loss of consciousness. The knack here is to recognize the early signs of word confusion before drowsiness takes over when it is easier to exert sufficient willpower to grab a dictionary for word study. Although this special effort is needed, once the meaning is clarified, the perceptible sense of relief makes the effort worthwhile. You may need to refer to more than one dictionary, diagram the word, or use it in sentences. But when you have finished you will find yourself more alert, with a renewed energy for continuing your work.

The definitions of key concepts in every chapter of this text are designed to emphasize the importance of gaining better word-understanding habits. However, you will also come across many unfamiliar words as you read this textbook. *It will remain your responsibility to use the dictionary to understand any unfamiliar words that you may find while reading this textbook and thus to reinforce this important critical thinking habit. Your instructor might even require that you keep a vocabulary notebook for this purpose.*

What Makes a Definition?

Definitions clarify words through boundaries.

The etymology, or history, of the word **definition** shows us something interesting. It comes from the Latin roots *de,* meaning off or away from, and *finis,* meaning end or boundary; the Latin word *definire* means to set bounds to. So when we *define* something, we discover or establish its boundaries. When we learn a new word, the definition shows us what boundaries separate it from every other word. For example, let's take the word *cheesecake.* If we only go for its meaning as a dessert, we see (Figure 2.1) how it can be defined through four boundaries that classify the word:

Baked desserts
Cakes that resemble pies
Egg-based, not flour-based, with crumb crust
Sweetened cottage or cream cheese as chief ingredient

In a definition, the word to be defined is called a **term.** Every term can be included in a **class,** or the largest family to which it is related within this particular boundary. Thus the term *cake* belongs in the class of baked desserts whose boundaries also include baked custard or baked Alaska. In addition, cheesecake has three other distinguishing characteristics, which create smaller boundaries that gradually separate it from every

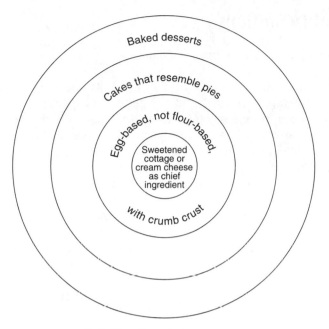

FIGURE 2.1 Definition Boundaries

other kind of baked dessert. Thus, when we define a thing, we methodically set it apart from everything else.

EXERCISE

Word Boundaries

Set up a piece of paper with three columns headed *Term, Class,* and *Characteristics*. Look up each of the words, list the class and characteristics, and diagram the boundaries as we did for *cheesecake*.

Example

Term	Class	Characteristics
1. Scissors	A cutting tool	Has two blades, each with a loop handle, joined by a swivel pin
2. Mailbag		
3. Moppet		
4. November		
5. Pneumonia		
6. Cat		

Kinds of Definitions

Not all definitions are dictionary definitions.

When you looked up the word *cat,* you probably found it described as a mammal of the family felidae, or of the genus and species *Felis catus.* This taxonomic description indicates the boundaries that differentiate cats from all other animals. The cat family includes lions and tigers as well as house cats, while a particular breed name distinguishes a Siamese from a Persian cat. The rules that govern this system of classification are based on a science called **taxonomy.** This science, established by an international commission, enables us to know what *agreements* have been made to identify all plants and animals so that no two can be confused. Just as taxonomy helps us distinguish one living thing from another, **dictionary definitions** describe terms according to the boundaries established by shared and separate characteristics. Both taxonomy and dictionary definitions owe their value to agreements that everyone can refer to.

This is especially important for **scientific definitions**, which remain more fixed than other kinds of definitions because they are specific and technical. Nurses or medical students who study the heart have to learn definitions of words such as *aorta, atrium, diastole,* and *endocardium.* Indeed, a large part of scientific training is word training in a vocabulary handed down from one decade to the next.

At the other extreme are **stipulative definitions** based on individual or group agreements. The term *middle class* no longer has any commonly agreed-upon meaning in the United States. Most Americans call themselves middle class whether they live in a mansion or a trailer. When considering a tax cut in 1995, the Democrats made a *stipulative* definition of the middle class as making up to $75,000 a year, whereas the Republicans set that amount at $200,000. Other commentators suggested that middle class could be better defined in terms of financial stability rather than income, and the debate continues. Other terms with stipulative definitions based on agreements include *functional illiteracy, disability,* and *sexual harassment.* In all these cases, definitions need to be established for reasons such as law, research, or policy implementation. In these instances, dictionary definitions are not of much use.

Definitions can also be **inventive**, describing previously unrecognized ideas, categories, or concepts. A new term *neuromarketing,* for instance, refers to new marketing methods based on laboratory studies of human brain responses to ads, brands, and cultural messages. Another inventive term is *echo boomers*, coined to describe the children of the "baby boomers" born in the 1980s and 1990s. Carl Jensen, a journalism professor at Sonoma State University, invented the term *junk-food news* to describe "sensationalized, personalized, and homogenized inconsequential trivia that is served up to the public on a daily basis." He gives examples of show business and celebrity stories, the stock market's ups and downs, fads, crazes and murders, anniversaries of events, and news about people in sports and politics.

People can also take familiar concepts and give them **personal definitions.** Consider this definition of the common word *hope* that Václav Havel derived from five years spent in prison for resisting the Soviet occupation. (After his release, he became the first president of the Czech Republic.)

> The kind of hope I often think about (especially in situations that are particularly hopeless, such as prison) I understand as a state of mind, not a state of the world . . . it is a dimension of the soul . . . an orientation of the spirit, an orientation of the heart; it transcends the world immediately experienced, and is anchored somewhere beyond its horizons. Hope . . . is an ability to work for something because it is good, not just because it stands a chance to succeed. The more unpropitious the situation in which we demonstrate hope, the deeper that hope is. Hope is definitely not the same thing as optimism. It is not the conviction that something will turn out well, but the certainty that something makes sense, regardless of how it turns out. (*Disturbing Peace*, 1990, p. 181)

"I don't know what you mean by 'glory,'" Alice said.

Humpty Dumpty smiled contemptuously. "Of course you don't—till I tell you. I meant 'there's a nice knock-down argument for you!'"

"But 'glory' doesn't mean 'a nice knock-down argument,'" Alice objected.

"When *I* use a word," Humpty Dumpty said in rather a scornful tone, "it means just what I choose it to mean—neither more nor less."

"The question is," said Alice, "whether you *can* make words mean so many different things."

"The question is," said Humpty Dumpty, "which is to be master—that's all."

(Lewis Carroll, *Through the Looking Glass*)

Definitions may also be **poetic** and **whimsical**, like "Happiness is a commute before the rush hour," or **philosophical**, like "Death is the invisible companion of life." Below this level are **eccentric** definitions that disregard the kind of agreements that make communication possible. A classic dialogue illustrating the eccentric definition takes place between Alice and Humpty Dumpty in Lewis Carroll's *Through the Looking Glass.*

A final category of definitions might be called **persuasive definitions.** These are definitions that advocate an opinion. Examples of these would be such statements as the following: "A state lottery is a form of voluntary taxation." "A state lottery is stealing from the poor." "Abortion is murder." "Women deserve the right to choose." All these equations are opinions offered as though they were given truths in order to win others over to the same opinion. Obviously, they are far removed from dictionary definitions.

The Connotations of Words

Word connotations are about feelings.

An important aspect of definitions is the **connotations** of words or the *associations* that they suggest to us. These associations can evoke reactions, images, emotions, or thoughts. For instance, let's take the word *snake.* The *denotation* of this word, or its literal meaning, is a reptile without legs. There it is: simply a "thing," nothing to get excited about. But for many people the word *snake* carries many negative connotations, such as being slimy, treacherous, poisonous, or evil. These common reactions can nevertheless be overcome through conscious familiarity with snakes.

Do dictionaries explain connotations? Not in the case of the snake, where such connotations are universally understood. A few, but not all, dictionaries help us understand the connotations a defined word carries by discussing subtle differences among its synonyms. For instance, if you look up the word *lying* in the *Webster's New World Dictionary of the American Language,* you will find explanations of the connotative differences among *lie, prevaricate, equivocate,* and *fib.* If you were to arrange these synonyms on a scale of their potential for emotional impact, *lying* would be at the top and *fibbing* at the bottom.

Class Discussion

1. Explain the meaning of and connotative differences among *disinformation, misspeaking,* and *falsifying.*
2. Make a list of synonyms for *cheating,* and rank their connotations as negative, positive, neutral, or phony neutral (a euphemism that hides a true negative meaning).
3. Repeat the procedure for the word *stealing.*

In later chapters of this book we will look at how connotations show our judgments of things and how they can be used to manipulate others to accept the same evaluations. But for now, simply consider connotations in your word choices and reading by asking questions or by dictionary study.

"*Miscegenation*. The word is humpbacked, ugly, portending a monstrous outcome: like antebellum or octoroon, it evokes images of another era, a distant world of horsewhips and flames, dead magnolias and crumbling porticos. In 1960, the year that my parents were married, *miscegenation* still described a felony in over half the states in the Union." (Barack Obama, Democratic Senator from Illinois, *Dreams of My Father: A Story of Race and Inheritance*, 2004, p. 11)

The Importance of Defining Key Ideas

Both study and debate need to begin with clear definitions.

The French philosopher Voltaire once said, "If you would argue with me, first define your terms." What he was talking about was not arguing in the sense of quarreling but in the sense of persuasive reasoning. He did not say *how* terms should be defined but that one should be very clear about what one has decided that key ideas mean. For example, if you want to argue in defense of the unregulated use of drugs, you should first define what you mean by *drugs*. Do you mean aspirin, or heroin, or both? How you define the term affects not only what you include within your boundaries to consider but also what remains outside to ignore. Undefined words have to be confronted sooner or later, and that is better done by you than by your opponent, because an argument based on undefined words collapses when challenged.

Clear definitions are an essential part of all fields of learning. For example, in law, definitions help juries decide the difference between *crimes* and *misdemeanors,* between *sanity* and *insanity*. In public affairs, debates over definitions can generate controversy, as has become the case with the meaning of the word *privacy*. In addition, definitions comprise a large part of any subject of learning. If you study political science, you have to begin by asking what the familiar word *political* really means. From that point, you can move into learning more unfamiliar words like *plebiscite*. In order to study our terms, we must study more than one dictionary and use each well, beginning always with a good desk-sized college dictionary. Unfortunately, many students have already formed the habit of only using pocket dictionaries that are helpful for spelling, but not always helpful for understanding a word's meaning. Indeed, their terse definitions can be so oversimplified as to create misunderstandings. However, not all full-sized dictionaries are equally well written. Therefore it is desirable to have some knowledge about what kinds of dictionaries there are, including electronic versions, as well as having the skills to explore and evaluate each one.

Word Concepts

Concepts abstract experience.

> **Concept:** A word that organizes and abstracts a body of related experience; a general idea. From the Latin *conceptus,* meaning a thing conceived.

The study of critical thinking begins with a review of many concepts. Each chapter of this book is titled by a concept. The word *concept* comes from the Latin *conceptus,* a thing conceived, suggesting a mental creation. Concepts convey abstractions of experience from the past such as *pluralism, aristocracy,* and *hegemony,* or they convey new ideas such as *sustainability, postmodern,* and *ergonomics.* Learning the key concepts from any field of learning comprises an important part of higher education. If we want to study economics, we begin by learning the difference between microeconomics and macroeconomics. Concepts help us make distinctions, as between a *heuristic* and an *algorithm* in problem solving. Concept learning not only conveys complex ideas but also enables us to talk about them.

If we want to truly understand new concepts, it can be helpful to begin with the word's etymology or history, with its earliest root idea. This idea can give us a concrete sense of the word's original conception. Traditional aids for concept study are encyclopedias, textbooks, and books written by leading thinkers in their special fields of knowledge. Yet even scholars cannot always agree on the definition of a term. *Critical thinking,* as mentioned earlier, has as many definitions as people who write on the subject or teach it. Yet each definition contributes to a dialogue that eventually will reach consensus as to which boundaries this new field of study should include or exclude.

Defining terms is a dynamic process in any field of learning. And there are some words that challenge each new generation. Two of these words, *truth* and *reality,* are discussed in boxes on these pages. They are both ordinary but profound words; they both remain elusive, yet they are the standards for measuring our ways of knowing and proceeding in the world and for thinking critically about the world. However, before going on to these terms, one example will serve to show how the grasp of a concept can totally change a person's life. In the *Narrative of the Life of Frederick Douglass,* first published in 1845, its author tells the story of how he was born into bondage on an American plantation. As a young man, he secretly taught himself to read and write (a crime punishable by death), then gradually made his escape into freedom and a life of renown.

> I often found myself regretting my own existence and wishing myself dead; and but for the hope of being free, I have no doubt but that I should have killed myself, or done something for which I should have been killed. While in this state of mind, I was eager to hear any one speak of slavery. I was a ready listener. Every little while, I could hear something about the abolitionists. It was some time before I found what the word meant. If a slave ran away and succeeded in getting clear, or if a slave killed his master, set fire to a barn, or did anything very wrong in the mind of a slaveholder, it was spoken of as the fruit of *abolition.* Hearing the word in this connection very often, I set about learning what it meant. The dictionary afforded me little or no help. I found it was "the act of abolishing;" but then I did not know what was to be abolished. Here I was perplexed. I did not dare to ask anyone about its meaning, for I was satisfied that it was something they wanted me to know very little about. After a patient waiting, I got one of our city papers, containing an account of the number of petitions from the north, praying for the abolition of slavery in the District of Columbia, and of the slave trade between the States. From this time I understood the words abolition and abolitionist, and always drew near when that word was spoken, expecting to hear something of importance to myself and fellow-slaves. The light broke in upon me by degrees.

Defining Reality

Reality comes from the Latin word *res,* which means thing, property, or possession. Related to *res* is *reri,* which means to reason and from which we derive the words *reason, ratio,* and *realize.* The past participle of *reri* is *ratus,* which means fixed by calculation or established for certain. The ideas etymologically involved in the word *reality* therefore involve reasoning and certainty. Here is what other noted thinkers have said about reality:

Everything flows. (Heraclitus, Greek philosopher)

The world was created by the word of God so that what is seen was made out of things which do not appear. (St. Paul)

Reality is what we bump against. (William James, American psychologist)

Reality is something as it actually is, independent of our thoughts about how it is. (Mortimer J. Adler, American philosopher)

Reality is an unknown and undefinable totality of flux that is the ground of all things and of the process of thought itself, as well as the movement of intelligent perception. (David Bohm, philosopher and physicist)

Defining Truth

The word *true* comes from the Old English form *troewe,* which means loyal or trustworthy, which in turn comes from the Indo-European base *deru,* meaning firm, solid, or steadfast. Related to the base word *deru* is *dru,* meaning firm as a tree or hard as wood. This etymology suggests that *truth* is something as hard and firm and as steadfast as a tree or its wood. Here are some definitions and descriptions of truth:

> *Truth suggests conformity with the facts or with reality, either as an idealized abstraction ("What is truth?" said jesting Pilate) or in actual application to statements, ideas, acts, etc. ("There is no truth in that rumor.")* (The American Heritage Dictionary)

> *Truth is a correspondence or agreement between our minds and reality.* (Mortimer J. Adler)

> *The ordinary mode of language is very unsuitable for discussing questions of truth and falsity, because it tends to treat each truth as a separate fragment that is essentially fixed and static in its nature. . . . However, truth and falsity have to be seen from moment to moment, in an act of perception of a very high order.* (David Bohm)

> *Truth is what stands the test of experience.* (Albert Einstein)

What Is Critical Reading?

Critical reading begins with a resolve to aim for a neutral and accurate comprehension of the material.

When we read a detective story, we enjoy getting lost in another world; when we read a training manual, we follow and memorize. In both cases, we rarely question what we read. Such reading is like boarding a bus; we get on and we get off. However, if we were to apply this attitude to newspaper reading (or watching TV news), we would always believe—or doubt—the last thing we read or heard. A critical reader does not soak up information like a sponge but interacts and asks questions based on clear standards that assess information reliability.

Yet critical reading cannot *begin* with these questions but rather with making sure that our reading has been accurate—that we have not substituted words and ideas not there, nor misunderstood ideas that were there. This first phase then requires an *attitude of receptivity.* The problem is that remaining receptive is not easy when the topic goes against our own experiences, opinions, and beliefs. If we strongly disagree with what we read—or hear—it can actually feel painful to remain attentive or true to the goal of faithfully recording the message, regardless of our opinions. Yet we cannot adequately respond to any material that we have not correctly understood. Thus the *critical reading phase* of challenging and questioning has to wait until we have achieved a faithful reconstruction of the information given. And achieving accurate comprehension can take more than one reading and include the use of a dictionary.

In reading this book you will not always feel receptive to the different viewpoints it presents. When an argument goes against our beliefs and values, we cannot help reacting. Many psychological studies have shown that in reading we tend to accept the views we already hold and minimize those we do not. Thus exercising control over our biases in order to maintain neutrality, even on issues we favor, can be a struggle. It may help to remember that perfect neutrality is rarely achieved. At best, we might only be able to admit to our biases and restrain our habitual personal reactions. Objectivity need not mean that we have changed what we feel; it does mean that we can set aside our prior convictions in order to make the effort to hear, read, and understand exactly what is being told to us. Thus, only when the material has been accurately understood can the critical reading phase truly begin. This second stage also cannot be hurried; it is a slow and careful process led by questions. Again we return to the definition of *critical,* whose original idea was to *sift* and *separate*. When one reads critically, one studies and reflects in order to sift words and ideas. When we become critical too soon, we lose the focus needed to make an accurate reading. And a criticism of information or arguments based on an inaccurate reading is a waste of time.

As you study each chapter of this book, you will be considering some key questions designed to help you critically assess information. The content of this Word Skills chapter can be summed up in four questions:

- Am I making the best word choice?
- Do I fully understand this word or concept?
- Is this word well defined?
- What are the connotations of this word?

The reading selections offered in this text are intended to stimulate critical thinking. You are encouraged to read each selection at least twice— once for comprehension and once for critical interaction. The study/writing/ discussion questions are intended to take you to deeper stages of critical analysis. Remember also to consult your dictionary regularly as you read, and write down your questions. As you follow these steps, you will find that your reading has become an active thinking endeavor.

Building Arguments
Word Choices

When we make a **claim**, each word appearing in the claim needs careful thought and definition. (*"If you would argue with me, first define your terms."* Voltaire) Word choices vary according to the values and purposes of the speaker. Notice how this author uses his definition of *Indians* to sway others to accept his beliefs.

Mr. Baily:

With the narrative enclosed, I subjoin some observations with regard to the animals, vulgarly called Indians. (definition of key term)

In the United States Magazine in the year 1777, I published a dissertation denying them to have a right in the soil. (principal claim, conclusion, or thesis)

The whole of this earth was given to man, and all descendants of Adam have a right to share it equally. There is no right of primogeniture in the laws of nature and of nations. (moral reasoning made through further claims to back principal claim)

What use do these ringed, streaked, spotted and speckled cattle make of the soil? Do they till it? Revelation said to man, "Thou shalt till the ground." . . . I would as soon admit a right in the buffalo to grant lands, as in Killbuck, the Big Cat, the Big Dog, or any of the ragged wretches that are called chiefs. . . . What would you think of going to a big lick or place where the beasts collect to lick saline nitrous earth and water, and addressing yourself to a great buffalo to grant you land? (analogy used to support principal claim) (H. H. Brackenridge, 1782)

Exercise

1. The issue here is whether Indians should have the right to their land. What is the author's claim on this issue?

2. How does the author use his definition of Indians to help his argument?

3. What reasoning does he offer to prove Indians are not human?

4. What is *primogeniture?*

5. What is unfair about this argument?

6. Write a one-paragraph argument in which you make a claim about anything. Give either a neutral or a controversial definition of your key term or subject. Then offer two reasons to support your definition.

Chapter Summary

1. An accurate use of words improves our thinking. Words give form to our thoughts so that we can make use of them. Words enable us to communicate with others and ourselves. Knowing the words for things and experiences helps us see and perceive more.

2. Writing helps us learn more about words and how to use them. When we struggle to select words that will describe our experiences, we realize that words are only *translations* of experience and not the experience itself.

3. Clear thinking depends on a clear understanding of the words we use. Word confusion leads to less consciousness, or disequilibrium, which can only be restored through word clarification.

4. We need to understand what dictionaries can and cannot offer us; we need to use them skillfully and frequently.

5. The thesaurus helps us when we are writing and translating nonverbal experiences and ideas into words; the dictionary helps us when we are reading and interpreting the words of others.

6. Definitions set boundaries for word ideas and show us their specific and general characteristics and how they are related to or distinguished from one another.

7. Dictionary definitions show us the agreements that society has made about a word's meaning. But we may also compose our own personal or stipulative definitions of experiences or compose persuasive definitions to sway the opinions of others. In critical thinking it is important not to confuse these different kinds of definitions, or to believe that personal, persuasive, or stipulative definitions carry the same agreements as those found in a dictionary.

8. The test of our understanding of a word is our ability to define it. This ability is particularly important for words representing key ideas that we wish to explain or defend. Taking the time to define the words we use is an essential preliminary to genuine communication.

9. A study of a word's etymology can help us trace a word back to its earliest root idea and can give us an image that conveys a more concrete sense of the word's logic. Learning a word's etymology can also help us recognize its relationship to other words with the same root meanings.

10. The connotations of a word are its associative meanings, which can be positive, negative, or neutral. These associations can take the form of feelings, ideas, images, or thoughts. Thus, although politicians might rarely admit to *lying* or being *confused*, it is quite acceptable for them to admit they *misspoke*.

11. The first stage of critical reading is objective receptivity to the material; this means having the technical ability as well as the willingness to accurately reproduce its content without alterations or distortions. If we question and interact with material that we have not accurately interpreted, our criticisms will not be fair or worthwhile.

Chapter Quiz

Rate each of the following statements as *true* or *false*. To answer some of these questions, you will need to consult your dictionary.

_____ 1. When Frederick Douglass grasped the concept of abolition, he understood it was possible for him to become free.

_____ 2. Words can be used to do a better or worse job of describing experiences but can never be more than translations of the experiences themselves.

_____ 3. A dictionary can help us think better when we use it to clear up word confusion.

_____ 4. Definitions of a word show the word's boundaries.

_____ 5. Knowing the words for things helps us see them better.

_____ 6. We do not fully understand a word unless we can define it.

_____ 7. When people debate a topic, understanding is greatly helped by their taking the time to define the key terms.

_____ 8. Etymology gives us word histories.

_____ 9. Pocket dictionaries are sufficient guides for a critical study of word meanings.

_____ 10. The word *ohm* comes from the Sanskrit language and means the sound of creation.

_____ 11. According to most dictionaries, there is more than one acceptable spelling of the word *cooperate*.

_____ 12. The term *French leave* means to say good-bye with a big kiss.

_____ 13. The prefix *in* in the words *insignificant* and *inflammable* means *not* in Latin.

_____ 14. The following words all contain the sound called a *schwa: mass, polite, placement, bogus, visible.*

_____ 15. The word *nausea* can be pronounced at least three different ways.

_____ 16. The word *round* can function as six different parts of speech: adjective, noun, transitive and intransitive verb, adverb, and preposition.

_____ 17. *Egregious* comes from a Latin word meaning standing out from the herd.

_____ 18. The word *nadir* in the phrase "the nadir of politics" means the highest point.

_____ 19. A *cogent* argument is a convincing one.

_____ 20. The word *decimate* means to dice something up into pieces.

Composition Writing Application

■ A Short Essay of Definition

Write an essay based on an extended definition or full discussion of a word or phrase supported by examples. It should also be an **essay of exposition,** which is a form of writing that explains something. In this case you will want to explain your definition fully through stories, examples, or specific information.

The thinking tasks of making definitions followed by explanations play a frequent part in our daily conversations. If you are having a conversation with a friend and say, "She just isn't mature," your friend may reply, "What do you mean by *mature?*" Thus, you are challenged to respond with a definition together with an explanation of how you use that term.

The directions for this assignment, and for all the other writing assignments in this book, are designed to make you conscious of the thinking elements involved in solving it as a given problem, much like a problem in mathematics. However, you must follow the instructions exactly as they define its parameters.

Summary of Instructions for This Assignment

1. *Objective:* To give your own definition of a word and to explain that word's meaning through your own experience.

2. *Form and length:* At least one typed page.

3. *Structure:* Begin with a topic sentence and end with a conclusion.

Step 1 Suppose you choose as your topic defining *adult.* Think of what the word has come to mean to you in your own life. Think about how you have heard others use this word. Look up its definition in several dictionaries. Now turn back to the diagram of the word *cheesecake.* Draw and define the boundaries for the word *adult* using dictionary definitions or whatever you can add in terms of your own experience.

Step 2 Now try *clustering* with the word *adult.* Clustering (or mapping) is a warm-up exercise that invites both hemispheres of the brain to work with

Clustering

To begin **clustering**, place an oval in the center of a page and write your key word inside that oval. Focus on that word. As thoughts, symbols, memories, or new word associations come, draw lines to new ovals that contain these new words. As words stimulate still further associations, draw lines to these. In time you will have a number of new clusters, all radiating from the key word. Notice how this is done with the word *family*.

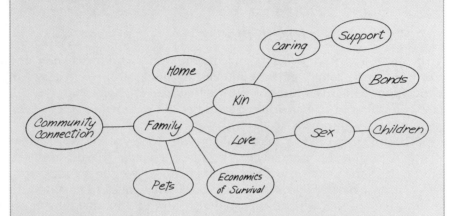

   Clustering allows us to use both of our brain hemispheres at once. This method can feel more natural than restricting ourselves to the left brain by making an outline first. When we list or outline thoughts, we use our left brain to force our thinking into a sequence before we know all we could think about the subject. In clustering, we invite input from the right brain as well as from the left at the beginning of our work and thus achieve a visual sense of the whole picture. Clustering is a free-association method that is best done without censorship, allowing discoveries and surprises at the results.

an idea. It can be a magical way to quickly release all the ideas, memories, and associations you have on a particular subject.

Step 3 Next, take the information you discovered from your cluster and begin to write a good paragraph about the various meanings and boundaries of the word *adult*. Contrast what you feel to be the true meaning of the word with some false meanings. Bring together your findings into one sentence that announces all you want to say about the definitions and boundaries of *adult.* This is a *topic sentence,* which generalizes your findings into a kind of conclusion. The rest of the sentences in the paragraph should support, or provide examples that support, the topic sentence. In this paragraph you can see how well you think about words while also working on the college level in expository writing.

■ *Peer Review*

In class read your essays of definition to one another in small groups. For each paper, write a critique that answers these questions:

1. Was each of the parameters observed?
2. Did you understand all that was said? Did anything need to be explained more?
3. Did you honestly find the writing interesting?

Scoring for Essay of Definition
1. Essay shows dictionary study of word. *10 points*
2. Body of essay defines and explains word from own experience. *30 points*
3. The exposition seems complete and easy to follow. *10 points*
4. Topic sentence opens essay. *10 points*
5. Conclusion is clearly stated. *10 points*
6. At least one full typed page. *20 points*
7. Work reasonably free of spelling and sentence errors. *10 points*

■ STUDENT WRITING EXAMPLE

MUSIC
Gary Aguirre

The word *music* comes from the Greek word *mousike,* meaning "art of the muses." Its simplest dictionary definition is "a rhythmic sequence of pleasing sounds." However, neither the original word idea nor these simplest definitions suggest the meaning of music in my life. To me music is the axle around which all human spiritual experience revolves. It is the common thread linking all religions and cultural expressions. From Spanish cante hondo, or deep song, to Balinese gamelan, to American jazz, musicians use song to define their heritage and their interpretation of the human experience. Music is a tangible representation of what I consider to be the unexplainable central creative force in the world that some call God.

The word *music's* deeper meaning becomes clearer when you find that some synonyms given in *Roget's Thesaurus* are *order* and *universe*. Music is an improvised creative expression, or melody, skillfully woven over a tapestry of mathematically juxtaposed rhythms and harmonies. It mimics the relationship of an individual's life experience against the solid background of history and culture. For instance, when American jazz great John Coltrane plays the standard "My Favorite Things," he begins with the familiar melody that accompanies the words "raindrops on roses and whiskers on kittens." The audience is drawn in because they have experienced this "place" before; in other words, they recognize the tune. From this starting point Coltrane soars into a whirl of spontaneous improvisation, while the drums, piano, and bass continue to pound out the original background collage of sound and rhythm. When he sees fit, Coltrane returns to the original melody, completing a cycle not unlike that of birth and death. The musician, in his expertise, provides a higher order to a world of sound that can, at times, seem completely chaotic.

Songs begin, travel through time and space, and then end. They live and die, like everything in the universe, serving no practical purpose. But like Coltrane's "My Favorite Things," the universe began, and may eventually end, also serving no practical purpose but to host those of us who were lucky enough to be here. To me music is not just "the art of combining tones to form expressive compositions" but a universe within itself that we humans can use to define our place in the infinite. Growing up in a non-religious family, music was my sole (or soul) connection with spirituality. The painstaking hours of teaching myself to play have afforded me the opportunity to worship in the only way I know how. As a song composer, I can offer my little bit to that which was here long before me and will continue long after I'm gone. Making music to me is prayer. Life and music are not separate entities; neither reflects the other, nor could either continue without the other. They are two parts of the greater whole, the everything.

Used with permission of Gary Aguirre.

• R E A D I N G S •

The Professor and the Madman: A Tale of Murder, Insanity, and the Making of the *Oxford English Dictionary*

Simon Winchester

The following reading is a miniature short story that introduces the book summarized in its intriguing subtitle: "A Tale of Murder, Insanity, and the Making of the Oxford English Dictionary." *After reading this story you might find yourself motivated to read a book that reads like a detective suspense story while relating a true account of two eccentric, dedicated men who participated in the most ambitious intellectual undertaking in English history. Simon Winchester is a journalist who writes on many diverse subjects.*

Mysterious (mistīə-riəs), *a*. [f. L. mystērium MYSTERY[1]+ OUS. Cf. F. *mystérieux*.]
1. Full of or fraught with mystery; wrapt in mystery; hidden from human knowledge or understanding; impossible or difficult to explain, solve, or discover; of obscure origin, nature, or purpose.

Popular myth has it that one of the most remarkable conversations in modern literary history took place on a cool and misty late autumn afternoon in 1896, in the small village of Crowthorne in the county of Berkshire.

One of the parties to the colloquy was the formidable Dr. James Murray, the editor of the *Oxford English Dictionary*. On the day in question he had traveled fifty miles by train from Oxford to meet an enigmatic figure named Dr. W. C. Minor, who was among the most prolific of the thousands of volunteer contributors whose labors lay at the core of the dictionary's creation.

For very nearly twenty years beforehand these two men had corresponded regularly about the finer points of English lexicography, but they had never met. Dr. Minor seemed never willing or able to leave his home at Crowthorne, never willing to come to Oxford. He was unable to offer any kind of explanation, or to do more than offer his regrets.

Dr. Murray, who himself was rarely free from the burdens of his work at his dictionary headquarters, the famous Scriptorium in Oxford, had nonetheless long dearly wished to see and thank his mysterious and intriguing helper. And particularly so by the late 1890s, with the dictionary well on its way to being half completed: Official honors were being showered upon all its creators, and Murray wanted to make sure that all those involved—even men so apparently bashful as Dr. Minor—were recognized for the valuable work they had done. He decided he would pay a visit.

5   Once he had made up his mind to go, he telegraphed his intentions, adding that he would find it most convenient to take a train that arrived at Crowthorne Station—then actually known as Wellington College Station, since it served the famous boys' school situated in the village—just after two on a certain Wednesday in November. Dr. Minor sent a wire by return to say that he was indeed expected and would be made most welcome. On the journey from Oxford the weather was fine; the trains were on time; the auguries, in short, were good.

At the railway station a polished landau and a liveried coachman were waiting, and with James Murray aboard they clip-clopped back through the lanes of rural Berkshire. After twenty minutes or so the carriage turned up a long drive lined with tall poplars, drawing up eventually outside a huge and rather forbidding red-brick mansion. A solemn servant showed the lexicographer upstairs, and into a book-lined study, where behind an immense mahogany desk stood a man of undoubted importance. Dr. Murray bowed gravely, and launched into the brief speech of greeting that he had so long rehearsed:

"A very good afternoon to you, sir. I am Dr. James Murray of the London Philological Society, and Editor of the *Oxford English Dictionary*. It is indeed an honour and a pleasure to at long last make your acquaintance—for you must be, kind sir, my most assiduous helpmeet, Dr. W. C. Minor?"

There was a brief pause, a momentary air of mutual embarrassment. A clock ticked loudly. There were muffled footsteps in the hall. A distant clank of keys. And then the man behind the desk cleared his throat, and he spoke:

"I regret, kind sir, that I am not. It is not at all as you suppose. I am in fact the Governor of the Broadmoor Criminal Lunatic Asylum. Dr. Minor is most certainly here. But he is an inmate. He has been a patient here for more than twenty years. He is our longest-staying resident."

10   Although the official government files relating to this case are secret, and have been locked away for more than a century, I have recently been allowed to see them. What follows is the strange, tragic, yet spiritually uplifting story they reveal.

Saved

Malcolm X

Interest in the life and work of Malcolm X continues to grow. The recognition he achieved during his lifetime as a provocative thinker and public speaker was short; he died, at age 40, the victim of a political assassination. In this selection, now a classic, Malcolm X describes how he managed through self-education to pull himself out of a life of street hustling and prison into literacy and power.

It was because of my letters that I happened to stumble upon starting to acquire some kind of a homemade education.

I became increasingly frustrated at not being able to express what I wanted to convey in letters that I wrote, especially those to Mr. Elijah Muhammad. In the street, I had been the most articulate hustler out there—I had commanded attention when I said something. But now, trying to write simple English, I not only wasn't articulate, I wasn't even functional. How would I sound writing in slang, the way I would *say* it, something such as, "Look, daddy, let me pull your coat about a cat, Elijah Muhammad."

Many who today hear me somewhere in person, or on television, or those who read something I've said, will think I went to school far beyond the eighth grade. This impression is due entirely to my prison studies.

It had really begun back in the Charlestown Prison, when Bimbi first made me feel envy of his stock of knowledge. Bimbi had always taken charge of any conversation he was in, and I had tried to emulate him. But every book I picked up had few sentences which didn't contain anywhere from one to nearly all of the words that might as well have been in Chinese. When I just skipped those words, of course, I really ended up with little idea of what the book said. So I had come to the Norfolk Prison Colony still going through only book-reading motions. Pretty soon, I would have quit even these motions, unless I had received the motivation that I did.

5   I saw that the best thing I could do was get hold of a dictionary—to study, to learn some words. I was lucky enough to reason also that I should try to improve my penmanship. It was sad. I couldn't even write in a straight line. It was both ideas together that moved me to request a dictionary along with some tablets and pencils from the Norfolk Prison Colony school.

I spent two days just riffling uncertainly through the dictionary's pages. I'd never realized so many words existed! I didn't know *which* words I needed to learn. Finally, just to start some kind of action, I began copying.

In my slow, painstaking, ragged handwriting, I copied into my tablet everything printed on that first page, down to the punctuation marks.

I believe it took me a day. Then, aloud, I read back, to myself, everything I'd written on the tablet. Over and over, aloud, to myself, I read my own handwriting.

I woke up the next morning, thinking about those words—immensely proud to realize that not only had I written so much at one time, but I'd written words that I never knew were in the world. Moreover, with a little effort, I also could remember what many of these words meant. I reviewed the words whose meanings I didn't remember. Funny thing, from the dictionary first page right now, that "aardvark" springs to my mind. The dictionary had a picture of it, a long-tailed, long-eared, burrowing African mammal, which lives off termites caught by sticking out its tongue as an anteater does for ants.

10   I was so fascinated that I went on—I copied the dictionary's next page. And the same experience came when I studied that. With every succeeding page, I also learned of people and places and events from history. Actually the dictionary is like a miniature encyclopedia. Finally the dictionary's A section had filled a whole tablet—and I went on into the B's. That was the way I started copying what eventually became the entire dictionary. It went a lot faster after so much practice helped me to pick up handwriting speed. Between what I wrote in my tablet, and writing letters, during the rest of my time in prison I would guess I wrote a million words.

I suppose it was inevitable that as my word-base broadened, I could for the first time pick up a book and read and now begin to understand what the book was saying. Anyone who has read a great deal can imagine the new world that opened. Let me tell you something: from then until I left that prison, in every free moment I had, if I was not reading in the library, I was reading on my bunk. You couldn't have gotten me out of books with a wedge. Between Mr. Muhammad's teachings, my correspondence, my visitors—usually Ella and Reginald—and my reading of books, months passed without my even thinking about being imprisoned. In fact, up to then, I never had been so truly free in my life.

The Norfolk Prison Colony's library was in the school building. A variety of classes was taught there by instructors who came from such places as Harvard and Boston universities. The weekly debates between inmate teams were also held in the school building. You would be astonished to know how worked up convict debaters and audiences would get over subjects like "Should Babies Be Fed Milk?"

Available on the prison library's shelves were books on just about every general subject. Much of the big private collection that Parkhurst had willed to the prison was still in crates and boxes in the back of the library—thousands of old books. Some of them looked ancient: covers faded, old-time parchment-looking binding. Parkhurst, I've mentioned, seemed to have been principally interested in history and religion. He had the money and the special interest to have a lot of books that you wouldn't have in general circulation. Any college library would have been lucky to get that collection.

As you can imagine, especially in a prison where there was heavy emphasis on rehabilitation, an inmate was smiled upon if he demonstrated an unusually intense interest in books. There was a sizable number of well-read inmates, especially the popular debaters. Some were said by many to be practically walking encyclopedias. They were almost celebrities. No university would ask any student to devour literature as I did when this new world opened to me, of being able to read and *understand.*

15   I read more in my room than in the library itself. An inmate who was known to read a lot could check out more than the permitted maximum number of books. I preferred reading in the total isolation of my own room.

When I had progressed to really serious reading, every night at about ten P.M. I would be outraged with the "lights out." It always seemed to catch me right in the middle of something engrossing.

Fortunately, right outside my door was a corridor light that cast a glow into my room. The glow was enough to read by, once my eyes adjusted to it. So when "lights out" came, I would sit on the floor where I could continue reading in that glow.

At one-hour intervals the night guards paced past every room. Each time I heard the approaching footsteps, I jumped into bed and feigned sleep. And as soon as the guard passed, I got back out of bed onto the floor area of that light-glow, where I would read for another fifty-eight minutes—until the guard approached again. That went on until three or four every morning. Three or four hours of sleep a night was enough for me. Often in the years in the streets I had slept less than that.

● ● ●

Study/Writing/Discussion Questions

1. Why do you think Malcolm X could be so confident and articulate as a hustler, yet have so much difficulty writing "simple English"?
2. What do you think of his practice of copying out every word in a dictionary?
3. Why did Malcolm X find it so empowering to learn new words?
4. What motivated him to read in his cell in semidarkness late through the night?
5. Why do you think Malcolm X wanted others to hear this story?

● ● ●

What Privacy Is—and What It Is Not

Charles J. Sykes

This excerpt, taken from the Introduction to the 1999 book The End of Privacy, *explores the meaning of the word* privacy *and how this meaning has changed over time. Charles J. Sykes is a journalist with a conservative perspective.*

For some of us, privacy is simply the right to be let alone; but having said that, what precisely does it mean? Is privacy simply a matter of protecting our solitude? Is privacy something we can expect only when we are by ourselves, when no one else can see us, or gain access to us? Or does privacy extend beyond solitude to our relations with others—our family, friends, and associates? Are there times we can expect a modicum of privacy even when we are in public or engaged in public affairs? Is privacy the right to control information about ourselves? If so, what information? Can we really hope to control what impression we make? Can we regulate others' reactions to our behavior?

Our experience of privacy is also likely to vary widely. For some of us, it is the ability to live a life unobserved, or to have a zone where we can develop intimate relations, blow off steam, relax and be ourselves in a way that is impossible in public. For others, it is to have a room or a life of their own, where they are freed from interference, judgment, and social pressure to pursue their interests, develop their talents, and take the sorts of chances that can be risked only in private. For some, privacy is what gives them a chance to repair their psyches and accumulate the moral and psychic capital they rely on when they emerge into public. For some of us, privacy is experienced in anonymity, the pleasure of being unknown or unrecognized when we travel to another city or take a vacation. (Surely one of the most significant losses of privacy for the modern celebrity is the inability to go *anywhere* without being recognized.) For some of us, privacy simply allows us to live in the twilight of public and private where we can go out unshaven, change jobs, and even relationships without being subject to publicity. For others, privacy may simply mean not being walked in on by parents or siblings; or it may be the power to choose what they reveal about themselves to others.

Each of us will react differently to violations of our privacy; we not only have different standards, we also calibrate our responses depending on our closeness or relationships with others. But we all have our own ladders of privacy, beginning with our closest relations, moving downward in descending orders of intimacy. For some, the ladder might look like this:

spouse
[priest, minister, rabbi]
brothers and sisters
parents
children
friends
in-laws
coworkers
neighbors
marketers
employers
government
news media
ex-spouses
potential rivals/enemies

Our willingness to share information declines with each rung. Information we would share with a sister, we might be unwilling to share with a parent, much less an in-law or a neighbor. We might have no qualms about giving our neighbor information about our habits that we would be very reluctant to share with our employer; and though we might share details of our sex lives with a friend, we would be horrified to share it with a government agent or (God forbid) the media. Certainly, our greatest fear would be for an enemy to compile a detailed and damaging dossier on us. Each person probably has a slightly different ladder, and different criteria for sharing information. But everyone has such limits and measures, because it is nearly impossible to live without them.

THE RISE AND FALL OF PRIVACY

5   Until modern times, of course, people had remarkably little privacy; many of them led their whole lives without ever really being alone. Every detail of their lives was subject to the scrutiny of family members, members of the tribe, or community. Over the past two centuries, the rise of the modern has been the rise of the individual. The literature of the last 200 years is a chronicle of what it meant to discover the power and the freedom of being alone. Undoubtedly, other societies and ages have done without much privacy, but we cannot. Even

so, a fair history of the state of privacy would not resemble anything like an even sweep either of rise or decline; there was no golden age from which we have fallen. Although we can chronicle the technologies that have enhanced the possibilities of privacy in our lives, every development and milestone has been shadowed by another taking us in quite a different direction.

The spread of prosperity, the single-family home, the automobile, the invention of television and computers have all made it possible for us to live private lives unimaginable to previous generations. We no longer live cheek by jowl with our neighbors, we can move about without crowding into buses or trains; our entertainment comes to us virtually one on one; we do not have to go to theaters or share our tastes with our neighbors. Once, our lives were hedged about by neighbors who would watch us nearly as closely as members of our own family; they would be silent—or not so silent—audience to our lives, acting sometimes as a support network, other times as a chorus of censure or unsolicited advice. They knew how we dressed, how we shopped, whom we dated, and the meaning of the various noises and odors coming from our homes.

Today, we may not even know their names. Many of us can go through life with only a nodding acquaintance with the people who live around us and even work with us. As Janna Malamud Smith notes, an adult living in a modern suburb is unlikely to have more than a few people who know her across time in different settings.

But this account runs parallel to another story: the same technologies that help separate us from the crowds also make it possible to monitor and record our behaviors. Although fewer people have intimate knowledge of our lives, many people—mostly unknown to us—know something about us. Here is the rub. The very technology that was supposed to free us from mass society and the conformity of mass media, has turned out to be as much a fishbowl as an information highway. In modern society, we have discovered that being free often means also being naked. The same society that allows us to live anonymously relies on surveillance to keep track of us because we are a society of strangers. We can close the blinds on our neighbors, but we have also opened doors to strangers who now know what we eat, what we wear, how we shop, who our doctor is, how much we earn, where we work, what drugs we take, and what we read.

Historical comparisons are useful, but also limited because the conditions of privacy in the modern technological world are, in fact, radically different from the challenges it faced in the past. Some critics dismiss concerns about massive commercial databases that track individual purchases and buying habits, by saying that such information was really no different from small-town gossip. But this misses the fundamental difference between being known by neighbors and friends, and being monitored by a faceless database. As intrusive as small-town gossip might have been, it was always shaded by some personal knowledge and connection. Being watched by a neighbor is not at all of the same magnitude as being watched by a bureaucracy, or tracked by a dataweb that misses little and forgets nothing.

10   The second paradox of privacy is that even though most of us have far more physical privacy, many of us seem extraordinarily anxious to get rid of that privacy. A man can reasonably expect to be left alone in his home, safe from prying eyes. But that same man can turn on the television set on any given afternoon and find a window into the most graphic, embarrassing details of the lives of others.

From *The End of Privacy* by Charles J. Sykes. Copyright ©1999 by the author and reprinted by permission of St. Martin's Press LLC.

Small Group Discussion or Writing Questions

1. Can you state the author's definition of privacy in one sentence?
2. Make an outline of his essay showing how each paragraph develops, illustrates, and clarifies his definition of privacy.
3. Name a few current social and political issues related to privacy that are not discussed in this excerpt.

Advanced Optional Writing Assignment

Write an essay of about three typed pages in which you describe a significant learning experience in your life that involved your use of language. What was easy for you? What was difficult? Explain how your sense of self and personal power changed through a greater or lesser mastery of language.

Optional Internet Research Assignment

1. Go to the site refdesk.com. Explore the possibilities this site offers for studying words through electronic dictionaries, thesauri, and encyclopedias. Write up your discoveries.
2. Using a search engine such as Google, find out more about the lives and works of Frederick Douglass, Barack Obama, Václav Havel, and Malcolm X.
3. Using your favorite search engine, see what more you can learn about the making of the *Oxford English Dictionary* or about current social and political issues related to personal privacy.

CHAPTER 3

Facts:

What's Real?

NO EXIT © Andy Singer

BILL'S HOMEMADE ICE CREAM

BILL'S

BILL'S

Used with permission of Andy Singer.

SINGER

Now why would it seem funny to discover that, in fact, Bill's "Homemade" Ice Cream is not homemade but manufactured? This question may be easy to answer compared to some of the other problems we can run into while learning more about facts. Because facts are judged on the

75

basis of "truth" and "reality," establishing them can be a tricky business. But we can avoid some pitfalls as we gain more clarity about the standards involved. This is the knowledge, together with some skills, that this chapter aims to teach.

DISCOVERY EXERCISES

The following three Discovery Exercises can be done on an individual or collaborative basis; they can be done outside class in preparation for discussion or in class itself.

▪ Beginning with the Word Fact

After consulting one or more dictionaries, write down your own definitions of the following words:

1. Know
2. Certain
3. Verified
4. Existence
5. Real
6. Fact

Read your definitions of *fact* aloud in class. Which definitions seem to cover all kinds of facts? Does your definition contain some of the following elements?

1. **Fact** comes from the Latin *factum,* meaning a deed, something done.
2. A fact is something known with certainty through experience, observation, testimony, record, or measurement.
3. A fact is something that can be objectively demonstrated and verified.
4. A fact is something that people will agree corresponds to a reality.

▪ Learning to Recognize Facts

Answer the following questions in writing, in preparation for a class discussion.

1. Make a list of five facts about yourself, beginning with your birth date.

2. How many chairs are in your classroom? Write down your total and when your instructor gives the signal, call out your number. Did you all agree?*

3. List five facts about the room you are in right now. Do not just name objects or events (such as lights, door), but make statements describing what you see in its context. For instance, do not say "Four windows" but "There are four open windows on the south wall of this room."

4. Which of the following are statements of facts?

   a. Human blood is grouped into four types: A, B, AB, and O.

   b. One centimeter is the equivalent of 0.3937 inch.

   c. The major religion in Mexico is Roman Catholicism.

   d. The food is awful in the cafeteria.

   e. Amelia Earhart was the first woman to fly solo around the world.

   f. Everybody should have health insurance.

   g. He must have forgotten his keys; they are on the table.

   h. Advertisement: Big 6 offers you the best buys in camping equipment.

5. Explain why items 4d through 4h are not facts.

■ Verifying Facts

One characteristic of facts is that they can be objectively verified—proven to be true—through the testimony of witnesses, through observations, or through records or documentation. Read the following list of facts. Select three to study. Aside from using the Internet, how would you go about verifying that each is indeed a fact?

1. A tornado is a dark funnel-shaped cloud made up of violently rotating winds that can reach speeds of up to 300 miles per hour.

2. One tablespoon is the equivalent of three teaspoons.

3. Mars rotates on its axis in nearly the same period as the Earth—24 hours, 37 minutes—so that a Mars day is almost identical to an Earth day.

4. Vermont was admitted to statehood March 4, 1791.

5. The nickname of Kansas is Sunflower State.

6. The highest mountain peak in the world is Mt. Everest at 29,035 feet.

7. Eritrea was formerly the northernmost province of Ethiopia.

8. The actor John Wayne was born in Iowa.

*Credit goes to Professor Jerry Herman of Laney College, who uses this question in his classes.

9. The word *bible* comes from the Greek word *biblia,* meaning a collection of writings.
10. There is a job available as a receptionist in the college president's office.

Facts and Reality

What we call facts do not necessarily represent what is real and true.

If you were to stand on a street corner and ask each passerby to tell you what a **fact** is, most people would tell you that a fact is what is real and true. However, this common notion is mistaken. Facts are our *interpretations* of what is real and true. Yet the problem with interpretations is that they can be dead wrong. Human history provides us with many examples.

Every schoolchild knows that the long-accepted "fact" that the earth was flat was an error based on limited perception. In every century mistaken notions taken for fact come and go, such as the idea that bathing is unhealthy, that blood-letting cures the sick, that women are inferior to men, that some races are inferior to others. Toward the end of the twentieth century, science and government assured us that pesticides would not harm human beings, nor would lead paint, nor buried toxic wastes. Such false notions remind us that what we call facts are the creations of human minds and, for this reason, subject to error. Most of us grew up believing that 98.6 degrees Fahrenheit represented normal body temperature. This medical "fact" was commonly accepted until 1992, when new investigations revealed that 98.6 wasn't normal at all; indeed, it was downright unusual. Indeed, it was found that healthy people thrive between 96.0 and 99.9, depending on the individual, time of day, sex, and race. Science moved forward in this case because facts long assumed to be true were reexamined. We need to continually reevaluate our "facts" in light of the feedback received from their tests against reality.

What, then, is reality?

Reality is another term that we all use every day, yet few of us can define. It remains a mystery elusive of a definition that can be agreed upon. In the previous chapter, you were offered a number of very different definitions, some by philosophers who have long debated the nature of reality. Philosophers have divided themselves into two camps: those who consider reality to be relative and those who view reality as absolute. In other words, some say the observer determines what reality is, while others say that reality is what it is—regardless of what people may think about it. Yet, no matter what side we may lean toward ourselves, we must concede that our judgments do change about the truth of some facts.

In summary, facts are not the equivalent of truths or reality; they are, at best, only our decisions about what seems to be most real. Human beings need facts because they need certainties in order to proceed through the world. But we should not forget that human beings are fallible.

Discussion Break Questions

1. State two facts that you are certain are true.
2. State two facts that you are certain will never change.
3. State two facts that you are certain will change.

Facts Are Not Absolutes

The most we can say about any fact is that its certainty is higher or lower in probability.

Facts that are most useful to us are those that have been repeatedly verified by many sources over time. Our lives and welfare depend on these certainties. On this planet we know that the fact of gravity limits what we can do and not do safely; we know that we can plan our daily schedules around the rising and the setting of the sun. But none can say that the orbit of this planet or its condition of gravity will always remain the same. We live in a physical universe that is eternally changing—from the invisible-to-the-eye subatomic level to obvious levels of wrinkles in our skin, the courses of rivers, the growth of children, and the motion of the sun and stars. Furthermore, modern technology is accelerating all kinds of unexpected environmental changes.

The sciences have their own way of coming to terms with the problem of certainties. Many statements that most of us would call facts are considered *probability* statements by the sciences. If a thermometer says the temperature is 65 degrees, a scientist would say that there is a 99 percent chance that the temperature is between 62.5 and 67.5 degrees. This would take into account any inaccuracies of the instrument. *Certainty* in science is usually considered to be a probability that is approaching certainty. In our human social history, beliefs that have often been mistaken for facts sometimes change as human knowledge evolves. In the eighteenth century and earlier, the belief that witches existed and caused malevolent harm to others was assumed to be fact. In nineteenth-century England, parents believed it necessary to "break the wills" of their children and beat them regularly in order to "civilize"

Used with permission of Anne Dowie, photographer.

them. Today neither of these beliefs is commonly considered true. Thus, many of our present cultural assumptions, thought to represent facts, may also be discovered mistaken over time. It is because of this human tendency to confuse beliefs with facts that a healthy society needs to preserve the freedom to debate, the right to disagree, the right to investigate one another's claims about facts, truths, and realities. Indeed, this is the only kind of environment in which critical thinking can flourish. A government that seeks absolute power over its citizens suppresses every stimulus to critical thinking. It buys out the media, censors a dissident press, discourages public protests, closes down schools, and imprisons those who dissent. Critical thinking is a fragile product of civilizations that value the freedom to search for truth. For the advancement of human knowledge and welfare, we need to value the right to continually reexamine whatever equations are made between reality, truth, and "facts."

Discussion Break Questions

1. Discuss a belief that you feel absolutely certain about. Discuss a belief that you are uncertain about.
2. Give an example of some methods used to suppress critical thinking.

Distinguishing Facts from Fiction

Surprisingly enough, we can sometimes be led to believe that the
difference between fact and fiction doesn't really matter.

Commercial advertising uses a lot of sophisticated knowledge about how
to get consumers to accept fakery. Actors in television commercials have
to convince us that they are not actors; they should look "real"—like one
of us. They have to persuade us that it is natural for two homemakers
doing aerobics together to share advice on laundry detergents or that a
celebrity is sincere in making a product testimonial. The blurring of fact
and fiction extends beyond commercials, sometimes with little concern
for the distinction. We watch documentaries that alternate between
actual news footage and reenactments. We watch adventure stories that
use news footage with pseudo-newsreels. Consider the following instances
of fact mixed with fiction.

1. Ronald Reagan was known for his "presidency by photo ops."
   When he went to the demilitarized zone in Korea, his video managers wanted to get footage of Reagan at the most exposed American bunker, Guardpost Collier, which overlooked North Korea.
   However, the Secret Service vetoed the idea for fear of sharpshoot-
   ers or infiltrators. After several days of negotiation, protection was
   provided for the president by erecting posts strong enough to hold
   30,000 yards of camouflage netting in front of the bunker. Then, to
   get the most dramatic shots, the army built camera platforms on

the hill beyond the guardpost so Reagan could be snapped standing there at the front. In the final shot, he was to be seen surrounded by sandbags, peering with his binoculars toward North Korea, evoking the memory of General Douglas MacArthur (from "The Storybook Presidency," *Power Game: How Washington Works,* by Hedrick Smith, 1988).

2. In a newspaper cartoon a father is changing a flat tire in the rain while his two children complain from the car window. The father says, "Don't you understand? This is *life;* this is what is happening. We *can't* switch to another channel."

3. Some TV stations regularly reenact true local crime events for the news, using actors to play the parts on the exact locations. They claim this is done as a public service.

4. A film star who regularly played the surgeon Colonel Potter on the TV series *M*A*S*H* appeared, wearing a doctor's white coat, in an aspirin commercial to endorse the product.

5. "The enduring legend of Enron can be summed up in one word: propaganda. . . . In a typical ruse in 1998, a gaggle of employees was rushed onto an empty trading floor of the company's Houston headquarters to put on a fictional show of busy trading for visiting Wall Street analysts being escorted by Mr. Lay. 'We brought some of our personal stuff, like pictures, to make it look like the area was lived in,' a laid-off Enron employee told *The Wall Street Journal* in 2002. 'We had to make believe we were on the phone buying and selling' even though 'some of the computers didn't even work.'" (Frank Rich, *The New York Times,* March 20, 2005)

6. "The Bush administration has a special flair for elaborately staged events, such as the President's jet landing on the aircraft carrier *USS Abraham Lincoln* declaring the end to major combat operations in Iraq. Sforsza [former ABC News producer] reportedly spent days planning the event, creating the perfect lighting and backdrop for television shots, including the now infamous 'Mission Accomplished' banner." (Ben Fritz, *All the President's Spin,* 2004, p. 23)

Feelings Can Be Facts

Feelings can deceive as well as illuminate.

We often hear that we should be objective and not subjective in order to determine facts. This warning is needed to remind us that anger, fear, envy, and prejudice can distort our perceptions and keep us from seeing things fairly as they really are. However, many interpret this familiar

© Eve Arrold/Magnum Photos

advice to mean that all feelings are "subjective"—and therefore irrational and unreliable—or that they invariably keep us from knowing what is true. This is a false assumption. There are times when feelings lead us to make a more careful investigation of a situation, such as when we feel mistrust. Therefore, it would seem wiser not to deny or suppress our feelings but instead to examine our *attitude* toward an issue. Is it objective or subjective? We can hate the taste of a bitter medication, yet decide to take it because our health depends on it. This would be assuming an objective attitude in spite of our feelings. A subjective attitude, on the other hand, would only choose what feels most comfortable despite long-term consequences. Thus, attitude can be objective, in the sense of being under conscious control, or subjective, in terms of remaining under unconscious influence. Ambulance attendants, police officers, or firefighters may flinch when they see a maimed or burned person, but nevertheless carry on with their work. Personal reactions of aversion cannot be allowed to interfere with such professional duty. Yet this does not mean that professionals need to deny what they are feeling in order to function well.

There are many circumstances in which a careful consideration of our feelings offers vital information. We need this sensitivity in human relationships, and we need sensitivity to interpret art. Look for instance at the photo on this page.

Suppose that you first react to the photo by feeling startled, then amused and curious. Such feelings might draw you to look more closely in order to learn more. You might even wonder if the photographer intended to lure your interest in this way.

When we are studying art, we give attention to our feeling reactions, because they can lead us to better understand a work's meaning. Artists, like the photographers whose pictures appear in this book, intentionally try to provoke reactions. Indeed, you cannot come into objective contact with a work unless you first assess how it affects you. When we listen to a salsa, our mood is affected and we feel enticed to dance. The release of joy we feel inside, when recognized, becomes a fact. Such experiences, when shared with others, can be especially powerful. We have all attended public performances where we laughed and cried together in an audience that was sharing the same feeling response. Here the feelings became a shared reality, a fact.

Let's now go back to the terms *objective* and *subjective*. Some believe that in order to be objective, a person must deny or suppress any feelings, because feelings keep one from being coolly rational and observant. Certainly this belief expresses an ideal. But, without faking, can it be achieved? Let us then consider how we might proceed with more honest realism about our feelings. We can learn how to observe, rather than react to, our feelings—to observe while feeling them at the same time. This means simply allowing feelings to be present without ignoring, denying, or suppressing them. When we are subjective about feelings, we are driven by them, we are unaware of how they are influencing our thoughts and decisions, and we react blindly to their directives. Unrecognized feelings can distort our reasoning and lead us to deceive others and ourselves. When subjectivity rules us, we cannot clearly discern what is real and true. However, when we take our feelings into account, staying present both with them and in what lies before us, we come closer to that ideal of objectivity.

Facts and Social Pressure

> Our need to have our perceptions verified by others also makes us susceptible to manipulation.

We only need to use our senses and perceptions to determine some facts. However, to be sure of their accuracy, we need confirmation from other sources.

1. JOHN: "Tell me, am I asleep or awake?"
   MARY: "You are awake."

2.   BILL: "Did that woman make a pass at me or did I imagine it?"
     JANE: "She made a pass, alright."
3.   EMILY: "I think this suit is too large for me. What do you think?"
     MAY: "Much too large."
4.   VERNA: "My checking account balances."
     NORMA: "My figures show you are correct."

In each of these examples, a personal examination alone could not determine what was real. To test the perception accuracy, confirmation was needed from others. Confirmation takes us out of disequilibrium and restores us to equilibrium. The reverse side of this principle is that someone who contradicts perceptions we feel certain about can make us feel uncomfortable, angry, even crazy.

5.   JOSE: "I didn't have too much to drink last night."
     WANDA: "Yes, you did! You were drunk!"
6.   CHILD: "I don't want to eat my carrots. They taste icky."
     PARENT: "Yes, you do want to eat them. You are just imagining things. They taste good."

As these examples illustrate, disagreements about perceptions result in conflicts. Sometimes conflicts can be settled by arbiters: an umpire in a game, a speedometer in a car, or a thermometer on the wall. But without an arbiter, we can be left feeling off balance and unsettled.

This human need for confirmation leaves us vulnerable to manipulation. The truth of this principle was demonstrated by American psychologist Solomon Asch, who conducted some simple experiments to test how a group could affect the perceptions of an individual. He found that in a small group, people are willing to deny the evidence of their own senses if the other members of the group interpret reality differently. In one experiment, Asch assembled groups of seven to nine college students in what was described as a test of visual judgment. In each group, only one of the students was actually a subject in the experiment; the others were the researcher's secret accomplices. The researcher informed the students that they would be comparing the lengths of lines. He showed them two white cards. On the first was a single vertical black line—the standard—whose length was to be matched. On the second white card were vertical lines of various lengths. The subjects were to choose the one line of the same length as the standard line (see Figure 3.1).

A series of eighteen trials was conducted. When the first pair of cards was presented, the group gave a unanimous judgment. The same thing happened on the second trial. In twelve of the remaining sixteen trials,

Standard   Comparison

FIGURE 3.1 Standard and Comparison Lines
in the Asch Experiment

however, all of Asch's accomplices agreed on what was clearly an incorrect answer. The real subject of the experiment was left to react. In about a third of the cases, the subject yielded to the majority and conformed to its decision. In separate experiments with a control group consisting of only genuine subjects, Asch found that people made mistakes less than one percent of the time. Subsequent interviews with those who yielded to the majority revealed that only a few of them had actually believed that the majority choice was correct. They admitted that they thought they had judged the length of the lines correctly but did not want to "rock the boat" or "spoil the results" by giving the right answer. And then there were those who had doubted their own perceptions and had concluded that they had better hide this from the others. The test provided a significant demonstration of the power of consensus to bring about conformity and to make a person invalidate his or her own perception.*

Class Discussion

1. Why did a third of the subjects in Asch's experiments conform to the incorrect majority even when their perceptions told them they were correct?

2. Did these subjects have any other means of judging the correctness of their perceptions than from the others in the group?

3. If group pressure can affect us this much in such a simple problem as determining the relative length of a line, what do you think are the implications in more complex problems such as public opinion on controversial issues?

4. If you are familiar with the story "The Emperor's New Clothes," what parallels do you see between its theme and Asch's experiment?

*Figure and text adapted from Solomon Asch, "Effects of Group Pressure upon Modification and Distortion of Judgments," in H. Proshansky and B. Seidenberg (Eds.), *Basic Studies in Social Psychology* (New York: Holt, Rinehart & Winston, 1965), pp. 393–401. Used with permission of CBS College Publishing.

Facts and Our Limited Senses

Both science and wisdom are needed to help us compensate for the
limitations of our senses.

We have seen how consensus and conformity influence perception and thus
limit our ability to know the facts. But even aside from the influence of
social pressure, we are limited in our ability to know the facts because of the
limits of our senses. We now know that dogs can hear levels of pitch that we
cannot and that butterflies can see colors invisible to us. If we look at a chart
of the electromagnetic spectrum, the portion visible to us is only a tiny slit
in the whole band. We have to use instruments—X rays, radar, the seismo-
graph, smoke detectors—to compensate for our sense limitations.

But aside from all this, our senses are affected by many other variables such as mental preoccupations, distractions, or our varying degrees
of alertness in different circumstances. How much do you actually see on
your commute route? How much attention do you pay to background
sounds when you live in the city? Has a friend ever complained you
didn't notice when he shaved off his beard?

Another human failing is that we interpret what we perceive on the
basis of our experience. Moreover, this experience may be too narrow and
limited to embrace what lies before us. The Buddha once succinctly
illustrated this point and more in the following wise parable.

● R E A D I N G ●

The Blind Men and the Elephant

Once upon a time a king gathered some blind men about an elephant and
asked them to tell him what an elephant was like. The first man felt a tusk and
said an elephant was like a giant carrot; another happened to touch an ear
and said it was like a big fan; another touched its trunk and said it was like a
pestle; still another, who happened to feel its leg, said it was like a mortar; and
another, who grasped its tail, said it was like a rope. Not one of them was
able to tell the king the elephant's real form.

● ● ●

Study Questions

1. What do you think the elephant represents?
2. Why did each of the blind men think in terms of comparisons?

3. What was wrong with their comparisons?

4. Can you think of examples in your life where you could not experience something new because you were comparing it to something familiar?

Statements of Fact

How we state a fact makes all the difference.

As the preceding sections have demonstrated, it is not always easy to determine some facts. Moreover, facts depend on the language used to express them. When we make statements of fact, our language needs to be quite specific and guarded against assumptions. This does not mean we must use tentative language all the time. But if we are stating facts, our language has to reflect the limits of our data as well as the measure of our certainty.

Study the photograph on page 89. Then read the following statements; notice how those in italics differ from those in regular type.

1. *A puppy has jumped up onto a car's running board.*

   In the near center of this rectangular black-and-white photo, a small white-spotted furry animal stands with four feet resting on two horizontal lines, one dark and one light. The head, ears, and legs of this little creature suggest those of a young dog. Behind and above him are two rectangular planes that share the same gray metallic-smooth reflecting surface. In front of his head a dark vertical hollow-seeming line extends to the top of the photo, leading the eye to two shiny overlapping disks that resemble a car's door lock and lock cover as well as to a shiny arc that suggests a car door handle. Below the horizontal lines that could comprise a car's running board, there appears a wide dark surface area such as one finds beneath a standing car. This darkest area becomes lighter as it moves into a speckled foreground of a rougher texture reminiscent of a dirt road surface.

2. *Someone put the puppy up there as a joke. He could not have jumped up there on his own.*

   The distance between the running board and the ground cannot be measured, but in this photo the distance appears to be almost twice the height of the dog. The width of the running board also cannot be seen, but it accommodates the four feet of the puppy. No people appear in the picture, nor do any human shapes appear in reflection.

From Anonymous by Robert Flynn Johnson, Thames & Hudson, London and New York. Used with permission of Thames & Hudson, Ltd.

3. *Although he can't jump down, the puppy does not appear afraid; someone outside the photo is reassuring him.*

   We see the small dog in profile with his head and body facing the photo's left border. He stands with his back feet together and his front feet apart. His gaze and stance suggest curiosity but not tension.

4. *Trees and clouds are reflected in the car door.*

   The medium grey metallic planes behind the puppy appear overlaid with darker shaded images consisting of wispy, smoky shapes forming a pyramid and two columns. Horizontal cloudlike formations rest suspended between these shapes.

5. *This is an old photo, probably from the 1920s or 1930s.*

   Wide running boards were featured on motor car sedans during the 1920s and 1930s. The craftsmanship of the car's door fixtures and sculptured door also suggest the elegance of that era. Moreover, during that time, dirt roads and rural scenes were more common.

As you probably have guessed, the italicized sentences are hasty interpretations of the photo, whereas the statements appearing in regular type offer objective descriptions derived from a careful study of the photo. The interpretations are *inferences* that may or may not be carefully drawn, whereas the objective *descriptions* offer perceptions and information that can be verified—that is, tested for factual accuracy. You yourself will be engaging in verification when you compare your own visual study of the photo to these statements. Moreover, you will be questioning whether they support such inferences. All in all, however, no study of the photo alone will be able to tell you with certainty how or why the puppy got on the running board, how the puppy is reacting, or where or when the picture was taken.

In preparation for writing your own description of different photos, it can be useful to pause in order to study some of the characteristics of factual statements.

1. Factual statements show an awareness of context and limitations. If a photo is being described, the writer does not pretend it is a life situation in which one can see all angles and ask questions.

   "In the near center of this black-and-white photo a small white-spotted furry animal stands with four feet resting on two horizontal lines, one dark and one light."

2. Factual statements use appropriate qualifiers to indicate uncertainties.

   "two shining overlapping disks that resemble . . . "

   "below the horizontal lines that could comprise . . . "

3. Factual statements state the obvious.

   "We see the small dog in profile."

4. Factual statements show a disciplined effort to describe what is present while restraining the impulse to jump to conclusions.

   "darker shaded images consisting of wispy, smoky shapes . . . "

5. Factual statements are not inappropriately cautious, such as to say, The dog appears to have legs.

6. Factual statements are *not* guesses assumed to be certainties.

   "Someone outside the photo is reassuring him."

7. Factual statements provide specific details that others can verify.

   "In this photo the distance appears to be almost twice the height of the dog."

Class Discussion

1. How do the detailed statements resemble police reports? Why are police taught to write like this?

2. If you were on a jury, how could it be useful to know the difference between factual statements and claims that are interpretations of data?

3. Why would it be important to know the difference if you were an attorney, a judge, a witness, or a defendant?

4. Why would a reporter be concerned with the difference between facts and interpretations?

5. Why would the difference matter to (a) a doctor, (b) a car mechanic, (c) a biologist, (d) a pharmacist?

Core Discovery Writing Application

▪ *Using a List of Facts to Describe a Photograph*

This is an exercise that challenges your mental and verbal awareness. Its task seems simple: to describe a photograph by making a list of at least ten factual statements about it. This exercise is best done first by the whole class working together on one photograph. Then small groups can work with other photographs.

1. Choose one photograph from this book for your group to study that has not already been described by the author. Each person should work quietly alone, then discuss his or her effort when everyone is finished. Spend some time absorbing the photograph, then take notes. Imagine that you are writing for someone who cannot see the photograph. Be as specific and detailed as you can, even about the picture's most obvious aspects. Be on guard against jumping to conclusions. Stay with your evidence. Arrange your list in some kind of logical order. (Don't jump around from the background to a person's clothes to another's hair.)

2. Write out your list of ten or more factual statements. Then compare your list to others in your group who worked on the same picture. How do you agree or differ about the facts you found? Star the facts you can agree upon.

Scoring for Using a List of Facts to Describe a Photograph

1. Obvious details not ignored. *20 points*
2. Things are described, not just labeled. (To say "bus" is not to describe the evidence of the clues you actually see; besides, this label could be a mistaken inference.) *20 points*
3. Facts are stated in at least 10 sentences. *10 points*
4. Inferences are not stated. *30 points*
5. Systematic presentation of data. *10 points*
6. No distracting errors of spelling, punctuation, or sentence structure. *10 points*

Standards We Use to Determine Facts: *Verifiability, Reliability, Plausibility, Probability*

In any situation, when we need to think critically, the first thing we have to determine is what the facts are. We solve practical problems through facts, such as proving the payment of a bill; we seek facts in every form of investigation, whether in a court of law or a geographical survey. This primary need for facts has led to the development of standards for determining both their existence and their reliability. When we think critically, we fully understand and use these standards, many of which have already been suggested in this chapter. Let's now look directly at four of them: verifiability, reliability, plausibility, and probability.

Verifiability means the data can be confirmed by another source. This source can be a reference source (such as a dictionary), a record (such as a marriage license), or a standard (such as Greenwich mean time). Another source could be the testimony of a witness or an expert. Data can be verified by the senses, by agreements, by measurements, or by documentation.

A second standard for determining facts is **reliability.** When we obtain agreements or disagreements about facts, we have to consider their degree of dependability. To do this we have to ask some critical questions. Is the witness biased? Do we need a larger survey? Were the senses used carefully and consciously? Were they adequate to the task? Were the measurements accurate? Were the documents genuine?

Probability, as tested through time and repetition, represents another standard used to determine the reliability of a fact. If the weather pattern in one region alters radically over a period of several years, this phenomenon of change becomes a fact. If over a ten-year period, the prices of homes in your neighborhood have risen 10 percent a year, this is a fact.

However, that rate of increase may not hold true next year. Thus, facts depend on our observation of the recurrence of things over time as well as on our assessment of the probability of their continuation.

Plausibility is a fourth standard for facts, meaning they undergo the test of credibility. If a friend tells you that he "totaled" the car you loaned him, you would want to ask a lot more questions. The same might be said for a car insurance salesperson who offers you a special $100-per-year deal on your new car. In both these cases, since neither claim seems totally plausible, you might well decide that you would have to check out what they told you. Should you find contradictions, such as spotting your car parked on the street without a dent, then you would know for certain that you had not been given the facts. Likewise, you might learn that the insurance person is not employed by the company she claims to represent. In both of these cases, you could also have been conned by more plausible arguments. Nevertheless, for facts to be accepted, they have to be plausible, make sense, or seem to be the most likely possibility.

In conclusion, these four standards suggest a few useful rules to follow:

1. Don't believe any facts given to you unless sufficient information is provided about their source to allow verification.
2. Don't totally accept—or take action on the basis of—facts given to you until you verify them for yourself.
3. Don't accept facts that appear implausible, that contain discrepancies or contradictions. (You will read more on the subject in Chapter 9.)
4. When you have an important decision to make, verify all the facts given you even if they come from someone you trust.

Chapter Summary

1. By definition, a fact is something known with certainty through experience, observation, or measurement. A fact can be objectively demonstrated and verified. A fact is something that people agree corresponds to reality.
2. It is not easy for us to determine whether facts correspond to reality. This can only be determined over time with repeated feedback and testing.
3. The difference between facts and fiction does matter.
4. Feelings are facts; they can distort or enhance our perceptions, depending on how conscious we are of their presence.
5. Facts are not absolutes but statements of probability.
6. Because we are dependent on confirmation from others in our search for facts, social pressures can lead us to distrust or distort our own perceptions.

7. Our senses are limited both in range and capacity and are affected by many factors, such as selective focus and mental preoccupations.

8. Facts must be expressed in carefully formulated statements that have the following characteristics:

    a. They define their own limitations.

    b. They are objectively stated.

    c. They use appropriate qualifiers.

    d. They state the obvious.

    e. They are not inappropriately cautious.

    f. They do not include guesses or inferences.

    g. They are specific and offer their evidence for others to verify.

9. The standards traditionally used to determine facts are verifiability, reliability, probability, and plausibility. Facts have to undergo the test of time and repetition and not contradict other known facts.

Chapter Quiz

Rate each of the following statements as *true* or *false*. In class discussion or in writing, give an example to substantiate your answer in each case.

_____ 1. Some facts can be determined by measurements.

_____ 2. Some facts can be confirmed by the senses, others by records.

_____ 3. The most reliable facts are those that have been repeatedly confirmed by tests over time.

_____ 4. Facts often consist of obvious details that are seen but not consciously recognized.

_____ 5. Sometimes what we claim to be facts are untrue because the human perceptions used to determine them are limited and fallible.

_____ 6. A person educated in critical thinking qualifies statements to reflect probabilities and uncertainties using provisional phrases such as "it appears that. . . . "

_____ 7. The only standards we use to determine facts are verifiability, reliability, plausibility, and credibility.

_____ 8. The study of many subjects consists of memorizing facts, because they are the nearest things we have to certainties.

_____ 9. All newspapers can be depended upon as reliable sources of facts about world events.

_____ 10. An atmosphere that permits disagreements about widely accepted perceptions and beliefs helps critical thinking to flourish.

Composition Writing Application

■ *Writing a Short Fact-Finding Report*

Think of a problem that you might solve by getting whatever facts you may need to make a decision or take effective action. This could involve buying a used car, selecting a college, agreeing to a date, getting insurance, finding affordable housing, or making a complaint before the city council. Write a simple report on the subject. Here is a summary of the parameters:

1. *Objective:* Write a report concerning a problem that could be solved through knowing or verifying more facts. Also describe how determining and verifying these facts helped you make a better decision or take more effective action.

2. *Structure:* Begin with a topic sentence and end with a summary statement. Your content should include three parts:

   a. Describe the problem.

   b. Describe what facts you needed, where you found them, and how you interpreted them.

   c. Describe the final outcome. Explain how getting these facts affected your perspective of the problem and helped you make a decision or take action toward solving the problem.

3. *Length:* The length of your report will be from one to four typed pages.

Scoring for the Fact-Finding Report

1. The problem is clearly explained. *10 points*
2. There is a systematic assessment of the missing or needed facts. *20 points*
3. There is a description of how the facts were found, what information was discovered, and how these facts were verified and interpreted. *20 points*
4. A conclusion shows how these facts aided understanding, made a decision or action possible, or solved the problem. *20 points*
5. The report is from one to four typed pages in length. *20 points*
6. There are no distracting errors of spelling, punctuation, or sentence structure. *10 points*

A PROBLEM SOLVED BY FACTS
Anthony Choy

I am an auto mechanic; a large part of my job requires skills in observing, investigating, and determining facts. Often people bring in cars with problems they can't identify, much less repair. In such cases, they hire me to get the facts. And the final test of whether or not I got the facts right is a car that runs right. Let me illustrate this with a story.

One day a customer brought in a 1977 Ford Pinto. His complaint was about the awful noise in his V-6 engine, which was louder when it revved high and quieter when it revved low. I began my inspection by locating the noise at the front of the engine area. I checked the alternator, water pump, valve adjustment, cam gears. Nothing was out of the ordinary. I was stumped.

I then removed the timing chain cover. I noticed there was a gear-to-gear system that is known to make a racket, but nothing comparable to the sound this engine was producing. Again the gears checked out okay. I was stumped again.

Then I started looking at the obvious. I retraced my diagnosing steps to study the engine some more. I noticed an excessive amount of silicone on the oil pan gasket where the bottom of the timing chain cover meets the oil pan. I noticed some broken gears inside the oil pan. I wondered: "Why didn't the last mechanic take care of this?" I examined the gears again and noticed how hard it was to remove the crank gear. The only way to remove that gear would be to remove the oil pan by lifting the engine off its mounts first. I realized then that the last mechanic who replaced the cam and crank gears did not do the job correctly: if the mechanic had removed the gears, there would not have been an excessive amount of silicone on the oil pan gasket. The gasket had not been replaced, otherwise the broken pieces in the oil pan would have been cleaned out. Why did the mechanic omit doing this? I realized it was probably because he or she could not figure out how to remove the oil pan.

5   Well, I replaced the parts and proceeded to repair the vehicle the way I was taught. I started up the engine, checked for leaks, and there were none. Then I revved the engine high for a moment and left it at idle, and the noise was completely gone. It purred like a kitten. I felt good to have corrected the problem. When my customer returned, he shook my hand and gave me a bonus.

Used with permission of Anthony Choy.

● R E A D I N G S ●

The Debt Explosion

Elizabeth Warren and Amelia Warren Tyagi

This excerpt is taken from the book The Two-Income Trap, *published in 2003. The authors are Harvard professor Elizabeth Warren, who specializes in bankruptcy law, and her daughter, Amelia, a consultant in health care and public education. In your first reading, make a list of what they claim to be facts. (Note: This excerpt does not include the many footnote citations provided by the authors to back up their claims.)*

In the new world of unregulated lending, families are barraged with advertisements and offers for a new product: all the debt they could ever want, and more. Now, in a single year, more than five *billion* preapproved credit card offers—totaling over $350,000 of credit *per family*—pour into mailboxes all across America. Magazine ads, telephone calls during dinner, and flyers at the bottom of grocery store bags barrage families with even more offers of credit, while roving bands of credit card marketers haunt college campuses and shopping malls. Credit card debt has increased accordingly: from less than $10 billion in 1968 (inflation adjusted) to more than $600 billion in 2000, an increase of more than *6,000 percent*. It would seem that once Americans got a first bite of the debt apple, they just couldn't get enough.

But what are families spending all that money on? Did they blow it on "vacations and luxury items," as one columnist claimed? This explanation might gratify the self-righteous bill-payers, but it doesn't square with the facts. Undoubtedly, all that easy credit dangling under everyone's noses enticed a few more Americans into buying things they could have lived without. As we showed in chapter 2, today's families are spending more on some goods, such as computers, home electronics, and pet food, than they did a generation ago. But they are spending less on food, clothing, appliances, home furnishings, and tobacco—a lot less. There is no evidence of an increase in impulse buying or luxury acquisitions over the past thirty years—certainly nothing that could account for a 6,000 percent increase in credit card debt. Moreover, the expenditures that have shown the biggest increases—e.g., housing, health insurance, college tuition, preschool— are the purchases *least* likely to appear on a credit card bill.

If families aren't buying more goods, then what are they using all that debt for? They get into debt trying to buy their way out of the Two-Income Trap. The bidding war has inflated the cost of middle-class life to the point that once they have paid the mortgage and other fixed expenses, families have little discretionary income left—and even less margin for error. What to do when something goes wrong, as it increasingly does? Since the two-income family does not have a stay-at-home mom to call on to help make ends meet when emergency strikes, the family turns to debt to make it through to the next payday.

No advertisements trumpet, "When your husband leaves you, there's MasterCard." Nor do we hear: "American Express: Don't lose your job without it." But those slogans would be closer to the truth about how credit is used today. When corporate layoffs loom, workers apply for as many credit cards as possible to see them through until they can find a new job. When health insurance lapses, the family hands a MasterCard to the doctor and prays for the best. And when Dad walks out, that "E-Z check" stuffed in with the latest credit card bill looks like just the thing to tide Mom over until the child support checks arrive. Later, when the credit card payments become unmanageable, the family takes on a second mortgage to consolidate all that debt. No one would suspect it from looking at the ads, but for every family taking out a second mortgage to pay for a vacation, there are sixty-one more families taking on a second mortgage so they can pay down their credit card bills and medical debts.

5　　　The bankruptcy court offers a peek at those in the most trouble with debt. The Myth of the Immoral Debtor would have us believe that these families consumed their way into bankruptcy, running up their credit cards to cover their "reckless spending." They are at least half right; families in bankruptcy are choking on credit card debt. Ninety-one percent of the families in bankruptcy were carrying balances on their cards by the time they filed. A third of homeowners were carrying second or even third mortgages or had refinanced their mortgages to get some cash. The amount of debt was truly staggering. Nearly one-third of bankruptcy filers—more than 400,000 families—owed *an entire year's salary* on their credit cards, a hole that was virtually impossible to dig a generation ago.

But the critics are off the mark on one point—the role played by overconsumption or its ubiquitous cousin, "trouble managing money." By 2001, those two reasons combined to account for less than 6 percent of families in bankruptcy. What about the rest? The overwhelming majority of bankrupt families faced far more serious problems. As we showed in chapter 4, nearly 90 percent had been felled by a job loss, a medical problem, or a family breakup, or by some combination of all three.

Potential Supreme Court nominee Judge Edith Jones asserts that "overspending and an unwillingness to live within one's means 'causes' debt." She is probably right. These families certainly overspent, accepting medical care they could not afford and making child support payments that left them with too little to pay the rent. They also lived beyond their means, trying to hold on to their houses and cars even after they lost their jobs. But we are forced to wonder, what would Judge Jones suggest those families have done? Not gone to the emergency room when the chest pains started? Moved the kids into a shelter the day their father moved out? Paid MasterCard and Visa, even if it meant not feeding their children? It is doubtlessly satisfying to point the long finger of blame at personal irresponsibility and overspending. But only the willfully ignorant refuse to acknowledge the real reasons behind all that debt.

Class Study/Writing/Discussion Questions

1. Why do you think that U.S. credit card debt has increased 6,000 percent since 1968?

2. In this excerpt the authors present some facts about the reasons families go into credit card debt that may counter what is commonly believed. Which of these facts surprised you?

3. The title of the book is *The Two-Income Trap*. In this excerpt, the authors do not fully explain why they would consider two incomes to be a trap. However, what entrapment aspects are discussed here?

4. According to these authors, how have credit cards come to serve as "safety nets" for American families?

5. According to these authors what facts point to the major causes of debt and bankruptcy in middle-class America?

Fast Food Nation: The Dark Side of the All-American Meal

Eric Schlosser

This excerpt is taken from the Introduction to a recent New York Times *bestseller. Its author is a correspondent for the* Atlantic Monthly. *As you read, notice how this journalist bases his work on the facts he has gathered and interpreted.*

Over the last three decades, fast food has infiltrated every nook and cranny of American society. An industry that began with a handful of modest hot dog and hamburger stands in southern California has spread to every corner of the nation, selling a broad range of foods wherever paying customers may be found. Fast food is now served at restaurants and drive-throughs, at stadiums, airports, zoos, high schools, elementary schools, and universities, on cruise ships, trains, and airplanes, at K-Marts, Wal-Marts, gas stations, and even at hospital cafeterias. In 1970, Americans spent about $6 billion on fast food; in 2001, they spent more than $110 billion. Americans now spend more money on fast food than on higher education, personal computers, computer software, or new cars. They spend more on fast food than on movies, books, magazines, newspapers, videos, and recorded music—combined.

Pull open the glass door, feel the rush of cool air, walk in, get in line, study the backlit color photographs above the counter, place your order, hand over a few dollars, watch teenagers in uniforms pushing various buttons, and moments later take hold of a plastic tray full of food wrapped in colored paper and cardboard. The whole experience of buying fast food has become so routine, so thoroughly unexceptional and mundane, that it is now taken for granted, like brushing your teeth or stopping for a red light. It has become a social custom as American as a small, rectangular, hand-held, frozen, and reheated apple pie.

This is a book about fast food, the values it embodies, and the world it has made. Fast food has proven to be a revolutionary force in American life; I am interested in it both as a commodity and as a metaphor. What people eat (or don't eat) has always been determined by a complex interplay of social, economic, and technological forces. The early Roman Republic was fed by its citizen-farmers; the Roman Empire, by its slaves. A nation's diet can be more revealing than its art or literature. On any given day in the United States about .one-quarter of the adult population visits a fast food restaurant. During a relatively brief period of time, the fast food industry has helped to transform not only the American diet, but also our landscape, economy, workforce, and popular culture. Fast food and its consequences have become inescapable, regardless of whether you eat it twice a day, try to avoid it, or have never taken a single bite.

The extraordinary growth of the fast food industry has been driven by fundamental changes in American society. Adjusted for inflation, the hourly wage of the average U.S. worker peaked in 1973 and then steadily declined for the next twenty-five years. During that period, women entered the workforce in record numbers, often motivated less by a feminist perspective than by a need to pay the bills. In 1975, about one-third of American mothers with young children worked outside the home; today almost two-thirds of such mothers are employed. As the sociologists Cameron Lynne Macdonald and Carmen Sirianni have noted, the entry of so many women into the workforce has greatly increased demand for the types of services that housewives traditionally perform: cooking, cleaning, and child care. A generation ago, three-quarters of the money used to buy food in the United States was spent to prepare meals at home. Today about half of the money used to buy food is spent at restaurants— mainly at fast food restaurants.

5   The McDonald's Corporation has become a powerful symbol of America's service economy, which is now responsible for 90 percent of the country's new jobs. In 1968, McDonald's operated about one thousand restaurants. Today it has about thirty thousand restaurants worldwide and opens almost two thousand new ones each year. An estimated one out of every eight workers in the United States has at some point been employed by McDonald's. The company annually hires about one million people, more than any other American organization, public or private. McDonald's is the nation's largest purchaser of beef, pork, and potatoes—and the second largest purchaser of chicken. The McDonald's Corporation is the largest owner of retail property in the world. Indeed, the company earns the majority of its profits not from selling food but from collecting rent. McDonald's spends more money on advertising and marketing than any other brand. As a result it has replaced Coca-Cola as the world's most famous brand. McDonald's operates more playgrounds than any other private entity in the United States. It is responsible for the nation's

bestselling line of children's clothing (McKids) and is one of the largest distrib-
utors of toys. A survey of American schoolchildren found that 96 percent could
identify Ronald McDonald. The only fictional character with a higher degree
of recognition was Santa Claus. The impact of McDonald's on the way we
live today is hard to overstate. The Golden Arches are now more widely recognized than the Christian cross.

In the early 1970s, the farm activist Jim Hightower warned of "the
McDonaldization of America." He viewed the emerging fast food industry as a
threat to independent businesses, as a step toward a food economy dominated
by giant corporations, and as a homogenizing influence on American life. In
Eat Your Heart Out (1975), he argued that "bigger is *not* better." Much of what
Hightower feared has come to pass. The centralized purchasing decisions of
the large restaurant chains and their demand for standardized products have
given a handful of corporations an unprecedented degree of power over the
nation's food supply. Moreover, the tremendous success of the fast food industry
has encouraged other industries to adopt similar business methods. The basic
thinking behind fast food has become the operating system of today's retail
economy, wiping out small businesses, obliterating regional differences, and
spreading identical stores throughout the country like a self-replicating code.

America's main streets and malls now boast the same Pizza Huts and Taco
Bells, Gaps and Banana Republics, Starbucks and Jiffy-Lubes, Foot Lockers,
Snip N' Clips, Sunglass Huts, and Hobbytown USAs. Almost every facet of
American life has now been franchised or chained. From the maternity ward at
a Columbia/HCA hospital to an embalming room owned by Service Corporation International—"the world's largest provider of death care services,"
based in Houston, Texas, which since 1968 has grown to include 3,823
funeral homes, 523 cemeteries, and 198 crematoriums, and which today
handles the final remains of one out of every nine Americans—a person can
now go from the cradle to the grave without spending a nickel at an independently owned business.

The key to a successful franchise, according to many texts on the subject,
can be expressed in one word: "uniformity." Franchises and chain stores strive
to offer exactly the same product or service at numerous locations. Customers
are drawn to familiar brands by an instinct to avoid the unknown. A brand
offers a feeling of reassurance when its products are always and everywhere
the same. "We have found out . . . that we cannot trust some people who are
nonconformists," declared Ray Kroc, one of the founders of McDonald's,
angered by some of his franchisees. "We will make conformists out of them in
a hurry. . . . The organization cannot trust the individual; the individual must
trust the organization."

One of the ironies of America's fast food industry is that a business so dedicated to conformity was founded by iconoclasts and self-made men, by entrepreneurs willing to defy conventional opinion. Few of the people who built fast
food empires ever attended college, let alone business school. They worked

Building Arguments
Facts

One powerful form of argument is to simply state the facts, allowing the facts to support an inevitable but implied conclusion. (This is generally known as "letting the facts speak for themselves.") Notice how this is accomplished in the reading given below. It offers the words of a Blackfoot woman from the year 1835, who offers only (her version of) the facts to explain why she left her husband to live with a white trapper.

I was the wife of a Blackfoot warrior, and I served him faithfully. (principal claim) I brought wood in the morning, and placed water always at hand. I watched for his coming; and he found his food cooked and waiting. If he rose to go forth there was nothing to delay him. I searched the thought that was in his heart, to save him the trouble of speaking. When I went abroad on errands for him, the chiefs and warriors smiled upon me, the braves spoke soft things, in secret; but my feet were in the straight path, and my eyes could see nothing but him.

    When he went out to hunt, or to war, who aided to equip him but I? When he returned I met him at the door; I took his gun; and he entered without further thought. When he sat and smoked, I unloaded his horses; tied them to stakes, brought in their loads, and was quickly at his feet. If his moccasins were wet I took them off and put on others which were warm and dry. I dressed all the skins that were taken in the chase. . . . I served him faithfully; and what was my reward? A cloud was always on his brow, and sharp lightning on his tongue. I was his dog; and not his wife. Who was it scarred and bruised me? It was he.

Exercise

1. Put into words the conclusion the Blackfoot woman leads you to draw for yourself from her story. (This is called an **implicit conclusion.**) What claims does she present as fact in order to support this conclusion?

2. Compose an argument in which you state two paragraphs of facts that give compelling support to a conclusion.

hard, took risks, and followed their own paths. In many respects, the fast food industry embodies the best and the worst of American capitalism at the start of the twenty-first century—its constant stream of new products and innovations, its widening gulf between rich and poor. The industrialization of the restaurant kitchen has enabled the fast food chains to rely upon a low-paid and unskilled workforce. While a handful of workers manage to rise up the corporate ladder, the vast majority lack full-time employment, receive no benefits, learn few skills, exercise little control over their workplace, quit after a few months, and float from job to job. The restaurant industry is now America's largest private employer, and it pays some of the lowest wages. During the economic boom of the 1990s, when many American workers enjoyed their first pay raises in a generation, the real value of wages in the restaurant industry continued to fall. The roughly 3.5 million fast food workers are by far the largest group of minimum wage earners in the United States. The only Americans who consistently earn a lower hourly wage are migrant farm workers.

Study/Writing/Discussion Questions

1. What facts surprised you most in Schlosser's essay?

2. In paragraph 4, what parallels does he draw between the growth of the fast food industry and fundamental changes in American society?

3. What does he have to say about standardization, uniformity, and conformity on the one hand, and nonconformist entrepreneurs on the other?

4. What final facts does he conclude with? How do they lend a dramatic effect to his conclusion?

Advanced Optional Writing Assignment

Write an essay of about four typed pages in which you describe an event in your own life or family life that involved facing and dealing with "hard facts." Were the facts subject to different interpretations? Did you go through different stages before you could come to acceptance? What changes resulted in your life because of these facts?

Optional Internet Research Assignment

1. Using Google or your preferred search engine, type in *Fact Checking* and see what sites you come up with. Visit several of these sites or

book references and write up what you discovered about available fact-checking resources.

2. Perhaps you would like to learn more about one of the authors who provided readings for this chapter. Begin by making a search for Eric Schlosser or Elizabeth Warren.

3. Professional reporters and fact-checkers use two online subscriber series sites (LexisNexis.com and FactsonFile.com) to verify information. If your library has a subscription to either of these sites, make a visit and write a short report on your discoveries.

CHAPTER 4

Inferences:
What Follows?

"If I am right in my guess that this is the Atlantic then we're the biggest fish in the world."

Used with permission of Richard Gundon.

Of course the fish are only the biggest fish in their own world, but they don't know that—only we do. We can be excellent observers, we can have some facts plainly before us, but still go wrong in the making of inferences. The problem is that inferences stand on even shakier ground than facts. When we learn to give them conscious attention, our thinking becomes more skillful. This chapter is dedicated to helping you do just that.

DISCOVERY EXERCISE

■ Recognizing Inferential Thinking

Study the cartoons on preceding pages. What kind of thinking is going on in the cartoons? How does the humor relate to this kind of thinking?

■ Defining Infer

After consulting a dictionary, write down your own definitions of the following words:

1. Reasoning
2. Conclusion
3. Guess
4. Explanation
5. Imagine
6. Infer
7. Inference
8. Interpret

Understanding the Words *Infer* and *Inference*

When we infer, we imagine, reason, guess, surmise, speculate, estimate, predict, and conclude.

> **Infer** The word *infer* comes from the Latin root *inferre*, meaning to bring in or to carry.
>
> When we infer, we bring in our imaginations to fill in for missing facts. We make guesses to form a bridge between what we know and don't know. We connect the dots.

We use inferences every hour of our lives in all its forms of imagining, guessing, estimating, predicting, and concluding. Inferences govern our simplest actions. If we see dark clouds (it must be going to rain), we take out our umbrellas. We devise complex chains of inferences in order to make decisions: what products to buy, apartments to rent, jobs to take, people to trust. Sometimes we connect the dots correctly, and sometimes we don't. The following two discovery exercises are designed to make this inference-making process more aware and conscious.

DISCOVERY EXERCISES

■ *Drawing Inferences from Evidence*

Read the following scenarios and think of three inferences you could make to explain each situation:

1. Your neighbors have regular habits and spend a lot of time at home. One day you notice that no lights have appeared in their house in the evenings for at least a week.

2. In an airport waiting room, you sit down next to a nun wearing a dark blue dress, starched white collar, and starched white headdress. You notice she is reading *Playboy* magazine.

3. Your child, age four, usually has a good appetite. However, she says no this morning when you offer her a dish of applesauce.

4. You are on a Greyhound bus. A man gets on and sits beside you. He is carrying an expensive briefcase, although he is shabbily dressed, unshaven, and perspiring heavily. When you suggest he place his briefcase on the rack overhead, he refuses, saying he doesn't mind holding it in his lap.

5. You are looking in your wife's closet for your missing shoe, and you notice a new and expensive man's sports jacket hanging there.

6. After a class you go to see your professor about an error in addition on your test score. You explain to him respectfully that 100 minus 18 is 82, not 79. He tells you to get the hell out of his office.

7. You are driving through a valley on a spring morning in a heavy rainstorm. You are on a two-lane highway, and you notice that only about half the cars that pass you head-on have their lights on.

TABLE 4.1 Safest and Most Dangerous U.S. Cities

Safest	Most Dangerous
1. Newton, Massachusetts	1. Camden, New Jersey
2. Brick Township, New Jersey	2. Detroit, Michigan
3. Amherst, New York	3. Atlanta, Georgia
4. Mission Viejo, California	4. St. Louis, Missouri
5. Clarkstown, New York	5. Gary, Indiana

Source: Morgan Quitno Corporation. Rankings based on city's rate for murder, rape, robbery, aggravated assault, burglary, and motor vehicle theft. Information Please Database © 2005 Pearson Education, Inc.

TABLE 4.2 US POPClock Projection

According to the U.S. Bureau of the Census, the resident population of the United States, projected to 04/17/05 at 17:34 GMT, is 295,905,121.

Component Settings

One birth every 8 seconds

One death every 12 seconds

One international migrant every 26 seconds

Net gain of one person every 13 seconds

Source: U.S. Census Bureau, Population Division.

TABLE 4.3 Average Cost of Tuition and Fees by U.S. Regions

Public Colleges and Universities		Private Colleges and Universities
Northeast	6,839	25,660
Middle States	6,300	21,439
Midwest	6,055	18,690
Southwest	4,569	15,867
South	4,143	17,317
West	4,130	19,998

Source: Trends in College Pricing 2004. CollegeBoard.com.

■ Drawing Inferences from Facts

When we interpret the meaning of facts, we draw inferences about them. How many inferences can you draw from the facts listed in Tables 4.1, 4.2, and 4.3? Note if you can experience your mind making inferences as they take place.

Distinguishing Inferences from Facts

> Good writing distinguishes inferences from facts, description from interpretation.

Inferences are very often confused with facts, as you may well have discovered from doing the Discovery Exercise on the mythical Johnson family in the Introduction.

From *Anonymous* by Robert Flynn Johnson, Thames & Hudson, London and New York. Used with permission of Thames & Hudson Ltd.

Moreover, as you learned when you described a photograph in the last chapter, the work of identifying the facts by stating details instead of substituting inferences made about these details is the primary challenge of descriptive writing. Usually, specific details are the most conspicuous and obvious information we can see; indeed, they can be so obvious that we do not even realize we are seeing them. One of the most difficult things about learning how to write descriptive reports is to remember to give the details and let them speak for themselves as much as possible instead of substituting our inferences or interpretations of what they mean.

To review the difference between statements of fact and inferences, suppose three people were asked to describe what they saw when they looked at a photograph of a man wearing overalls and lying with his eyes closed under a tree. Suppose each person just gave you one statement:

- This is a picture of a man who is dead drunk.
- This is a farmer resting during his lunch hour.
- This is a picture of a man who just had a car crash.

Although each person might think that he or she has sized up the situation correctly, none has carefully examined or described the evidence. Instead, only final *interpretations* are offered. Each statement might seem to be a plausible explanation of why the man is lying under the tree, but none of these conclusions can be verified. Therefore, we have to present our evidence carefully, which is what we do in description. Our facts are our evidence. And facts can often lie in the *obvious*—the ordinary details that we take for granted. When we describe, we need to set forth our perceptions without assuming that others see or interpret things as we do.

The practice of stating the obvious also helps the writer draw better inferences. When we review our evidence, we may discover that we had rushed to hasty conclusions such as those offered previously. A man dressed in overalls lying under a tree is just a man dressed in overalls lying under a tree; he is not a drunk, not a lunchtime loafer, and not a car wreck victim. Such labels are not facts, only interpretations. However, this does not mean we should never make interpretations. It is just that we need to draw only those that our facts can support. Yet such a practice goes contrary to human inclinations, or to the preference to rush to interpretations.

Thus, descriptive writing can become a discipline for the mind; it stretches our capacities to state our facts and think about them with care. And it requires slowing down and taking our time. Nevertheless, the results are worth it, for descriptive writing that presents its facts with responsible clarity is also *interesting* writing. When we clearly describe what we observe and think, our work naturally becomes concrete and specific, and therefore more alive and interesting to ourselves and to others.

Short Break Study Questions

Which of the following statements are descriptive statements and which are interpretations? Translate the latter into descriptive.

   a. She is a strange person.
   b. When you don't pass the ketchup when I ask, I wonder why.
   c. Whenever I see him, I feel angry inside.
   d. Instead of listening to me, she tore out of the room on a rampage.

From *Anonymous* by Robert Flynn Johnson, Thames & Hudson, Thames & Hudson, London and New York. Used with permission of Thames & Hudson Ltd.

How Inferences Can Go Right and Wrong

We make inferences to help us fill in for missing facts and in order to make sense of the facts we have. As we make inferences, we have to keep checking them against our facts; otherwise we can build one faulty inference on top of another.

We solve problems by asking questions, gathering facts, making inferences from them, and then letting these inferences suggest strategies for finding new facts, which in turn lead to new inferences. Each inference directs us toward our objective. When we use inferences consciously and imaginatively, they give us the certainties we need to move forward. Inferences are *essential* mental operations in the search for knowledge. But we have to learn how to make them soundly. The greatest difficulties occur when inferences are confused with facts or acted upon as though they were facts. Inferences used with conscious skill lead us to knowledge. When used without conscious awareness, they lead us to confusion and illusion.

Let us now consider contrasting examples of how inferences can create either knowledge or confusion. Let's begin with a reading selection showing the thinking of that master of skillful inference, Sherlock Holmes.

● R E A D I N G ●

The Adventure of the Speckled Band (1892)

Sir Arthur Conan Doyle (1859–1930)

"Good-morning, madam," said Holmes cheerily. "My name is Sherlock Holmes. This is my intimate friend and associate, Dr. Watson, before whom you can speak as freely as before myself. Ha! I am glad to see that Mrs. Hudson has had the good sense to light the fire. Pray draw up to it, and I shall order you a cup of hot coffee, for I observe that you are shivering."

"It is not cold which makes me shiver," said the woman in a low voice, changing her seat as requested.

"What, then?"

"It is fear, Mr. Holmes. It is terror." She raised her veil as she spoke, and we could see that she was indeed in a pitiable state of agitation, her face all drawn and gray, with restless frightened eyes, like those of some hunted animal. Her features and figure were those of a woman of thirty, but her hair was shot with premature gray, and her expression was weary and haggard. Sherlock Holmes ran her over with one of his quick, all-comprehensive glances.

5 "You must not fear," said he soothingly, bending forward and patting her forearm. "We shall soon set matters right, I have no doubt. You have come in by train this morning, I see."

"You know me, then?"

"No, but I observe the second half of a return ticket in the palm of your left glove. You must have started early, and yet you had a good drive in a dog-cart, along heavy roads, before you reached the station."

The lady gave a violent start and stared in bewilderment at my companion.

"There is no mystery, my dear madam," said he, smiling. "The left arm of your jacket is spattered with mud in no less than seven places. The marks are perfectly fresh. There is no vehicle save a dog-cart which throws up mud in that way, and then only when you sit on the left-hand side of the driver."

10   "Whatever your reasons may be, you are perfectly correct," said she. "I started from home before six, reached Leatherhead at twenty past, and came in by the first train to Waterloo. Sir, I can stand this strain no longer; I . . . ."

Excerpt from Sir Arthur Conan Doyle, "The Adventure of the Speckled Band," 1892.

● ● ●

Study/Writing/Discussion Questions

1. In this short excerpt, what three inferences does Sherlock Holmes make about the visiting lady? Are all three correct?

2. On what observations (clues) does he base these inferences?

3. Describe a situation in which one of the following individuals would need to make skillful inferences:

   a. A physician   d. A cook

   b. A salesperson   e. An antique appraiser

   c. A car mechanic

The fascination that Holmes holds for us lies in his uncanny ability to draw correct inferences. He is a fictional hero, not of physical but of mental prowess. His appeal endures because we all know that wrong inferences can hurt us, whereas correct inferences give us power, vision, and speed. The danger is that even one faulty inference can get us into trouble. Moreover we can build a wobbly leaning tower of inferences on the foundation of one mistaken one. Let's look at a simple example of how two different people confronted this challenge.

Neighbor 1	Neighbor 2
Facts observed	**Facts observed**
1. I see John sitting on the front steps of his house.	1. I see John sitting on the front steps of his house.
2. It is Monday morning. He usually is at school by this time.	2. It is Monday morning. He usually is at school at this time.
Chain of inferences	**Chain of inferences**
1. He could be sick.	1. He's pretending to be sick.
2. He could be playing hooky.	2. He was probably out late partying last night.
3. Maybe he has some good reason to be at home.	3. I'll bet he is hung over from drugs and alcohol.
4. In any case, I don't think he'd mind talking to me.	4. I'll bet his parents don't know.
Conclusion	**New chain of inferences**
I'll go over and ask him what's up.	1. If this keeps up, he'll get kicked out of school.
	2. Maybe he's been suspended already.
	Conclusion
	I had better call up his parents at work and tell them he's in real trouble.

Class Discussion

1. Why do the inferences drawn by Neighbor 1 and Neighbor 2 go in such different directions?
2. What is the difference between the way Neighbor 1 and Neighbor 2 work with their facts and inferences?
3. Give an example of a time when you jumped to a conclusion, or made a hasty inference, then went way off course as a result when you built a whole structure of reasoning on top of that first faulty inference.

Drawing Inferences from Careful Observation

Though we may not have all the facts about a photograph, we can learn a lot by recording the details we can observe and by drawing careful inferences from them. Since it is easier to show than describe how this is done, we'll examine how one person used observation and inference to describe the photo on page 117. As you read the description, notice these features:

1. The facts appear first, followed by the inferences that can reasonably be drawn from them.
2. More than one inference can be drawn from each set of facts.
3. The factual information groups together the details of one segment or feature of the photograph at a time.
4. The conclusion draws together the facts and the possible inferences into a plausible explanation of the message, purpose, and meaning of the photograph.

Facts

This black-and-white photo centers on two individuals seen from the waist up; their heads are bent a little forward and their eyes appear directed downward toward a row of small raised black rectangles above a lined white surface. This black-and-white area is encased within curved and rectangular wooden-textured surfaces.

Inferences

1. They are both seated and looking down at a piano keyboard.
2. They are both concentrating.

Facts

The individual seen in profile in the foreground has shoulder-length, thick, straight, dark hair extended to cover her forehead and most of one ear. The one eye visible has a full eyelid and the cheeks hang soft, smooth, and childlike.

Inferences

1. She is a young girl around 12 years old.
2. She is of Asian descent.

Facts

To the girl's left, in the direct center of the photograph, the second individual's head appears slightly above the dark head of the girl. The hair is in a man's cut, white, and appears thinner over a broad forehead. The eyebrows are also white and shaggy over his dark downward-gazing eyes. The skin seems lighter than that of the girl. A fold of skin beneath his chin hangs above a dark tie and white shirt. Lapels and medium-valued folds along sides and arms suggest a man's suit.

Inferences

1. He is a Caucasian male in his 60s.
2. He is a professional who dresses somewhat formally.

Facts

His left arm is bent with two fingers stretched forward over the keyboard.

Inferences

1. He is resting his elbow on the piano.
2. He is her piano teacher.
3. He is giving very close attention.
4. He is prepared to help her hit the right keys.

Facts

The young girl is wearing a shirt in white and some middle-value color; her sleeves extend to her elbows. Her left arm reaches toward the piano with her fingers and thumb poised above the keys. Her right arm, visible in the foreground, seems wrapped a plastic casing with large white dots on its surface. In the place of a right hand is long knob of wooden texture that has a dark thin rectangular slot on the side facing the camera. A cable line extends from her elbow to a bobbin at the end of this slot. A second slot appears on top of this wooden knob from which a small white object with a sharp point extends.

Inferences

1. The girl has lost her right hand and some, or all, of her right arm. She wears a prosthetic device both plastic and wooden.
2. The white spots on her arm are holes in the plastic.
3. She is able to play the piano through use of this cable. By placing a pencil in the wooden "hand" device, she can hit the notes with the pencil's eraser end.
4. She has experienced a terrible injury but that is past.
5. She is dressed informally, wearing an oversized T-shirt.

Facts

Her lips, seen in profile, have the slight curve of a smile. Her body posture appears soft rather than tense. The mouth of the teacher is slightly open; the direction of his gaze is toward her hands on the keyboard.

Inferences

1. The teacher is about to say something.
2. His hands are poised to help her hands.
3. The girl is confident and glad of her accomplishment.
4. Both are too absorbed to notice the photographer.

Facts

The piano lacks sheen; its texture is marred by random light ragged-edged spots. The area behind the pupil and teacher is dark and rectangular. Silver lines appear at top and bottom. Horizontal and vertical blonde shapes appear that suggest a table and chair. No other people appear in the background.

Inferences

1. They are alone in a schoolroom that has a blackboard, student tables, and chairs.
2. She is playing a beat-up upright classroom piano.
3. They are having an after-school lesson in a classroom.

Conclusion

This photo presents three separate contrasting entities—the girl, the man, and the piano—in a revolving circle. The scene is a simple one: that of a piano lesson. What cannot be seen or heard is the music they have made, the limitations overcome. Without pity or sentimentality, the photo presents their intelligent collaboration.

Core Discovery Writing Application

■ Using Facts and Inferences to Describe a Photograph

1. This is a mental exercise that uses writing. Choose a photograph in this book not already described by the author. For your notes, make yourself a page with columns like this:

Facts of the Photograph	Inferences I Make about This Fact
My description of a detail: a form, texture, shade, relationship, or configuration that I see.	What I imagine this detail represents or what I interpret it to mean.

2. Survey the photograph in a systematic way, beginning with what is central, then moving to relationships of the parts and the background.

3. Write out your list using the columns in step 1 to match each statement of fact with an inference. (Actually, in your thinking, the inference will probably come to mind first. If so, write it down, then restudy the photo to discover and describe the evidence upon which this inference was based.)

4. Write a conclusion that draws your list of facts and inferences together into an explanation of the photograph. (See the example on page 119). This concluding summary should not introduce new information or provide a story that your evidence cannot support.

5. Now write your description in the form illustrated for you in the preceding exercise on pages 116–119. Remember to end with a summary.

6. The length should be at least two typed pages.

Scoring Using Facts and Inferences to Describe a Photograph

1. Obvious details not ignored. *10 points*

2. Statements of fact described rather than just named or interpreted. *20 points*

3. Systematic organization of data: systematic sectioning of photo—small groupings of related facts, shown with inferences clearly drawn from each grouping. *20 points*

4. Some imaginative use of inferences beyond the obvious. *10 points*

5. Conclusion brings given facts and inferences together in a logical interpretation (not introducing new facts or a fantasy). *20 points*

6. No distracting errors of spelling, punctuation, sentence structure. *10 points*

7. Minimum length of two typed pages. *10 points*

Generalizations Are Inferences

A good scientist, like a good writer, knows how much evidence is needed to support a generalization.

Samuel Scudder, whose encounter with a fish was described in Chapter 1, stated that "Agassiz's training in the method of observing facts and their orderly arrangement was ever accompanied by the urgent exhortation not to be content with them. 'Facts are stupid things,' he would say, 'until brought into connection with some general law.'" We can apply this statement to our concerns about thinking and writing. It is not enough to collect and state facts and inferences alone; we need to look for patterns in them and see how we can make generalizations to describe their organizing principles or "laws."

> "Do you perhaps mean," I asked, "that the fish has symmetrical sides with paired organs?"
> His thoroughly pleased "Of course! Of course!" repaid the wakeful hours of the previous night.

In science, laws are **generalizations** that are based on observations and that deal with recurrence, order, and relationships. Generalizations, in turn, relate individual members of a class or category to a whole. To arrive at laws or generalizations, we must look for information, then look for patterns or configurations, analyze them, and finally draw conclusions about the relationships, recurrences, and order of the gathered data. These were the complex mental actions you followed when drawing conclusions in the last exercise.

It takes experience to know when you have gathered enough information to make accurate generalizations. Beginners, like Scudder, may decide they have seen everything after ten minutes or, at the other extreme, refrain from drawing conclusions for too long. A good scientist, like a good writer, recognizes how much evidence is needed to support reliable generalizations.

When you first listed only facts about a photograph, you may have experienced the sense of the "stupidity" of facts that Agassiz referred to. Perhaps you had a sense of not knowing where to stop or how to separate the relevant details from the irrelevant. However, this first stage of simple-minded observing and collecting is important.

In the second stage of writing and of thinking, we begin to separate, compare, categorize, and organize our information. In the photograph description our intuition may first put everything together. Eventually, we are able to formulate all this into a generalization that is a summary statement. In paragraph writing, this statement becomes our **topic sentence**. This (usually first) sentence states in a general way the main idea to be proven or explained. What then follows is the evidence—the facts and inferences that support the main idea. Therefore what we do is present our topic sentence, which is actually our conclusion, *first* in our writing, although we arrived at it *last* in our thinking. This is exactly what you did in the exercise where you first wrote down your facts and inferences in columns and then drew a conclusion at the end that summarized all your information.

The topic sentence serves both as a statement of commitment and as a guide, aiding us in sorting out what support is needed and relevant. A topic sentence functions like a magnet in this respect. It also *tests* our facts and our inferences about them. We may even discover that the evidence we have selected does not support our topic sentence very well at all. In such cases, we stop and begin again.

The willingness to loop back and forth between the evidence and the generalization takes persistence fueled by a resolve to arrive at truth as best we can. Such a process must be familiar to you from your own writing experience, although you may never have looked at what you were doing in this conscious way before. The following exercise is designed to have you write with this conscious awareness in mind.

Composition Writing Application

■ Writing a Paragraph from Facts, Inferences, and Generalizations

Choose a photograph from this chapter that you have not described before or study the *Doonesbury* cartoon on page 123. Working alone, observe your photograph or cartoon for a while, noticing what is plainly visible.

Make notes by listing your facts and seeing what inferences you can draw from them. Putting this information together, draw a conclusion about the whole. What message, what statement about life do you think is being conveyed here? Write this conclusion at the top of your page. Use this sentence as a topic sentence for a paragraph to follow that makes a general statement or conclusion about your evidence.

Now write the rest of the paragraph in sentences. Describe the photograph or cartoon using all the facts you can to support your topic sentence. Link these facts to your inferences appropriately throughout. At the end, bring everything together into a second conclusion or a summary of what you have demonstrated.

Read your paragraph aloud to one to three other students who selected the same photo or cartoon. Did you find that you supported your topic sentence adequately?

■ Questions about the Doonesbury Cartoon

1. What is the professor trying to teach his students?
2. What inferences does he expect them to make?
3. What inferences do they make?
4. What clues led you to your own conclusions about this cartoon?
5. How would you describe the professor's teaching style?

Doonesbury

G. B. TRUDEAU

Core Discovery Writing Application

■ Analyzing the Use of Facts and Inferences in a Newspaper Article

1. Work with the article on pages 125–127 called "Tougher Grading Better for Students" or with another article assigned to you by the instructor. Read the article carefully. Then make a chart with four columns, as shown in Table 4.4. After you read each sentence, choose

TABLE 4.4 Analyzing Facts and Inferences

Data Claimed to Be Factual in This Sentence	Inferences Expressed in This Sentence	Pertinent Missing Information	My Own Inference about This Sentence
	"Tougher Grading Better for Students"		Wow! I didn't know that. This must be true since it is based on research.
	"America's high school students may not be getting smarter, but their teachers are getting more generous—at least when it comes to grading."	Who arrived at this conclusion? Was that the unanimous opinion of the teachers surveyed? Or is it the opinion of one or more researchers?	This statement is a rather broad unqualified generalization. Surely there must be a significant number of exceptions.
A national survey released this month showed that a record 28 percent of incoming college freshmen had A averages, up from only 12.5 percent in 1969.		Both private and public college freshmen? And do students take the same high school courses now with the same content and standards offered in 1969?	Maybe teachers don't grade as hard as they used to because students complain more about their grades. Maybe students receive better instruction and training in how to improve their study habits now than in 1969.

the column that seems appropriate for entering quotes or comments. The examples in Table 4.4 should help you get started. Proceed as in this example, working sentence by sentence, analyzing each one.

2. To save time, you can make a photocopy of the article and cut and paste some sentences into the appropriate columns. When working with quotations, note that although the public statement may be a fact, its content could be an inference. In such cases, put the quote in the first column, and in the second column, note that it expresses an inference.

3. Line for line, as you proceed through the article, notice if you find any information missing. Consider what you or an ordinary reader would need to have in order to understand and believe its claims. Is enough information given about the sources of facts so that they could be verified? Are there enough facts, enough inferences, sufficient explanations? As you read, notice the times you feel puzzled, curious, confused, or suspicious. Then consider if these reactions could be due to pertinent missing information.

4. In the last column, record your thinking about each recorded fact and/or inference. Write down your conclusions, questions, comments, and reactions.

5. When you have finished going through the whole article systematically, prepare your chart in final form by typing and/or by cutting and pasting.

6. On a final sheet of paper, sum up what you learned through your analysis in one paragraph. Did you conclude that the article offers reliable information? Did your final impressions differ from your first?

● R E A D I N G ●

Tougher Grading Better for Students

America's high school students may not be getting much smarter, but their teachers are getting more generous—at least when it comes to grading.

A national survey released this month showed that a record 28 percent of incoming college freshmen had A averages, up from only 12.5 percent in 1969. During much of that period, ironically, student scores on standardized tests actually declined.

Higher grades and lower test scores may be related, according to new research by economists Julian Betts and Stefan Boedeker at the University of California, San Diego. They find a strong relationship between school grading standards and student achievement: The tougher a school grades, the harder its students work and the more they learn.

Their finding is enormously significant. "For thirty years, social scientists have been trying to decide why some schools are good and some are bad," said Betts. "They looked at class size, teacher education and per pupil spending, none of which seem to matter much. So I decided to look at standards set in the schools."

5 If Betts and Boedeker are right, spending more money on schools may help a lot less than simply changing the incentives facing students. If they are allowed to slack off and still earn good grades, most will take it easy. But holding them to higher standards costs nothing and can motivate them to achieve more.

Betts and Boedeker studied the math and science performance of roughly 6,000 middle- and high-school students nationwide over five years, starting in 1987. Students were tested each year to measure how much they were learning. The researchers also had information on grading standards, amount of homework assigned and other factors.

The two scholars found large differences in grading standards between schools and a strong relationship between those standards and how much students learned each year. Over five years, otherwise similar students at tough schools scored about 6 points more than students at easy schools on standardized tests with 100 as the top score. A 6-point difference is huge, Betts said.

Stronger students seem to benefit the most from tougher standards, suggesting that other policies must also be sought to "help the weaker students match the gains in achievement of their (better) prepared counterparts."

One solution to uneven grading standards would be to hold standardized state or national graduation exams to test high school achievement and thus give students more incentive to take their studies seriously. Such exams are routine in Europe and Japan, where graduating students are much further advanced than their American counterparts.

10 Bishop tested this theory by comparing the math performance of 13-year-olds (measured by an international test administered in 1991) in Canadian provinces that have standardized graduation exams and in those that don't.

His findings were striking. In Canadian provinces with testing, students learned about two-thirds of a grade level more than those in provinces without.

"One of the most cost-effective methods of improving achievement in American schools would be to create curriculum-based exams for each state," Bishop said.

Reprinted with permission. ©1995 *San Francisco Chronicle.*

● ● ●

Scoring for Analyzing Facts and Inferences in a Newspaper Article

1. Correct identification of all facts and inferences appearing in the article. *30 points*
2. Does not confuse own inferences with those made in article. *10 points*
3. Shows an understanding that although a quotation may be presented as fact, its content may express an inference. *10 points*
4. Shows understanding that estimates, predictions, and opinions are inferences. *10 points*
5. Missing information column shows thoughtful reflection on *pertinent* missing data. *10 points*
6. Own inferences are drawn systematically, item for item, and show careful reflection on the data. *10 points*
7. Format is systematic, methodical, and easy to read. *10 points*
8. Final conclusion assesses how the information is presented in the article. *10 points*

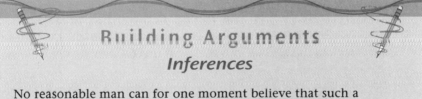

Building Arguments

Inferences

No reasonable man can for one moment believe that such a Beautiful country [America] was intended by its Author [God] to be forever in the possession and occupancy of serpents, wild fowls, wild beasts and savages who derive little benefit from it. (Caleb Atwater, 1850)

Exercise

1. The previous is a claim based on an inference. Put the claim into your own words. Explain how its reasoning is an inference.
2. What conclusion is implied?
3. What evidence is offered in support of the claim?
4. Explain how the claim justifies the author's values.
5. Make a claim that is based on an inference.

Chapter Summary

1. The word *infer* means (a) to derive by reasoning, (b) to conclude, (c) to guess. When we infer, we use imagination or reasoning to provide explanations for situations in which all the facts are either not available or not yet determined.

2. Responsible report writing or descriptive writing lets the facts speak for themselves as much as possible. This often means taking the time to find the right words to describe the obvious and abandoning inferences drawn too hastily that cannot be supported.

3. Writing that offers specific detailed support for its conclusions makes interesting writing. When we perceive and think clearly, we interest both ourselves and others.

4. Reasonable inferences can be used in descriptive writing to tie facts together. Care must be taken to distinguish facts from inferences, nevertheless.

5. In solving problems, inferences can be used as a strategy in planning and choosing alternatives. When we think well, we assess all facts, derive as many inferences as we can, and devise strategies for confirming or obtaining more information.

6. Detectives and consultants of all kinds are valued for their ability to examine facts and make the best inferences from them.

7. Inferences tend to build on inferences in chains of association. Unless each inference is tested for its support of evidence, a series of inferences can mislead us into flights of imagination, away from reliable knowledge.

8. Facts and inferences are linked together through generalizations. Facts have little significance in themselves until generalizations or laws can be derived from them. Generalizing too soon, before we have gathered a sufficient number of facts, is hazardous. This does not mean that we should not generalize at all; it simply means that we should learn how to draw generalizations that can be supported.

9. The topic sentence of a paragraph is a generalization that summarizes the main idea to be demonstrated in that paragraph. When we think, we usually arrive at this generalization last, after we have examined all our facts and inferences; nevertheless, we state it first, at the beginning of the paragraph. The topic sentence is a kind of conclusion, which is repeated again in another form at the end of the paragraph.

10. By the time you have finished this chapter, you should understand more about the thinking operations involved in constructing a paragraph or engaging in descriptive writing. You will understand how observation helps determine facts, imagination, and reasoning to link the facts with explanations, and how a generalization ties all this information together into a meaningful whole.

Chapter Quiz

Write two inferences to explain each of the following events:

1. You see a little girl pushing an elderly woman down Main Street in a large baby carriage.
2. Your best friend leaves you a note saying she has joined the Marines.
3. You have received no mail for the past two weeks.
4. A recent study found that men between fifty and seventy-nine years old married to women one to twenty-four years younger tended to live longer, with a mortality rate 13 percent below the norm.
5. The same study found that men married to older women died sooner; their death rate was 20 percent higher than the norm.

Rate each of the following statements as *true* or *false*. Explain your choice in each case or give an example to defend your choice.

_____   6. To state that "annual beef consumption in the United States is 96.8 pounds per capita in 1998, as compared to 11 pounds in China" is to make a generalization without facts.

_____   7. To state the obvious is to state the sensory details of what is actually seen, as opposed to what is *thought* or interpreted about what is seen.

_____   8. Good thinking does not continue to build inferences on top of inferences but stops whenever possible to check these inferences against the original facts or to find new ones.

_____   9. One should always avoid making inferences in every kind of writing.

_____   10. To state that the United States has the highest per capita use of motor vehicles in the world is to make a generalization without offering the supporting facts.

● R E A D I N G S ●

The Three Perceptives

Idries Shah

This is an old teaching story of the Sufis, a mystic Muslim sect that claims to be far older than Islam. Their stories are parables told to help people understand the nature of the mind and how to use it to gain wisdom. The term perceptives *might also be translated as "wise men." This reading was translated by Idries Shah, one of the leading interpreters of Sufi philosophy in the West. As you read it, take note of how accurately the three men connect their inferences to both their observation skills and past experiences.*

There were once three Sufis, so observant and experienced in life that they were known as The Three Perceptives.

One day during their travels they encountered a camelman, who said, "Have you seen my camel? I have lost it."

"Was it blind in one eye?" asked the first Perceptive.

"Yes," said the cameldriver.

5   "Has it one tooth missing in front?" asked the second Perceptive.

"Yes, yes," said the cameldriver.

"Is it lame in one foot?" asked the third Perceptive.

"Yes, yes, yes," said the cameldriver.

The three Perceptives then told the man to go back along the way they had come, and that he might hope to find it. Thinking that they had seen it, the man hurried on his way.

10   But the man did not find his camel, and he hastened to catch up with the Perceptives, hoping that they would tell him what to do.

He found them that evening, at a resting-place.

"Has your camel honey on one side and a load of corn on the other?" asked the first Perceptive.

"Yes," said the man.

"Is there a pregnant woman mounted upon it?" asked the second Perceptive.

15   "Yes, yes," said the man.

"We do not know where it is," said the third Perceptive.

The cameldriver was now convinced that the Perceptives had stolen his camel, passenger and all, and he took them to the judge, accusing them of the theft.

The judge thought that he had made out a case, and detained the three men in custody on suspicion of theft.

A little later, the man found his camel wandering in some fields, and returning to the court, arranged for the Perceptives to be released.

20   The judge, who had not given them a chance to explain themselves before, asked how it was that they knew so much about the camel, since they had apparently not even seen it.

"We saw the footprints of a camel on the road," said the first Perceptive.

"One of the tracks was faint; it must have been lame," said the second Perceptive.

"It had stripped the bushes at only one side of the road, so it must have been blind in one eye," said the third Perceptive.

"The leaves were shredded, which indicated the loss of a tooth," continued the first Perceptive.

25   "Bees and ants, on different sides of the road, were swarming over something deposited; we saw that this was honey and corn," said the second Perceptive.

"We found long human hair where someone had stopped and dismounted, it was a woman's," said the third Perceptive.

"Where the person had sat down there were palm-prints, we thought from the use of the hands that the woman was probably very pregnant and had to stand up in that way," said the first Perceptive.

"Why did you not apply for your side of the case to be heard so that you could explain yourselves?" asked the judge.

"Because we reckoned that the cameldriver would continue looking for his camel and might find it soon," said the first Perceptive.

30   "He would feel generous in releasing us through his discovery," said the second Perceptive.

"The curiosity of the judge would prompt an enquiry," said the third Perceptive.

"Discovering the truth by his own enquiries would be better for all than for us to claim that we had been impatiently handled," said the first Perceptive.

"It is our experience that it is generally better for people to arrive at truth through what they take to be their own volition," said the second Perceptive.

"It is time for us to move on, for there is work to be done," said the third Perceptive.

35   And the Sufi thinkers went on their way. They are still to be found at work on the highways of the earth.

From Idries Shah, *The Caravan of Dreams.* New York: Penguin Books, 1972. Author and date of origin of "The Three Perceptives" unknown. Reprinted with permission of The Octagon Press Ltd., London.

● ● ●

Study/Writing/Discussion Questions

1. Make a list with two columns. On one side, state the inferences made by the three men. On the other side show the facts to which they related these inferences.

2. Why were the men so restrained in defending themselves?

3. What do you think of their statement: "It is our experience that it is generally better for people to arrive at truth through what they take to be their own volition." Can you apply this to learning and teaching?

4. What would you say is the most important value of the three men?

• • •

The Stone Boy

Gina Berriault

This story was first published in Mademoiselle magazine; it was then scripted by Berriault into a Hollywood film—with a happy ending—in 1984. The author has received many awards and has served on the faculty of San Francisco State University. In your first reading of this story, look at (1) how the plot of this story revolves around the inference making of its characters and (2) how your own inference making enables you to "participate" in the story, thus achieving a deeper understanding of it.

Arnold drew his overalls and raveling gray sweater over his naked body. In the other narrow bed his brother Eugene went on sleeping, undisturbed by the alarm clock's rusty ring. Arnold, watching his brother sleeping, felt a peculiar dismay; he was nine, six years younger than Eugie, and in their waking hours it was he who was subordinate. To dispel emphatically his uneasy advantage over his sleeping brother, he threw himself on the hump of Eugie's body.

"Get up! Get up!" he cried.

Arnold felt his brother twist away and saw the blankets lifted in a great wing, and, all in an instant, he was lying on his back under the covers with only his face showing, like a baby, and Eugie was sprawled on top of him.

"Whassa matter with you?" asked Eugie in sleepy anger, his face hanging close.

5   "Get up," Arnold repeated. "You said you'd pick peas with me."

Stupidly, Eugie gazed around the room as if to see if morning had come into it yet. Arnold began to laugh derisively, making soft, snorting noises, and was thrown off the bed. He got up from the floor and went down the stairs, the laughter continuing, like hiccups, against his will. But when he opened the staircase door and entered the parlor, he hunched up his shoulders and was quiet because his parents slept in the bedroom downstairs.

Arnold lifted his .22-caliber rifle from the rack on the kitchen wall. It was an old lever-action Winchester that his father had given him because nobody else used it any more. On their way down to the garden he and Eugie would go by the lake, and if there were any ducks on it he'd take a shot at them.

Standing on the stool before the cupboard, he searched on the top shelf in the confusion of medicines and ointments for man and beast and found a small yellow box of .22 cartridges. Then he sat down on the stool and began to load his gun.

It was cold in the kitchen so early, but later in the day, when his mother canned the peas, the heat from the wood stove would be almost unbearable. Yesterday she had finished preserving the huckleberries that the family had picked along the mountain, and before that she had canned all the cherries his father had brought from the warehouse in Corinth. Sometimes, on these summer days, Arnold would deliberately come out from the shade where he was playing and make himself as uncomfortable as his mother was in the kitchen by standing in the sun until the sweat ran down his body.

Eugie came clomping down the stairs and into the kitchen, his head drooping with sleepiness. From his perch on the stool, Arnold watched Eugie slip on his green knit cap. Eugie didn't really need a cap; he hadn't had a haircut in a long time and his brown curls grew thick and matted, close around his ears and down his neck, tapering there to a small whorl. Eugie passed his left hand through his hair before he set his cap down with his right. The very way he slipped his cap on was an announcement of his status; almost everything he did was a reminder that he was eldest—first he, then Nora, then Arnold—and called attention to how tall he was (almost as tall as his father), how long his legs were, how small he was in the hips, and what a neat dip above his buttocks his thick-soled logger's boots gave him. Arnold never tired of watching Eugie offer silent praise unto himself. He wondered, as he sat enthralled, if when he got to be Eugie's age he would still be undersized and his hair still straight.

10   Eugie eyed the gun. "Don't you know this ain't duck-season?" he asked gruffly, as if he were the sheriff.

"No, I don't know," Arnold said with a snigger.

Eugie picked up the tin washtub for the peas, unbolted the door with his free hand and kicked it open. Then, lifting the tub to his head, he went clomping down the back steps. Arnold followed, closing the door behind him.

The sky was faintly gray, almost white. The mountains behind the farm made the sun climb a long way to show itself. Several miles to the south, where the range opened up, hung an orange mist, but the valley in which the farm lay was still cold and colorless.

Eugie opened the gate to the yard and the boys passed between the barn and the row of chicken houses, their feet stirring up the carpet of brown feathers dropped by the molting chickens. They paused before going down the slope to the lake. A fluky morning wind ran among the shocks of wheat that covered the slope. It sent a shimmer northward across the lake, gently moving the rushes that formed an island in the center. Killdeer, their white markings flashing, skimmed the water, crying their shrill, sweet cry. And there at the south end of the lake were four wild ducks, swimming out from the willows into open water.

15   Arnold followed Eugie down the slope, stealing, as his brother did, from one shock of wheat to another. Eugie paused before climbing through the wire fence that divided the wheatfield from the marshy pasture around the lake. They were screened from the ducks by the willows along the lake's edge.

"If you hit your duck, you want me to go in after it?" Eugie said.

"If you want," Arnold said.

Eugie lowered his eyelids, leaving slits of mocking blue. "You'd drown 'fore you got to it, them legs of yours are so puny," he said.

He shoved the tub under the fence and, pressing down the center wire, climbed through into the pasture.

20   Arnold pressed down the bottom wire, thrust a leg through and leaned forward to bring the other leg after. His rifle caught on the wire and he jerked at it. The air was rocked by the sound of the shot. Feeling foolish, he lifted his face, baring it to an expected shower of derision from his brother. But Eugie did not turn around. Instead, from his crouching position, he fell to his knees and then pitched forward onto his face. The ducks rose up crying from the lake, cleared the mountain background and beat away northward across the pale sky.

Arnold squatted beside his brother. Eugie seemed to be climbing the earth, as if the earth ran up and down, and when he found he couldn't scale it he lay still.

"Eugie?"

Then Arnold saw it, under the tendril of hair at the nape of the neck—a slow rising of bright blood. It had an obnoxious movement, like that of a parasite.

"Hey, Eugie," he said again. He was feeling the same discomfort he had felt when he had watched Eugie sleeping; his brother didn't know that he was lying face down in the pasture.

25   Again he said, "Hey, Eugie," an anxious nudge in his voice. But Eugie was as still as the morning about them.

Arnold set his rifle on the ground and stood up. He picked up the tub and, dragging it behind him, walked along by the willows to the garden fence and climbed through. He went down on his knees among the tangled vines. The pods were cold with the night, but his hands were strange to him, and not until some time had passed did he realize that the pods were numbing his fingers. He picked from the top of the vine first, then lifted the vine to look underneath for pods and then moved on to the next.

It was a warmth on his back, like a large hand laid firmly there, that made him raise his head. Way up the slope the gray farmhouse was struck by the sun. While his head had been bent the land had grown bright around him.

When he got up his legs were so stiff that he had to go down on his knees again to ease the pain. Then, walking sideways, he dragged the tub, half full of peas, up the slope.

The kitchen was warm now; a fire was roaring in the stove with a closed-up, rushing sound. His mother was spooning eggs from a pot of boiling water and putting them into a bowl. Her short brown hair was uncombed and fell forward across her eyes as she bent her head. Nora was lifting a frying pan full of trout from the stove, holding the handle with a dish towel. His father had just come in from bringing the cows from the north pasture to the barn, and was sitting on the stool, unbuttoning his red plaid Mackinaw.

30   "Did you boys fill the tub?" his mother asked.

"They ought of by now," his father said. "They went out of the house an hour ago. Eugie woke me up comin' downstairs. I heard you shootin'—did you get a duck?"

"No," Arnold said. They would want to know why Eugie wasn't coming in for breakfast, he thought. "Eugie's dead," he told them.

They stared at him. The pitch cracked in the stove.

"You kids playin' a joke?" his father asked.

35   "Where's Eugene?" his mother asked scoldingly. She wanted, Arnold knew, to see his eyes, and when he had glanced at her she put the bowl and spoon down on the stove and walked past him. His father stood up and went out the door after her. Nora followed them with little skipping steps, as if afraid to be left alone.

Arnold went into the barn, down along the foddering passage past the cows waiting to be milked, and climbed into the loft. After a few minutes he heard a terrifying sound coming toward the house. His parents and Nora were returning from the willows, and sounds sharp as knives were rising from his mother's breast and carrying over the sloping fields. In a short while he heard his father go down the back steps, slam the car door and drive away.

Arnold lay still as a fugitive, listening to the cows eating close by. If his parents never called him, he thought, he would stay up in the loft forever, out of the way. In the night he would sneak down for a drink of water from the faucet over the trough and for whatever food they left for him by the barn.

The rattle of his father's car as it turned down the lane recalled him to the present. He heard voices of his Uncle Andy and Aunt Alice as they and his father went past the barn to the lake. He could feel the morning growing heavier with sun. Someone, probably Nora, had let the chickens out of their coops and they were cackling in the yard.

After a while another car turned down the road off the highway. The car drew to a stop and he heard the voices of strange men. The men also went past the barn and down to the lake. The undertakers, whom his father must have phoned from Uncle Andy's house, had arrived from Corinth. Then he heard everybody come back and heard the car turn around and leave.

40   "Arnold!" It was his father calling him from the yard.

He climbed down the ladder and went out into the sun, picking wisps of hay from his overalls.

Corinth, nine miles away, was the county seat. Arnold sat in the front seat of the old Ford between his father, who was driving, and Uncle Andy; no one spoke. Uncle Andy was his mother's brother, and he had been fond of Eugie because Eugie had resembled him. Andy had taken Eugie hunting and had given him a knife and a lot of things, and now Andy, his eyes narrowed, sat tall and stiff beside Arnold.

Arnold's father parked the car before the courthouse. It was a two-story brick building with a lamp on each side of the bottom step. They went up the wide stone steps, Arnold and his father going first, and entered the darkly paneled hallway. The shirt-sleeved man in the sheriff's office said that the sheriff was at Carlson's Parlor examining the Curwing boy.

Andy went off to get the sheriff while Arnold and his father waited on a bench in the corridor. Arnold felt his father watching him, and he lifted his eyes with painful casualness to the announcement, on the opposite wall, of the Corinth County Annual Rodeo, and then to the clock with its loudly clucking pendulum. After he had come down from the loft his father and Uncle Andy had stood in the yard with him and asked him to tell them everything, and he had explained to them how the gun had caught on the wire. But when they had asked him why he hadn't run back to the house to tell his parents, he had had no answer—all he could say was that he had gone down into the garden to pick the peas. His father had stared at him in a pale, puzzled way, and it was then that he had felt his father and the others set their cold, turbulent silence against him. Arnold shifted on the bench, his only feeling a small one of compunction imposed by his father's eyes.

45   At a quarter past nine, Andy and the sheriff came in. They all went into the sheriff's private office, and Arnold was sent forward to sit in the chair by the sheriff's desk; his father and Andy sat down on the bench against the wall.

The sheriff lumped down into his swivel chair and swung toward Arnold. He was an old man with white hair like wheat stubble. His restless green eyes made him seem not to be in his office but to be hurrying and bobbing around somewhere else.

"What did you say your name was?" the sheriff asked.

"Arnold," he replied; but he could not remember telling the sheriff his name before.

"Curwing?"

50   "Yes."

"What were you doing with a .22, Arnold?"

"It's mine," he said.

"Okay. What were you going to shoot?"

"Some ducks," he replied.

55   "Out of season?"

He nodded.

"That's bad," said the sheriff. "Were you and your brother good friends?"

What did he mean—good friends? Eugie was his brother. That was different from a friend, Arnold thought. A best friend was your own age, but Eugie was almost a man. Eugie had had a way of looking at him, slyly and mockingly and yet confidentially, that had summed up how they both felt about being brothers. Arnold had wanted to be with Eugie more than with anybody else but he couldn't say they had been good friends.

"Did they ever quarrel?" the sheriff asked his father.

60 "Not that I know," his father replied. "It seemed to me that Arnold cared a lot for Eugie."

"Did you?" the sheriff asked Arnold.

If it seemed so to his father, then it was so. Arnold nodded.

"Were you mad at him this morning?"

"No."

65 "How did you happen to shoot him?"

"We was crawlin' through the fence."

"Yes?"

"An' the gun got caught on the wire."

"Seems the hammer must of caught," his father put in.

70 "All right, that's what happened," said the sheriff. "But what I want you to tell me is this. Why didn't you go back to the house and tell your father right away? Why did you go and pick peas for an hour?"

Arnold gazed over his shoulder at his father, expecting his father to have an answer for this also. But his father's eyes, larger and even lighter blue than usual, were fixed upon him curiously. Arnold picked at a callus in his right palm. It seemed odd now that he had not run back to the house and wakened his father, but he could not remember why he had not. They were all waiting for him to answer.

"I come down to pick peas," he said.

"Didn't you think," asked the sheriff, stepping carefully from word to word, "that it was more important for you to go tell your parents what had happened?"

"The sun was gonna come up," Arnold said.

75 "What's that got to do with it?"

"It's better to pick peas while they're cool."

The sheriff swung away from him, laid both hands flat on his desk. "Well, all I can say is," he said across to Arnold's father and Uncle Andy, "he's either a moron or he's so reasonable that he's way ahead of us." He gave a challenging snort. "It's come to my notice that the most reasonable guys are mean ones. They don't feel nothing."

For a moment the three men sat still. Then the sheriff lifted his hand like a man taking an oath. "Take him home," he said.

Andy uncrossed his legs. "You don't want him?"

80 "Not now," replied the sheriff. "Maybe in a few years."

Arnold's father stood up. He held his hat against his chest. "The gun ain't his no more," he said wanly.

Arnold went first through the hallway, hearing behind him the heels of his father and Uncle Andy striking the floor boards. He went down the steps ahead of them and climbed into the back seat of the car. Andy paused as he was getting into the front seat and gazed back at Arnold, and Arnold saw that his uncle's eyes had absorbed the knowingness from the sheriff's eyes. Andy and his father and the sheriff had discovered what made him go down into the garden. It was because he was cruel, the sheriff had said, and didn't care about his brother. Was that the reason? Arnold lowered his eyelids meekly against his uncle's stare.

The rest of the day he did his tasks around the farm, keeping apart from the family. At evening, when he saw his father stomp tiredly into the house, Arnold did not put down his hammer and leave the chicken coop he was repairing. He was afraid that they did not want him to eat supper with them. But in a few minutes another fear that they would go to the trouble of calling him and that he would be made conspicuous by his tardiness made him follow his father into the house. As he went through the kitchen he saw the jars of peas standing in rows on the workbench, a reproach to him.

No one spoke at supper, and his mother, who sat next to him, leaned her head in her hand all through the meal, curving her fingers over her eyes so as not to see him. They were finishing their small, silent supper when the visitors began to arrive, knocking hard on the back door. The men were coming from their farms now that it was growing dark and they could not work any more.

85   Old Man Matthews, gray and stocky, came first, with his two sons, Orion, the elder, and Clint, who was Eugie's age. As the callers entered the parlor, where the family ate, Arnold sat down in a rocking chair. Even as he had been undecided before supper whether to remain outside or take his place at the table, he now thought that he should go upstairs, and yet he stayed to avoid being conspicuous by his absence. If he stayed, he thought, as he always stayed and listened when visitors came, they would see that he was only Arnold and not the person the sheriff thought he was. He sat with his arms crossed and his hands tucked into his armpits and did not lift his eyes.

The Matthews men had hardly settled down around the table, after Arnold's mother and Nora had cleared away the dishes, when another car rattled down the road and someone else rapped on the back door. This time it was Sullivan, a spare and sandy man, so nimble of gesture and expression that Arnold had never been able to catch more than a few of his meanings. Sullivan, in dusty jeans, sat down in the other rocker, shot out his skinny legs and began to talk in his fast way, recalling everything that Eugene had ever said to him. The other men interrupted to tell of occasions they remembered, and after a time Clint's young voice, hoarse like Eugene's had been, broke in to tell about the time Eugene had beat him in a wrestling match.

Out in the kitchen the voices of Orion's wife and of Mrs. Sullivan mingled with Nora's voice but not, Arnold noticed, his mother's. Then dry little Mr. Cram came, leaving large Mrs. Cram in the kitchen, and there was no chair left for Mr. Cram to sit in. No one asked Arnold to get up and he was unable to rise. He knew that the story had got around to them during the day about how he had gone and picked peas after he had shot his brother, and he knew that although they were talking only about Eugie they were thinking about him and if he got up, if he moved even his foot, they would all be alerted. Then Uncle Andy arrived and leaned his tall, lanky body against the doorjamb and there were two men standing.

Presently Arnold was aware that the talk had stopped. He knew without looking up that the men were watching him.

"Not a tear in his eye," said Andy, and Arnold knew that it was his uncle who had gestured the men to attention.

90 "He don't give a hoot, is that how it goes?" asked Sullivan, trippingly.

"He's a reasonable fellow," Andy explained. "That's what the sheriff said. It's us who ain't reasonable. If we'd of shot our brother, we'd of come runnin' back to the house, cryin' like a baby. Well, we'd of been unreasonable. What would of been the use of actin' like that? If your brother is shot dead, he's shot dead. What's the use of gettin' emotional about it? The thing to do is go down to the garden and pick peas. Am I right?"

The men around the room shifted their heavy, satisfying weight of unreasonableness.

Matthews' son Orion said: "If I'd of done what he done, Pa would've hung my pelt by the side of that big coyote's in the barn."

Arnold sat in the rocker until the last man had filed out. While his family was out in the kitchen bidding the callers good night and the cars were driving away down the dirt lane to the highway, he picked up one of the kerosene lamps and slipped quickly up the stairs. In his room he undressed by lamplight, although he and Eugie had always undressed in the dark, and not until he was lying in his bed did he blow out the flame. He felt nothing, not any grief. There was only the same immense silence and crawling inside of him; it was the way the house and fields felt under a merciless sun.

95 He awoke suddenly. He knew that his father was out in the yard, closing the doors of the chicken houses so that the chickens could not roam out too early and fall prey to the coyotes that came down from the mountains at daybreak. The sound that had wakened him was the step of his father as he got up from the rocker and went down the back steps. And he knew that his mother was awake in her bed.

Throwing off the covers, he rose swiftly, went down the stairs and across the dark parlor to his parents' room. He rapped on the door.

"Mother?"

From the closed room her voice rose to him, a seeking and retreating voice. "Yes?"

"Mother?" he asked insistently. He had expected her to realize that he wanted to go down on his knees by her bed and tell her that Eugie was dead. She did not know it yet, nobody knew it, and yet she was sitting up in bed, waiting to be told, waiting for him to confirm her dread. He had expected her to tell him to come in, to allow him to dig his head into her blankets and tell her about the terror he had felt when he had knelt beside Eugie. He had come to clasp her in his arms and, in his terror, to pommel her breasts with his head. He put his hand upon the knob.

100 "Go back to bed, Arnold," she called sharply.

But he waited.

"Go back! Is night when you get afraid?"

At first he did not understand. Then, silently, he left the door and for a stricken moment stood by the rocker. Outside everything was still. The fences, the shocks of wheat seen through the window before him were so still it was as if they moved and breathed in the daytime and had fallen silent with the lateness of the hour. It was a silence that seemed to observe his father, a figure moving alone around the yard, his lantern casting a circle of light by his feet. In a few minutes his father would enter the dark house, the lantern still lighting his way.

Arnold was suddenly aware that he was naked. He had thrown off his blankets and come down the stairs to tell his mother how he felt about Eugie, but she had refused to listen to him and his nakedness had become unpardonable. At once he went back up the stairs, fleeing from his father's lantern.

105 At breakfast he kept his eyelids lowered as if to deny the humiliating night. Nora, sitting at his left, did not pass the pitcher of milk to him and he did not ask for it. He would never again, he vowed, ask them for anything, and he ate his fried eggs and potatoes only because everybody ate meals—the cattle ate, and the cats; it was customary for everybody to eat.

"Nora, you gonna keep that pitcher for yourself?" his father asked.

Nora lowered her head unsurely.

"Pass it on to Arnold," his father said.

Nora put her hands in her lap.

110 His father picked up the metal pitcher and set it down at Arnold's plate.

Arnold, pretending to be deaf to the discord, did not glance up but relief rained over his shoulders at the thought that his parents recognized him again. They must have lain awake after his father had come in from the yard: had they realized together why he had come down the stairs and knocked at their door?

"Bessie's missin' this morning," his father called out to his mother, who had gone into the kitchen. "She went up the mountain last night and had her calf, most likely. Somebody's got to go up and find her 'fore the coyotes get the calf."

That had been Eugie's job, Arnold thought. Eugie would climb the cattle trails in search of a newborn calf and come down the mountain carrying the calf across his back, with the cow running down along behind him, mooing in alarm.

Arnold ate the few more forkfuls of his breakfast, put his hands on the edge of the table and pushed back his chair. If he went for the calf he'd be away from the farm all morning. He could switch the cow down the mountain slowly, and the calf would run along at its mother's side.

115 When he passed through the kitchen his mother was setting a kettle of water on the stove. "Where you going?" she asked awkwardly.

"Up to get the calf," he replied, averting his face.

"Arnold?"

At the door he paused reluctantly, his back to her, knowing that she was seeking him out, as his father was doing, and he called upon his pride to protect him from them.

"Was you knocking at my door last night?"

120 He looked over his shoulder at her, his eyes narrow and dry.

"What'd you want?" she asked humbly.

"I didn't want nothing," he said flatly.

Then he went out the door and down the back steps, his legs trembling from the fright his answer gave him.

From Gina Berriault, "The Stone Boy," *Mademoiselle*, 1957. Copyright © 1957 by Condé Nast Publications, Inc. Reprinted courtesy *Mademoiselle*.

●   ●   ●

Study/Writing/Discussion Questions

1. What inferences did you make, before the tragic incident, about the relationship between Arnold and Eugie? What evidence did you base your inferences on?

2. What did Arnold do immediately after the shooting? What inferences did you make about that?

3. What inferences did his parents and the sheriff and the family's friends make about Arnold's behavior?

4. What information does the author give you about how well Arnold understands his own feelings and behavior?

5. What inferences did you make by the end of the story about Arnold's needs? Explain your evidence.

6. What inferences did you make by the end of the story about Arnold's future?

Objectives Review of Part I

When you have finished Part I, you will understand:

1. The following concepts on an experiential basis: observing, labeling, describing, interpreting, facts, inferences, sensing, perceiving, thinking

2. That it is possible to maintain awareness of one's own thinking–feeling–perceiving process

3. How clear thinking depends on "staying awake" to what is

And you will have had practice in developing these skills:

1. Suspending thinking in order to freshly sense and gather data

2. Describing the obvious evidence without substituting labels and interpretations

3. Recognizing when you and others are formulating facts and when you are formulating inferences

4. Recognizing how facts and inferences can become confused with one another

PART II

Problems of Critical Thinking

CHAPTER 5

Assumptions:
What's Taken for Granted?

"...so we began asking ourselves, does it really make sense to pay you fifty million when there are C.E.O.'s in Korea and Mexico who would do the same job for twenty-five."

The discovery of an assumption can be amusing, if not shocking. In this chapter, we will take a fresh look at that familiar term, *assumption*, and see how it operates in our thinking. We will study types of assumptions, building on what we have already learned about aware observing and inferences. In short, we will continue to build the skills of critical thinking.

Used with permission of Richard Guindor.

DISCOVERY EXERCISES

The following three exercises can be done with a partner or alone, depending on your instructor's directions.

▦ Defining Assumption

Using at least two dictionaries, write your own definition of *assumption*.

▦ Finding Assumptions in Cartoons

Study previous cartoons and state in words what assumptions brought humor to these situations.

> The word **assume** comes from the Latin *assumere*—to take up. When we assume, we take up or accept something. In reasoning, we assume when we take something for granted or accept an idea without sufficient proof of its truth or certainty.

▦ Finding Assumptions in Stories

As you read the stories told in each of the following paragraphs, think how each depends on one or more assumptions. In preparation for class discussion, write your answers to the questions that follow each paragraph.

1. You are a guard at Alcatraz. One day a prisoner is found to be missing. When you inspect his cell you find a hole dug through the concrete under his bed. All that is next to the hole is a bent metal spoon. What assumptions of the guards did the prisoner exploit in order to escape?

2. While visiting Sweden you go with a friend to a grocery store. You are surprised to notice that although the cashier takes the money, the customers bag their own groceries. You take two plastic bags off a hook nearby and begin to fill them. Your friend tells you that you need to pay the cashier for the bags. What assumptions did you make?

3. You have a dinner guest from a foreign country who belches loudly all through the meal. You find him disgusting and want to get rid of him. But he insists that he be allowed to return your hospitality. So you go to his house for dinner. There everyone but you belches loudly all through the meal. Before you leave, your host says, "I am sorry you did not like my dinner, but you didn't have to be so rude about it." What was the assumption of the foreign guest?

4. A woman once proposed marriage to George Bernard Shaw, a witty and erudite English dramatist. "Imagine a child," she said, "with my body and your brains." "Yes," he said, "but what if the child has my body and your brains?" What was his assumption?

5. In his struggles to receive backing for the voyage of his ships to the Far East by sailing west, Christopher Columbus once spent some hours trying to persuade a nobleman to lend his support. The nobleman maintained that he was trying to do the impossible, like making an egg stand on end. Then the nobleman called for an egg and handed it to Columbus, who was sitting across from him at a table. Taking up the challenge, Columbus tried wobbling the egg on one end and then the other, while the nobleman laughed in derision. Then, picking up the egg, Columbus gently smashed its end on the table, allowing it to stand firmly in position, while its contents oozed out. What assumption about the problem did the nobleman make that Columbus did not?

6. On a remote Wyoming highway, a European tourist drives his rental car into a small gas station. An attendant comes out, opens the hood of his car, props up the supporting rod, and looks inside at the engine. Suddenly, without warning, he smashes down the hood, causing the rod to rip through the metal hood. Startled, the tourist puts his head out the window and screams: "What did you do to my car?"

    "Get the hell out of here!" yells the attendant. Frightened, the driver turns on the ignition and pulls out of the station, muttering to himself: "Now I know why they call it 'the Wild West.'" What were the tourist's assumptions?

7. In Oakland, California, a gang of teens—some as young as 13—were arrested in connection with sixty burglaries. All the teens were Asian Americans and the homes they robbed were all in Asian American neighborhoods. Two girls from the gang would knock at the doors. If someone came to the door, they would ask for someone who did not live there, then leave. If no one answered, the girls would signal to two boys, who would go around to the back of the house and break in. The police said, "They acted with impunity because they didn't look out of place in the neighborhood. . . . At times they would wave at neighbors, who would wave back." What assumptions are evident here?

Understanding Assumptions

Assumptions can be forgotten inferences.

Our study of inferences in Chapter 4 leads us naturally into assumptions. We use assumptions in our reasoning, like inferences, to help us bridge what we know with what we don't know. Usually when we infer, we are aware of our reasoning. We infer actively and consciously when we make plans, such as deciding what to pack when we go on a trip. We get into trouble when we make wrong assumptions, however, meaning that we draw some conclusions too hastily, lack some crucial information, or mistake some uncertainties for certainties. For example, it is easy to spot the tourists who visit San Francisco in the cool and foggy summer months. They are the people shivering on the streets dressed in light summer clothing. They only packed for warm weather because most places in North America are warm in July and California has a sunny weather reputation. They would not remember what they took for granted until faced with the fact of the cold damp fog typical of the northern coast's summer season. Thus, many San Francisco shops thrive on catering to tourists' needs for warm clothing because every year new tourists arrive having made the same wrong assumption.

Yet critical thinkers can learn from wrong assumptions by mulling them over. Exactly when and why did I think that? What else might I have considered? Not all assumptions can be prevented, of course, but taking some time out for reflection might prevent their reoccurrence:

- When did I assume my roommate would always pay his half of the rent?
- Why didn't I read the small print in my apartment lease?
- When I bought that car, why did I think I could do without air-conditioning?

Our ability to survive as a species depends on our ability to learn from wrong assumptions. We live on a collective foundation of hard-learned lessons. Each child has to be taught that humans can drown in water, that some mushrooms are poisonous, that we have to protect ourselves from too much heat or cold. Collectively, one reason that we watch the news each day is to learn about new wrong assumptions. Consider these examples:

- In 2005 an Italian journalist, who had been kidnapped and held for months by Iraqi insurgents, was freed by a group of Italian intelligence agents. However, while they were rushing to the Baghdad airport, U.S. soldiers fired on their car. The journalist and two of the agents were wounded; one agent was killed when he threw himself over the journalist.
- A demolition crew in Florida bashed in the roof of a house before learning not only that they had the wrong address but that a family was inside at the time having dinner.
- A woman allowed a longtime friendly neighbor to water her plants while she was on vacation. A year later the woman discovered she

was the victim of identity theft. Her friendly neighbor had gone into her personal files and stolen the necessary private information.

- A Catholic university agreed to accept a donation of several million dollars from an anonymous donor who was vouched for by several board members. Because the money was promised within a year, the university went ahead to contract for some new buildings. A year later the university discovered it was caught in a complex scam with no donation and a large debt.

- In late 2004 the public learned that their favorite star athletes routinely used steroids and other banned substances.

Discussion Break or Writing Questions

1. Which of these examples challenged your assumptions about justice? Which challenged your assumptions about trust?
2. Which situations might have been prevented in some way?
3. Write or describe to a classmate about a time you came to distrust something previously trusted. How was an assumption involved here?
4. Did you learn anything from making this wrong assumption?

Types of Assumptions

Assumptions can be conscious or unconscious, warranted or unwarranted.

The examples of assumptions discussed so far in this chapter have been **unconscious assumptions.** They were assumptions only recognized as such after circumstances revealed their errors. A reading offered in Chapter 2 dramatizes the revelation of an unconscious assumption made by Dr. John Murray about one of his collaborators.

Yet assumptions need not always be unconscious; they can also be intentionally conceived in the form of **working assumptions,** or theories designed to serve as strategies or trial ideas. These assumptions are conscious in that it is clear from the outset that these ideas may not succeed. Let's continue with the example of Dr. James Murray. In 1870, after more than twenty years of working on what was to become the *Oxford English Dictionary*, James Murray realized that the project was too ambitious for his limited staff. Murray then developed the working assumption that the task might be completed if thousands of amateur volunteers could be recruited to work at home on specific assignments. The experiment turned out to be highly successful although the dictionary was not ready for publication until 1928, thirteen years after the death of Dr. Murray.

Working assumptions, however, need not be so elaborate; they can be everyday simple assumptions.

• You agree to meet your date in front of the local movie theater at 6:00. You arrive but she is not there. You wait until 6:15. You call her on her cell phone. She does not answer. You quickly decide to assume she is on her way. You decide to buy both tickets, save some seats in the theater, and return to wait outside.

Working assumptions help us plan our lives.

• You wonder whether you should pursue a career as a basketball star or a basketball coach. You decide to proceed on the assumption that you will become a basketball star. Then if you don't have what it takes, or get injured, you can always fall back on being a basketball coach. You have an intentional strategy.

Here is another example of a conscious assumption.

• Your parents want to make an investment decision. They decide to invest in real estate, *assuming* that property values will continue to rise in the years to come. Because their assumption is conscious, they recognize there is a risk that they may be wrong. Should property values fall, they may be disappointed, but they will not be left with the shock or surprise of having taken a profit for granted.

The same factors operate in any area of life where people take action based on calculated risks. In mathematics, conscious assumptions are essential. For example, $2 + 2 = 4$ is not a fact but a conclusion or theorem based on axioms that are assumed to be fundamental. An **axiom** is defined as a statement assumed as a basis for the development of a subject. Usually, axioms are very acceptable assumptions—not outlandish ones—that can be applied to the real world. Sometimes, as in this case, they are said to be self-evident, but still they are assumptions. We will return in the chapter on Inductive Reasoning (Chapter 11) to the topic of creating working assumptions, or **hypotheses.**

Warranted and unwarranted assumptions have some parallels to conscious and unconscious assumptions. A warranted assumption is based on some knowledge of pertinent standards, codes, customs, or agreements. These agreements make it possible for a group of people to take certain things for granted, as we all must do, in order to proceed efficiently through life together. If a family invites you over to their house for dinner, you can assume that you will not pay for the meal. On the other hand, if you go to a restaurant, it would be unwarranted to expect a free meal. However, if your friends owned a restaurant and invited you over there for dinner, you might not be sure what to expect.

Because many situations can be equally uncertain, we need to stop sometimes to clarify expectations. In public life we form agreements, sometimes in the form of laws or regulations, to help us know what we can assume. Thus if you buy a carton of milk in a grocery store dated for use within one week, your assumption is warranted that it will not be sour when you open it. If you do find the milk to be sour, you can return it to the store for a refund. The same can be said of assumptions that the city buses will arrive and leave on schedule, that the post office will be open on weekdays but not holidays, and that gas and electricity will be available at the flick of a switch. When such events do not occur, citizens can and do complain to those responsible for their maintenance. Thus, warranted assumptions enable societies to proceed through many activities in a routine manner. Nevertheless, it is possible to be unfamiliar with some standard, code, or agreement. If you expect milk to remain fresh in your refrigerator for a month, that would be an unwarranted assumption. If you expect city buses to arrive every half-hour after midnight, that would be unwarranted; and if you go to the post office expecting to mail a package on Christmas day, that assumption would be unwarranted.

Above all, our common safety depends upon warranted assumptions, such as that our pharmacies will not give us bogus medications, that the police will not rob us, that laws will be enforced, and that our own government will not harm us. Training in critical thinking can help us avoid making as many unconscious assumptions as well as unwarranted ones.

Discussion Break Question

1. Write down or explain to your neighbor the difference between a conscious and an unconscious assumption and between a warranted and an unwarranted assumption. Give your own examples of each.

Identifying Hidden Assumptions in Reasoning

Hidden assumptions exert a powerful effect on our reasoning; however, identifying them is not always easy.

- If your friend is Japanese, she must be moody.
- He is a good candidate for mayor; he looks sincere.
- If you love her, you'll give her diamonds.

All of these statements contain hidden assumptions. The first hangs on a stereotype, assumed to be true, about the moodiness of all Japanese people. The second depends on two questionable assumptions: (1) that the appearance of sincerity is actual sincerity; (2) that sincerity is the best qualification for holding office. Finally, the third example is an advertising slogan designed to persuade consumers to accept many assumptions.

If we accept any of these statements, then, we have also agreed to swallow their hidden assumptions. When we think critically, we do not accept and believe statements that hinge upon unspoken, unproven ideas.

Learning how to identify hidden assumptions is a complex skill comparable to catching fish by spotting their shadows underwater. The bait that brings the fish to the surface is the question "What would someone have to believe in order to come to this conclusion?" When we bring forth the words that make hidden ideas explicit, we bring the fish ashore so that its logic and truth can be tested.

All three opening examples depend on hidden stereotypical assumptions. **Stereotypes** are **hasty generalizations** about life that are assumed to be true and are placed in a mental file for further use. To return to two of the opening examples—the sincere mayor and the gift of diamonds— each also represents ideas based on stereotypical assumptions.

He is a good candidate for mayor; he looks sincere.

The claim assumes that people who appear sincere are honest people. Yet a person could also be sincerely deluded or sincerely malevolent. Moreover, many other more substantial qualifications are needed to hold public office.

If you love her, you'll give her diamonds.

For more than a century, the diamond industry has succeeded in persuading millions to believe (1) that crystalline carbons are rare and deserve their high price and (2) that they are the perfect symbol of a pledge of love. The advertising slogan asks you to assume that (1) a gift of diamonds gives a woman proof of her worth and (2) men who don't give women diamonds don't love them. Thus the consumer might be left feeling guilty for not conforming to the expectations cultivated by such propaganda.

Discussion Break Questions

Identify and express the hidden assumptions underlying each of the following statements or situations. The first one is provided as an example.

1. What's a nice girl like you doing in a place like this?

   Hidden underlying assumptions: (1) I am a nice girl. (2) This is a bad place. (3) You can offer me protection. (4) I should trust you. (5) I would fall for a pick-up line as old as this one.

2. I couldn't visit a Buddhist temple because they worship idols there.

3. How can that marriage counselor help people if he himself is divorced?

4. You go into a pharmacy and see a young woman standing behind the counter. You ask her if you can speak to the pharmacist. She tells you she is the pharmacist.

5. I can't understand why I haven't met my soul mate this year. My astrologer said I would.

6. Villagers in the Fiji Islands live in poverty and hardship. They do not have running water, baths, and toilets in their homes. It will take them a hundred years to catch up with the rest of the world.

7. In a television program about earthquake preparedness, an expert demonstrated his gas-driven generator. "In the event of a major disaster," he said, "this generator would run our children's television set so that they would have something to do."

Hidden Assumptions in Arguments

Good arguments are not based on assumptions.

> The purpose of an **argument** is to be persuasive. A good argument consists of **claims** supported by reasoning, by facts, examples, and evidence.
>
> **Facts** take the form of statistics, testimony, records, and verified information.
>
> A **good argument** sets forth its claims and reasoning clearly and openly; it examines its own assumptions.

Arguments, as the term is used in this text, are structures of reasoning designed to be persuasive. A good argument has a structure of claims supported through reasoning, facts, examples, and evidence. Moreover, all of these elements are made clear and explicit. A poor argument may lack any of these factors. A clever debater can topple the structure of any argument that rests on a rug of hidden assumptions (see Figure 5.1). When critical thinkers compose an argument, they put it to the rug test; they don't wait for their opponents to do it for them.

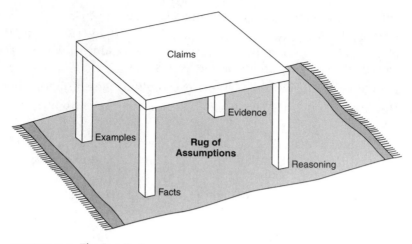

FIGURE 5.1 The Rug Test

DISCOVERY EXERCISE

▪ *Articulating Hidden Assumptions Underlying Arguments*

Write down the hidden assumptions you find in the following quotations, to share in a later class discussion. The first is done for you by way of example.

1. A Senator, concerned about the high mortality rate of children in the United States from gunshot wounds, introduced legislation that would require manufacturers to install childproof locks on all handguns.
   a. It is all right for adults to shoot guns but not for children to shoot guns.
   b. Children fire the guns that kill children.
   c. Adults know how to use guns with discretion.
   d. Parents will procure their guns from law-abiding manufacturers and dealers.
   e. Only handguns shoot children.
2. I am worthless; I do not have a college degree.
3. "I'm nothing," he said. "You understand that, nothing. I earn $250,000 a year, but it's nothing, and I'm nobody. My expenses range from maintaining an apartment on Park Avenue for $20,400 a year to

$30,000 a year for private schools for my children. My total expenses come to over $300,000 a year, leaving nothing left over for dinner parties, paintings, furniture, a mistress, psychiatrists, or even a week in Europe." (From Lewis Lapham, "The Gilded Cage," *Money and Class in America,* New York: Random House, 1988.)

Value or Belief Assumptions

Value assumptions are the beliefs we take for granted. Although we may not be aware of their presence and influence, they greatly affect our reasoning.

Value assumptions are the beliefs we never or rarely question, the beliefs we assume everyone shares. When first adopted, they may not have been examined at all, especially if they were absorbed through family or culture. Sometimes a visit to another culture can bring them into conscious awareness and reconsideration. An example from the life of the author Jean Liedloff will serve as an illustration.

Liedloff spent two-and-a-half years living with a Stone Age tribe, the Yequana Indians of the rain forests of Brazil. One thing that puzzled her was that the tribe did not have a word for *work,* nor did members distinguish work from other ways of spending time. She observed the women thoroughly enjoying the task of going down to a stream for water several times a day, even though they had to descend a steep bank with gourds on their heads and babies on their backs. Gradually the author came to realize that the idea that work is hard and leisure is fun is only a Western value assumption. She had to consider that this idea was not necessarily a truth about life, but a cultural attitude. This insight led her to reexamine other Western beliefs, such as the idea that progress is good and that a child belongs to its parents.

Other examples of cultural value assumptions emerged in a PBS "reality" series called *Frontier House* that depicted the lives of three families who had agreed to go back in time to 1883 Montana homesteading life for six months. They had to fell trees to build their own homes and furniture, raise their own food, brave a blizzard to care for livestock, wash their clothing in a creek, and barter for food and supplies. Many lost weight from hunger and there were fights over food hoarding. Yet in spite of all their hardships, video interviews made after their return to their modern lives revealed a sense of less vitality, less kinship with other family members, and more boredom and emptiness. Their common value assumption had been that modern city life, with all its comforts, possessions, and conveniences, offered the best possible life. Many were surprised to realize that they had found more satisfaction in a life requiring a lot of physical work together with communal activities directed toward common survival.

Used with permission of Kirk Anderson.

Thus our lives are shaped and guided by our value assumptions—sometimes well, sometimes poorly. The cartoon labeled "The 7 Virtues of Consumer Culture" depicts some values commonly accepted in our time. Their effect can be startling when we recognize that these values are what our great grandparents called the seven deadly sins. It awakens us to the possibility that, without awareness, we have transformed what once were sins into virtues. Moreover, the implication is that past traditional virtues (such as thrift, sobriety, generosity, and modesty) are now sins in a consumer culture. Thus, value assumptions differ not only from culture to culture but even reverse themselves over time within a society. Bringing these value assumptions to conscious awareness allows us to choose whether we want to continue to live by them.

Discussion Break Questions

1. What do you think about these two examples of value assumptions as they relate to work and the conveniences of modern life?
2. Do you agree with what this cartoon says about the seven virtues of consumer culture? Why or why not?

Assumption Layers in Arguments

A value assumption can form the base of a pyramid that supports many layers of hidden assumptions, all of which provide support for one idea expressed at the top.

Once we understand the meaning of both hidden assumptions and value assumptions, we can find them, like archeologists, by sifting through layers beneath a stated claim (see Figure 5.2). Consider this statement

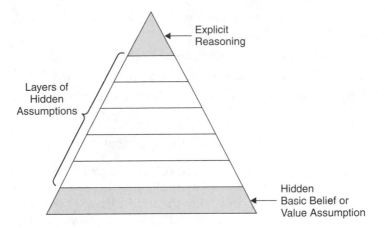

FIGURE 5.2 Pyramid of Value Assumptions

once made by Ronald Reagan. When he heard that 12 million Americans were unemployed, this is how he responded:

If you women would stay at home, maybe we could solve America's unemployment problem.

Now why, you may wonder, would he make such a statement? First we have to list some of the assumptions he was making.

1. All women could have men to support them.
2. Women are taking jobs away from men.
3. Women do not really need jobs because they can stay at home.
4. Men want and will take women's jobs (and pay).
5. Work for women is a kind of indulgence allowed by their men.

What basic belief would underlie so many assumptions? One belief that Reagan might have held, common to his generation, was this idea: *A woman's place is in the home.* It would appear that he never reexamined this belief in light of the social and economic changes that occurred during his lifetime. He never asked himself whether this belief was forever true.

We can also learn a lot about hidden assumptions by studying the disagreements that people have, disagreements expressed in arguments. Notice as you read the following examples how these differences depend upon opposing values and priorities that may not even be recognized.

Today the UN spends more than $10 billion each year and has become a tool for anti-American, anti-democratic tyrannies and third-world kleptocracies. (Mark W. Smith, *The Official Handbook of the Vast Right-Wing Conspiracy*, p. 74.)

Hidden Assumptions

1. The UN spends too much money.
2. The United States should not support the UN.
3. The UN allows other countries to harm the United States.
4. Affiliation with the UN is dangerous for the United States.

Value Assumption

The United States is not safe in a situation that it cannot dominate.

The Kleptocrats [a ruling class of thieves] have taken over. Look at America's leadership today—not just political, but corporate too. Tell me you wouldn't trade the whole mess of them for one good kindergarten teacher. (Jim Hightower, *Thieves in High Places*, p. xiii.)

Hidden Assumptions

1. America's new leadership consists entirely of thieves.
2. Americans are fed up with them.
3. A good kindergarten teacher is honest and provides public service with humility and integrity.
4. We need people with such qualifications to lead the country.

Value Assumption

America's leaders, both political and corporate, are wrong when they put private interests before public interests.

Discussion Break or Writing Questions

Divide the class into six groups and have each group consider one of the following controversies.

1. War is never justifiable unless in self-defense.
   Preemptive war is justifiable.
2. Abortion denies an infant's right to life.
   Abortion allows a woman the right to control her own body.
3. Gay couples should be able to marry if they wish.
   Gay couples should not have the right to marry.
4. A total of $165 million in public funds was spent to build and furnish the Clinton Library in Arkansas. The dedication of this library was a widely celebrated media event. A woman wrote a letter to the editor saying that the money would have been better spent on affordable housing units for low-income families rather than for the glorification of a past president about whom we already had a glut of information.

5. A city council proposed placing a 17-cent tax on plastic bags used by grocery stores in order to cut down on consumer use and thus save millions of dollars in litter control and waste management. Trade groups representing the grocers and plastic industry argued that this was a regressive tax that would harm their industry and also burden lower-income consumers.

6. Congress created a compensation fund for families shortly after the 9/11 attacks on New York City, granting awards on the basis of potential life earnings. The more affluent families of financial executives who died in the World Trade Center received far greater payouts than did the families of janitors or emergency personnel. The 2,880 individual payouts ranged from $250,000 to $7.1 million. In order to receive compensation, each family had to agree not to sue the airline or airline security companies.

In discussion or writing, answer the following questions:

1. What beliefs or value assumptions shape the reasoning on each side of this issue?
2. What priorities are at stake here and how do they conflict?
3. Which side speaks more to your own values?

Assumptions, Incongruities, and Thinking

First we have to be alert enough to recognize incongruities; then we need to do the thinking needed to explain them.

> **Incongruity** is something that does not meet our expectations about what is correct, appropriate, logical, or standard. The word comes from the Latin *incongruent*, meaning "not in agreement."

When we see two little girls dressed up in their Sunday best to have their picture taken, we expect to see happy smiling faces as well. But what we see in the photo on the next page instead challenges our stereotypical assumption. This photo may even make us feel uncomfortable. Yet, if instead of turning away, we become curious, we might then come to discover some interesting things about this incongruity. When we can allow ourselves to endure the discomfort of having our assumptions challenged, we learn and grow.

Photo by Arthur Rothstein. Courtesy Library of Congress.

Terms Used by Piaget to Describe Cognitive Development

Equilibrium is the stable inner feeling of balance and well-being we have when the schemas—or mental constructs—of our experiences and beliefs enable us to understand our environments and function well within them.

Assimilation is the process we use when we can explain new events satisfactorily through our existing schemas, thus maintaining equilibrium.

Disequilibrium is the confusion and discomfort we feel when a new experience cannot be adequately explained by our existing schemas.

Accommodation is the process whereby we modify our old schemas in such a way as to improve our understanding and functioning, thus restoring equilibrium.

This topic brings us back to Chapter 1 and the ideas of psychologist Jean Piaget about learning. Piaget says that when we have experiences that we cannot easily assimilate, we then are provoked to think.

We think when we reorder old mental categories. This process is what Piaget calls *accommodation*. It is provoked by an inner sense of disequilibrium. We experience disequilibrium when our assumptions are challenged by momentous experiences, such as witnessing a birth or a death, or more mundanely, discovering we have a flat tire. When our assumptions are challenged, we feel actual physical discomfort; but when we can reorganize our mental categories to accommodate a new experience, our equilibrium is restored. Thus, a feeling of equilibrium is a reward for successful thinking. While describing many of the photographs in this book so far, you may have felt especially uncomfortable. This is because all of them, whether you realized it or not, are based on *incongruities*. In studying the photographs, you have had the choice of either avoiding the disequilibrium they aroused or staying with the task long enough to reach a satisfactory explanation for their incongruities—and thus finding a way to restore your equilibrium.

To return to the picture of the little girls, you might imagine some explanations for their frowns. You could infer (1) they were given dolls they didn't like; (2) they did not want to pose for the picture; (3) the picture was taken when they were off guard; or (4) the photographer only wanted to make a statement of ironic contrasts. If this last explanation seems the most promising, you might wonder if perhaps the photographer was purposely playing with some incongruities. Perhaps the whole composition was intentional: to contrast Hollywood play dolls against two girls dressed up as dolls; to contrast a false concept of little girls with real little girls; to contrast false faces with real faces reflecting the stresses of life.

Sometimes we have to hang in there through a period of doubt and confusion before we can reach an explanation that reconciles all our facts, or until we can bring our information into a satisfying pattern of order. And although we may never be able to confirm the final truth of our explanation, at least we have the satisfaction of having reconciled all the available information. Piaget says that persistence in this process of moving from disequilibrium to equilibrium develops our thinking skills.

Thinking comes about in life through provocation: when we meet situations that do not fit a familiar pattern, that do not fall into familiar stereotypes, that do not meet expectations. In such cases, we have the personal choice to deny or ignore—or to think, to learn, and to grow. When we were toddlers, if we touched a hot stove, the experience of being burned was an unpleasant encounter with reality. And yet, even then, if we had not stopped to analyze even in a simple way what caused the pain, we would have had to suffer the same pain over and over again. Even if we decided to always depend on someone else to think for us and protect us, we would eventually find such a solution to be impractical. We survive best when we can think for ourselves. And the more we think, the more willing, open, and able we are to accept life's challenges of our assumptions.

Discussion Break Questions

1. Give an example of some incongruity that you have experienced that challenged you to recognize one of your assumptions.
2. Can you describe the disequilibrium you felt when you could not resolve this incongruity?
3. How did you restore your equilibrium?
4. Have you experienced disequilibrium at times while studying this textbook? How was your equilibrium restored?

Chapter Summary

1. An assumption is something we take for granted, something we accept prematurely as being true, something we do not check out carefully. Often, we do not recognize that we have made an assumption until it causes a problem for us.

2. Assumptions can be conscious or unconscious, warranted or unwarranted. Unconscious and unwarranted assumptions can lead to faulty reasoning, whereas conscious and warranted assumptions can be useful tools for problem solving. We need to recognize the difference.

3. Hidden assumptions are unconscious assumptions that greatly influence a line of reasoning. One form of hidden assumptions is stereotypes, where we try to fit new experiences into old or prejudiced categories. Another type is value assumptions, or basic unexamined beliefs that unconsciously influence our thinking.

4. Arguments are the use of reasoning to defend an idea or to persuade someone else to believe in the idea. Good arguments do not rest upon unexamined assumptions.

5. We perceive incongruities when we observe situations that do not meet our expectations or assumptions. This can cause a feeling of disequilibrium. We restore our equilibrium when we reach a new understanding through the process of reexamining our assumptions. This is a familiar and continuous process that results in growth and learning.

6. Someone who brings a fresh perspective to a problem that has stumped others is often able to find a solution because he or she does not buy the assumptions that restrain others. As a conscious tool, we can look for assumptions when we are confronted with a problem to solve.

Building Arguments
Assumptions: Building an Argument

Some of our chiefs make the claim that the land belongs to us. It is not what the Great Spirit told me. He told me that the lands belong to Him, that no people owns the land; that I was not to forget to tell this to the white people when I met them in council. (Kannekuk, Kickapoo prophet, 1827)

Exercise

1. What claim is being refuted here?
2. What assumption lies in the claim?
3. What counterclaim is being made?
4. State a claim that you feel contains an assumption. State why you believe it is an assumption. Formulate your own counterclaim.

Chapter Quiz

Rate each of the following statements as *true* or *false*. Justify your answer with an example or explanation.

_____ 1. When we articulate hidden assumptions, we simply read what we find in print before us.

_____ 2. A good argument invariably contains a few hidden assumptions.

_____ 3. A value assumption is a belief assumed to be true and shared by everyone.

_____ 4. "Can you believe it? She is twenty-three years old and not even thinking of getting married." This statement, made by a Puerto Rican mother, contains no value assumption.

_____ 5. Assumptions are often recognized only in retrospect because of the problems they cause.

_____ 6. In mathematics, conscious assumptions are called *axioms*.

_____ 7. A conscious assumption can be used as a strategy to lead us to new information. If a child does not come home from school at the usual time, we might first decide to call the homes of the child's friends; if that turns up no information, we might call the police.

_____ 8. Stereotypes contain no assumptions.

_____ 9. To be uncomfortable is to be in disequilibrium. Thinking through a problem restores the comfort of our mental equilibrium.

_____ 10. Incongruities can provoke us into thinking in order to resolve their conflict with our assumptions and expectations.

Composition Writing Application

■ Expository Essay: Solving a Problem by Uncovering Assumptions

Think of a major problem from your own life (or someone else's) that was solved by the discovery of one or more hidden assumptions. If you prefer to use historical examples from the lives of explorers, artists, or scientists, do some research on the kinds of problems they succeeded in solving. (Besides using ordinary encyclopedias, you might also look for some special science encyclopedias in the library.) Write in sketch form your basic findings, searching for the following elements to develop and emphasize:

1. What particular problem concerned your subject?
2. What assumptions were embedded in the problem?
3. How were these assumptions discovered?
4. What restraints did these assumptions impose?
5. What, if any, wrong assumptions were made?

Prepare a working outline for an essay of about three typewritten pages. Then begin your essay with a thesis statement that explains what you concluded from your research and analysis:

The **thesis statement**, also called the *thesis,* has some similarity to the topic sentence in that it states a generalization. However, as it is introduced, it may be stated through several sentences instead of one, as it proposes an idea that will be developed, explained, and illustrated over many paragraphs and pages. By definition, the thesis is the idea that the essay intends to prove. Again, in the process of thinking, the

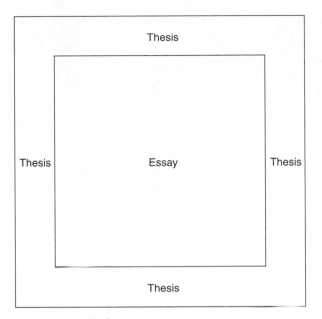

FIGURE 5.3 Thesis as a Frame

thesis, like the topic sentence, may only be mentally formulated after some time has been spent studying the subject. However, when the essay is written in an academic style, the thesis is stated in the first paragraph. A thesis is also called the *controlling idea* because everything written in the essay is based on the dictates of its objective. We can visualize the thesis as a frame, like a picture frame; everything that will appear in that picture—the essay—is contained in and limited by the thesis (see Figure 5.3).

The act of stating the thesis helps us organize our thoughts around one main purpose; it can also serve as a magnet to help us decide what information is relevant for support. Every statement and every fact appearing in the essay should either support or develop the thesis.

Let's look at an example of a thesis. Suppose you decided to write an expository essay to explain a problem you solved at work through the discovery of a hidden assumption. Your thesis might be introduced in this manner:

(1) All of us have heard fables about villages that suffered long and hard from a particular problem, like a famine or a wayward dragon. (2) Then one day a stranger appeared and solved the problem simply, quickly, and miraculously. (3) In such stories, what seemed to be a miracle to

the villagers was only a matter of a newcomer's bringing a fresh perspective, unbiased by any past assumptions. (4) My own life had a parallel situation several years ago when I went to work for the municipal utilities district. (5) And although I did not arrive on a horse or in a suit of armor, I did bring a fresh perspective that solved an "insoluble problem."

These five sentences comprise the thesis statement. The first two introduce the topic and invite reader interest. The third states a principle and a limitation of focus. The fourth makes the transition to a personal incident that will illustrate this principle. And the fifth sentence states the actual thesis that the narrative will develop, support, and illustrate.

Here is a summary of the parameters for this assignment:

1. *Topic:* How one creative individual challenged the restraints of some mistaken assumptions in solving a problem.
2. *Objective:* To describe and explain, through a narrative, a personal or historical achievement from the perspective of how inherent assumptions were worked through.
3. *Form:* Essay using personal or researched information for illustration and exposition to support the thesis statement.
4. *Length:* At least three typed pages.

Submit your working outline with your paper if your instructor requests that you do so. To follow up in class, read your essays to one another in pairs or small groups. Check over one another's work to see whether the parameters were followed. Critique each essay with the following questions.

Scoring for Expository Essay on Assumptions

1. Does the writer state the thesis clearly and develop it through narrative and exposition? *40 points*
2. Does the essay really stay with the topic of illustrating how an individual solved one major problem through working with some mistaken assumptions? *25 points*
3. Is the length at least three typed pages? *10 points*
4. Is the thesis supported with personal or researched information? *15 points*
5. Is the work free of distracting errors in punctuation, spelling, and sentence structure? *10 points*

● **STUDENT WRITING EXAMPLE**

A MISPLACED ASSUMPTION

Terry Ruscoe

All of us have heard fables about villages that suffered long and hard from a particular problem, like a famine or a wayward dragon. Then one day a stranger appeared and solved the problem simply, quickly, and miraculously. In such stories, what seemed to be a miracle to the villagers was only a matter of a newcomer's bringing a fresh perspective, unbiased by any past assumptions. My own life had a parallel situation several years ago when I went to work for the municipal utilities district. And although I did not arrive on a horse or in a suit of armor, I did bring a fresh perspective that solved an "insoluble problem."

My work as a storekeeper was to receive and distribute merchandise, such as plumbing supplies, to our work crews. Here was the problem: after our trucks rolled out of the yard to make deliveries, we would often get calls asking for a modification in the order. But, we had no way of getting in touch with the trucks once they left. This could mean even more frustration for the frantic caller who needed just one more of those special pipeline fittings to complete the job and get traffic moving again.

"Radios, that's what we need," said the foreman as he burst into the office. He had just been chewed out by the supervisor of maintenance for a work delay of two hours that was due to some missing material. "The only problem is the budget. How can we afford $800 right away to put a radio in each of the trucks?" Carl, the receiving clerk, who was instructing me on the proper manner of keeping stock records, looked up and quipped, "Yeah, not only is that too much money, but say the driver is out of his truck unloading . . . he may not even hear the thing."

Later that day at lunch, several of us were in the break room. We began tossing the problem around. One of the guys came up with a good idea, suggesting that we augment the radios with an attachment to automatically sound the horn of the truck when it was called. But this would be even more expensive and still be useless if the driver was out of range or was out in a pool vehicle.

5   Another problem that arose was the lack of firsthand communication; every message would have to be channeled through the base station operator unless we bought our own base station transmitter, which would cost even more money. And then there was the question of privacy: what if we wanted the driver to stop on the way back to pick up some doughnuts? We didn't need the whole district to know about it. "It's the same old problem," moaned one driver. "Face it, we're just going to have to pop for the whole deal, base station and all, and be done with it. Consider it a long-term investment into our sanity."

I had been listening, just listening, for about twenty minutes when I realized that what we had here were two misplaced assumptions: the first was that we had to reach the truck; and the second was that we had only one way of communicating. It's the driver we need to reach, I reasoned. And what else was there besides radios? Telephones? He couldn't carry a phone around with him, but . . . what about a beeper? That way, when he got our message, he could go to any nearby phone and call us. (Remember that this was back in the times when cell phones were not yet invented and only doctors carried beepers.) "Okay," I said, "why not supply each driver with a remote-controlled beeper, so that when he gets our message he can go directly to a phone and call us. As they say, 'phoning is the next best thing to being there.'" And guess what? It worked. If we wanted to contact a driver we simply beeped him. It was far less expensive, and we were able to rent the beepers immediately. Above all, the troops could now get what they wanted without any of those old-fashioned glazed-or-chocolate mix-ups.

Used with permission of Terry Ruscoe.

● R E A D I N G S ●

Lateral and Vertical Thinking

Edward de Bono

Edward de Bono has been a professor at Cambridge, Oxford, and Harvard Universities. He has written many innovative books about thinking, maintaining it is a learnable and teachable skill. He was the first to develop the term lateral thinking, *which is particularly useful for creative problem solving. Lateral thinking allows a person to overcome binding assumptions and see a problem in an entirely different way, thus allowing novel solutions. In the illustrative story presented here, Edward de Bono explains the differences between lateral and vertical thinking.*

Many years ago when a person who owed money could be thrown into jail, a merchant in London had the misfortune to owe a huge sum to a money-lender. The money-lender, who was old and ugly, fancied the merchant's beautiful teenage daughter. He proposed a bargain. He said he would cancel the merchant's debt if he could have the girl instead.

Both the merchant and his daughter were horrified at the proposal. So the cunning money-lender proposed that they let Providence decide the matter. He told them that he would put a black pebble and a white pebble into an empty money-bag and then the girl would have to pick out one of the pebbles. If she chose the black pebble she would become his wife and her father's debt would be canceled. If she chose the white pebble she would stay with her father and the debt would be canceled. But if she refused to pick out a pebble her father would be thrown into jail and she would starve.

Reluctantly the merchant agreed. They were standing on a pebble-strewn path in the merchant's garden as they talked and the money-lender stooped down to pick up the two pebbles. As he picked up the pebbles the girl, sharp-eyed with fright, noticed that he picked up two black pebbles and put them into the money-bag. He then asked the girl to pick out the pebble that was to decide her fate and that of her father.

Imagine that you are standing on that path in the merchant's garden. What would you have done if you had been the unfortunate girl? If you had to advise her what would you have advised her to do?

5   What type of thinking would you use to solve the problem? You may believe that careful logical analysis must solve the problem if there is a solution. This type of thinking is straight-forward vertical thinking. The other type of thinking is lateral thinking.

Vertical thinkers are not usually of much help to a girl in this situation. The way they analyze it, there are three possibilities:

1. The girl should refuse to take a pebble.
2. The girl should show that there are two black pebbles in the bag and expose the money-lender as a cheat.
3. The girl should take a black pebble and sacrifice herself in order to save her father from prison.

None of these suggestions is very helpful, for if the girl does not take a pebble her father goes to prison, and if she does take a pebble, then she has to marry the money-lender.

The story shows the difference between vertical thinking and lateral thinking. Vertical thinkers are concerned with the fact that the girl has to take a pebble. Lateral thinkers become concerned with the pebble that is left behind. Vertical thinkers take the most reasonable view of a situation and then proceed logically and carefully to work it out. Lateral thinkers tend to explore all the different ways of looking at something, rather than accepting the most promising and proceeding from that.

The girl in the pebble story put her hand into the money-bag and drew out a pebble. Without looking at it she fumbled and let it fall to the path where it was immediately lost among all the others.

"Oh, how clumsy of me," she said, "but never mind—if you look into the bag you will be able to tell which pebble I took by the colour of the one that is left."

10   Since the remaining pebble is of course black, it must be assumed that she has taken the white pebble, since the money-lender dare not admit his dishonesty. In this way, by using lateral thinking, the girl changes what seems an impossible situation into an extremely advantageous one. The girl is actually better off than if the money-lender had been honest and had put one black and one white pebble into the bag, for then she would have had only an even

chance of being saved. As it is, she is sure of remaining with her father and at the same time having his debt canceled.

Vertical thinking has always been the only respectable type of thinking. In its ultimate form as logic it is the recommended ideal towards which all minds are urged to strive, no matter how far short they fall. Computers are perhaps the best example. The problem is defined by the programmer, who also indicates the path along which the problem is to be explored. The computer then proceeds with its incomparable logic and efficiency to work out the problem. The smooth progression of vertical thinking from one solid step to another solid step is quite different from lateral thinking.

If you were to take a set of toy blocks and build them upwards, each block resting firmly and squarely on the block below it, you would have an illustration of vertical thinking. With lateral thinking the blocks are scattered around. They may be connected to each other loosely or not at all. But the pattern that may eventually emerge can be as useful as the vertical structure.

●　●　●

Study/Writing/Discussion Questions

1. What role do assumptions play in vertical thinking?

2. How does lateral thinking work with assumptions?

3. "Vertical thinkers take the most reasonable view of a situation and then proceed logically and carefully to work it out. Lateral thinkers tend to explore all the different ways of looking at something, rather than accepting the most promising and proceeding from that." Look again at the story of Columbus and the egg cited in the Discovery Exercises at the beginning of this chapter. Was Columbus a vertical or lateral thinker?

4. Is the author saying that vertical thinking is wrong? Explain why or why not.

5. Edward de Bono once gave this example of lateral thinking: "A granny complains that she can't continue with her knitting because Suzy the three-year-old keeps playing with her wool. A vertical solution would be to put Suzy in a play pen. A lateral solution would be to put the granny there." Explain the role of assumptions in this solution.

6. In the state-operated health care program offered in China, village physicians are paid not for their services to the sick but for the number of their assigned patients who stay well. How does this represent a lateral thinking solution?

7. A persistent problem in the United States is illegal drug use. One unsuccessful solution has been the "war on drugs." Do you think this was a vertical or lateral solution? If you feel it is vertical, suggest some lateral solutions. If you claim it is lateral, then describe some vertical solutions.

8. According to *Time* magazine (8/26/02) new ecologically sound products include inflatable sofas and chairs, the Flamp, a lamp that leeches light from other sources without using electricity, and the Eco-Flush Toilet with high, medium, and low settings. What assumptions had to be questioned in order to create each of these products?

● ● ●

Winterblossom Garden

David Low

The following is an excerpt from an autobiographical short story. Born in 1952 in Queens, New York, David Low now lives in the East Village of New York City. This story may be viewed from many perspectives, including as a study of the frustrations of a mother and son separated by their different value assumptions. The short story "Winterblossom Garden" appeared in an anthology, Under Western Eyes *(New York: Doubleday, 1995), edited by Garrett Hongo.*

My mother pours two cups of tea from the porcelain teapot that has always been in its wicker basket on the kitchen table. On the sides of the teapot, a maiden dressed in a jade-green gown visits a bearded emperor at his palace near the sky. The maiden waves a vermilion fan.

"I bet you still don't know how to cook," my mother says. She places a plate of steamed roast pork buns before me.

"Mom, I'm not hungry."

"If you don't eat more, you will get sick."

5   I take a bun from the plate, but it is too hot. My mother hands me a napkin so I can put the bun down. Then she peels a banana in front of me.

"I'm not obsessed with food like you," I say.

"What's wrong with eating?"

She looks at me as she takes a big bite of the banana.

"I'm going to have a photography show at the end of the summer."

10   "Are you still taking pictures of old buildings falling down? How ugly! Why don't you take happier pictures?"

"I thought you would want to come," I answer. "It's not easy to get a gallery."

"If you were married," she says, her voice becoming unusually soft, "you would take better pictures. You would be happy."

"I don't know what you mean. Why do you think getting married will make me happy?"

My mother looks at me as if I have spoken in Serbo-Croatian. She always gives me this look when I say something she does not want to hear. She finishes the banana; then she puts the plate of food away. Soon she stands at the sink, turns on the hot water and washes dishes. My mother learned long ago that silence has a power of its own.

15   She takes out a blue cookie tin from the dining-room cabinet. Inside this tin, my mother keeps her favorite photographs. Whenever I am ready to leave, my mother brings it to the living room and opens it on the coffee table. She knows I cannot resist looking at these pictures again; I will sit down next to her on the sofa for at least another hour. Besides the portraits of the family, my mother has images of people I have never met: her father, who owned a poultry store on Pell Street and didn't get a chance to return to China before he died; my father's younger sister, who still runs a pharmacy in Rio de Janeiro (she sends the family an annual supply of cough drops); my mother's cousin Kay, who died at thirty, a year after she came to New York from Hong Kong. Although my mother has a story to tell for each photograph, she refuses to speak about Kay, as if the mere mention of her name will bring back her ghost to haunt us all.

My mother always manages to find a picture I have not seen before; suddenly I discover I have a relative who is a mortician in Vancouver. I pick up a portrait of Uncle Lao-Hu, a silver-haired man with a goatee who owned a curio shop on Mott Street until he retired last year and moved to Hawaii. In a color print, he stands in the doorway of his store, holding a bamboo Moon Man in front of him, as if it were a bowling trophy. The statue, which is actually two feet tall, has a staff in its left hand, while its right palm balances a peach, a sign of long life. The top of the Moon Man's head protrudes in the shape of an eggplant; my mother believes that such a head contains an endless wealth of wisdom.

"Your Uncle Lao-Hu is a wise man, too," my mother says, "except when he's in love. When he still owned the store, he fell in love with his women customers all the time. He was always losing money because he gave away his merchandise to any woman who smiled at him."

I see my uncle's generous arms full of gifts: a silver Buddha, an ivory dragon, a pair of emerald chopsticks.

"These women confused him," she adds. "That's what happens when a Chinese man doesn't get married."

20   My mother shakes her head and sighs.

"In his last letter, Lao-Hu invited me to visit him in Honolulu. Your father refuses to leave the store."

"Why don't you go anyway?"

"I can't leave your father alone." She stares at the pictures scattered on the coffee table.

"Mom, why don't you do something for yourself? I thought you were going to start taking English lessons."

25   "Your father thinks it would be a waste of time."

While my mother puts the cookie tin away, I stand up to stretch my legs. I gaze at a photograph that hangs on the wall above the sofa: my parents' wedding picture. My mother was matched to my father; she claims that if her own father had been able to repay the money that Dad spent to bring her to America, she might never have married him at all. In the wedding picture she wears a stunned expression. She is dressed in a luminous gown of ruffles and lace; the train spirals at her feet. As she clutches a bouquet tightly against her stomach, she might be asking, "What am I doing? Who is this man?" My father's face is thinner than it is now. His tuxedo is too small for him; the flower in his lapel droops. He hides his hand with the crooked pinky behind his back.

I have never been sure if my parents really love each other. I have only seen them kiss at their children's weddings. They never touch each other in public. When I was little, I often thought they went to sleep in the clothes they wore to work.

Copyright 1982 by David Low. Used with permission of David Low.

Study/Writing/Discussion Questions

1. Working individually or in small groups, take a piece of paper and draw a vertical line down the center in order to make two columns. Write the word *Mother* at the top of one column and *Son* at the top of the other. Then reread the story carefully, this time taking particular note of the value assumptions that underlie their thinking. As you read, compose statements that express these assumptions. (They will usually take the form of "shoulds," as in "People should like to eat.") In the first column, write out the assumptions the mother holds about what her young Chinese American son should do, how he should live, and what he should understand. In the second column, write down the assumptions held by the son about what the Mother should do, how she should live, and what she should understand.

2. When you have finished, compare and discuss your lists.

3. Do you find that one is more aware than the other of these assumptions? How does this awareness level affect their relationship?

Advanced Optional Writing Assignment

Write an autobiographical essay of about four typed pages in which you show how you discovered some of your value assumptions through conflicts with another person, your own culture, a visited culture, or a newly adopted culture. Explain what the conflicts were and explain how they resulted from different value assumptions that you may or may not have been aware of at the time. Show how you were able to resolve or not resolve these differences.

Begin the essay with a thesis that involves some statement about value assumptions. Work from an outline that will appear on the first page of this assignment. Construct a draft outline or cluster to help you set up the symmetries for your comparison (how alike) and contrast (how different). You might decide to use a story to describe the conflict, contrasting your value assumptions in conclusion. Or you might want to state the value assumptions first, then compare and contrast people on the basis of each assumption, and end with a summary conclusion.

Optional Internet Research Assignment

1. William McDonough, architect and industrial designer, appears to be a lateral thinker. His goal is to help companies discover that profits and sustainability are not antithetical to one another. He also challenges the assumption that industries must create waste. He cites, for instance, the possibility of creating edible grocery bags. For more information about his work, see McDonough.com. Write a short report on your findings.

2. Make a search into the lives and inventions of Nicholas Tesla and Thomas Edison. Write up a report based on these questions: How did they differ in their education and styles of creative thinking? How did Edison flout so many assumptions about how to engage in invention? How did Tesla flout Edison's assumptions about the use of alternating currents? How does Edison's behavior toward Tesla call into question some assumptions about his integrity? How does Tesla's death in poverty and obscurity defy some common assumptions about justice and rewards? (Your class might also enjoy seeing two excellent PBS videos on the lives of Tesla and Edison.)

CHAPTER 6

Opinions:
What's Believed?

"What is the point of having an opinion if you don't email
it to everyone you know?"

This chapter explores that familiar word *opinion* and examines how it affects our ability to think critically. By definition, opinions express our decisions about life. We collect them from experiences, or adopt them from others, and store them in our memory files. They may be based on a careful study of evidence, or they may not. They may even be confused with facts. In this chapter, we will take an irreverent look at opinions, their characteristics, and their problems.

DISCOVERY EXERCISES

The three discovery exercises that follow can be done either alone or with a partner in preparation for class discussion of this chapter.

■ Comparing a Sample of Opinions

Study the following statements of opinion:

1. My psychiatrist said I need a vacation, not medication.
2. "Why not go to war for oil? We need oil." (Ann Coulter)
3. "Most Americans who are considered 'poor' today have routine access to a quality of housing, food, health care, consumer products, entertainment, communications, and transportation that even the Vanderbilts, the Carnegies, the Rockefellers, and the nineteenth-century European princes, with all their wealth, could not have afforded." (Stephen Moore and Julian Simon, *It's Getting Better All the Time*, Washington, DC: Cato Institute, 2000)
4. "All this . . . persuades us that the word 'person' as used in the Fourteenth Amendment does not include the unborn. . . . We need not resolve the difficult question of when life begins. When those trained in the respective disciplines of medicine, philosophy, and theology are unable to arrive at any consensus, the judiciary, at this point in the development of man's knowledge, is not in a position to speculate as to the answer." (U.S. Supreme Court, *Roe v. Wade*, 1973)

In writing or class discussion, answer these questions about the statements:

1. What do these opinions have in common?
2. How are they different?
3. Do they all have equal weight and value?

■ Why Do We Get Confused by the Word Opinion?

Find at least three different meanings in a dictionary for the word *opinion*. (Be sure to look at the word's etymology.) Write down each definition and compose a sentence that clearly expresses each meaning. Do you find that some of these meanings of *opinion* seem to contradict one another? Explain exactly how.

After you have finished, compare your different meanings to those given here:

1. A judgment that, though open to dispute, seems probable to the *speaker.* "No one can say if our weather has changed permanently for the worse or not, but it's my *opinion* that it has."
2. A belief held with confidence but not substantiated by proof. "There'll always be an England."
3. A claim or statement about what is considered to be true, supported by reasoning. "Americans are overworked. Their average work hours have continued to increase over the past thirty years. It is now not only commonplace in families for both parents to work, but the working poor hold three and four jobs just to make ends meet."
4. A judgment formed by an expert. "As your doctor of long standing, it is my opinion that you should not have surgery at this time."
5. Prevailing sentiment. "Public opinion supports more environmental protection."
6. A formal judgment drawn after a legal hearing. "It is the opinion of the court that the defendant is guilty."

■ An Exercise in Evaluating Opinions

Rate the following opinions as:

A. An opinion I would accept and act on
B. Worthy of consideration
C. I'd want another opinion
D. Forget it!

_____   1. Your doctor says you need surgery immediately.
_____   2. A psychiatrist testifies in court that the defendant is not guilty by reason of insanity.
_____   3. The weather forecaster says it will rain tomorrow.
_____   4. Your attorney says you should sue your neighbor for damages.
_____   5. You want to rent an apartment but the neighbor next door says the landlord is a weirdo.
_____   6. Your best friend tells you your fiancée is tacky.
_____   7. Your English instructor says you don't know how to think and should see a psychiatrist.

_____   8. Your astrologer tells you not to go on any long trips in May.

_____   9. The judge says you are guilty of driving under the influence of alcohol.

_____   10. An engineer says you can prevent your basement from flooding by blasting holes for drainage in your foundation.

_____   11. Your utility energy advisor says you can conserve energy by having your floors insulated.

_____   12. A Pentagon general advises bombing Mexico.

Types of Opinions

Opinions take many forms: judgments, advice, generalizations, personal preferences, and general public sentiment.

Let's review what you may have discovered so far by categorizing opinions into types. First, there are the *judgments:* this is *good,* this is *bad;* this is *right,* this is *wrong;* this *should be,* this *should not be.* Look at the following two examples and provide a third example of your own.

1. Men and women should not share college dorms.
2. That car you bought was a lemon.
3.

A second type of opinion involves giving advice: *You should do this; you should not do this.* Examples of such opinions appear as follows:

1. I wouldn't advertise for a roommate if I were you.
2. You need a new car.
3.

As you must have concluded from the earlier rating exercise, whether one chooses to accept advice is an individual matter.

A third category of opinions includes simple *generalizations,* typically preceded by the word *all, no,* or *some.* In this case, the opinion is stated as a generalization in order to suggest that it represents a general truth.

1. Children in the United States are pressured to grow up too fast.
2. Nothing comes without a price.
3.

Here again, support for the opinion may be offered or not. Those who take more responsibility for their opinions do offer reasons and evidence. A critical thinker draws generalizations from evidence and, in turn, examines the generalizations provided by others for their basis in evidence.

A fourth category of opinion involves *personal taste* or *personal preferences: I like this; I don't like this.* Personal preferences need not be rational; they also do not necessarily need to be explained or justified.

1. I can't explain why, but I love the *Survivor* television series.
2. The only shoes I will wear are Caterpillar boots.
3.

A final category of opinion, close to personal taste, is *public sentiment.* Often obtained from polls, public sentiment is a gauge of prevailing public impressions on current issues. Like personal preferences, public sentiment need not be rational or even knowledgeable. Top-of-the-head impressions are as welcome to pollsters as studied opinions. Here are some examples:

1. The president is doing a good job.
2. Global warming is just an unproven theory.
3.

Distinguishing Between Responsible and Irresponsible Opinions

Not all opinions deserve careful consideration.

You are probably wondering at this point how we can manage to communicate about opinions when we use the same word to convey so many different meanings:

1. An expert's judgment
2. An unsubstantiated belief
3. An argument that is well supported
4. A final legal judgment
5. Personal preferences
6. Public sentiment

When we study critical thinking, we take these differences into account and recognize that we have to evaluate each type differently. A popular truism, which would seem to contradict this idea, states "Everyone is entitled to an opinion." Some might believe that this expression means that all opinions are relative truths and should therefore not be judged. Others believe that "Everyone is entitled to an opinion" only means that every person has a right to free speech. Critical thinkers might be willing to give most opinions a full hearing, but they need not feel compelled to offer blanket tolerance. Moreover, a critical thinker would expect any opinion to measure up to the standards of a good argument if the opinion's intent is to persuade.

Let's give an ordinary example that illustrates the need to evaluate opinions. Suppose you want to decide how to vote on a safe drinking water bond issue. After reading a number of pro and con arguments in the Voter Information Pamphlet, you wonder whose opinion you should respect the most. Would it be that of the League of Women Voters? Of your assembly representative? Of the Save-Us-from-More-Taxes Association? Of your Uncle George? Actually, from all these four choices, your Uncle George might turn out to be the most knowledgeable source you could find. To determine the value of his contribution, you would need to know how well and recently he had studied the subject, how much inside knowledge he had, and what sources he had consulted. You would also want to know whether his viewpoint was independent of vested interests and how sound his reasoning appeared. These questions represent the same standards that we use for a serious evaluation of any opinion offered to influence us.

On the other hand, opinions that are only expressions of personal taste or belief do not require justification or evaluation. If you prefer yogurt to ice cream, jazz to pop music, you do not really need to explain why. The same may be said of personal beliefs. You do not have to defend a statement that you believe in God. However, if you wanted to persuade someone to agree with you, then you would want to use the standards of an argument—that is to say, you would offer the support of reasons. In evaluating opinions, therefore, the first step is to distinguish between opinions that require responsible support and those that do not.

To sum up, critical thinkers have standards for judging which opinions are worthy of their time and consideration and which are not. Thus, when we read a newspaper editorial, we expect it to meet the standards of an argument. When we go to a physician, attorney, or financial advisor, we assume they have the training and experience to offer sound opinions. We can assume they know what facts are available and which are missing, what the variables are, and how much risk is involved in judging and predicting the odds. However, as critical thinkers, we do not assume that all the authorities we consult are always right; in the last analysis, we make our own decisions on the basis of our own judgments about others' opinions.

Looking at Public Opinion Polls

Public opinion polls can be used not just to determine public opinion but to manipulate it.

Some congressional representatives and senators regularly poll their constituents by sending questionnaires with questions like the following:

Of every dollar now spent by state government, how much do you feel is wasted?

1. None
2. 0–10 cents
3. 10–20 cents
4. 20–40 cents
5. 40–50 cents
6. Over 50 cents

On the whole, do you consider the following institutions and people to be trustworthy and credible?

1. Major industry and corporations	Yes	No
2. Small businesses	Yes	No
3. Labor unions	Yes	No
4. Government bureaus and agencies	Yes	No
5. Elected officials	Yes	No
6. Judges	Yes	No
7. Print journalists	Yes	No
8. TV journalists	Yes	No

Here, the constituent is asked to give opinions without the assistance of any facts. Moreover, judgments are requested on the basis of general impressions or feelings. The government representative who formulated this poll appears to have relinquished the expectation that an electorate should give informed consent. And thus the polled constituents might also draw the same conclusion. In tabulating the poll's results, legitimacy and weight will be given equally to conclusions based on vague impressions and to those based on study and knowledge.

Unfortunately, such polling practices are becoming more common in the United States. Indeed, with citizens voting less and less, polls provide at least some kind of feedback for representatives. Nevertheless, polls carry none of the legal safeguards of a public vote or election. Poll results can also be influenced by many factors that do not affect voting, such as how the question was phrased, how the sample was chosen, and how the poll was interpreted. Finally, although election results must be released, the release of poll results is at the discretion of individuals. Poll results can be published for the calculated purpose of *creating* public opinion. (Remember what Solomon Asch taught us?) Thus, their purpose need not necessarily be simply to reflect public sentiment. In sum, polls are not equivalent to public elections in terms of legal safeguards, the extent of their representativeness, or even the measure of responsibility assumed for them by either pollsters or the public.

Discussion Break Questions

1. If the president announces that a recent poll has shown that three out of every five Americans favor invading Canada, do you think this should give the president a mandate to go ahead?
2. Do you think it is becoming too complex for most Americans to be well informed on public issues and that this is why many tend to fall back on sentiments and feelings?

Opinions as Claims in Arguments

> Opinions function as primary claims in arguments that are supported by facts, other claims, and reasoning. In an essay, the thesis is a statement of opinion.

Arguments begin with opinions. Having an opinion that we want to express and defend motivates us to build an argument. Yet a mere statement of opinion alone is not an argument.

Americans are overworked.

To serve as an argument, this statement needs support. *An opinion only becomes an argument when it provides supporting reasons that might persuade others to agree with this opinion.*

> Unemployment in Americans is growing while the employed are overworked. (*opinion that is a conclusion or principal claim*) Employers are hiring fewer workers because they can use their existing workforce for more hours. (*supporting claim or reason*) In the Detroit area the average workweek is 47.5 hours; Saturn workers have a regular 50-hour week, and in some plants, workers are doing 60 hours a week. The United Auto Workers (UAW) estimates that 59,000 automobile jobs would be created if the plants were on a 40-hour week. (*supporting claims offering verifiable statistics*) (Juliet Schor, *A Sustainable Economy for the Twenty-First Century*, 1995)

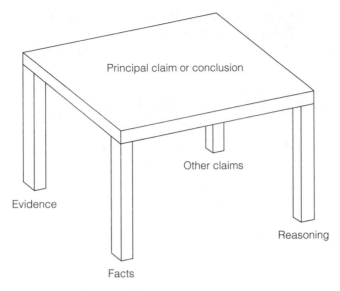

Principal claim or conclusion

Other claims

Evidence

Reasoning

Facts

FIGURE 6.1 Argument Structure

Thus, an argument consists of an opinion supported by reasons. To explain an argument we return again to the metaphor of a table: the table-top holds the opinion or principal claim; its legs are supporting claims, also known as reasons (Figure 6.1). More simply, an argument is a conclusion supported by reasons.

The principal claim in an essay is called a **thesis:**

Unemployment in America is growing while the employed are overworked.

In the language of argument, this thesis is also called a **conclusion.** It is not a conclusion in the sense that it is a final summary but in the sense that it is the conclusion of a line of reasoning:

Employers are hiring fewer workers because they can use their existing workforce for more hours.

The argument's credibility is greatly increased by the support of additional claims offering verifiable statistics about the working hours of autoworkers. This is known as **evidence**—data that can be verified as factual. Evidence includes statistics, testimony, personal experience, witnesses, and records—information whose accuracy can be examined independently.

In the Composition Writing Application that follows, you are asked to write an essay in which you make a short argument in support of an opinion, express an opinion, or analyze three opinions. Such an exercise can remind you how opinions function as primary claims in an argument and how the support of evidence, other claims, and reasoning gives these opinions credibility and persuasiveness.

Composition Writing Application

■ First Option: A Short Argument Supporting an Opinion

Write a one- to two-page essay stating and defending an opinion you believe in. Follow these steps:

1. *What:* State the opinion or principal claim in one sentence.
2. *Support:*
   a. Give three or more reasons why you believe this opinion to be true.
   b. Also provide evidence in the form of facts, statistics, or specific examples to support your claim.
3. *Persuasion:* Explain why you believe others should accept this opinion.
4. *Conclusion:* Bring your ideas together in a summary or a generalization.

■ Second Option: A Short Expository Essay about an Opinion

Write a short essay describing an opinion of your own. Follow these steps:

1. *What:* State an opinion.
2. *Source:* Was this opinion based on your own experience or something you heard or read? Be specific about the circumstances in which you formulated it.
3. *Reasons:* Why is it a good opinion or a poor one? What tests of life and time has it survived? Have any experiences suggested that you need to alter this opinion?

The length of your essay should be two to three typed pages. It should take the form of an essay with a thesis. The first paragraph should cover step 1. The second or next two paragraphs should cover step 2. The main part of your essay (two to three paragraphs) should offer the support of reasons described in step 3. The final paragraph should sum up the whole.

■ Third Option: A Short Essay Analyzing Three Opinions

Study your local newspaper's editorial pages to find some editorials and letters to the editor that interest you. Select three to analyze and photocopy them. For each, paste your photocopy at the top of a page and then analyze the piece of writing by answering these questions:

1. Is the opinion a judgment, advice, an expression of taste or sentiment, a belief, or a generalization? Support your answer in each case, providing an example and explaining it fully in these terms.

2. Is this opinion just a personal expression of taste or sentiment, or is it offered in an attempt to influence others? Explain fully.

3. Does the person giving this opinion show any special expertise regarding the subject or have any special qualifications? Explain what information you have and what is lacking.

4. Is the opinion backed up by evidence and sound reasoning? Show why or why not.

5. Does this opinion appear to be based on an objective study of the facts, or does it seem to be motivated by vested interests or a profit motive? Explain your judgment.

6. Would you call this a responsible opinion? Why or why not?

■ Peer Review

To follow up in class, form groups of two or more and read your papers aloud. Check one another's work to determine whether all the parameters given were observed. Evaluate the assignment according to the scoring box given below.

Scoring Sheet for Any One of the Three Opinion Essay Options

1. The opinion or opinions are clearly stated. *10 points*
2. The support offered is adequate and relevant (or, in the case of option three, clearly stated and analyzed). *30 points*
3. Each parameter is followed and/or each question considered. *30 points*
4. The essay is clearly organized around a purpose to describe, state and defend, or analyze, depending on the option chosen. *20 points*
5. There are no distracting errors of punctuation, spelling, or sentence structure. *10 points*

Chapter Summary

1. Although the word *opinion* is a common one, it is just as commonly misunderstood, because the same word covers so many varieties of thoughts, ranging from expert judgments to expressions of sentiment or personal taste.

2. Opinions can be well substantiated or not. They can be based either on reasons or solely on whim, feelings, emotions, or prejudice.

3. Critical thinking requires that we recognize the difference between responsible and irresponsible opinion and that we distinguish statements based on evidence from statements based solely on feelings.

4. People enjoy expressing and reading opinions.

5. Expert opinion is based on an understanding of evidence and risks in a situation and is important and highly valued.

6. Public opinion polls can be used to *determine* public sentiment on social and political issues but also to *manipulate* public sentiment. This occurs when we forget that sentiment is not the same as informed opinion and that opinion polls are not subject to the same safeguards as public elections.

7. Opinions should not be confused with facts.

8. Arguments consist of supported opinions; the intent of an argument is to persuade.

9. In an essay, a statement of opinion can be the thesis or its principal claim.

Building Arguments
Opinions

Indians ought not to buy whiskey. It is hot in his heart for a little while, then it is gone; the Indian is cold, his head is sore, and he does not remember what he did when the poison was in him. Whiskey is hot poison for the Winnebagoes. My head is like the snow with age, I have seen the ruin that it has brought upon our nation, and I advise them to buy no more whiskey. (Decori, Winnebago chief, 1828)

Exercise
1. What is the principal claim made here?
2. What reasons are given to support it?

Chapter Quiz

Rate each of the following statements as *true* or *false*. Justify each answer.

_____   1. Expert opinion calculates the risk involved in bridging the gap between the known and the unknown for a particular situation.

_____   2. Giving advice is not a way of offering an opinion.

_____   3. The results of public opinion polls are equivalent to votes in elections.

_____   4. Opinions in the form of judgments state what is right and wrong, bad and good.

_____   5. Some opinions are based on generalizations, such as stereotypes, as in the statement "All Chinese look alike."

_____   6. Responsible opinions are based on a careful examination of the evidence.

_____   7. Opinions are the same as facts.

_____   8. Gossip is opinion sharing without any requirement for substantiation.

_____   9. Everyone is entitled to his or her own opinion because all opinions carry equal value.

_____   10. Prevailing sentiment refers to popular opinion that changes with the times.

● R E A D I N G S ●

The Loss of Innocence

James P. Steyer

This essay is taken from Steyer's recent critique of television, a book called The Other Parent. *In 1977 when Marie Winn wrote* The Plug-in Drug, *a parallel critique describing television's effects on children's behavior and consciousness, she could assume that parents were supervising their children's viewing and were able to do something about the situation. Today, according to Steyer, the problem is that the human parent is either absent (and working) or standing by helpless as their children become raised by a machine that completely corrupts their tastes, morals, and sensibilities. Note, as you read, how he presents and supports his opinion.*

For me, as a parent of three young children and as a longtime teacher, the loss of innocence at too early an age is perhaps the highest price that American kids pay in this new media environment. Ever since the Hays Office began monitoring Hollywood morals in the 1920s, Americans have worried about the media's impact on "family values." But before our mass-media culture became so explicit and so pervasive, before large media companies began to realize huge profits by pushing sex and sensationalism, things were different. Parents were much better able to control what their children learned about and when. I'm hardly a prude, having grown up in the "free love" era of the late 1960s and 1970s, but I am deeply troubled by this aspect of today's media culture. Our kids are bombarded with language, messages, and images that far exceed the most outrageous forms of pop culture we experienced. And instead of making a social or political statement, they aim to shock and titillate for commercial reasons.

Traditionally, childhood was guarded by what Neil Postman, chairman of New York University's Department of Culture and Communication and a respected media observer, calls a "sequence of revealed secrets." Kids were routinely protected from information that they were not yet ready to understand. That innocence is priceless. It's an essential element of childhood and growing up. But today, such gatekeeping is virtually impossible. In the course of a single year, the average American child is exposed to about ten thousand episodes of sexual intercourse or references to sex on television alone. We're not even talking about their repeated exposure to sex in movies, ads, magazines, music, radio shows, and easily accessed Web sites. In a recent two-week survey of TV shows by the Henry J. Kaiser Family Foundation, *more than two-thirds* of the shows that aired in what used to be "family hour"—from 7:00 to 9:00 P.M.—contained sexual content inappropriate for kids. And this was only broadcast television, not the more extreme content routinely available on cable.

This constant and overwhelming exposure to sexual messages is coming at a time when splintered families, the decline in organized religion, and struggling public schools have left many kids without other clear messages when it comes to sexual behavior and values. Should parents be the first line of defense? Absolutely. But the media has some serious responsibility too, especially when they are using publicly owned airwaves to make billions of dollars.

If we don't start taking responsibility—as parents first, but also by demanding it from the huge media interests as well as the government officials who are supposed to regulate them on behalf of the public interest—then we put our children at continued risk. We will raise generations of kids desensitized to violence, overexposed to reckless sex, and commercially exploited from their earliest years. And our culture will pay an ever-increasing price.

● ● ●

Study/Writing/Discussion Questions

1. What is the thesis of this essay? Can you find it stated in one sentence?

2. Make an outline showing how Steyer organizes facts and claims to support this thesis.

3. State your agreement or disagreement with his opinion and defend it. Do you think innocence is a value worth preserving?

4. In another chapter of the same book, Steyer writes, "A steady diet of media sex can have other troubling effects on adolescents. The fact is that while sex is pervasive in the media, it is rarely accompanied by any discussion of the risks and consequences of sexual behavior." Agree or disagree with this statement and explain why.

• • •

A Modest Proposal

Jonathan Swift (1667–1745)

This essay by Jonathan Swift has long been regarded as a classic of English litera-ture; it has intrigued generations of college students. Swift both loved and hated his native Ireland, where he was born into Anglo-Irish aristocracy. At the time this essay was written, in 1729, the Irish had long suffered from British exploitation, corrupt Irish politicians, and absentee landlords. In your first reading, begin with this ques-tion. What exactly is this author's opinion?

It is a melancholy object to those who walk through this great town or travel in the country, when they see the streets, the roads, and cabin doors, crowded with beggars of the female sex, followed by three, four, or six children, all in rags and importuning every passenger for an alms. These mothers, instead of being able to work for their honest livelihood, are forced to employ all their time strolling to beg sustenance for their helpless infants, who, as they grow up, either turn thieves for want of work, or leave their dear native country to fight for the Pretender in Spain, or sell themselves to the Barbados.

I think it is agreed by all parties that this prodigious number of children in the arms, or on the backs, or at the heels of their mothers, and frequently of their fathers, is in the present deplorable state of the kingdom a very great additional grievance; and therefore whoever could find out a fair, cheap, and easy method of making these children sound, useful members of the commonwealth would deserve so well of the public as to have his statue set up for a preserver of the nation.

But my intention is very far from being confined to provide only for the children of professed beggars; it is of a much greater extent, and shall take in the whole number of infants at a certain age who are born of parents in effect as little able to support them as those who demand our charity in the streets.

As to my own part, having turned my thoughts for many years upon this important subject, and maturely weighed the several schemes of other projectors, I have always found them grossly mistaken in their computation. It is true, a child just dropped from its dam may be supported by her milk for a solar year, with little other nourishment; at most not above the value of two shillings, which the mother may certainly get, or the value in scraps, by her lawful occupation of begging; and it is exactly at one year that I propose to provide for them in such a manner as instead of being a charge upon their parents or the parish, or wanting food and raiment for the rest of their lives, they shall on the contrary contribute to the feeding, and partly to the clothing, of many thousands.

5   There is likewise another great advantage in my scheme, that it will prevent those voluntary abortions, and that horrid practice of women murdering their bastard children, alas, too frequent among us, sacrificing the poor innocent babes, I doubt, more to avoid the expense than the shame, which would move tears and pity in the most savage and inhuman breast.

The number of souls in this kingdom being usually reckoned one million and a half, of these I calculate there may be about two hundred thousand couples whose wives are breeders; from which number I subtract thirty thousand couples who are able to maintain their own children, although I apprehend there cannot be so many under the present distress of the kingdom; but this being granted, there will remain an hundred and seventy thousand breeders. I again subtract fifty thousand for those women who miscarry, or whose children die by accident or disease within the year. There only remain an hundred and twenty thousand children of poor parents annually born. The question therefore is, how this number shall be reared and provided for, which, as I have already said, under the present situation of affairs, is utterly impossible by all the methods hitherto proposed. For we can neither employ them in handicraft or agriculture; we neither build houses (I mean in the country) nor cultivate land. They can very seldom pick up a livelihood by stealing till they arrive at six years old, except where they are of towardly parts; although I confess they learn the rudiments much earlier, during which time they can however be looked upon only as probationers, as I have been informed by a principal gentleman in the country of Cavan, who protested to me that he never knew above one or two instances under the age of six, even in a part of the kingdom so renowned for the quickest proficiency in that art.

I am assured by our merchants that a boy or a girl before twelve years old is no salable commodity; and even when they come to this age they will not yield above three pounds, or three pounds and half a crown at most on the Exchange; which cannot turn to account either to the parents or the kingdom, the charge of nutriment and rags having been at least four times that value.

I shall now therefore humbly propose my own thoughts, which I hope will not be liable to the least objection.

I have been assured by a very knowing American of my acquaintance in London, that a young healthy child well nursed is at a year old a most delicious, nourishing, and wholesome food, whether stewed, roasted, baked, or boiled; and I make no doubt that it will equally serve in a fricassee or a ragout.

10   I do therefore humbly offer it to public consideration that of the hundred and twenty thousand children, already computed, twenty thousand may be reserved for breed, whereof only one-fourth part to be males, which is more than we allow to sheep, black cattle, or swine; and my reason is that these children are seldom the fruits of marriage, a circumstance not much regarded by our savages, therefore one male will be sufficient to serve four females. That the remaining hundred thousand may at a year old be offered in sale to the persons of quality and fortune through the kingdom, always advising the mother to let them suck plentifully in the last month, so as to render them plump and fat for a good table. A child will make two dishes at an entertainment for friends; and when the family dines alone, the fore or hind quarter will make a reasonable dish and seasoned with a little pepper or salt will be very good boiled on the fourth day, especially in winter.

I have reckoned upon a medium that a child just born will weigh twelve pounds, and in a solar year if tolerably nursed increaseth to twenty-eight pounds.

I grant this food will be somewhat dear, and therefore very proper for landlords, who, as they have already devoured most of the parents, seem to have the best title to the children.

Infant's flesh will be in season throughout the year, but more plentiful in March, and a little before and after. For we are told by a grave author, an eminent French physician, that fish being a prolific diet, there are more children born in Roman Catholic countries about nine months after Lent than at any other season; therefore, reckoning a year after Lent, the markets will be more glutted than usual, because the number of popish infants is at least three to one in this kingdom; and therefore it will have other collateral advantage, by lessening the number of Papists among us.

I have already computed the charge of nursing a beggar's child (in which list I reckon all cottagers, laborers, and four-fifths of the farmers) to be about two shillings per annum, rags included; and I believe no gentleman would repine to give ten shillings for the carcass of a good fat child, which, as I have said, will make four dishes of excellent nutritive meat, when he hath only some particular friend or his own family to dine with him. Thus the squire will learn to be a good landlord, and grow popular among the tenants; the mother will have eight shillings net profit, and be fit for work until she produces another child.

15   Those who are more thrifty (as I must confess the times require) may flay the carcass; the skin of which artificially dressed will make admirable gloves for ladies, and summer boots for fine gentlemen.

As to our city of Dublin, shambles may be appointed for this purpose in the most convenient parts of it, and butchers we may be assured will not be wanting; although I rather recommend buying the children alive, and dressing them hot from the knife as we do roasting pigs. . . .

I can think of no one objection that will possibly be raised against this proposal, unless it should be urged that the number of people will be thereby much lessened in the kingdom. This I freely own, and it was indeed one principal design in offering it to the world. I desire the reader will observe, that I calculate my remedy for this one individual kingdom of Ireland and for no other that ever was, is, or I think ever can be upon earth. Therefore let no man talk to me of other expedients: of taxing our absentees at five shillings a pound: of using neither clothes nor household furniture except what is of our own growth and manufacture: of utterly rejecting the materials and instruments that promote foreign luxury: of curing the expensiveness of pride, vanity, idleness, and gaming in our women: of introducing a vein of parsimony, prudence, and temperance: of learning to love our country, in the want of which we differ even from Laplanders and the inhabitants of Topinamboo: of quitting our animosities and factions, nor acting any longer like the Jews, who were murdering one another at the very moment their city was taken: of being a little cautious not to sell our country and conscience for nothing: of teaching landlords to have at least one degree of mercy toward their tenants: lastly, of putting a spirit of honesty, industry, and skill into our shopkeepers: who, if a resolution could now be taken to buy only our native goods, would immediately unite to cheat and exact upon us in the price, the measure, and the goodness, nor could ever yet be brought to make one fair proposal of just dealing, though often and earnestly invited to it.

Therefore I repeat, let no man talk to me of these and the like expedients, till he hath at least some glimpse of hope that there will ever be some hearty and sincere attempt to put them in practice.

But as to myself, having been wearied out for many years with offering vain, idle, visionary thoughts, and at length utterly despairing of success, I fortunately fell upon this proposal, which, as it is wholly new, so it hath something solid and real, of no expense and little trouble, full in our own power, and whereby we can incur no danger in disobliging England. For this kind of commodity will not bear exportation, the flesh being of too tender a consistence to admit a long continuance in salt, although perhaps I could name a country which would be glad to eat up our whole nation without it.

20   After all, I am not so violently bent upon my own opinion as to reject any offer proposed by wise men, which shall be found equally innocent, cheap, easy, and effectual. But before something of that kind shall be advanced in contradiction to my scheme, and offering a better, I desire the author or authors will be pleased maturely to consider two points. First, as things now stand, how they will be able to find food and raiment for an hundred thousand useless mouths and backs. And secondly, there being a round million of creatures in human figure throughout this kingdom, whose sole subsistence put into a common stock would leave them in debt two millions of pounds sterling, adding

those who are beggars by profession to the bulk of farmers, cottagers, and laborers, with their wives and children who are beggars in effect; I desire those politicians who dislike my overture, and may perhaps be so bold to attempt an answer, that they will first ask the parents of these mortals whether they would not at this day think it a great happiness to have been sold for food at a year old in this manner I prescribe, and thereby have avoided such a perpetual scene of misfortunes as they have since gone through by the oppression of land-lords, the impossibility of paying rent without money or trade, the want of common sustenance, with neither house nor clothes to cover them from the inclemencies of the weather, and the most inevitable prospect of entailing the like or greater miseries upon their breed forever.

I profess, in the sincerity of my heart, that I have not the least personal interest in endeavoring to promote this necessary work, having no other motive than the public good of my country, by advancing our trade, providing for infants, relieving the poor, and giving some pleasure to the rich. I have no children by which I can propose to get a single penny; the youngest being nine years old, and my wife past childbearing.

Study/Writing/Discussion Questions

1. At what point in this essay did you realize that Swift was writing satire?

2. Using at least two dictionaries, write down your own definitions of the words *irony* and *satire*.

3. Outline the reasoning used to support the "modest proposal." What is so immodest about it?

4. Does the "modest proposal" represent Swift's own opinion or that of a persona, or fictional identity? If you think he has constructed a persona, then what clues suggest the presence of a very different opinion that would seem to be his own?

5. What opinions are expressed appear here about Catholics (Papists), abortions, and population control?

6. In paragraph 17 Swift begins a new section in which he anticipates objections to his proposal and rejects alternative proposals. What proposals are these? How is this presentation ironic?

7. De Bono describes a lateral thinker as provocative, generative, and unconventional. What problem was Swift trying to address, and how did he approach it in a lateral rather than vertical manner?

8. Describe any parallels you might have recognized in this essay to problems, issues, and attitudes existing in our own time. Would you say that the message of this 1729 essay still has value for us today?

Optional Internet Research Assignment

1. Learn more about public opinion polling by visiting the website of the National Council on Public Polls. See the questions listed for determining the validity of polls as well as its ethics and standards guide. Write up your findings.

2. In the past several years opinion websites called *blogs* have become extremely popular; on occasion they have even exercised a decisive influence on American politics and the media. Put in a search for blogs and see what directories you come up with. Then describe what you learned by visiting some different interest area sites with labels such as religion, family, politics, finance, and rants.

3. Make a search that will give you more background information on the life and times of Jonathan Swift. Explore what Swift meant when he said that the Irish poor would "leave their dear native country to fight for the *Pretender* in Spain, or sell themselves to the *Barbados.*"

CHAPTER 7

Evaluations:
What's Judged?

© 2000 DAVID COHEN

This is a chapter about one variety of opinion called **evaluations.** They can be baldly honest, as in this cartoon, or hidden and manipulative. Their basis can be explicit or vague criteria, clear or vague feelings. Their effects are powerful. When we mistake them for facts or are influenced by them unawares, we get into trouble. This chapter teaches how to both recognize and detach from evaluations.

DISCOVERY EXERCISES

Both Discovery Exercises can be studied either alone or with a partner in preparation for class discussion.

■ *Defining* Evaluate

First, study the etymology of the word *evaluate*. What do its prefix and root mean? Then, write out definitions of the following words:

1. Judge
2. Appraise
3. Estimate
4. Value
5. Evaluate

Based on your work, answer these questions either in writing or in class:

1. What does *evaluate* mean?
2. Is an evaluation an inference?
3. Is an evaluation an opinion?
4. Can an evaluation be based on an assumption?

■ *Recognizing Evaluative Words*

Circle the words in the following passages that express evaluations that pass judgments on the worth of something. Note whether any evidence or reasons are given to support the evaluations.

A reminder before you begin: These Discovery Exercises are not tests in which you are expected to know all the answers; they are meant only to help you acknowledge what you already know and to inspire you to learn more.

1. "Cyclo-cross has got an old-school feel to it, a wacky, super-fun, rad, community feel." (Rachael Lloyd, *San Francisco Chronicle*, November 28, 2004)
2. "Take Howard Dean's tax-hiking, government-expanding, latte-drinking, sushi-eating, Volvo-driving, *New York Times* reading, body-piercing, Hollywood-loving, left wing freak show back to Vermont where it belongs." (TV commercial, Club for Growth, 2004)
3. "Florida's system for restoring civil rights to ex-felons is unjust, capricious and unsustainable. It should be scrapped." (Debbie Cenziper and Jason Grotto, *The Miami Herald*, June 12, 2005)

4. *SIGNS.* "The number 1 Movie in America Again. . . and Again! One of the best movies of the year, engrossing, terrifying, and intelligent. A Very Scary Movie. Spooky. Suspenseful. A Wonderful Movie! A Dazzling White Knuckler! Two Thumbs Up! Thrilling, Frightening!" (Advertisement)

5. "*Quintuplets*, a moronic dull-fest that is, in turns, physically painful to watch and jaw-droppingly, stupendously stupid." (Tim Goodman, sitcom review, *San Francisco Chronicle*, June 16, 2004)

On Evaluations

Our values shape our ideals, decisions, and judgments.

Evaluate comes from the Latin *ex* = from, and *valere* = to be strong, to be of value. To evaluate, then, is (1) to determine or fix the value or worth of something or (2) to examine and judge, appraise, estimate.

SIPRESS

Something really bad has happened.
Details at eleven.

It takes some hard thinking to evaluate, appraise, and estimate value. We make comparisons and measure them against ideals, yet our standards may be conscious or unconscious. When we do "comparison shopping," we evaluate. We decide what car to buy, what apartment to rent, what school to attend. Using criteria that depend upon our needs, values, and priorities, we decide what candidates to vote for, what beliefs to hold, what friends to spend time with, what movies to attend, what books to read. In addition, our lives are affected by the evaluations of others: the teacher who assigns grades, the boss who hires or fires us, the friends who give or withhold their loyalty. Thus, given the effects of evaluations on our lives, it can be worthwhile to take time to learn how to make the evaluating process more skilled and conscious.

Premature Evaluations

> Our minds tend to evaluate situations before we have had the time to look them over.

If a stranger were to grab your arms and throw you down to the sidewalk, you would immediately think that this person was a thug. But suppose this person was protecting you from being hit by a swerving car? All of a sudden the label "thug" would disappear as you looked up into the face of a new friend. Your first evaluation was understandable, but it turned out to be premature and unfair. Here is another example:

> ALEX: "I knew before I spoke to him that he was too young for the job."
> COREY: "How do you know he is too young for the job?"
> ALEX: "Well, he has acne, for one thing . . . Okay, okay, I'll give him an interview."

Sometimes an evaluator may not be that willing to concede the possibility of prejudice.

> JULIA: "I just can't go out with someone who looks like a *nerd*."
> JANE: "What do you mean by a nerd?"
> JULIA: "You know—a *NERD!*"

Here Julia keeps repeating her evaluation as though it were a fact. A nerd is a nerd is a nerd. She commits the *fallacy of circular reasoning*. (We will learn more about this fallacy in Chapter 10.) It is more common than uncommon for evaluations to be passed off as facts: "He's a genius." "She's a screwball." "He's a scumbag."

Discussion Break Questions

Premature evaluations are snap judgments made before the situation has been adequately studied. Look at the statements below. What questions would you ask the evaluator in each case?

1. Your boyfriend doesn't have a job? He must be a loser.
2. She drives a dirty old clunker. We'd better not take her in as a housemate.
3. Those who share music files are thieves.

Evaluations Are Not Facts

> Critical thinkers try to be fair in their use of evaluations. They don't mistake evaluative words for facts.

JEANIE: Leonardo DiCaprio is a has-been. That's just a fact!

SUZY: Why do you say that?

JEANIE: Well, in *Titanic* he was luscious and divine. DiCaptivating we called him. But now, after he starred in *The Aviator*, . . . well, it spoiled everything to see him play a stingy eccentric who worried all the time about germs. Also I didn't like his haircut.

SUZY: So an actor always becomes a has-been when he plays a role his fans don't like?

JEANIE: Well, there might be some exceptions. What I mean is that *The Aviator* shattered my fantasies about him. That really is a fact.

In this example Jeanie is showing how our minds tend to work: the evaluation pops up first strong and clear, while the basis for the evaluation may take a little effort to uncover.

Yet this human tendency to evaluate first and think afterwards has a survival function. If we see a car headed toward us in the same lane, the only apt thought is *danger!* Without having to think, we can swerve to avoid an accident. Yet afterwards, other evaluations might come to mind, such as calling the other driver an idiot. Yet although name-calling can let off the steam of anger, it can also lead to more trouble and confusion.

Thus our innate tendency to rush to judgment might save our lives in some situations but endanger us in others.

Suppose you go to a lot of effort to persuade your brother to enroll in college; he finally agrees to take one English course. Five weeks into the semester, he drops his English class. He tells you he can't stand the instructor. When you question him, he says the instructor is a phony: he

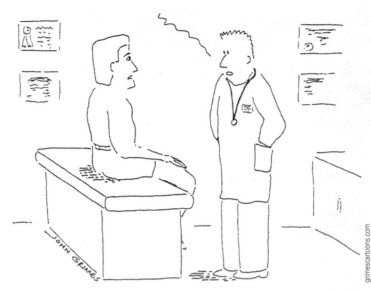

KEVIN, THE TESTS CAME BACK POSITIVE. I'M AFRAID YOU'RE A JERK.

wears tweed jackets and horn-rimmed glasses. But as you question him further, he confesses his disappointment with his progress in class. If he had received the help he needed to feel successful, perhaps he would not have cared how the instructor dressed.

To think critically, we need to be aware of how feelings influence evaluations and result in judgments that may not be fair. It is for this reason that most countries have developed courts of law for those who cannot settle their own disagreements. Fair judgments, or evaluations, are achieved by set procedures that require emotions to be controlled and judgments suspended until all testimony has been heard and all evidence considered. Finally, it must be said that although our human tendency to rush to judgment can make it very difficult for us to be fair, nevertheless we still must continuously evaluate our experiences in order to survive.

Discussion Break Questions

1. Share some examples of situations in which you changed your initial evaluation from positive to negative or vice versa. Explain how this occurred.

2. Explain, in your own words, why it is so difficult for us to make fair evaluations.

3. Share some examples of evaluations that you or others made that turned out to be "spot on."

Expectations Influence Evaluations

Expectations influence our perceptions as well as our evaluations.

Psychologist John Enright tells the following story that illustrates the influence of expectations on our perceptions as well as our evaluations.

> This morning I had a longing for some orange juice. I knew there must be some in the freezer since my roommate went shopping yesterday. I took an orange-labeled can out of the freezer and made myself a glass; as I did so, I noticed that it was a little darker than usual, but I concluded that it was just a different variety of orange or a different mix of rind and juice. Then when I tasted it, it was just awful. I spit it out in the sink and really made a mess of things, but I was sure that it was spoiled, and I didn't want to make myself sick. Then I decided that I might as well take it back to the grocer's and get our money back. I fished the can out of the garbage and looked at the label. To my surprise it said "Tangerine Juice." I couldn't believe it. I tasted some of the juice left in the glass and . . . *it was good tangerine juice!*

Discussion Break Questions

1. Neither the liquid nor the taste buds of the person changed. How can you explain what happened?
2. What information was missing in the first evaluation?
3. Describe an instance in which expectations influenced your perceptions and evaluations.

Recognizing Evaluations in Word Connotations

Word connotations can be manipulative evaluations.

Evaluations are opinions that can be openly or covertly expressed. Compare these two statements:

- I believe electric cars are impractical because they can't be driven on the freeway at high speeds and they can only be driven a limited number of miles before needing a recharge.
- Electric cars are kiddy-cars for environmental Puritans.

The first example is an up-front evaluation that clearly expresses a personal opinion. It allows us to agree or disagree. The second example is a covert opinion because it evaluates through a choice of words with negative connotations: "kiddy-cars" and "environmental Puritans." It does not invite us to agree or disagree because it implies that these words represent facts.

Word connotations were introduced in Chapter 2. At that time we were studying how to select words with connotations appropriate for what we wanted to communicate. In this chapter we are focusing on the ways in which word connotations carry evaluations that influence our feelings, and thus the formation of our opinions. Sometimes these connotations are so subtle as to influence us unawares. Let's look now at some simple word choices that carry positive or negative word connotations.

Discussion Break Questions

1. Show how the connotations of the following words differ by writing a plus or minus beside each word that carries either a positive or a negative connotation. Then answer the questions that follow either in writing or with your neighbor in class.

Girl	Chick	Slut
Guy	Dude	Stud
Dismissed	Kiss-off	Abandoned
CEO	Boss	Honcho
Alcoholic	Dipso	Drunkard

2. What kind of differences lie in the meanings of the words within each set of three?

3. If you call me "a flake," does that mean that I am, in fact, "a flake" or does it simply mean you see me in a negative light?

DISCOVERY EXERCISE

■ Recognizing Evaluative Words' Persuasive Powers

Underline the words in the following passages that contain connotations that could influence feelings, and thus opinion as well.

1. Editor: Your editorial "Added Peril at the Border" criticizes the Minuteman Project for organizing to help our government stop the massive influx of illegal aliens into our country from Mexico. You are

wrong in characterizing the Minutemen as vigilantes and extremists. They are just good citizens trying to help our government protect its borders. (Adapted from a letter to the *San Francisco Chronicle,* April 6, 2005)

2. The mayor has used this city as a trampoline to further his own eccentric career. His public style is aloof, capricious, adversarial, and profoundly egocentric.

3. "Liberals promote immoral destructive behavior because they are snobs, they embrace criminals because they are snobs, they oppose tax cuts because they are snobs, they adore the environment because they are snobs. Every pernicious idea to come down the pike is instantly embraced by liberals to show how powerful they are." (Ann Coulter, *Slander, Liberal Lies About the American Right,* 2002)

4. "Backlash theorists . . . imagine countless conspiracies in which the wealthy, powerful, and well connected—the liberal media, the atheistic scientists, the obnoxious eastern elite—pull the strings and make the puppets dance. And yet the backlash itself has been a political trap so devastating to the interests of Middle America that even the most diabolical of stringpullers would have had trouble dreaming it up." (Thomas Frank, *What's the Matter with Kansas?* 2004)

Skilled Use of Evaluations

An expert is a person with a reputation for making skilled evaluations.

So far in this chapter we have looked mainly at examples of premature or manipulative evaluations; however, that does not mean that evaluations are wrong. On the contrary, skilled evaluations are highly important and often prized achievements. Experts in any profession, such as law or medicine, are highly paid for their evaluation skills. We visit a physician to get a diagnosis, recommended treatments, and estimates of the time needed for recovery. We go to an attorney to find out whether or not there might be a chance of winning a case. We read editorials in newspapers because we respect editors' evaluations of public issues. We read film, book, art, and music reviews to learn from the reviewers' expertise.

The following reading is an excerpt from a review written by a skilled evaluator, the journalist Vicki Haddock. In this article she offers (1) a movie review, (2) an evaluation of the public response to an Oscar-winning film, and (3) an evaluation of the sport of boxing.

• R E A D I N G •

Million Dollar Brutality

Boxing's violence is unrelenting and, in movies, unremarkable.

Vicki Haddock

What a curious comment on humanity it is that the Oscar-winning best picture *Million Dollar Baby* has ignited fierce debate outside the ring, but not about the subject at its core: professional boxing.

Among inherently treacherous sports, boxing is unique—the only one in which a contestant achieves the pinnacle of success by pummeling an opponent into a state of unconsciousness. It encourages actions that would warrant assault charges if they occurred on the street.

In the multimillion dollar sport of boxing, the violence is unvarnished. There is no ball, no net, no goal lines. Just fists. One database lists 1,200 fighters killed in matches worldwide, and many pro boxers who do survive must cope with some degree of brain damage.

Boxer Mike Tyson has been quoted describing his technique: "I try to catch my opponent on the tip of his nose because I try to punch the bone into his brain."

5 The very premise of boxing is barbaric to the American Medical Association and its counterparts in dozens of other countries. They have clamored, in vain, for a ban on pro and amateur boxing.

The celluloid verdict about the sport by *Million Dollar Baby* director Clint Eastwood is an enigma. Some moviegoers see his film as an unmistakable condemnation of the business. It ultimately renders a spunky prize fighter a helpless quadriplegic. Yet the film also imbues boxing with nobility. Along with figurative sweat and spattering blood, the audience is hit with a string of rationalizations: "Boxing is about respect—getting it for yourself and taking it away from the other guy." Also "The magic of boxing is fighting beyond endurance, through cracked ribs and detached retinas. The magic of risking everything for a dream that no one sees but you."

More significantly, *Million Dollar Baby* seems to absolve the fighter's trainer/manager of blame. The God-like narrator Morgan Freeman reassures us, basso profundo, that the fighter was disabled doing what she *loved* to do.

© *San Francisco Chronicle.* Reprinted by permission.

• • •

Study/Writing/Discussion Questions

1. What evaluations does the author offer in her title and subtitle?
2. How does the author open this essay by finding irony in two situations?

3. What three facts does she offer to support her evaluation of boxing as a brutal and violent sport?

4. What contradictory evaluations does she describe in the last two paragraphs of this review?

Propaganda and Hidden Evaluations

The best defense against propaganda is to stay conscious.

Propaganda

1. Publicity to promote something. 2. Deceptive or distorted information that is systematically spread. (*Encarta Dictionary*)

Propaganda connotes deliberately false or misleading information that supports a political cause or the interest of those in power. (*Wikipedia*)

Propaganda involves the dexterous use of images, slogans and symbols that play on our prejudices and emotions. (*The Age of Propaganda*)

The word **propaganda** means the manipulation of public opinion for the benefit of the propagator. One thing is certain about propaganda: it shows no respect for truth and rational argument. Instead, psychologically sophisticated maneuvers are used to affect the unconscious mind and sway emotions toward a predetermined purpose.

The influence of propaganda is not as distant as an airplane dropping pamphlets on the enemy, but as close as your television set or the checkout stand in your neighborhood supermarket. While you are waiting your turn in line, bored and tired, even the magazine rack's accounts of lurid gossip and familiar celebrities can have their appeal. Consider these magazine headlines:

Thugs Mourn the Death of Their Dictator

Senator X Grovels for Votes

The First Lady, Our Comforter in Times of War

In each case, evaluations offer to do our thinking for us. Advertisers also prefer to persuade us into accepting their own evaluations of their products. One useful technique is just to keep repeating the desired evaluative words. "Reach for aspirin for relief, aspirin for relief, for relief. Reach for aspirin for relief whenever you have those awful headaches, those awful headaches. Aspirin for relief." This technique has the additional advantage of not requiring evidence. It is only necessary to get the message imprinted in the readers' or viewers' brains within the few seconds required to turn a page or glance at a TV commercial.

"Tiggerrific! What a gem! A fun, heart warming story for the whole family. A gem of a movie! The Tigger Movie. What a gem!"

In order to be most effective, propaganda should not be easily recognizable. Early attempts at propaganda, as seen in old World War II movies, seem ludicrous to us now. Today propaganda can entice our attention with the latest styles in entertainment. It holds our eyes and touches our feelings with colorful, stirring, even frightening images. It provides us with well-dressed experts or authority figures who tell us what we should know, who comfort us with reassurances that they are taking the best care of our interests. Today's propaganda is created by highly sophisticated public relations firms. Celebrities and public figures hire them to shape their images, tell them how to dress, write their speeches, prepare them for talking to the press, plant articles about them in the newspapers, arrange for talk show appearances. At present, public relations firms are hired routinely by organizations wishing to influence the larger American public. They include not only large corporations, but also the Catholic Church, the Pentagon, and foreign governments such as those of Kuwait and Saudi Arabia. At present, PR advisors are even hired to plan and carry out publicity campaigns for U.S. presidents that will influence public perceptions, gain consent, and thus advance the policies of their administrations.

Modern public relations firms have a sophisticated knowledge of human psychology. They play on our dreams and desires, our secret unconscious wishes, and even our fatigue and lethargy. The television viewer who lies down on his sofa to "relax" at the end of a hard day is especially prone to manipulation. According to the book *The Plug-In Drug* (by Marie Winn, Bantam, 1978), television itself induces an immediate trance state in viewers, regardless of the content shown. Perhaps you have become aware of this phenomenon yourself when you found you had to make an extreme effort to get up out of your chair and turn the television off. The next day you might not even wake up to the realization that you had been hypnotized to reach for that bottle of aspirin on the grocery shelf or cast a vote for that sincere-looking politician. Thinking critically requires that we simply *wake up*. If you want to retain the power of making your own choices, you need to learn to recognize propaganda strategies. In short, you have to continuously reclaim the right to think for yourself.

Building Arguments
Evaluations

Yet, while there were whites who preferred to live like Indians, there were few, if any, Indians who regarded a completely civilized form of living as superior to their own way of life. This is true even of Indian children who were educated in the schools of the white colonists and who were later permitted to return to their own people. With the opportunity of choosing between the two ways of life, they rarely cast their lot with civilization.

The reason for this decision was because the Indian was convinced that the white man's style of life, with its lack of freedom; innumerable laws and taxes; extremes of wealth and poverty; snobbish class divisions; hypocritical customs; private ownership of land; pent-up communities; uncomfortable clothing; many diseases; slavery to money and other false standards, could not possibly bring as much real happiness as their own ways of doing. The great mass of white people and the great mass of Indians realized that their two ways of life were directly opposed. Each race looked upon the other as inferior; neither felt inclined to adopt the ways of the other; and that is why the Indians and the whites could not get along together. (Alexander Henry, American trader, 1764)

Exercise

1. What is the principal claim made in the first paragraph?
2. What behavior is cited to support this claim?
3. What characteristics of the white man did the Indians find objectionable?
4. What do these evaluations tell us about the values of the Indians?

Short Discussion Break Questions

1. What images do you remember most from commercial advertisements?
2. What words, or advertisement jingles, stay in your mind?
3. What advertised products do you buy? Do you think you were hypnotized?

Chapter Summary

1. Evaluations make judgments about worth on the basis of standards that may be conscious or unconscious.

2. Evaluations can help us react quickly to situations in which our survival is at stake. But this same tendency to evaluate first instead of last may be problematic when we don't reexamine our evidence to make sure our evaluation is warranted.

3. Evaluations are not facts. Factual reports keep the distinction between facts and evaluations clear.

4. Premature evaluations are hasty evaluations that contain unexamined or faulty support.

5. Feelings and expectations affect both our perceptions and our evaluations.

6. All of us need to learn how to make fair and sound evaluations because they affect our lives constantly. Experts are those who have a reputation for offering skilled and reliable evaluations.

7. Connotative words convey evaluations that can be used to sway our opinions. When we think critically, we recognize how these connotations affect our feelings so that we can choose or not choose to accept the opinions they contain.

8. Evaluations are used in advertising and journalism to persuade us, sometimes hypnotically, to make positive associations with products and purchase them.

9. Critical thinking requires that we stay alert to manipulative advertising techniques that are most effective when we can be enticed to enter into a trance state.

10. Propaganda uses many sophisticated manipulative techniques of persuasion. One of these is the use of hidden evaluations. A critical thinker knows how to recognize and detach from the influence of propaganda.

Chapter Quiz

Rate the following statements as *true* or *false*. Give an example to substantiate your answer in each case.

_____   1. Evaluations are not facts but judgments based on conscious or unconscious standards.

_____   2. Premature evaluations can result from hasty observing and thinking.

_____ 3. Opinion can be influenced unawares by the use of highly connotative words.

_____ 4. Evaluations should never be used in writing reviews, such as of films and books.

_____ 5. Repeating evaluations, as is done in advertising, can serve as a hypnotic technique.

_____ 6. A critical thinker notices when evaluations are substituted for facts, information, and evidence.

_____ 7. Prior expectations influence perceptions and our evaluation of these perceptions.

_____ 8. Our first reactions, before we have had time to examine the evidence, are always the most reliable.

_____ 9. To evaluate wisely, we need to observe and think carefully while also being clear about our standards.

_____ 10. Many advertisements want us to let them do the evaluating for us.

Composition Writing Application

■ First Option: Observing and Analyzing Evaluations in Advertisements

Select two printed advertisements of the same product or type of product and make a list of all the evaluative words used. Also consider the images that accompany these words and how the two interact to persuade you to buy this product. Photocopy the ads to hand in with your paper, or attach the originals. Write at least a one-page analysis of each advertisement; then compare the ads to one another in a final page. Write a summary at the end that states your thesis.

In your one-page analysis of each ad, go over every major evaluative word you have listed and thoroughly discuss both its literal and connotative (associative) meanings. Notice what appeals these words carry to make you want to buy the product. Do the words make a pattern of evaluation that conveys a subliminal message? Is one key or primary evaluation repeated a lot, reinforced by secondary or lesser evaluations?

In your conclusion, rate each ad for its trickery or honesty and effectiveness.

In review, the parameters are:

1. *Topic:* Comparison of the use of evaluative language and imagery in two advertisements of the same or related products. The original ads, or photocopies of them, should be attached.

2. *Method:* Descriptive analysis using exposition, comparison, and evaluation.

3. *Length:* Three typed pages.

4. The summary at the end states your conclusion as a thesis.

■ Second Option: Writing a Critical Review

Write a review that evaluates a film, music album, or concert. Be conscious of your standards for evaluation. Try working with just three criteria that you discuss at the beginning, such as exciting, instructive, and entertaining. Be sure to define each one. Describe the strengths of the work as well as weaknesses.

Make this into a short essay of about three pages. Let your thesis be your recommendation for (or against) buying or going to see this work. In review, the parameters are:

1. *Topic:* A review of a film, music album, or concert.

2. *Method:* A summary and evaluation of an event or product on the basis of three criteria. The thesis states your recommendation as a reviewer.

3. *Length:* Three typed pages.

Scoring for Evaluative Words in Advertising or a Critical Review

1. Directions followed for choice of comparison of two advertisements or the writing of a review. *25 points*

2. Method directions followed for descriptive analysis, or a summary and evaluation in the review on the basis of three explicit criteria. *30 points*

3. Length of three typed pages. *20 points*

4. Summary states thesis. *15 points*

5. No distracting errors of spelling, punctuation, or sentence structure. *10 points*

● R E A D I N G S ●

Prices Without Values

Frank Ackerman and Lisa Heinzerling

This short excerpt is taken from the opening chapter of the 2004 book Priceless: On Knowing the Price of Everything and the Value of Nothing. *Robert F. Kennedy Jr. has called it "a damning indictment of cost-benefit analysis applied to health and*

*environmental protection." Frank Ackerman is an economist at the Global Develop-
ment and Environmental Institute at Tufts University and Lisa Heinzerling is a professor
at the Georgetown University Law Center specializing in environmental law.*

Right up to the day they died, Russian immigrants Mariya Diment and Liya Murkes
loved to take long walks together along the oceanfront near the senior residence
where they lived in Santa Monica. One summer day in the year 2000, Cheryl
Chadwick, reportedly talking on a cell phone while driving her Mercedes-Benz,
plowed into Diment and Murkes while they were strolling, killing them both.

What happened to Mariya Diment and Liya Murkes is not unusual, and
almost certainly will become less so; as many as 1,000 people a year now die
in car accidents caused by what some are calling "phoneslaughter."
Researchers have found that people who are talking on cellular phones while
driving are four times more likely to get into car accidents than people who are
not—about the same as the increased risk from driving after several drinks
(around the legal threshold for drunk driving in most states). Ten years ago, only
10 million people worldwide had ever even used a cell phone; by now, cell
phone users number a billion and counting. The vast majority of Americans with
cell phones talk on them while driving.

Most states, and many cities and towns, are deciding whether to do something to prevent these accidents. Some places have banned cell phone use while
driving. Others have used laws already on the books—even homicide laws—
to try to get at the problem.

Some of the country's most influential economists, however—based on
research conducted with the help of generous funding from wireless
providers—have concluded these restrictions are a bad idea. Why? Because
the people who are talking while driving are willing to pay a lot to talk on the
phone—more than many people who face deadly risks are willing to pay to
avoid the risk of being killed. What these researchers have done is compare
the price of phone calls made while driving with the "price" of deadly risks.
Since risk is not, like cell phones and calling plans, directly bought and sold
in the marketplace, economists have tried to find places where it is sold *indi-
rectly.* They have focused mainly on risky workplaces, where extra wages
are, in theory, required to convince workers to accept increased risks of
death. In comparing levels of wages and risk, economists have estimated that
groups of workers doing dangerous jobs are paid, on average, a total of
about $5–6 million more, per work-related death. By comparing the price of
cell phone use with this "price" of risky work, economists have concluded that
banning cell phone use in cars makes no economic sense.

5   The technique of translating lives into dollars is complex, but the bottom line
of the cell phone studies is simple to state: the Cheryl Chadwicks of the world
can go on talking into their cell phones while driving their Mercedes-Benzes,
even though it means that quite a few of the Mariya Diments and Liya Murkeses

of the world end up in the morgue. All based, amazingly enough, on the price of someone else's phone call.

● ● ●

Study/Writing/Discussion Questions

1. What are the authors evaluating in this essay?
2. What are they saying about the value economists place on human life as compared to cell phone profits?
3. What is the authors' implied thesis?

● ● ●

Porn, Pervasive Presence: The Creepy Wallpaper of Our Lives

William F. Buckley Jr.

This excerpt is taken from an article of the same title published in the National Review *in November 2001. William F. Buckley Jr. is the founder of this conservative magazine and its former editor. The author of many books, a journalist, and a TV personality (on the program* Firing Line*), Buckley was born in New York City, the son of a wealthy oilman; he attended Yale University. In this essay he evaluates a clothing store's catalog, moving from there to evaluate pornography as a big business. Note as you read how he uses specific detail and humor to set a scene from which to bring the reader into its larger implications.*

I stopped by at the local Abercrombie & Fitch for sailing wear. I waited, at the counter, for my package and looked down on the A&F Summer Catalogue. You could see the handsome young man on the cover, but the catalogue itself was bound in cellophane. My eyes turned to the card alongside. "To subscribe: Fill out this card and head to the nearest A&F store with a valid photo ID." *With a valid photo ID?* I thought that odd and asked the young man behind the counter, who was perhaps 19 years old, why IDs were required for purchasers of an Abercrombie & Fitch catalogue. He said, "Well, uh, it's kind of porny inside."

Abercrombie & Fitch has been from time immemorial a sportswear store renowned for its wholesome regard for the outdoor life. I smile still at the story recorded in *The New Yorker* generations ago. It was of a gardener in Long Island who yearned to buy a genuine A&F barometer and finally saved up the money to do so. He brought the beautiful thing back from Manhattan to his little house on the south shore, tapped it a few times impatiently, and stormed back to Manhattan to complain to the salesman that it was defective, its needle stuck at the mark "Hurricane." Abercrombie returned his money and the plaintiff returned to Islip to find that his house had been blown away.

Abercrombie's barometric needle had pointed resolutely at the impending hurricane of 1938, and presumably the company's current managers are confident that its current clothes line is also pointed surely, though the summer A&F catalogue seems to be suggesting that young men and women are better off wearing no clothes at all.

It is introduced by a 150-word essay under the title, "The Pleasure Principle." A definition ensues: "In psychoanalysis, the tendency or drive to achieve pleasure and avoid pain is the chief motivating force in behavior." And then an amplification: "Summer being our favorite time of the year and all, we've worked extra hard to bring you our best issue yet by letting the pleasure principle be our guide through the hottest months."

5   The lead page gives us a jaunty blonde clutching her hair, wet from the ocean she has just emerged from. If she is wearing anything, it would be below her pelvic joint. Above it, which is all the viewer can see, there are no clothes.

Next, a two-page spread of above-the-navel photos, six young men and one girl. One does spot a shoulder strap on the girl that may be a part of a bathing suit, subterranean and not reached by the camera. But lo, she does wear a watch, sheltering the wrist's nudity. The men wear nothing. A few pages on, a boy wears tennis shoes (unlaced) and a towel over his head. On his knee a camera rests. His shorts are given perspective by the young man's erection.

Whereas the young man a few pages on is entirely naked, leaning slightly over one knee. Across the page are worshipful photos of his windblown face in six differing exposures. . . . On to another young man entirely naked, one knee (the windward knee) held up. He is reposing on the deck of a sailboat, his back resting on an unfurled mainsail. The very next page gives us a girl wearing a T-shirt on which one can actually make out the name of our hosts: "Abercrombie" is discernible, and then something on the order of "Open Beauty Pageant." That shirt tapers off at the lady's waist. Below the waist there is nothing at all, except, of course, her naked body. A few pages later the young man is naked again on the boat, but wearing a drenched jacket which reaches only as far as his waist. A few pages later we have five beautiful blondes in full summer wear, draped about a Byronic young man evidently lost in the poetry of his reflections, a loose towel over his crotch.

There was never a pitch more nakedly designed than Abercrombie's to stimulate erotic appetites. The last part of the catalogue actually depicts clothes of one kind or another, but the reader, getting that far, is hotly indignant: What are all those shirts and shorts and pants doing, interrupting my view of the naked kids! I mean, I showed you my ID, didn't I?

The Number-One Sport

Neither of us (I am co-opting the reader) is suffering simply from being the last guy in town to get the word. Erotomania is *the* phenomenon. The ubiquity of merchandised sex is hinted at by such displays as *Esquire's* and Abercrombie's, which are merely byways to full-blown porn.

10   Frank Rich did a thorough piece, in May 2001, for *The New York Times Magazine*, nicely titled, "Naked Capitalists: There's No Business Like Porn Business." The raw figures he assembled astonish. We learn that $4 billion a year is spent on video pornography, that this sum of money is greater than what is spent on major league baseball; indeed that pornography is a bigger business than professional football or basketball. That 700 million rentals of porn movies occur every year, and that people pay more money for pornography in America than they do for movies. Perhaps we should say, more carefully, than for "non-adult" movies. Every year, 400 regular movies are made. The porn people make 11,000.

There used to be laws—not of the kind that would interfere with *Esquire* or Abercrombie, but laws that said: That product is obscene; and you can't peddle it in *our* marketplace.

● ● ●

Study/Writing/Discussion Questions

1. What are William Buckley's expectations as he enters the clothing store and how are they disappointed?

2. What do you think would be the sales psychology behind requiring that customers show their ID before viewing the catalog? Why do you think the catalog begins with an essay on "The Pleasure Principle"? What audience are they trying to reach?

3. How does this author seem to define pornography? How would that differ from nudity?

4. What does he mean by the term *erotomania*?

5. In the next to final paragraph, he gives some facts about the porn business in the United States. How do these facts affect the tone of his essay?

6. What does the final statement reveal about his underlying values? Explain why you agree or disagree with his point of view.

Advanced Optional Writing Assignment

Get a copy of the book *Priceless* to study more of the examples it offers of dollar estimates made on the value of life and public health in the United States. Or read the whole of William F. Buckley's essay on pornography in the *National Review* for November 19, 2001. Write an essay that formulates a generalization, followed by support, on the values of either William Buckley or the authors of *Priceless*.

Optional Internet Research Assignment

1. William Bennett (formerly U.S. Secretary of Education) is a conservative commentator who strongly believes that the survival of the United States is endangered by those who teach what he considers to be "easygoing moral and culture relativism." Such relativism, he says, will not call "good" what is good, such as the superior goodness of the American way of life, or "evil" what is evil, by which he means America's enemies. Do some Internet research on his book *Why We Fight* or get a copy from your local library to study for a report.

2. In this chapter we have been mainly concerned with the power of evaluative words. Yet images can be far more persuasive—and devious in their ability to have an immediate effect on the unconscious mind. Political as well as commercial propagandists take full advantage of this phenomenon. Here are some exercises that may lead you to make some discoveries about how images can be used as tools for persuasion.

   a. Consider some photo ops of political figures. How do they evoke positive evaluations? Exactly how do they convey trustworthiness, power, and authority? Using news photos or Google's photo search, print out some photographs for written analysis. (Or bring in clippings from daily newspapers.)

   b. Collect some photographs of celebrity actors. Exactly what about each one is appealing or attractive? How do these images affect your feelings and imagination? Why would you want to buy a product they might endorse or go to see one of their films?

   c. Consider some of the online advertisements that compel your interest. Print out some of these ads for study and analysis.

   d. One website, called PRwatch.org, discusses PR firms that design propaganda campaigns intended to manipulate public opinion for the benefit of wealthy individuals, foreign nations, corporations, and the U.S. government. Write up a report describing how the PR industry presented one client to the public.

CHAPTER 8

Viewpoints:
What's the Filter?

When one's own viewpoint is mistaken for reality, there are no other viewpoints. In this cartoon, we see how such narrow awareness affects our lives on this planet. We might also wonder if the animals have the wiser perspective.

The ability to detach from one's own point of view and assume another's is an important skill; it enables us to communicate better with others and gain new perspectives. However, if we forget that all information must flow through the filters of human biases, we confuse information with reality. A person trained in critical thinking always looks for the source of any piece of information and evaluates that information within the context of its viewpoint and inherent bias. The purpose of this chapter is to demonstrate the benefits of such attitudes and skills.

DISCOVERY EXERCISES

■ *Understanding the Term* Viewpoint

Using at least two dictionaries, formulate your own definitions of the following words:

1. Viewpoint
2. Point of view
3. Attitude
4. Bias
5. Perspective
6. Frame of reference
7. Opinion

■ *Discussion or Writing Questions*

1. Explain how viewpoints can be both collective and individual.
2. Explain why the term *viewpoint* is far more than a synonym for the word *opinion.*

■ *What Types of Viewpoints Are There?*

This is an exercise that will involve the whole class working in small groups. Each group will use brainstorming to construct one cluster or mind map illustrating a viewpoint. The mind maps may be drawn on sections of the blackboard or be drawn with crayons or felt-tip pens on large sheets of paper. Each group will begin by choosing one of the categories in the following list. Each mind map will record all the different viewpoints the group can imagine would fit under the chosen category.

Type of Viewpoint	Examples to Get You Started
Socioeconomic	Homeless, working class
Political	Red states, blue states
National	Chinese, Korean
Ethnic	Native American, Armenian
U.S. high school youth	Skaters, thugs

Type of Viewpoint	Examples to Get You Started
Religious	Islam, Catholicism
Financial world	Stock market, banking
Education	Students, administration
Occupation	Plumber, journalist
Citizenship	Immigrant, voter
Pastimes	Bikers, shopping mall visitors
Consumer groups	Internet users, Harley-Davidson owners

■ Study Questions

1. What did you learn from this exercise?
2. Take any one subgroup within a viewpoint (such as bikers) and describe how its members identify themselves through clothing, symbols, possessions, language, or shared opinions.

Viewpoints in Literature

When we study the elements of literature—such as plot, theme, and character—a crucial element is the point of view that tells the story. In literature an author can choose a third person to tell the story with omniscient or limited understanding. Other choices of viewpoint include a first-person narrative told by one character or the multiple points of view shared by several characters. In each case, the author must decide how much information and sensitivity this viewpoint will allow and how this perspective will shape the story and affect the reader. The science fiction novel *Flowers for Algernon,* by Daniel Keyes, is a first-person narrative told through the diary of a young man whose range of awareness expands and then contracts. By reading the diary entries, we learn that he is the subject of a scientific experiment that gradually raises his I.Q. from 70 to 185. He goes through a career change—from being a baker's assistant to becoming a linguistic scientist; he also enters into more complex social interactions. In time, however, his intelligence allows him to discover that the scientific experiment of which he is the subject will fail. The diary then reveals a gradual return to retardation. Thus, the plot hangs on distinct changes in his consciousness reflected through his writing. Here are three entries from this diary.

Progris riport 1 martch 3

My name is Charlie Gordon I werk in Donners bakery where Mr. Donner gives me 11 dollars a week and bred or cake if I want. I am 32 yeres old and next munth is my brithday . . . (p. 1)

Progress report 13

Am I a genius? I don't think so. Not yet anyway. I'm exceptional—a democratic term used to avoid the damning labels of gifted and deprived (which used to mean bright and retarded) and as soon as exceptional begins to mean anything to anyone they'll change it. Exceptional refers to both ends of the spectrum, so all my life I've been exceptional. (p. 106)

Nov. 21

I don't know why Im dumb agen or what I did rong. Mabye its because I din't try hard enuf or just some body put the evel eye on me. Anyway I bet Im the frist dumb persen in the wrold who found out some thing inportent for sience. I did something but I don't remembir what. (p. 216)

(Quotes taken from *Flowers for Algernon* by Daniel Keyes (New York: Bantam, 1975). © by Daniel Keyes.)

Discussion Break Question

1. Most of you will probably have read this story in middle school or have seen it on film. What did this story teach you about the way in which lives are shaped by awareness and intelligence?
2. Describe some other films and stories that enabled you to enter into unfamiliar viewpoints and thus learn more about yourself and other human beings as a result.

On Unconscious Viewpoints

Viewpoints, like assumptions, opinions, and evaluations, may or may not be consciously recognized.

In earlier chapters of this text, distinctions were drawn between the conscious and the unconscious uses of assumptions, opinions, and evaluations. To understand assumptions, we have to know that an assumption can be unconscious. To appreciate well-supported opinions, we need to distinguish them from superficial sentiment or fixed opinions that defy reexamination. To make sound evaluations, we need to guard against premature judgments. In this chapter, as we work with viewpoints, the issue of conscious and unconscious use appears again.

Both conscious and unconscious viewpoints are illustrated in the excerpts from *Flowers for Algernon*. In the first entry, Charlie only identifies himself through his work, his salary, and his age. One might say that he is not even aware that he has a viewpoint, nor at that time would he have been able to grasp the concept of viewpoint. By the time of the second diary entry, he has long since learned that he has a personal viewpoint, that other viewpoints exist beyond his own, and that he can enter into them or step out of them. Nevertheless, learning how "to step into others' shoes" does not require a genius I.Q.

The psychologist Jean Piaget, who studied learning stages in children, theorized that before the age of seven most young children lack the ability to see the world through any viewpoint other than their own. The ability to move beyond this cognitive limitation varies from one individual to another, depending on a number of educational, cultural, and emotional factors. As we grow out of egocentrism, we also develop the ability to be *exterior* to our own viewpoint—to see and recognize it from the outside, objectively. We learn how to see the world through the eyes of others. Such a capacity enables us to respect life more and to separate who we are as human beings from how we sometimes think and behave. We learn the meaning of the word *compassion* and move from the unconsciousness of egocentrism to the consciousness of objectivity.

Other less conscious viewpoints that share this feature of self-identification include ethnocentrism and religiocentrism. *Ethnocentrism*, in its milder forms, is an attitude that judges other people by one's own cultural practices, values, and standards, as though these were the only reasonable norms. The relativity of ethnocentrism becomes clearer to us when we go to live in another country and find that we can adapt to new cultural mores, such as eating with our hands, that we might have judged as backwards before. However, ethnocentrism also has tragic consequences, as in the case of Yugoslavia's "ethnic cleansing." The United States, in turn, shows its ethnocentricity when it justifies morally questionable actions as being "in America's best interests." Thus, ethnocentricity is always easier to see in other nations, especially if they are considered enemies.

Religiocentrism is a word used to describe an attitude that assumes one's own religion is the only religion, or the only religion with the right beliefs. Of course, usually this assumption is based on unfamiliarity with other religions. Here are two examples of religiocentric reasoning:

1. All any couple needs to have a happy marriage is to be good Christians.
2. Women are morally crooked because they came from Adam's rib. It is best for a girl not to come into existence, but being born she had better be married or buried.

Now notice how the religiocentrism disappears when the same idea is recognized as representing a viewpoint:

1. Christians believe that happiness in married life is inevitable when a couple lives by Christian values.
2. According to more fundamentalist Islamic sects, women are morally inferior. Because the Koran states that Eve was not created directly by God, as was Adam, it follows that women need to remain under the absolute domination of men.

Discussion Questions

1. Cite some ideas that represent ethnocentric or religiocentric thinking.

2. Those who believe it is important to strongly advocate the truth of nationalist or religious beliefs might argue that at least they are not *relativists*. Compare several dictionary definitions of *relativism* and share your views on this subject.

3. What do the terms *androcentric, anthropocentric, Eurocentric,* and *biocentric* mean? Would you call these unconscious viewpoints?

DISCOVERY EXERCISE

▪ *Recognizing Political and Social Points of View*

Read the following passages and notice how they express very different viewpoints based on different concerns, values, and priorities. See if you can assign each a political or social label, such as "radical left," "right con-servative," or "feminist," on the basis of the language used and the ideas expressed.

1. I say without any pride that I did my job as a soldier [in Iraq]. I commanded an infantry squad in combat, and we never failed to

accomplish our mission. But those who call me a coward are also right. I was a coward, not for leaving the war, but for having been a part of it in the first place. (Camilo Mejia, *Stop the Next War Now,* 2004)

2. If tens of millions of American girls and young women are determined not to have children, or to have no more than one, America must accept either mass immigration or the fate of Japan and Europe. But America has time to act. If Americans wish to preserve their civilization and culture, American women must have more children. (Patrick Buchanan, *The Death of the West: How Dying Population and Immigrant Invasions Imperil Our Country and Our Civilization,* 2002.)

3. Anyone who picks up a newspaper or turns on the television will recognize the sustained assault in the US and Europe on Christmas and Christianity. In New York, religious floats have been banned from the "holiday parade." And last week brought the news that the pope himself had been greatly startled to find the Nativity scene in an elementary school of the town Treviso replaced by a display featuring Little Red Riding Hood. (Helle Dale, The Heritage Foundation, December 23, 2004)

4. Janet Jackson's "garment glitch" emboldens the prevalent stereotype that black women are nothing more than hypersexual beings guided by no moral or ethical compass. (*FEM L.A.'s Feminist News Magazine,* May 8, 2005)

5. I confuse Earth Day and May Day because May Day is where the Communists celebrate. You know, it's one and the same to me. (Rush Limbaugh, radio broadcast, April 22, 2005)

6. The legacy that I left behind was a vision of a better world. We protected a grove of old-growth forest. And we left a living embodiment of what that vision of a better world is all about . . . I have to tell you that the coolest people I have ever met, young and old, are the ones who are out there giving their life for a good cause. . . . That's honor. Money is not honor. Doing something of real value with one's life is honor. (Julia Butterfly Hill, *The Legacy of Luna,* 2001)

Discuss these questions in writing or in class:

1. Which quotes were the most difficult for you to identify?

2. What were the clues that helped you decide how to label the viewpoint?

Recognizing Viewpoints: Left and Right

Even though their meanings keep shifting, the terms *liberal* and *conservative, left* and *right,* are still used as yardsticks to describe political viewpoints.

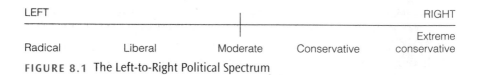

LEFT   RIGHT

| | | | | Extreme |
| Radical | Liberal | Moderate | Conservative | conservative |

FIGURE 8.1 The Left-to-Right Political Spectrum

Today's students often find it both frustrating and confusing to under-stand, use, and apply the labels "left" and "right" to categorize shifting world patterns of political, social, economic, and religious values. In years past, the left-to-right political spectrum shown in Figure 8.1 seemed ade-quate. This one-dimensional model is further amplified in Figure 8.2.

Today this paradigm (model of reality) appears too limited. Besides the left-to-right spectrum, other models of political viewpoints have been offered, such as the two-axis model depicted in Figure 8.3. This model has the advantage of including perspectives that do not fit on the single-axis left-to-right paradigm, such as anarchism, populism, libertarianism, and environmentalism.

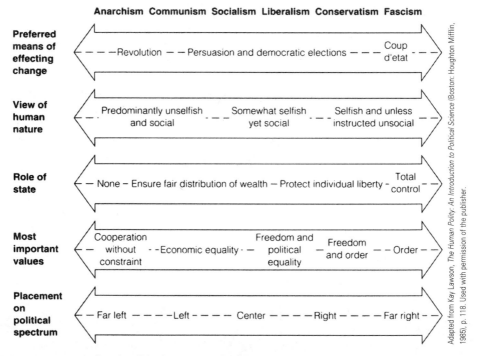

FIGURE 8.2 Traits of Political Systems on Left-to-Right Spectrum

From Michael Marien, "The Two Post-Industrialisms and Higher Education," *World Future Society Bulletin*, May 1–June 1982, p. 20. Used with permission of World Future Society.

(**Hamiltonian:** favors nationalization, global interdependence, government-corporation cooperation)

BIG

Liberal

Neoconservative

Democratic

Conservative

Socialist

(favors equality and collective control) LEFT

RIGHT (favors liberty and private control)

Utopian communalist

Libertarian

Guild socialist

Anarcho-capitalist

Left-anarchist

SMALL

(**Jeffersonian:** populist, green perspective [peace and environmentalism]: favors liberty and equality, small cooperatives, community self-reliance)

FIGURE 8.3 The Two-Axis Model of Political Views

For many complex reasons, third parties have rarely gained power in the United States, leaving us with a two-party system of Republicans and Democrats. Nevertheless, right, left, and centrist perspectives exist within these two parties. During some government administrations these perspectives coalesce; in others they split and divide. For instance, during the Clinton administration of the 1990s, the Democratic party shifted focus from representing labor and the working class to becoming more centrist and pro-business. In the twenty-first century, conservative Republicans united behind the neoconservative policies of the George W. Bush administration in coalition with the moral agenda of the Christian Right. In response, the Democrats wavered between centrism and their progressive wing.

Table 8.1 attempts some generalizations about the values that traditionally have distinguished U.S. conservatives from liberals. However, in order to fully understand the viewpoints presently shaping American politics, both time and study are needed to examine definitions of such words as *liberal, conservative, neoconservatism, the religious right, progressivism, libertarian,* and *green.* One good place to begin is with an online

TABLE 8.1 Traditional Values of U.S. Conservatives and Liberals

U.S. Conservatives	U.S. Liberals
1. Chief concern is preserving and generating wealth, assets, and resources, both personal and national. Belief in personal initiative and responsibility. Dedication to free market capitalism.	1. Chief concern is government protection of the public from the inequities and excesses of the capitalist economic system.
2. Concern about safety, law, and order—personal, national, and international. Belief in strong police and military force and strong punishment of offenders.	2. Concern for law, order, and safety, but equally concerned about ensuring justice and respect for civil rights. Tendency to believe more in prisoner rehabilitation than punishment.
3. Concern about personal freedom: least taxation of wealth, least government regulation. Right and left Republicans divided on how much government regulation they want of personal life.	3. Concern about social responsibility. Support for regulations and funding to assure community needs are fairly met.
4. Preference for traditional social conformity. Opposition to abortion and gay marriage.	4. Greater tolerance of nonconformity and alternative lifestyles, ethnic diversity, and other religious orientations.
5. Support for a high military budget and military solutions to problems.	5. Support for a strong military defense but more wary of military-industrial complex and more critical of military interventions.
6. Support for pro-business legislation, less gun control, school vouchers, tax reductions for those with higher incomes, elimination of capital gains taxes, expansion of military spending, government deregulation, privatization of government programs.	6. Support for legislation such as minimum wage increases, stricter gun control, equitable taxation, universal health care, federal subsidies to public schools and farmers, labor protection, public financing of elections.
7. Wary of federal spending and administration of programs dealing with welfare and health care. May or may not oppose Social Security, affirmative action, student loans, public housing, public education, environmental protections.	7. Opposed to tax loopholes and subsidies for corporations, low fines for environmental pollution, federal deregulation of banks, huge corporate mergers, media monopolies.
8. Committed to furthering the interests of corporations.	8. Committed to furthering the interests of corporations but more wary of how they can harm the public good.
9. Prominent in the Republican Party.	9. Prominent in the Democratic Party.

encyclopedia such as Wikipedia. Such a source will list each group's characteristic issues of concern as well as provide lists of their publications, think tanks, and chief commentators. In addition, the Discovery Exercise on page 229 is designed to enable you to arrive at your own conclusions about their characteristic beliefs, concerns, and rhetoric.

Today our so-called "mainstream" city newspapers and corporate network radio and television stations fall far short of fully reflecting this country's diverse range of opinion. Nevertheless, this vacuum has become filled by the Internet's offering of an ever growing range of viewpoints. Libraries also offer access to viewpoints both online and in print that are underrepresented in the mainstream media. Most of these publications clearly identify their social, religious, or political affiliations. Browsing through such small newspapers and magazines can help you reach your own understanding of what values, ideas, and rhetoric characterize right-wing opinion, left-wing opinion, green opinion, and so on.

In the next discovery and writing assignments you will have an opportunity to carry out this kind of exploration, while finding provocative and stimulating reading as well. Before getting into these next assignments, however, take some time out to study the following reading and consider the discussion questions that appear at its end.

• R E A D I N G •

> Objectivity, n (Apparently,) The practice of presenting both sides of an issue.

Beyond the Myth of Objectivity

Jay Davis

The following short essay by Jay Davis, a staff member for the Center for Media and Values, appeared on the Center's website.

Spend a week watching any of the network news reports and you are likely to conclude that all issues have only two sides and that middle-aged, white males have the only insight on them. From Sunday afternoon interview programs to ABC's *Nightline*, satisfying the U.S. media's standards of "objectivity" seems to require bringing opposing personalities together to debate issues of foreign and domestic policy. The ensuing dialogue, usually between Democrats and Republicans or some equivalent, suggests that all sides of the issue are covered. This dualism is one way media interpret news in North America. It seems clear, however, that "presenting both sides" tends to undermine creative discussion of the many shades of belief that actually represent opinion on complex issues.

If all issues are presented in black-and-white, yes-and-no terms, if one is either pro-life or pro-choice, pro-intervention or anti-intervention, what happens to discussion of cases that fail to fit the neatly established dichotomy?

Another traditional definition of *objectivity* focuses on the idea of impartiality. In this view, objectivity means keeping one's own beliefs, opinions or feelings separate from the story. This definition is more textbook than honest, however. Most journalists would agree that true impartiality is impossible. Even the most evenhanded reporter is subject to personal bias.

Objectivity is stressed and stretched today by the growth of new media and the shrinkage of mass media markets. Its surviving forms carry the weight of tradition. The unwary viewer can be left with the impression that media dualism represents all the sides there are to current issues.

5   The limits of objectivity make the search for alternative viewpoints crucial. Still, there's no doubt that in the immediate future, most readers, viewers and listeners will depend on mainstream media for the basic facts that shape their opinions.

What to watch for, then, in media news? Look for creativity. Look for journalists and media that stretch to find unusual perspectives. Watch for the foreign correspondent who takes the trouble to interview refugees when another power invades their country. Pay attention to the broadcaster who takes precious time to explore the history of the debate over rights, pointing out how today's opinions echo historical questions. Read the writer whose editorial on nuclear energy in Tennessee includes an interview with an elderly Appalachian trout fisherman who remembers what the fish were like before the power plant was built.

Journalists are well aware that any story will change with the number of people interviewed, but not enough of them follow this principle on all stories. Those who go the extra mile are worth watching for. A truly effective journalist shouldn't be satisfied with the views of the experts. Neither should media consumers.

Used with the permission of the Center for Media and Values.

•   •   •

Study/Writing/Discussion Questions

1. According to the author, what strategies are used on television to provide the illusion of objectivity?

2. How and why do these strategies center on familiar dichotomies?

3. What support does the author give for his claim that maintaining true impartiality is impossible?

4. Why does he say that the search for alternative viewpoints is crucial?

5. List what he says to watch for in media news.

TABLE 8.2 Political Points of View

Neoconservative	Conservative	Christian Conservative	Mass Media Corporate
American Enterprise	*National Review*	*World Magazine*	*Life*
Weekly Standard	*American Spectator*		*Time*
FrontPage.com	*Wall Street Journal*		*Fortune*
Magazine.com	*Washington Times*		
NewsMax.com	*New York Post*		
Insight on the News	*New York Sun*		
Policy Review	*Commentary*		

Left Progressive	Left Centrist	Left Christian
Mother Jones	*The New Yorker*	*Sojourner Magazine*
In These Times	*Harpers*	*Christian Science Monitor*
The Progressive	*The Atlantic*	
The Nation	*The Washington Post*	

DISCOVERY EXERCISE

■ *Learning to Recognize Political Viewpoints*

This is an inductive exercise designed to enable you to arrive at your own conclusions about the differences between left and right viewpoints. Go to your library and sample a few—or all—of the magazines and newspapers from each column in Table 8.2. Most of these publications can also be sampled online. Note how their beliefs, issues of concern, and rhetoric differ. Report your findings to the class.

Composition Writing Application

■ *A Survey of Some Alternative Viewpoints*

This assignment is designed to introduce you to some viewpoints rarely heard on corporate-owned TV stations, newspapers, and radio stations. Most of these magazines or websites clearly identify their viewpoints and affiliations. Some offer information, some advocate ideas, some focus on media criticism. A few appear as publications available in your local library or bookstore; all can be found online.

First skim through the following list of magazines, then read the assignment directions that follow.

Adbusters

The Advocate

Aljazeera.com

Arab American News

Arms Sales Monitor

Asia Times

The Beat Within

Bioneers

*Black Issues in Higher Education
   (blackissues.com)*

Censorship News

Chicano.org

Common Dreams News Center

Earth Island Journal

Fairness and Accuracy in Reporting

Feminist Weekly News

*Foundation for Individual Rights
   in Education*

Guerilla News Network

Independent Media Center

Indian Country Today

The Korea Times

Mexican Labor News & Analysis

MoveOn.org

News India

Public Citizen (consumer news from
   Ralph Nader)

Rapture Index

Teen Voices Magazine

Tikkun

Tricycle: The Buddhist Review

Utne Reader

WatchingAmerica.com

Zines Directory

■ Assignment Directions

Choose four publications from the list and write down your notes about each in the following order:

1. *Name, date, and form* of publication (print or online).
2. *Cover or home page.* Describe the magazine cover or website home page, concluding with a statement about the mood or impact that it might have on the reader.
3. *Purpose.* Does this magazine openly state its mission or purpose? If so, what is it?
4. *Table of contents or headlines.* Study the feature topics of this magazine and summarize them. How would you describe the magazine's overall slant, values, and interests?
5. *Advertising.* If there are any advertisements, note what products are featured. If this is a print magazine, generalize about the types of

advertisers, their products, and their presentation. Note also the ratio of articles to advertisements. Describe a typical advertisement.

6. *Audience.* What might you infer, on the basis of the topics chosen and language used, about (a) the political and/or ethnic group to whom this publication seems directed and (b) the readers' level of education, social class, and income.

7. *Content.* Does this publication offer perspectives rarely found in mainstream publications, national TV networks, and radio stations? Explain why or why not.

8. *Other.* Write down anything remarkable that you learned from studying this magazine.

Select *two* of these magazines to write up for an oral or written report. If the instructor agrees, you can write up your notes in outline form based on your answers to these eight questions. The report should be at least four typed pages. Attach to your report photocopies of the cover and table of contents of each magazine or attach printouts of some pages from each website. Be sure to review the criteria given in the scoring box before you turn in your final draft to the instructor.

Scoring for Survey of Some Alternative Viewpoints

1. Choice of two publications whose unfamiliarity poses some challenge. *10 points*

2. Description of cover or home page conveys its calculated effort to attract readers through mood, choice of images, symbols, words, and topics. *20 points*

3. Table of contents or headlines are not just listed; discussion shows thoughtful attention to the details that give evidence of the publication's interests, slant on life, values, and ideology. *20 points*

4. Advertisements: Specific examples show the types of advertisers, the types of products, and how they are presented. Speculation may be offered about what the ads, or lack of ads, suggest about the values of the magazine and its readers. *20 points*

5. Audience: Thoughtful conclusions are drawn about the social, ethnic, income, and educational characteristics of readers. *10 points*

6. Content: Thoughtful conclusions are offered about the uniqueness of this perspective. *10 points*

7. No distracting errors of spelling, punctuation, sentence use, word use. *10 points*

Hidden Viewpoints: The Use of News Framing

News framing describes the way an editor uses layout design, placement, and headlines to sensationalize, downplay, exaggerate, or convey importance.

When we begin to understand that information is filtered through human viewpoints, we begin to ask more questions about "the daily news." We begin to wonder *who* decides *what* is news? Are they truth seekers dedicated to public service? The book *How To Watch TV News,* by Neil Postman and Steve Powers, says "no" in answer to this last question, casting doubt even on the assumption that the intention of the news media is to keep you informed. The media's purpose, these authors maintain, is to keep you entertained and sell you products:

> You may think that a TV news show is a public service and a public utility. But more than that, it is an enormously successful business enterprise. The whole package is put together in the way that any theatrical producer would proceed, that is, by giving priority to show business values. (p. 161)

The authors then go on to say that acquiring media literacy means taking the time to inquire about the viewpoint, or the economic and political interests, of those who run TV stations:

> Keep in mind that other professionals—doctors, dentists, and lawyers, for example—commonly display their diplomas on their office walls to assure their clients that someone judged them to be competent. . . . But diplomas tell more than station "owners" and news directors and journalists tell. Wouldn't it be useful to know who these people are? Where they come from? What their angle is? And, especially, where they stand in relation to you? (p. 163)

Learning the identity of the owners of any given TV network (as well as magazines or newspapers) remains a challenge in this decade of constant and overlapping media mergers. It can require ongoing research to learn what combinations of business conglomerates (including banks, insurance companies, industries, publishers, and individuals) control which newspapers or television stations or which of these media groups are merging with still other media groups.

The Discovery Assignment that follows is designed to introduce you to the technique of *news framing analysis.** A news frame is basically the

---

*The author is indebted to Ralph H. Johnson and William Dorman for their lectures on how to teach frame analysis.

layout, placement, and prominence given to any story in a publication. The editor, representing the policies and values of the publishers, owners, and advertisers, chooses the frame for any given story. The editor must decide what stories go on the front page, which will have pictures, which will be short, which long, which sensationalized, which minimized. Although journalists may write the stories, editors decide on the wording of the headlines. A comparison of two newspapers from the same day will show how the same stories are given different prominence and treatment.

When we conduct frame analysis, we remove our attention from story content and bring our awareness to the influence of newspaper layout, story prominence, and headline language. Such analysis helps us recognize which information a given viewpoint will tend to emphasize, minimize, or omit. We then understand how all of these more subtle elements have a calculated effect on the reader. Frame analysis habits teach us to detach from the influence of the frame and gain a more objective perspective on the hidden viewpoint it expresses.

DISCOVERY ASSIGNMENT

■ *Observing How a Newspaper Frames Its Information*

1. Each student should bring a copy of that day's newspaper to class for this exercise, which will involve either small-group or general class discussion. Newspapers might include *USA Today*, the *Wall Street Journal*, the *New York Times*, a local city newspaper, or an online newspaper.

2. Study the front page of each newspaper. What subject was chosen for the main headline? How is the headline worded? What are the subjects of stories accompanied by pictures? Which stories are given less prominence? What are the differences in depth of treatment?

3. Now study the inside pages. Which news stories are given less prominence in each? Which stories do not appear in some papers? How do the editorials differ? How do the advertisements differ?

4. Choose one news item that appears in all the newspapers to compare how it is treated in each one. Consider the following items:

    a. How much prominence is given to this story?

    b. Does the headline use words that suggest evaluations?

    c. Does the story have balance, giving more than one point of view?

    d. Are opinions and judgments mixed in with the facts?

    e. Does the headline accurately reflect the article's data and conclusions?

5. What can you infer about the different values of each newspaper from the way in which each frames its information?

Building Arguments
Viewpoints

Much has been said of what you term Civilization among the Indians. Many proposals have been made to us to adopt your laws, your religion, your manners, and your customs. We do not see the propriety of such a reformation. We should be better pleased with beholding the good effects of these doctrines in your own practices than with hearing you talk about them, or of reading your newspapers on such subjects. You say, "Why do not the Indians till the ground and live as we do?" May we not ask with equal propriety, "Why do not the white people hunt and live as we do?"

(Old Tassel of the Cherokee tribe, 1777)

Exercise

1. What argument is Old Tassel refuting?
2. Given what you know about U.S. history from 1777 to the present, was Old Tassel's viewpoint heard or understood by the white men?
3. How can you explain that Old Tassel could describe and compare the two opposing viewpoints while the white men only saw their own?

Chapter Summary

1. Critical thinking means learning to recognize viewpoints and how they shape the content of any message.
2. Viewpoints—like assumptions, opinions, and evaluations—can be either conscious or unconscious.
3. We communicate best when we are aware of our own viewpoint and can understand and respect the viewpoints of others as well.
4. Writers shape their stories through their choice of a point of view; their choices include third-person, first-person, and multiple points of view. These viewpoints may be omniscient or humanly limited.
5. Unconscious viewpoints include the egocentric, ethnocentric, and religiocentric.
6. Left, right, and centrist perspectives exist within both the Republican and Democratic parties.

7. The Internet provides a vehicle for the expression of a wide range of viewpoints not well represented in the U.S. corporate media. Such viewpoints include third political parties, feminists, gays and lesbians, ethnic minorities, labor, environmentalists, religious groups, and immigrants.

8. Periodicals can express viewpoints through images, words, and in the framing given to information. Framing decisions made by an editor can exercise a hidden influence over the reader.

Chapter Quiz

Rate each of the following statements as *true* or *false*. Rewrite any false statements to make them true.

_____   1. Viewpoints can be either consciously or unconsciously assumed.

_____   2. To be exterior to one's own viewpoint is to see it objectively as just one viewpoint among many.

_____   3. Egocentrism means being absorbed in one's personal viewpoint without being able to put oneself in other people's shoes.

_____   4. Religiocentrism means believing one's country is morally superior to any other.

_____   5. Nations tend to become more ethnocentric in wartime.

_____   6. Authors only tell their stories from one viewpoint.

_____   7. Conservatives are prominent in the Republican party.

_____   8. Liberals are best known for their opposition to programs such as social welfare.

_____   9. A newspaper editor implies the relative importance of a news story by the framing given to the story.

_____   10. We communicate best when we ignore the viewpoints of others.

● R E A D I N G ●

Why Can't We Talk About Religion and Politics?

Jim Wallis

This reading comes from the Introduction to God's Politics: Why the Right Gets It Wrong and the Left Doesn't Get It, *a book that became a best-seller in 2005. Jim Wallis identifies himself as an editor of* Sojourners *magazine, designated as "progressive Christian" on the cover of the book. There Wallis is also described as an "evangelical, public theologian, nationally renowned preacher, and faith-based activist." Consider as you read how he seeks to shape a new perspective on the separation of church and state while also challenging some value assumptions of both left and right.*

Why can't we talk about religion and politics? These are the two topics you are not supposed to discuss in polite company. Don't break up the dinner party by bringing up either of these subjects! That's the conventional wisdom. Why? Perhaps these topics are too important, too potentially divisive, or raise the issues of core values and ultimate concerns that make us uncomfortable.

Sojourners magazine, where I serve as editor, commits the offense, in every single issue, of talking about faith, politics, and culture. Yet our subscriber and on-line lists are growing, especially among a younger generation. I am also on the road a lot, speaking almost every week to very diverse audiences of people. I hear and feel the hunger for a fuller, deeper, and richer conversation about religion in public life, about faith and politics. It's a discussion that we don't always hear in America today. Sometimes the most strident and narrow voices are the loudest, while more progressive, prophetic, and healing faith often gets missed. But the good news is about how all that is changing—really changing.

Abraham Lincoln had it right. Our task should not be to invoke religion and the name of God by claiming God's blessing and endorsement for all our national policies and practices—saying, in effect, that God is on our side. Rather, Lincoln said, we should pray and worry earnestly whether we are on God's side.

Those are the two ways that religion has been brought into public life in American history. The first way—God on our side—leads inevitably to triumphalism, self-righteousness, bad theology, and, often, dangerous foreign policy. The second way—asking if we are on God's side—leads to much healthier things, namely, penitence and even repentance, humility, reflection, and even accountability. We need much more of all these, because these are often the missing values of politics.

5 Of course, Martin Luther King Jr. did it best. With his Bible in one hand and the Constitution in the other, King persuaded, not just pronounced. He reminded us all of God's purposes for justice, for peace, and for the "beloved community" where those always left out and behind get a front-row seat. And he did it—bringing religion into public life—in a way that was always welcoming, inclusive, and inviting to all who cared about moral, spiritual, or religious values. Nobody felt left out of the conversation. I try to do that too in this book.

The night before I wrote this introduction, I was speaking in Denver, Colorado. A young man was waiting patiently in a greeting line after my talk. Finally we shook hands and he told me that he was an agnostic (not religiously affiliated).

But he said that he cared deeply about the moral issues at stake in his country. Then he told me he had been "spiritually inspired" by the evening. And he thanked me for making him feel included. "I just wanted to give you some feedback from outside the community," the sincere agnostic said. It was an encouraging word to me.

The values of politics are my primary concern in this book. Of course, God is not partisan; God is not a Republican or a Democrat. When either party tries to politicize God, or co-opt religious communities for their political agendas, they make a terrible mistake. The best contribution of religion is precisely not to be ideologically predictable nor loyally partisan. Both parties, and the nation, must let the prophetic voice of religion be heard. Faith must be free to challenge both right and left from a consistent moral ground.

God's politics is therefore never partisan or ideological. But it challenges everything about our politics. God's politics reminds us of the people our politics always neglects—the poor, the vulnerable, the left behind. God's politics challenges narrow national, ethnic, economic, or cultural self-interest, reminding us of a much wider world and the creative human diversity of all those made in the image of the creator. God's politics reminds us of the creation itself, a rich environment in which we are to be good stewards, not mere users, consumers, and exploiters. And God's politics pleads with us to resolve the inevitable conflicts among us, as much as is possible, without the terrible cost and consequences of war. God's politics always reminds us of the ancient prophetic prescription to "choose life, so that you and your children may live," and challenges all the selective moralities that would choose one set of lives and issues over another.

This book challenges both the Right and the Left—offering a new vision for faith and politics in America. To do that, we will enter into a new conversation of personal faith and political hope. I hope you will join the discussion.

● ● ●

Study/Writing/Discussion Questions

1. Do you prefer to avoid talking about religion or politics?
2. At what points do you agree or disagree with the author's line of reasoning in this essay?
3. How would you describe your own viewpoint on the issue of the separation of church and state?

Objectives Review of Part II

When you have finished Part II, you will understand:

1. The concepts and complexities of assumptions, opinions, evaluations, and viewpoints
2. How these concepts are mental experiences
3. How they are problematical when confused with facts
4. How a viewpoint frames information
5. The meaning of conscious and unconscious viewpoints

And you will have practice in developing these skills:

1. Recognizing the mental formation of assumptions, opinions, evaluations, and viewpoints
2. Assessing assumptions, opinions, evaluations, and viewpoints for strengths and limitations
3. Identifying underlying assumptions and value assumptions in discourse
4. Separating opinions and evaluations from facts
5. Recognizing hidden opinions within evaluative words
6. Identifying social and political viewpoint characteristics
7. Analyzing the news frame

PART III

Forms and Standards of Critical Thinking

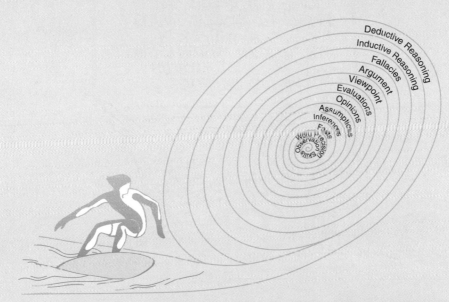

CHAPTER 9

Argument:
What's a Good Argument?

Used with permission of Ben Dib.

Fighting may be easier than arguing, but even fighting can't proceed when viewpoints and ideologies become entangled. This chapter shows you how to disentangle before the fighting starts, or better, how to make fighting unnecessary. It will show you models of good and poor arguments in order to lead you toward writing arguments that are well constructed, well supported, and persuasive. In short, you will learn the skills of argument building, argument analysis, and argument evaluation.

You have been prepared for this chapter by the Building Arguments boxes, by many references to argument components, and by some short argument writing assignments. When you finish studying this chapter, you will be able to prepare for the longer argument research assignments described in Appendix 1 of this book.

DISCOVERY EXERCISE

■ Reading and Judging Arguments

Read the nine points of view offered here on a controversial issue. Then answer the questions that follow, in writing or class discussion.

1. People are saying, well, we'll stop jobs from going overseas by making sure we put up walls and barriers between the United States and the rest of the world. That's lousy policy. Consumer prices will go up if we wall ourselves from the rest of the world. Economic isolationism is bad economic policy, and it will cost people jobs. (George W. Bush, March 11, 2004)

2. When I am president, and with your help, we're going to repeal every benefit, every loophole, every reward that entices any Benedict Arnold company or CEO to take money and the jobs overseas and stick the American people with the bill. (John Kerry, 2004 campaign speech)

3. There is a stark reality to outsourcing. Jobs will go wherever they cost employers less. . . . Without systemic reforms, shipping jobs overseas is not a winning formula for anyone except big business. (Michelle Chen, labor commentator on Znet, "The Reality Behind Job Outsourcing," March 14, 2004)

4. Does outsourcing benefit the United States? You better believe it does. Free trade works both ways. Jobs coming from other countries to the United States are called "insourced" jobs. While more jobs are outsourced from the U.S. than are insourced to the U.S., for the last 15 years insourced jobs grew by 117 percent, while outsourced jobs only grew by 56 percent. (Larry Elder, libertarian Los Angeles talk show host, from "Lou Dobbs to Outsourcing: Drop Dead," posted on *WorldNet Daily*, March 10, 2005)

5. We're not creating jobs in the private sector, and that's never happened before in our history. Our economists and politicians need to be coming up with answers, not dogma. . . . We've lost three million jobs in this country over the last three years, and millions more American jobs are being at risk of being outsourced to cheap overseas

labor markets. (Lou Dobbs, anchor and managing editor of CNN's *Lou Dobbs Tonight,* March 10, 2004)

6. Whether one regards the trend as disruptive or beneficial, one thing is clear. Corporate America no longer feels it can afford to ignore India. "There's just no place left to squeeze" costs in the U.S., says Chris Disher, a Booz Allen Hamilton Inc. outsourcing specialist. "That's why every CEO is looking at India." ("Is There a Way Out from Job Outsourcing?" Mapsofindia.com, no author or date)

7. What we're looking at today in terms of outsourcing—that is computer and service jobs—are precisely the jobs that were promised to previous generations of factory workers who were displaced. The notion was, "not to worry, you too will be in the computer industry." Well, now that industry isn't here, and it's being driven by low wages, and by government policies. It's a perversion of free trade, not its example. (Harley Shaiken, Professor of Labor and the Global Economy, University of California at Berkeley, from transcript of *Jim Lehrer NewsHour,* March 11, 2004)

8. Contracting jobs overseas is simply the latest manifestation of free trade. Public policy needs to help workers find new jobs, not retreat from the principles of free trade that have benefited the U.S. and economies around the world. (Greb Mankiw, Chairman, George W. Bush's Council of Economic Advisers, *The Business Times,* Singapore, January 24, 2004)

9. It doesn't do much good for a father to be able to buy a pair of shoes more cheaply if that father loses his job. (Participant in UN study of globalization from transcript of *Jim Lehrer NewsHour,* March 11, 2004)

Study Questions

1. What common issue do these arguments address?
2. How would you label each viewpoint here?
3. What is the basic pro or con position taken by each?
4. Take one viewpoint for analysis. What reasons are given to support its position?
5. Which arguments do you find to be the most persuasive and why?

Critical Reading of Arguments

What an argument first needs is an objective reading or hearing.
Afterwards criticism can begin with five questions.

As you will remember from the short discussion in the second chapter about critical reading, accurate comprehension must precede any criticism

of the material. In reading arguments, maintaining openness is not always easy, especially when the arguments express values that differ from your own. It can require a lot of restraint to slow down those inner objections in order to make sure that you really understand what is being said. You may have found it a struggle to give a fair hearing to some of the viewpoints expressed in the opening Discovery Exercise. Yet critical analysis cannot be fair unless it is based on a careful and accurate reading of the material.

In this chapter you will be guided by some questions that will help you fairly assess the arguments you read. By using these questions, you will be able to make rapid evaluations of newspaper editorials, letters to editors, voter information pamphlets, and any other form of persuasive writing. The skills of critical analysis will also enable you to write more effective arguments yourself, whether in the form of simple letters of complaint or in the longer argumentative essay assignments that appear in Appendix 1 of this book.

What follows are five guiding questions to help you quickly analyze any argument. After completing this analysis, you will know whether to accept the argument, reject it, or simply suspend judgment for the time being.

1. What viewpoint is the source of this argument?
2. What is the issue of controversy?
3. Is it an argument? Or is it a report?
4. How is the argument structured in terms of reasons and conclusion?
5. What are the argument's strengths and weaknesses?

What Viewpoint Is the Source of This Argument?

Arguments represent the bias, interests, and objectives of a viewpoint.

This chapter's opening Discovery Exercise gave you an opportunity to apply what you learned in the previous chapter about the way viewpoint shapes content. You might have begun by first skimming through each argument, reading the names, titles, and affiliations of each speaker, then rereading the argument in light of this information. From such clues, you might have been able to make inferences about the speaker's values, motives, and beliefs. You would have begun by asking the first question of critical reading: *What viewpoint does this argument express?*

What Is the Issue of Controversy?

To assess an argument, we first must determine the issue.

Argument: offering reasons to support a conclusion with the intent to persuade.

Issue: a problem of public concern that is subject to dispute or debate.

Debate question: a question that states an issue, providing a focus for pro and con positions on that issue. Debate questions are expressed in neutral terms, often beginning with such words as "should."

Arguments are based on *issues*. An issue is a controversial problem that evokes different arguments pro and con. A few examples of topics that each contain many controversial issues are water privatization, genetically modified foods, nuclear weapons, marijuana legalization, trade globalization, homelessness, a living wage, "preemptive strike" as a war policy. Newspapers offer information and opinions daily on new topics; each of these topics can contain many issues of controversy.

Thus every controversial topic generates many issues; moreover, surrounding these issues are many debate questions. The opening Discovery Exercise began with pro and con arguments on the issue of job outsourcing from the United States. A closer study of these arguments might uncover such debate questions as the following:

- Does job outsourcing benefit the United States?
- Should the U.S. federal government encourage job outsourcing?
- Is job outsourcing necessary?

As is customary in debates, the question both sides will address must be expressed in neutral language that does not favor either one side or the other. A good debate question is free of biased connotations. The question is also left open by the use of such words as *can, need,* or *should.* Like a good polling question, a debate question needs careful formulation.

Debate questions can also be less general than the three given previously; they can address more specific aspects of the larger problem:

- Is the United States losing too many jobs to outsourcing?
- Are lower consumer costs worth the social costs of job outsourcing?
- Should the U.S. government do more to help workers who lose their jobs to outsourcing?

Debate questions are clearly stated when we find pro and con arguments on newspaper editorial pages or in magazines such as the *Congressional Digest.* However, often the debate questions are not made explicit in arguments, requiring that we supply them from our own thinking.

Consider the following example:

Americans receive almost 2 million tons of junk mail every year. About 44% of the junk mail is never even opened and read. Nonetheless, the average American still spends 8 full months of his or her life just opening junk mail. (*50 Simple Things You Can Do to Save the Earth,* Earthworks Press, 1989)

These two sentences comprise an argument around which debate questions (addressing solutions) such as the following could be posed:

- Should junk mail be banned?
- Should consumers revolt against junk mail?

Class Discussion

Read each of the following arguments. For each one, first state the issue and then formulate one debate question that addresses this issue.

1. Good cocoa cannot be made properly with water. Milk is essential.
2. Today millions of forty- and fifty-year-old workers are being let go due to age discrimination. We need better enforcement of our discrimination laws.
3. Rail transportation carries at least ten times the number of people per hour as the average freeway. It should be obvious to city and state traffic planners that an investment in improved rail service is the best answer to traffic gridlock.

4. Republicans have been unfairly criticized for their vote against an international comprehensive test ban treaty. If we really want to eliminate the potential of a nuclear holocaust, the United States must continue to build up its military and thus persuade the rogue nations of the world to disarm.

5. Consumers who object to ATM fees can avoid payment by using the ATMs owned by their own banks.

Is It an Argument or a Report?

Arguments and reports are each structured differently and have different objectives. We cannot analyze one according to the standards of the other.

Although arguments and reports have very different objectives and forms (see Table 9.1), they can be mistaken for one another if their differences are not fully understood. Moreover, to add to the confusion, arguments can sometimes be disguised as reports while actually offering a biased perspective. (More will be explained about this hybrid later.)

The main purpose of a **report** is to offer information; this can be done by offering facts and findings or relating and explaining events. Its objective is not to advocate an opinion. If the situation is controversial, the reporter should present arguments from all sides, but not favor one argument or another. Likewise in writing scientific reports, the author might make recommendations, but not advocate.

Arguments, on the other hand, do advocate opinions; information may be used to explain an idea, to justify it, or to persuade others to accept that idea. Arguments are not supposed to be neutral but express a position. Let's review these differences by means of two examples on the subject of changing our national anthem.

Report

Andrew Jacobs, D-Ind., has introduced a bill that would change the national anthem to "America the Beautiful." He says that both musicians and the general public agree that "The Star-Spangled Banner" is just too difficult to sing correctly. However, although everyone might agree with him on this score, winning public support for the change might not be so easy. According to a recent telephone poll conducted by *Time* magazine, 67 percent were against this replacement.

Argument

I am in favor of replacing "The Star-Spangled Banner" with "America the Beautiful." Our present anthem, with its incredible range of octaves, makes it difficult even for an opera singer to perform. As a

TABLE 9.1 Arguments and Reports: Making the Distinction

Report	Argument
Purpose: To inform in a manner that wins trust in the reliability of the information.	*Purpose:* To persuade others to agree with an idea.
Structure:	*Structure:*
1. Data presented and explained.	1. Assertion of a thesis or conclusion.
2. Offers support to confirm data's accuracy and veracity, such as corroborating evidence, independent studies, examples, expert testimony, records, surveys, polls, investigations, statistics, analogies.	2. Reasons given to support this conclusion are offered in the same forms as in a report. However, material that supports the conclusion is emphasized, whereas material that does not is usually omitted or downplayed.
3. Offers hypotheses for interpreting the data. May or may not side with one hypothesis.	3. Clearly committed bias.
4. Summary of findings in manner that leaves final assessment up to the reader.	4. Summary argues for agreement with own conclusion.

result, most of us can only hum along. Moreover, the content of the lyrics is antiquated, hard to remember, and warmongering. "America the Beautiful" spares us all these problems.

Discussion Break Questions

1. The idea of changing our national anthem is a controversial proposal. Why is the first example a report on the subject and not an argument?

2. The second example is an argument and not a report. How is it significantly different? What makes it an argument?

A report can tell a story, as in the first example. It can present findings, interview supporters and detractors, and offer a hypothesis to predict a final outcome. Nevertheless, a report leaves the final conclusions up to the reader. When a report concerns a controversial subject, pro and con positions may be quoted, but the report itself remains objective.

Another difficulty we face in making the separation between arguments and reports is that arguments are sometimes disguised as reports. This practice is particularly prevalent in many of the so-called newsmagazines, which offer news reports that are actually opinion pieces because of their slanted language, selection of information, and emphasis. Here is a light-hearted example of a report with a biased perspective:

> To put audiences out of their pregame misery, many stadiums resort to canned versions of error-free performances of "The Star-Spangled Banner." . . . But a taped version takes away the thrill of victory and the agony of defeat inherent in every live performance, as well as the singers' inalienable right to get it wrong. (*Time,* February 12, 1990, p. 27)

Class Discussion

Identify the following as either reports or arguments:

1. The rate of population growth is slowing down, but the total numbers continue to rise. Each year, we add 80 million, the equivalent of the population of Germany, to the world total. In 2000, there will be more than six billion people in the world. During the 2060's, there may be 20 billion. (*The Macmillan Atlas of the Future,* 1998, p. 24)

2. Conservation to some people once implied sacrifice, deprivation and lower living standards. Now even many of them recognize that conserving energy is the cheapest, safest, cleanest and fastest way to avoid future energy crises. (Sen. Alan Cranston, D-Calif., newsletter to constituents, November 1984)

3. Too often the American economic system is looked upon as being a kind of battlefield between two opposing sides—consumers and the business/industrial community. This is a misguided but widely held viewpoint. It is wrong to believe that consumers are at the mercy of business and industry . . . what is good for business is good for the consumer. (Robert Bearce, "Free Enterprise," *Your Heritage News,* May 1984)

4. The tap water was so dark in Atlanta some days this summer that Meg Evans couldn't see the bottom of the tub when she filled the bath. Elsewhere in her neighborhood, Gregg Goldenberg puts his infant daughter to bed rather than lower her into a brew "the color of iced tea." . . . All try to keep tuned to local radio, TV to catch "boil water" advisories. ("The Coming Water Crisis," *U.S. News & World Report,* August 12, 2002)

5. Making Suicide Pay: There is finally good news for Mr. Milo Stevens, the 26-year-old incompetent who botched a suicide attempt in 1977 during which he launched himself into the path of a New York Transit Authority subway train. He has won a $650,000 negligence settlement and is still free to try again. (*American Spectator,* March 1984)

How Is the Argument Structured in Terms of Reasons and Conclusions?

A quick method for analyzing an argument is to disassemble its structure, first identifying its conclusion and then separating that statement from the reasons offered to support it.

Conclusion: A clear statement of what an argument intends to prove. This statement serves as the argument's thesis, final opinion, or judgment. It clearly shows the author's position on an issue.

Reason: Statements offered to explain, justify, or support the conclusion of an argument. Reasons can take the form of statements of facts, statistics, evidence, or reasoning. Any number of reasons can be offered to support one conclusion.

In the chapters that follow, you will be learning more about standards and forms for inductive and deductive reasoning. You will learn that with induction, arguments are structured in this manner:

- Data
- Data
- Data
- Data

Conclusion

In deduction we use the syllogism:

- Major Premise
- Minor Premise

Conclusion

Arguments use both inductive and deductive reasoning. Simplified models such as these reveal their structure. We will learn more about how these models help us understand the rules of reasoning in the next chapter. For now we only want to focus on the two essential aspects of an argument: (1) what point is being made and (2) how this point is supported. If we can identify these two elements quickly in an argument, we can size up its structure. Thus, when reading the chapter's opening arguments on outsourcing, you may have sensed that some of them were better reasoned than others, but you may not have been really sure how to explain why or why not. Seeing arguments in terms of their structure can help us begin to do that. It also helps us write better arguments.

The next few pages offer a rapid method for recognizing these two elements in arguments; this method explains arguments as structures consisting of *reasons* and *conclusions*. Both inductive and deductive arguments consist of both conclusions and reasons. As you will discover in the following chapters, the term *reasons* can be used to include both the premises of deduction and the factual evidence of induction, and the term *conclusion* includes inductive hypotheses as well as deductive conclusions. In both cases, separating conclusions from their reasons is not always easy. Yet we have to make this separation in order to determine what conclusion we are being asked to accept, and whether or not sufficient and adequate reasons are given in its support. This portion of the chapter will offer exercises for practice in identifying and analyzing arguments in terms of their reasons and conclusions.

Identifying the Conclusion of an Argument

The key to understanding any written argument is to first search for its conclusion. Although the word *conclusion* is generally understood as a final summary statement in an argument, the conclusion functions more like the thesis of a composition, which sometimes appears first. In the formal reasoning of induction and deduction, a conclusion is the *last step* in a reasoning process:

Inductive

> Yesterday I was happy singing.
>
> Last week I was happy singing.
>
> Every time in my life I sing, I feel happy.

Conclusion: Singing makes me happy.

Deductive

> Singing makes me happy.
>
> I am singing.

Conclusion: I am happy.

In an argument, a conclusion is the bottom line of a decision, while the reasons are the evidence and thoughts that support this decision. Yet the problem remains that although we know our own conclusions, it is not always that easy to find them in the written arguments of others, especially because statements of reasons can look like very much like conclusions:

> Over the past two years, actions by local governments against homeless people have risen sharply. [reason] A 16-city study released last week by the National Law Center on Homelessness & Poverty found that cities are increasingly passing and enforcing laws that criminalize conduct associated with homelessness, such as sleeping, begging, and even sitting in public places. [reason] But passing laws against the homeless will not end homelessness. [conclusion] (Column Left/Maria Foscarinis, Jim Scheibel, *Los Angeles Times,* December 16, 1993)

Here the first statement is a conclusion supported by the second sentence. Yet, in this context, both of the first two sentences serve as reasons to support the final sentence, which is the author's thesis, or the argument's conclusion.

One secret for recognizing conclusions is to look for the signals of the so-called inference indicator words that precede conclusions. Here are some examples of the way in which these words signal the conclusions of arguments:

1. *The truth of the matter is* that homelessness is the foe, not the homeless.
2. *In my opinion* homeless people must follow the rules just like anyone else.
3. *It all goes to show* we have to establish a bottom line of dignity and subsistence for all.
4. *Therefore* it's time we put an end to the problem of homelessness.

Identifying Reasons

Reasons are statements of opinion, propositions, premises, or statements of evidence offered to explain, justify, or support conclusions.

1. I am not in favor of accepting unsanitary and unregulated street camps for homeless people. [conclusion] Homelessness is not a healthy choice. [reason] It's important to reinforce their own desires to get off the streets and rejoin society. [reason]
2. Instead of attacking homeless people, cities should attack homelessness. [conclusion] Grocery carts can be donated instead of repossessed by police. [reason] Day jobs can be provided instead of making begging a misdemeanor. [reason]

As is the case with conclusions, reasons are easier to identify when we supply them ourselves than when we read or hear them in someone else's argument. Yet, we need to identify the reasons in order to decide if they provide adequate and sufficient support for the conclusion. In both arguments given in the previous examples, if only one reason had been offered, the support would have been insufficient. Both reasons together make for stronger arguments, although both will need more expansion and development to be convincing, as would occur in a longer complete argument.

The task of analysis then begins by flushing out the reasons, which means looking for the conclusion first. In a short argument, once we identify the conclusion, the reasons are simply what remain.

Another technique for identifying reasons is to look for the so-called inference indicator words that often introduce reasons. Here is an example of how such indicator words signal statements serving as reasons:

> I am in favor of sending the homeless to live in state-operated farm communities [conclusion] *first because* it would provide them with a healthier lifestyle than living on the streets [reason] *and second*, farming would allow them to raise their own food and give them something constructive to do.

Conclusion indicator words include *therefore, so, in fact, the truth of the matter is, in short, it follows that, shows that, indicates that, suggests that, proves that, we may deduce that, points to the conclusion that, in my opinion, and the most obvious explanation is.*

Reason indicator words include *because, first . . . second, since, for, for one thing, in view of the fact that, for the reason that, is supported by, for example, also.*

EXERCISE

■ Identifying Reasons and Conclusions

In the following statements, underline the conclusions and number the reasons:

1. Students who want well-paying careers upon graduation should train themselves to be computer programmers. Most cities are full of advertisements for computer programmers.

2. By the study of different religions we find that in essence they are one. All are concerned with revelations or breakthrough experiences that can redirect lives and empower them toward good.

3. I am not pro-abortion at all. I think that people nowadays use abortion as an easy form of birth control. It's also against my religion.

4. Guns kill people; that's why handguns should be banned.

5. Deep fat frying can greatly increase the calories of foods such as fish, chicken, and potatoes. Therefore, it is better to bake, boil, or steam foods.

6. "It is important that individual citizens equip themselves with a baloney detection kit to determine whether politicians, scientists, or religious leaders are lying—it's an important part of becoming a citizen of the world." (Carl Sagan)

7. America should put a freeze on immigration. Its first duty is to take better care of its own disadvantaged, poor, and unemployed.

8. America boasts about its wealth and prosperity as the world's most competitive economy. Yet its citizens are told there is not enough money for health care, environmental protection, for parks, safety nets for the poor and elderly, or public funding for the arts. Isn't there something wrong with this picture?

9. "If nothing happened, if nothing changed, time would stop. For time is nothing but change. It is change that we perceive occurring all around us, not time. In fact, time doesn't exist." (Julian Barbour, British physicist)

10. I don't drink because alcohol gives me a brief high followed by a longer depression.

More on Distinguishing Reasons from Conclusions

Implied Conclusions

Now that we have learned how to dismantle arguments and separate reasons from conclusions, we are ready to confront a few final complexities. To begin with, *sometimes the conclusion is not stated at all but merely implied.* Let's take this argument on gun control:

> I find that just as criminals can be deterred by higher arrest or conviction rates, they can also be deterred by the fact that would-be victims might be able to defend themselves with a gun. Criminals are less likely to commit a crime if the probability that a victim is going to be able to defend himself increases.

Here the implied conclusion is "I am opposed to more gun control legislation." In some arguments, however, the missing conclusion may be more difficult to formulate.

It has been claimed that 80–90% of all cancers may be caused by environmental pollutants. The incidence of cancer is increasing now and will continue to increase. Governments spend millions of dollars researching causes of cancer, leukemia, and inherited disease, but simultaneously spend billions of dollars in [the nuclear power] industry that will directly propagate these diseases. (Helen Caldicott, MD, "Medical Implications of Nuclear Power." Helen Caldicott website)

In this quotation, Dr. Caldicott provides reasons, only which she claims to be facts. Her conclusion, which is implied, could take many forms, such as

- Citizens should educate themselves about the medical dangers of nuclear power.
- Governments cannot be trusted to put the health of its citizens before those of industry.
- Citizens should demand that their governments stop supporting nuclear power and instead do all they can to prevent the environmental causes of cancer.

Conclusions in a Series

Sometimes a series of conclusions can be offered as reasons for an implied conclusion. In the following quotation, the speaker is offering a parody of the reasons given in the Preamble to the Constitution for the creation of that Constitution. These conclusions serve as his argument's reasons.

The arms race does not form a more perfect union. The arms race does not ensure domestic tranquility. The arms race does not provide for the common defense. The arms race does not promote the general welfare. And finally, the arms race does not secure the blessings of liberty to ourselves and to our posterity. (Bishop Walter F. Sullivan, testimony before special congressional ad hoc hearings on the full implications of the military budget, January 1982)

Conclusion at the Beginning

Conclusions do not always appear at the end of an argument; sometimes they appear in the beginning, as in newspaper headlines.

Mystery Traffic Jams

It's one of the great conundrums of commuting—you're sailing along a freeway at 50 miles per hour, when suddenly the brake lights go on in front of you and in seconds, you're down to stop-and-go. Creep, crawl. Creep, crawl. After a while, the traffic jam loosens, and you are back up to 40 or 50. (*San Francisco Chronicle*, December 6, 1999, p. A17)

Conclusion in the Middle

Sometimes a conclusion appears in the middle of a series of statements.

> Well drivers are not the only ones who wonder about this. In fact there are hundreds of people who get paid to study traffic jams. . . . *"It's the mystery traffic jam,"* [conclusion] says an airborne TV station traffic reporter . . . who spent the past 10 years watching the ebb and flow . . . from his lofty perch. (*San Francisco Chronicle,* December 6, 1999, p. A17)

As we stated earlier, when we want to analyze arguments, the first step is to identify the conclusion. Obviously, we need to determine clearly *exactly what the author is claiming to prove* before becoming involved in a reaction of agreement or disagreement. By identifying the conclusion, we know the author's exact position. We may agree or disagree with this position—but first we must know what it is. If we should mistake one of the reasons for the conclusion, we may find ourselves going off on a wrong track in our analysis and rebuttal. But once we have identified the conclusion, we can easily determine the reasons and isolate them for examination and evaluation.

The final advantage of learning how to identify conclusions and reasons is that it saves us the time of wrestling with poor arguments. When we have the skill to quickly survey and assess an argument's structure, then we can decide whether or not this argument is worth our serious consideration. Moreover, when we are writing our own arguments, we will know how to build them on a clear and aware foundation and thus demonstrate a visible structure of conscious thought.

EXERCISES

■ More Practice in Identifying Reasons and Conclusions

Analyze the following arguments by underlining the conclusions, or by supplying the conclusion in writing if it is only implied. Note that sometimes a conclusion may be part of a sentence, or the conclusion may be offered alone without any reasons attached.

1. Frequent snacks of high-energy food are not harmful to backpackers. Indeed, hikers are found to have more energy and less weariness if they snack every hour.
2. Broadcast television is not appropriate in the courtroom. The relentless pressure of the media threatens the balance between the First

Amendment's press freedom and the Sixth Amendment's fair trial rights.

3. Whereas birth is a cause for celebration, death has become a dreaded and unspeakable issue to be avoided by every means possible in our modern society. Perhaps it is that death reminds us of our human vulnerability in spite of all our technological advances. (Elisabeth Kübler-Ross)

4. Do not stop thinking of life as an adventure. You have no security unless you live bravely, excitingly, imaginatively; unless you choose a challenge rather than competence. (Eleanor Roosevelt)

5. There's nothing like the taste of fresh, hot brownies. Bake your own the easy way with Brownlee's Brownie Mix! (advertisement)

6. No doctor should have the right to allow a patient to die. No doctor is God.

7. Videos are a good way to entertain children. You can control what they watch, and there are many worthwhile films to choose from.

8. Since the 1920s, sperm counts have declined among American men. The underlying causes are uncertain, but the factors of stress and toxic chemicals are being considered.

9. If only 1 percent of the car owners in America did not use their cars for one day a week, they would save 42 million gallons of gas a year and keep 840 million pounds of CO_2 out of the atmosphere.

10. Because of their greater use of prescription drugs, women turn up in hospital emergency rooms with drug problems more frequently than men. (FDA consumer report)

■ More Practice with Longer Arguments

Analyze the arguments that opened this chapter by underlining the conclusions and numbering the reasons given. Then do the same for each of the following arguments:

1. People think non-violence is really weak and non-militant. These are misconceptions that people have because they don't understand what non-violence means. Non-violence takes more guts, if I can put it bluntly, than violence. . . . We are convinced that non-violence is more powerful than violence. We are convinced that non-violence supports you if you have a just and moral cause. If you use violence, you have to sell part of yourself for that violence. Then you are no longer a master of your own struggle. (Cesar E. Chavez)

2. An enigma presents itself which in all ages has agitated inquiring minds. How can it be that mathematics, being after all a product of human thought which is independent of experience, is so admirably appropriate to the objects of reality? Is human reason, then, without experience, merely by taking thought, able to fathom the properties of real things? In my opinion, the answer to this question is briefly, this: as far as the propositions of mathematics refer to reality, they are not certain; and as far as they are certain, they do not refer to reality. (Albert Einstein)

3. Many economists believe that water is a natural resource like any other and should be subject to the laws of supply and demand—and market pricing. Since the turn of the century, U.S. water use has risen at least six fold. . . . Nowhere is demand greater than in the West—whose population has soared nearly 70 percent in 25 years. Scarce water has been misdirected because of a hodge-podge of regulations and federal subsidies—which have created lot of waste. If farmers were encouraged by market pricing to use just 5 percent less water, the demands of urban users could be met for the next 25 years. ("Making Water Plentiful," *Investor's Business Daily,* February 17, 1997)

4. A growing movement of people believe that the imperatives of economic globalization—unlimited growth, a seamless global consumer market, corporate rule, deregulation, privatization, and free trade—are the driving forces behind the destruction of our water systems. These must be challenged and rejected if the world's water is to be saved. Water as a fundamental right is guaranteed in the Universal Declaration on Human Rights. ("Water as Commodity—The Wrong Prescription" by Maude Barlow, quoted in *Institute for Food and Development Policy Backgrounder,* Summer 2001)

Core Discovery Writing Application

■ Writing a Short Persuasive Argument: A Letter of Complaint

This assignment is about claiming your own power. It is a practical opportunity to stand up for something you believe in, to defend yourself or others against some injustice, and to initiate or restore communication with someone. This assignment will take the simple form of writing an effective argument in a short letter of complaint. In this letter, you will only need to describe what you consider to be an injustice and then communicate clearly what you want.

▪ *The Steps*

1. Address the letter to a specific individual: to a friend, a parent, an elected official, a landlady, or a newspaper editor. In short, address it to someone who has some power to do something about the situation that concerns you. It may take some research to determine who this person is, but that is a key part of the assignment.

2. As you outline your letter, use neutral, descriptive, and nonblaming language to explain

   a. What the situation is

   b. What is unfair about it

   c. What you want from the other person now

   Your final paragraph should serve to keep the two of you connected by asking for reactions, a call, an appointment, or an agreement within a time frame that you suggest. (For instance, you might conclude by saying "I would like very much to hear what you have to say in response, and I would welcome hearing from you by phone or letter. If I have not heard from you within a week, then I will call you.")

3. Use reasoning and evidence to support your case. Make your conclusions straightforward and simple. Be clear about what you want but also remain courteous and respectful.

4. The length of your letter should be one to two pages typed; use a business letter format.

▪ *Writing Preparation*

In choosing your topic, select a situation that feels genuinely unjust and unfinished to you, one that you have not been able to handle in a way that you would like. The more emotion you feel on the subject, the greater the challenge will be to formulate an effective, well-reasoned argument. When we feel very angry, sad, or apathetic, it is difficult to think clearly or make ourselves heard. Yet, writing and revising to work through your emotions can summon the clarity and power needed to present your case effectively. If at the beginning you feel overwhelmed by feelings, write them out or hit some pillows until you blow off steam. When you feel more collected, you can compose your argument. After you have finished your first draft, reread it, asking yourself whether your purpose was to make the other party feel ashamed, guilty, or wrong. Blaming the other person may make you feel better temporarily, but will not help you get what you really want. If you try to make people feel guilty, they will resist hearing what you have to say and not want to cooperate. Instead use neutral descriptive language; report what happened with objectivity. Be quite specific about how you see the problem and what you want the other person to do for you. Remain respectful both of yourself and of the person you are addressing. Do not make demands or give ultimatums, but make requests that the other party can meet.

■ Peer Review

To follow up on this exercise in class, exchange your letter or essay with a partner and do the following:

1. Underline the conclusion and circle the reasons.
2. Answer these questions on a sheet to attach to your partner's work:
   a. Which reasons clearly support, justify, or explain the conclusion? Which do not?
   b. Are more reasons needed? Explain.
3. If any portion is not clear to you, circle it and ask your partner to explain it to you.

When you receive your work back, consider the comments. If you cannot agree with the critique, seek another partner and go through the same process verbally. If you find the criticisms helpful, revise your work accordingly.

Scoring for Letter of Complaint

1. Letter is addressed to a specific person who has the power to do something about the situation. *10 points*
2. Organization is simple and clear, describes the situation and the complaint, and is requesting a specific action. *10 points*
3. Request made that is clear and possible to fulfill. *10 points*
4. Conclusion is clear; sufficient and adequate reasons are given. *10 points*
5. Topic chosen involves challenge of self-control. (Not a routine letter returning a defective product.) *20 points*
6. Language does not blame, make guilty, or cause defensiveness. *10 points*
7. A final connecting statement is made, requesting, but not demanding, a response within a stated period of time. *10 points*
8. No distracting errors of punctuation, sentence structure, spelling. *20 points*

What Are the Strengths and Weaknesses of This Argument?

To make a list of standards for judging the strengths and weaknesses of an argument would mean reviewing most of the material covered in the past several chapters of this text. These six questions summarize such standards:

1. Are the reasons adequate to support the conclusion?
2. Are there any hidden assumptions in this argument?
3. Are any central words ambiguous or slanted to incite prejudice?
4. Are there fallacies in the reasoning? (You will learn how to use this question in the next chapters.)
5. Is any important information omitted?
6. Is any information false, contradictory, or irreconcilable?

All but the final three questions have already been discussed in this text. Fallacies will be explained in the next chapters. What follows now is an explanation of the last two questions.

Is Any Important Information Missing?

Crucial information can be purposely or inadvertently omitted in an argument or a report. A critical thinker looks for what is missing.

Detecting missing information in arguments on unfamiliar subjects is not easy. Here we have to depend on our ability to observe, read carefully, and ask questions. It is especially important to recognize the following missing elements:

- Missing definitions
- Missing reasons and conclusions
- Missing facts or information

These categories, which also function as standards, have already been discussed in this text. The importance of *definitions* was emphasized in Chapter 2, where you learned how their absence confuses argumentation and general understanding. In this chapter, you have been learning about the need for both *reasons* and *conclusions*. In Chapter 4, on inferences, you encountered the problems caused by *pertinent missing facts or information*. Thus in each case, standards for clarity, completeness, and fairness were not met when important information was left out. All in all, it takes active concentration to detect the absence of crucial information. Oddly enough, such awareness begins by just paying more attention to our confusion. Our first reaction might be to blame ourselves; indeed, our reading may not have been sufficiently careful. But there are the instances in which our confusion results from the absence of crucial information. Consider, for instance, the following advertisement:

> *Our highest rate for five years. Guaranteed.* Now for a limited time only you can lock into our highest rate for up to five years with an Iowa Federal five-year C.D. If you're retired, think about what this could mean. You won't have to worry about dropping interest rates for a long time. And it's FSLIC insured. Completely safe.

If you don't feel tempted to rush right down to invest, you might realize that the actual interest rate is never mentioned. And here you are being asked to "lock into" it for a period of five years! Thus, it may be true after all that you won't have to worry about dropping interest rates; you may spend more time regretting missing the higher ones. To forget to read carefully for missing information may result in later being unhappily reminded of the adage "Let the buyer beware."

Class Discussion

What questions would you ask of the writers or speakers who said the following?

1. Weight problem? You've tried every kind of diet, exercise, pills and if you do lose a pound or two, it's back in no time. Everybody offers their advice, which is even more frustrating. Your weight problem is taking over your life. At our Health Spa, health specialists will work to take your weight off for good. Call us. Toll free. Georgetown Hospital Health Spa.

2. You are invited to my twenty-first birthday party. Prizes will be given for those who arrive Friday evening exactly at 7:07 P.M. in the Sigma Delta Dormitory lounge.

3. Oh, honey, by the way, my former boyfriend came into town today and gave me a call.

4. I have to go out now and take care of some business.

5. Spacious sunny apartment available! Great rent: $650. Secure building. Close to freeway connections. One block from buses and subway.

6. *Nuclear Power Is Cheaper Energy for Tomorrow*
   "The price of electricity from fossil fuel plants will always depend heavily on the cost of fuel, which is unpredictable. The cost of nuclear fuel is more stable; its supply is within our control; and there's plenty of it. As a

nuclear plant's construction costs are paid for, its lower fuel costs *hold down* the price of the electricity. Eventually, the lower cost of fuel more than makes up for the higher cost of construction." (advertisement, U.S. Committee for Energy Awareness)

Following Up on Missing Information

Sometimes you may come across a report that leaves you with a lot of questions. If you are in a rush, you might just set your questions aside. But let's consider a situation in which you might feel highly motivated to learn more. Suppose you have a two-year-old child who had a serious flare-up of eczema the week before. You decide to use the Internet to find out more about a medication prescribed by your family doctor, a medication whose generic name is tacrolimus and brand name is Protopic. You go to the site called Eczemanet, where you are shocked to find the following statement in bold type, announcing its opposition to an FDA "black box" warning against the two atopic dermatitis medications: tacrolimus and pimecrolimus.

> In a statement issued March 10, 2005, the Academy's president, dermatologist Clay J. Cockerell, M.D., said, "The American Academy of Dermatology is disappointed that the FDA has taken this action despite the fact that there is no data that proves proper topical use of these medications is dangerous in people.

You know that your doctor prescribed this medication for your son one week before the FDA issued this warning. Thus she may well not have known that this medication was under review. But before calling her, you can't stop wondering why the FDA would issue a black box warning against these two products if there were no data to prove that they were dangerous to people?

A quick return to the Internet takes you to Medline Plus, a service of the National Library of Medicine and National Institutes of Health. There you find the following Reuters health report dated the same day as the previous statement.

● R E A D I N G ●

Eczema Drugs Carry Cancer Risk, US FDA Says

Thursday, March 10, 2005

WASHINGTON (Reuters)—Two eczema creams—Novartis's Elidel and Fujisawa's Protopic—must carry a strong warning of cancer risk, the U.S. Food and Drug Administration said on Thursday.

Research shows the creams are absorbed into the body and can cause cancer, the FDA said. The creams will carry a "black box" warning—the strongest warning carried on medicines.

And babies should not be treated with the creams at all, the FDA said.

"The data showed that the risk of cancer increased as the amount . . . of the drug given increased. The data also included a small number of reports of cancers in children and adults treated with Elidel or Protopic," the FDA said in a statement.

5   In February members of an FDA advisory panel said they were concerned the companies were aggressively advertising the medicines to treat infants and others with skin problems the creams are not approved to treat.

Elidel, known generically as pimecrolimus, and Protopic known generically as tacrolimus, should be used only as directed and only after other eczema treatments have failed to work because of the risk, the FDA said.

Since the FDA approved Protopic in 2000 and Elidel in 2001, seven cases of lymphoma and six skin cancer cases have been reported in patients, the FDA said.

Animal tests have suggested the creams could cause cancer, the FDA added.

"The manufacturers of the products have agreed to conduct research to determine whether there is an actual risk of cancer in humans, and, if so, its extent," the FDA said.

10   "Both products are applied to the skin to control eczema by suppressing the immune system. FDA's Public Health Advisory specifically advises physicians to weigh the risks and benefits of these drugs in adults and children," the agency added.

Doctors who prescribe the drugs should remember they should be used only for the shortest time possible, it said.

"Elidel and Protopic are not approved for use in children younger than 2 years old," the FDA added.

"The long-term effect of Elidel and Protopic on the developing immune system in infants and children is not known. In clinical trials, infants and children younger than 2 years of age treated with Elidel had a higher rate of upper respiratory infections than those treated with placebo cream."

According to the National Institutes of Health (NIH), about 15 million Americans, including about 20 percent of children, suffer from eczema, a skin inflammation that can cause itchy thick skin with blisters or scaly patches.

● ● ●

Study/Writing/Discussion Questions

1. As a concerned parent, what questions would you now have after reading the Reuters report? Break into small groups to formulate your questions. See how many questions each group can come up with.

2. Where would you go to get answers to these questions? What other sources would you want to consult?

3. Why do you suppose the word *cancer* did not appear in the AAD announcement?

Is Any Information False, Contradictory, or Irreconcilable?

Although we may not be able to prove falsehoods, we can pay attention to such warning signs as discrepancies, contradictions, incongruities, and inconsistencies.

Discrepancy: Something diverges from what we expect: an inconsistency, as between facts and claims.
(American Heritage Dictionary)

Incongruity: Something that does not meet our expectations about what is correct, appropriate, logical, or standard. The word comes from the Latin *incongruent*, meaning *not in agreement.*

Consistency: Something that is consistent has constancy and therefore dependability. The term comes from the Latin *consistens,* meaning *to stand firmly.* Something that is **inconsistent** lacks constancy or logical coherence, and may contain contradictions.

Contradiction: To make claims that cannot both be true or both be false at the same time; to do or say something, then deny it was done or said; to say one thing but do the opposite.

Irreconcilable: Conflicting ideas, beliefs, or information that cannot be fully explained or resolved.

A final topic for this chapter concerns ways of approaching information suspected to be false. As critical readers, we cannot conduct court hearings to prove lies, but our knowledge of critical thinking standards can help us assess information reliability. An early signal that something may be wrong is the appearance of **discrepancies, inconsistencies,** or **contradictions.** Read the definitions of these and related terms given in the box. Then consider the following situations.

• Political candidate: "During my administration, millions of new jobs have been created. Why in this state of Arizona alone, in the last month, employment has increased from 5.9% to 5.7%."

- Federal Reserve Board Chairman Alan Greenspan: "It turns out we were all wrong to expect tax cuts to produce budget surpluses. . . . Yet knowing what I know today, I would have made the same decision."

  Hillary Clinton: "Just for the record, we were not all wrong, but many people were wrong." (Senate hearing, March 15, 2005)

- "Senator Kerry, you voted for the U.S. invasion of Iraq. Yet now you say that our president made a grave mistake and that you want to correct that mistake if you win the presidential election."

  Senator: "I voted for the invasion because I trusted my president."

- Today a prestigious peer-review journal of occupational and environmental medicine published the results of the largest study ever conducted on the effects of toxic PCB chemicals. The study, financed by XX Incorporated, found no significant increase in cancer deaths among plant workers. XX Incorporated faces potential liabilities of hundreds of millions of dollars for cleaning up waters contaminated by PCBs. For many years it vigorously opposed federal government requirements to dredge the sediments in waters contaminated by PCBs. It has frequently cited scientific studies that it says show no link between exposure to PCBs and cancer. The study did not address other health risks associated with PCBs such as neurological dysfunction, liver damage, skin irritation, and reproductive problems.

Class Discussion

Divide into four groups that will each consider one of the preceding examples. Then answer the following questions.

1. What exactly is the discrepancy here? Are there any contradictions? If so, what are they?
2. What critical thinking standards are not being met here?

As we all know, contradictions need not always signal a faulty cover-up; they can also stem from careless thinking. For our purposes as critical thinkers, however, it may not be necessary to determine whether carelessness or lying was involved. We need only refer to the standard that says that any argument that contains contradictions is unsound.

> A **sound argument** (or one that is both true and correctly reasoned) does not contain contradictions.

Contradictions appear not only in arguments but also in other situations, such as those that involve contradictions between

- Words and action
- Evidence and denials
- Different testimonies
- Different facts
- Claims and consequences
- What we are told and what we know to be true

The challenge of contradictions is that they don't appear with labels; their detection only results from alert perception and thinking.

Aside from the presence of contradictions, there are many other warning signs of possible dishonesty. We might encounter them in situations ranging from live encounters at home or work to events reported on the nightly news. Here are some signs that call for closer attention:

1. Person who, when confronted with a contradiction, either flatly denies it or engages in diversionary tactics such as name-calling, red herrings, and straw man arguments.
2. Person who makes a false statement and, when confronted with evidence that it is false, only continues to make the false statement.
3. Person who offers "facts" without citing sources, thus making it difficult to corroborate their veracity.
4. Person who uses "double-talk," choosing words that can mislead or deceive.

Class Discussion

Break into small groups. Share your knowledge of personal or public examples that illustrate any of these warning signs. In which cases was there a confirmation that some form of deceit had occurred?

Chapter Summary

1. The critical reading of arguments is an active endeavor that requires involvement, interaction with questions, and evaluation.
2. The questions asked in the critical reading of arguments are:
   a. What viewpoint is the source of this argument?
   b. What is the issue of controversy?
   c. Is it an argument or a report?

    d. How is the argument structured in terms of reasons and conclusions?

    e. What are the argument's strengths and weaknesses?

3. The analysis of arguments in terms of their reasons and conclusions applies to both inductive and deductive arguments. Reasons include data, evidence, and premises, while conclusions include those deductively drawn as well as hypotheses.

4. The conclusion of an argument is the last step in a reasoning process. However, it may be stated at any time during an argument or not at all.

5. Reasons support conclusions. They may be generalizations that could function as conclusions in another context. Once the argument's main conclusion is uncovered, the reasons offered in support becomes clear.

6. Arguments state and defend a claim in an attempt to persuade. Arguments disguised as reports slant the facts and language toward a bias.

7. Reports that only relate events or state facts cannot be analyzed as though they were arguments.

8. An issue is a topic of controversy upon which positions may be taken. Surrounding each issue are many debate questions.

9. The following questions can serve as guidelines for analyzing the strengths and weaknesses of arguments:

    a. Are the reasons adequate to support the conclusion?

    b. Are there any hidden assumptions?

    c. Are any central words ambiguous or slanted so as to incite prejudice?

    d. Are there fallacies of reasoning?

    e. Is any important information missing?

    f. Is any information false or contradictory?

● R E A D I N G S ●

Is Job Outsourcing Good for America?

Here are three pro and con arguments on the topic of U.S. job outsourcing. Michael Hussey's pro argument appeared on his own blog as well as in *Etalkinghead* on February 12, 2004. A second pro argument was written by Thomas L. Friedman of *The New York Times* on February 29, 2004. Thomas Friedman is a journalist who has written several books on globalization; more recently he has come to be known as "the globalization guru." The con argument was written by Rory L. Terry, Assistant Professor of Finance at Fort Hays State University. A condensed version of this argument appeared on *CNNmoney* on March 12, 2004.

Job Outsourcing Good for America
Michael Hussey

Meet the United States' newest faux victim in its long line of faux victims—the American programmer and information technology employee. Ever since this month's *Wired* magazine placed an attractive Indian female on the cover along with the words " Kiss Your Cubicle Goodbye," the idea that American high tech workers are facing desolation as more and more of their jobs are outsourced to Indian "IT Farms," has been granted a degree of undeserved legitimacy. Expect to hear more and more about this as the year progresses and millions of more Indian workers and American businesses benefit from these cost saving initiatives.

In fact, I know some of those facing this desolation. My old company recently laid off a significant number of engineers and replaced the team with an Indian outsourcing company at 25% of the cost. And while there is undoubtedly a short-term discomfort with any layoff, the word is, almost all of those employees have found new and improved employment.

Just like Mexican workers who come to the United States to "steal our jobs," the cost savings afforded to American businesses make us stronger, freeing up American capital and talent to create opportunities that are ever more interesting for all of us. There are currently a billion people in India and a billion more in China who will continue to "steal" our jobs. I wish there were a trillion of them.

At the dawn of the computer age, many intelligent people preached gloom and doom; altruistically warning us to beware of a future race of supercomputers which would obsolete human beings and drive the entire world's wealth into fewer and fewer hands. This notion was (and remains) derived from Marxist economic theory which states that the end game of capitalism is a greater concentration of wealth in fewer and fewer hands while every day, more and more people are left by the wayside. That millions of people still cling to this theory is pure blasphemy to economic reality. Rather than being left by the wayside, millions are getting in on this good action ($).

5   The skeptics preached a similar doom about industrial machinery replacing farm labor. Raise your hand if you would rather be tilling the soil right now or reading this column.

Trade and new technology have always freed us up to lead more and more interesting lives. In the case of Indian engineers working for less, from an economic perspective, this is the equivalent of discovering a new super computer that can produce more output using fewer resource inputs.

Throughout history, there have been certain subversive individuals chiefly responsible for creating, cultivating and finally manipulating particular groups of people to achieve their own ends—and one of the most effective tools for cultivating masses behind a would-be dictator's cause is to paint that person as a victim. A victim of "the system," a victim of "race," of "the Jews," of "the almighty dollar," of "religious persecution," of "technology," of your "parents," of "men," of "gun manufacturers," "a fast food culture," ad nauseam.

This latest uproar over Asian labor simply needs to be identified for what it is. The manipulators desire to curb the individuality out of some of the most individualistic members of the new economy— the computer geeks. I am not falling for it.

This nonsense will eventually cease. I look forward to seeing this culture of victimization become the final victim.

Used with permission of Michael Hussey.

• • •

30 Little Turtles

Thomas L. Friedman

Indians are so hospitable. I got an ovation the other day from a roomful of Indian 20-year-olds just for reading perfectly the following paragraph: "A bottle of bottled water held 30 little turtles. It didn't matter that each turtle had to rattle a metal ladle in order to get a little bit of noodles, a total turtle delicacy. The problem was that there were many turtle battles for less than oodles of noodles."

I was sitting in on an "accent neutralization" class at the Indian call center 24/7 Customer. The instructor was teaching the would-be Indian call center operators to suppress their native Indian accents and speak with a Canadian one—she teaches British and U.S. accents as well, but these youths will be serving the Canadian market. Since I'm originally from Minnesota, near Canada, and still speak like someone out of the movie *Fargo*, I gave these young Indians an authentic rendition of "30 Little Turtles," which is designed to teach them the proper Canadian pronunciations. Hence the rousing applause.

Watching these incredibly enthusiastic young Indians preparing for their call center jobs—earnestly trying to soften their t's and roll their r's —is an uplifting experience, especially when you hear from their friends already working these jobs how they have transformed their lives. Most of them still live at home and turn over part of their salaries to their parents, so the whole family benefits. Many have credit cards and have become real consumers, including of U.S. goods, for the first time. All of them seem to have gained self-confidence and self-worth.

A lot of these Indian young men and women have college degrees, but would never get a local job that starts at $200 to $300 a month were it not for the call centers. Some do "outbound" calls, selling things from credit cards to phone services to Americans and Europeans. Others deal with "inbound" calls— everything from tracing lost luggage for U.S. airline passengers to solving computer problems for U.S. customers. The calls are transferred here by satellite or fiber optic cable.

5   I was most taken by a young Indian engineer doing tech support for a U.S. software giant, who spoke with pride about how cool it is to tell his friends that

he just spent the day helping Americans navigate their software. A majority of these call center workers are young women, who not only have been liberated by earning a decent local wage (and therefore have more choice in whom they marry), but are using the job to get M.B.A.'s and other degrees on the side.

I gathered a group together, and here's what they sound like: M. Dinesh, who does tech support, says his day is made when some American calls in with a problem and is actually happy to hear an Indian voice: "They say you people are really good at what you do. I am glad I reached an Indian." Kiran Menon, when asked who his role model was, shot back: "Bill Gates—[I dream of] starting my own company and making it that big." I asked C. M. Meghna what she got most out of the work: "Self-confidence," she said, "a lot of self-confidence, when people come to you with a problem and you can solve it—and having a lot of independence." Because the call center teams work through India's night—which corresponds to America's day—"your biological clock goes haywire," she added. "Besides that, it's great."

There is nothing more positive than the self-confidence, dignity and optimism that comes from a society knowing it is producing wealth by tapping its own brains—men's and women's—as opposed to one just tapping its own oil, let alone one that is so lost it can find dignity only through suicide and "martyrdom."

Indeed, listening to these Indian young people, I had a déjà vu. Five months ago, I was in Ramallah, on the West Bank, talking to three young Palestinian men, also in their 20's, one of whom was studying engineering. Their hero was Yasir Arafat. They talked about having no hope, no jobs and no dignity, and they each nodded when one of them said they were all "suicide bombers in waiting."

What am I saying here? That it's more important for young Indians to have jobs than Americans? Never. But I am saying that there is more to outsourcing than just economics. There's also geopolitics. It is inevitable in a networked world that our economy is going to shed certain low-wage, low-prestige jobs. To the extent that they go to places like India or Pakistan—where they are viewed as high-wage, high-prestige jobs—we make not only a more prosperous world, but a safer world for our own 20-year-olds.

●   ●   ●

What's Wrong with Outsourcing?

Rory L. Terry

A great deal of effort is being expended to convince us all that the outsourcing of jobs under the rubric of free trade is a good thing. First I would like to briefly discuss two of these arguments.

We will create new jobs in highly paying fields. The United States has neither superiority in innovation nor comparative advantage in retaining skilled jobs. Innovation requires intellectual capital. Foreign students receive outstanding educations: consider our low rank in the education of mathematics and the sciences. Moreover, we freely transfer our knowledge to foreign workers. Consider the large number of international students enrolled in our most advanced technical degree programs at our most prestigious universities, or consider the number of new non-native Ph.D.'s that leave our universities each year. Innovation requires creativity. To assume that our workers are inherently more creative than foreign workers is both arrogant and naïve. Innovation requires access to knowledge and physical resources. Corporations are the owners of knowledge and resources, and they are rapidly transferring both overseas in the form of job outsourcing and foreign direct investment in research and manufacturing facilities. The capitalistic system is being implemented throughout the world, and with it will come creativity and innovation in foreign countries equal to our own. And, where is the comparative advantage that will allow us to retain the most desirable jobs? Our labor force is not better trained, harder working, or more innovative than that of our foreign competitors—but, it is more expensive. Labor arbitrage will continue to move jobs overseas, provided there is a sufficient supply of trained foreign workers. In short, creation is not preservation!

Outsourced jobs aren't good jobs. In truth most of our best, high-paying jobs can be exported. Any job that is tied to exportable capital (such as a manufacturing plant) or involves intellectual capital combined with communication of output can be exported. So what jobs can be (and are being) outsourced? They include doctors (even surgeons), mathematicians, accountants, financial analysts, engineers, computer programmers, architects, physicists, chemists, biologists, and researchers of all types.

There are many other arguments in favor of job outsourcing, but none of them prove that outsourcing does not destroy jobs. Rather these are arguments that the benefits of outsourcing outweigh the costs. I have no doubt that companies are better off because of outsourcing. Cost reductions and other benefits provide a strong incentive to outsource jobs. A company that decides to move its production overseas cuts its costs in many ways, including the following:

1. Extremely low wages.
2. The circumvention or avoidance of organized labor.
3. No Social Security or Medicare benefit payments.
4. No federal or state unemployment tax.
5. No health benefits for workers.
6. No child labor laws.
7. No OSHA or EPA costs or restrictions.
8. No worker retirement benefits or pension costs.

Besides cutting costs, there are other benefits to exporting jobs, including the following:

1. Tax incentives provided by our government.
2. Incentives from foreign governments.

3. The creation of new international markets for the company's products (which ultimately empowers the company to turn a deaf ear to this country's problems and influence)
4. The continued benefits of our legal system and the freedoms that we provide.

The net effect of all this is lower costs, higher revenue, higher profits, higher stock prices, bonuses for management, and the creation of wealth for a subclass (capitalists—owners) at the expense of the displaced worker and the taxpayer.

5   The dilemma we face is that while multinational corporations are fully benefiting from outsourcing, they are paying only part of the cost. An externality exists in economics whenever there is a separation of costs and benefits, and the decision maker does not incur the full cost but receives the full benefits of the decision. The fact is, there is no economic force, no supply and demand equilibrium, no rational decision process of either business or consumer that will make an externality go away. Classic examples of externalities are when a business dumps toxic waste into a nearby river and the downstream residents incur the environmental and medical costs. The business is able to lower its costs and pass those lower costs on to its customers, and never pay for the damages it inflicts on society. We have laws in this country against dumping and pollution because they are externalities—stopping them requires a legislative solution.

As a society, and as a country, we experience many costs from outsourcing, including the loss of jobs, social costs, higher costs of raw materials and endangerment of our sovereignty. Loss of jobs reduces the tax base, creates high unemployment benefit costs, and raises the cost of government retraining programs. Displaced unemployed workers have higher rates of child and spousal abuse, alcoholism, bankruptcy, divorce, etc. As China and India and other large populations grow, they demand huge quantities of oil, gas, steel and other basic raw materials. As global demand rises, so do prices and thus costs. These costs are borne by all of us—every time we fill our gas tanks, for example. As our trade deficits with emerging capitalistic systems such as China expand, we become increasingly dependent on their willingness to finance our trade deficits. And as a nation, we lose our ability to make independent decisions that are in our best interest when we are dependent on foreign debt and foreign manufacturing.

As a nation, we have entrusted the creation and preservation of wealth, and by implication, the creation of jobs, to our corporations. As such, American corporations have become our de facto agent with respect to job creation. But corporations fundamentally have one over-riding responsibility—to maximize shareholder wealth. There is apparently an inverse relation between domestic job creation and global production cost. Corporations view labor costs and shareholder wealth from a multinational perspective. Consequently, there can be inherent conflict between the job creation goals of our nation and the shareholder wealth maximization goal of the corporation. Outsourcing is clearly an example of the great lie: what's good for American business is good for America.

Used with permission of Professor Rory L. Terry.

● ● ●

Study/Writing/Discussion Questions

Working alone or with a partner or group, write an outline that analyzes one of the three preceding arguments.

Begin by stating the debate question addressed by all three arguments. Write your statement of the debate question at the top of your outline. Now begin your analysis by making an outline that answers the following questions:

1. What is the viewpoint of the writer? What are this writer's qualifications and affiliations?
2. What is the final conclusion of the argument? Quote or summarize.
3. What reasons does the writer give in support of this final conclusion? Number and summarize each, using quotes as needed.
4. Do you find any key words that are ambiguous (not clearly defined) or words with connotations that convey hidden evaluations, bias, or prejudice? Quote and discuss each.
5. Is any essential information missing in the argument?
6. Discuss any information you find that seems to be false, inconsistent, or irreconcilable.

CHAPTER 10

Fallacies:
What's a Faulty Argument?

"Hey, I'm not *crazy*. ... Sure, I let him drive once in a while, but he's never, *never* off this leash for even a second."

Of course the man's defense is absurd, but would you recognize his red herring fallacy? You will find twenty different types of fallacious reasoning discussed in this book; each has a different name to describe a different reasoning error. Fallacies may be accidental or intentional; many are amusing;

all are manipulative; each sidesteps the work of constructing a fair and well-reasoned argument. In order to make learning these twenty fallacies easier, they will be presented in two segments. Three groups of fallacies are presented in this chapter; a fourth group, fallacies of inductive reasoning, will be discussed at the end of Chapter 11. This placement, following a review of the principles of inductive reasoning, should make their fallaciousness more evident and therefore easier to understand. All in all, this division into two parts is intended to make it easier for you to recognize and remember each one.

> **Fallacy** comes from the Latin word *fallacia*, which means deceit or trick. A fallacy is a statement or argument that presents itself as soundly reasoned when it is not.

DISCOVERY EXERCISE

■ *Recognizing Fallacies*

Environmental zealots threaten four industries in California—agriculture, mining, timber, and construction—and the people will no longer tolerate what the zealots are doing to the ability of Californians to make a living. The zealots can shut down the American economy. (Rep. William Dannemeyer, R-Calif.)

1. Do you tend to agree with this opinion or not?
2. What exactly is right or wrong about the argument?
3. If you are familiar with some fallacies, do any of the following apply: poisoning the well, slippery slope, bandwagon, slanted language, appeal to fear, hasty generalization, use of ambiguous words?

The Fallacies

Since the times of the Greeks, fallacies of reasoning have been given names and categorized for study and identification. When we learn the names and characteristics of these fallacies, we gain the following advantages:

- We learn more about the rules for good reasoning.
- We avoid using them ourselves.
- We are not influenced by arguments that contain them.

The effectiveness of fallacies rests in their pseudo-reasoning, their use of hidden appeals to our emotions, and their ability to distract our attention from their weaknesses. On the surface their argument may appear plausible, but a closer study reveals confusion or intentional manipulation. Fallacies fan the smoke of fear, pity, or prejudice; they distract from the issue, play with language, and assume what they should prove. In this chapter, you will learn how to avoid using—or being influenced by—the following fallacies that manipulate through language, emotions, and distraction.

Manipulation Through Language

1. **Word ambiguity:** Seeks to gain an advantage in an argument by using vague or undefined words.
2. **Misleading euphemisms:** Hides meaning by creating words that make a less acceptable idea seem positive or unrecognizable.
3. **Prejudicial language:** Attempts to persuade through the use of loaded words that convey a bias.

Manipulation Through Emotions

4. **Appeal to fear:** Seeks to persuade by arousing fear.
5. **Appeal to pity:** Seeks to persuade by arousing pity.
6. **Appeal to false authority:** Seeks to persuade by citing a fake or inappropriate authority.
7. **Appeal to bandwagon:** Seeks to persuade by appealing to the wisdom of a popular momentum.
8. **Appeal to prejudice:**
   a. **Personal attack:** Attacks a person's character on matters irrelevant to the issue.
   b. **Poisoning the well:** Seeking to prejudice others against a person, group, or idea so that their arguments will not be heard on their own merits.

Manipulation Through Distraction

9. **Red herring:** Instead of proving a claim, diverts attention into other issues.
10. **Pointing to another wrong:** Distracts attention from an admitted wrongdoing by claiming that similar actions went unnoticed and unpunished.
11. **Straw man:** Misrepresents or caricatures an opponent's position, then refutes the false replica created; also attacks a minor point in an argument, then claims this maneuver invalidates the whole argument.

12. **Circular reasoning:** Assumes what it is supposed to prove by reasserting a conclusion as though this claim needs no supporting reasons or by repeating the same conclusion in different words.

Fallacies That Manipulate Through Language

Fallacies that use deceptive language include the fallacies of word ambiguity, misleading euphemisms, and prejudicial language.

Fallacious arguments can be based on an inept use of words or a purposeful selection of words that are vague, ambiguous, and prejudicial in connotation. When the selection is intentional, such words can ward off questioning and hide the weaker aspects of an argument. Three fallacies that attempt persuasion through deceptive word use are called the fallacies of word ambiguity, misleading euphemisms, and prejudicial language.

Word Ambiguity

The **fallacy of word ambiguity** occurs in an argument when a key word with several meanings is left undefined; as a result, the reader must assume what meaning was intended.

A good argument makes careful and conscious word choices. It wants to persuade, and to make its language as clear as possible. A faulty argument tries to gain an unfair advantage by using words that might confuse others and lead them to agree with a claim they don't fully understand. The fallacy of ambiguity uses vague or ambiguous words for this purpose: "We should treat *drug* use as a private right that harms no one but the user." Here, what is meant by *drug* is undefined. The reader trained in critical thinking will stop and wonder what substances the author would include under the term *drugs*. If such a question cannot be answered, then the argument is not worth further study.

Let's consider some more examples.

Long Beach, Calif.—Gov. Arnold Schwarzenegger, speaking Tuesday to open an annual conference celebrating women's contributions to the state, dismissed California nurses who protested his health care policies as "special interests" who are mad because "I kick their butt." (Carla Marinucci, *San Francisco Chronicle*, December 9, 2004)

Later in the following year the governor was to dismiss, as *special interests*, union-represented teachers, firefighters, and police. For the governor, the term *special interests* seemed to apply to any citizens that he did not want to represent. By making them into enemies, he further confused the public by using a term usually reserved for self-serving lobbyists seeking advantages not necessarily in the public interest.

> School prayer will not help as long as students are taught *immorality*, e.g., basic condom training. Returning to teaching students *basic morality* will help. If public schools insist on teaching immorality, parents must have the choice to send their children to a school that teaches *fundamental morality*.

Here, the writer defines *immorality* as public education in condom use. However, it is not clear what the writer means by *basic morality* or *fundamental morality*. Does she mean abstinence education? Does she mean birth control? Does morality only apply to sexual behavior? A thoughtful reader will not be able to proceed beyond these questions.

Class Discussion

Explain why the italicized words in the following statements are ambiguous and what purpose such ambiguity serves.

1. Our *modern lifestyle* is the radical environmentalist's ultimate target.
2. Those who engage in demonstrations are *anti-American*.
3. *Society* is to blame for crime, not *criminals*.
4. You should be willing to do anything for *love*.

Weasel words are words that appear to say one thing when in fact they are saying nothing at all. (Weasels are predators who steal into the nests of other animals, make small holes in their eggs, suck out the insides, and leave the hollow eggs standing.)

Ambiguous words can be not only words with more than one meaning, but also words that say nothing at all. Advertisers frequently use weasel words in order to lure buyers into projecting their own desires onto advertising claims. The advantage of this approach for advertisers is that they can later deny responsibility for the buyer's interpretations. Such ambiguities may take the form of such hollow words such as *helps,* as in

"Helps prevent cavities," or *as much as*, as in "Saves as much as 1 gallon of gas." A few other familiar weasel words appear in the following ads:

- Save on typewriters from a leading maker! SALE! SALE! $200! Made to sell for $495! (Here the word *sale* only tells you the store has something to sell. Perhaps it was overpriced in the first place.)
- Women's coats—$54. A $75 value. (The word *value* is relative. Perhaps the store bought the coats especially for the sale and set the previous value arbitrarily.)
- These blouses have the *feel* of silk. (That an item has the *feel* of silk does not mean it is silk.)
- Come see our sheepskin-look seat covers. (Remember, they are not saying that the items *are* sheepskin.)

Class Discussion

Identify the ambiguous words in the following sentences by underlining the words and stating how they function for persuasion.

1. All ingredients in this ice cream are natural and nutritious.
2. These pies are made from locally grown cherries and have that old-fashioned country taste.
3. Ace aspirin provides relief up to eight hours.
4. Ida Insect Spray helps fight mosquitoes.
5. Tony's Tonic helps you feel and look ten years younger.
6. You can save as much as 1 quart of oil a day.
7. Wear a jacket that has the feel of leather.

Misleading Euphemisms

> **Euphemism** comes from the Greek word meaning "good voice," or to use words of good omen. Euphemisms are inoffensive words used to maintain a level of social formality. All of us know what is meant when we hear *remains* for corpse or *bathroom* for toilet. **Misleading euphemisms**, on the other hand, are deliberately created for the purposes of evasion and manipulation.

Ordinary euphemisms allow us to avoid taboo subjects and maintain polite social interactions. Misleading euphemisms manipulate and deceive;

they are the staples of commercial and political propaganda. They can make the bad seem good and the good seem bad.

Misleading euphemisms perform the tasks of promoting and lying (also known by the euphemism of "public relations"). They sanitize and camouflage actions, things, or events that could appear unacceptable in light of professed values. They intentionally distort truth and meaning. In George Orwell's novel *1984,* misleading euphemisms are grimly parodied in his creation of a state built on the slogans "War Is Peace," "Freedom Is Slavery," and "Ignorance Is Strength." Here the government ministries include the Ministry of Truth (which produces lies and propaganda), the Ministry of Love (which practices imprisonment, brainwashing, and torture), and the Ministry of Peace (which concerns itself with war).

The term *double-talk* is also used to describe misleading euphemisms, as when politicians speak of "disinformation" to describe lies planted in media releases. Public relations employees, both inside and outside the U.S. government, specialize in creating euphemisms. In the U.S. military, lists of official euphemisms are distributed to military officers for their use in relating to the public. Sometimes euphemisms serve as code words to sanitize military actions that might raise uncomfortable questions and offend our professed national values. Here are some examples of misleading euphemisms:

Misleading Euphemism	Conventional Term
Acceptable losses	Number of our own soldiers expected to die in battle
Friendly fire	Shooting our own soldiers by mistake
Unconventional warfare	Combat methods violating Geneva Convention agreements
Hot zone	Area exposed to nuclear fallout or biological or chemical agents
Rigged or amped out	Describes soldier who has taken narcotics or amphetamines
Black ops	Officially unsanctioned activities such as kidnapping or assassinating enemy leaders
Effecting a regime change	Attacking a country in order to set up a new government favorable to the attacker
Detainee	Prisoner of war
Insurgents	Resistance
Preemptive strike	Unprovoked attack

Class Discussion/Writing Assignment

Following are some recently coined controversial terms. To some they represent valuable new concepts; to others they are intentionally misleading euphemisms. Divide into groups, with each group selecting a few of these words; if you decide that one is misleading, explain why.

Clear Skies Initiative

Healthy Forests Initiative

Leave No Child Behind Act

Personal Investment Accounts

Ownership Society

Entitlement Society

Zone of Autonomy

Extraordinary Rendition

Prejudicial Language

> The **fallacy of prejudicial language** is an attempt to persuade through the choice of slanted or loaded words that convey a bias. The implication in such a tactic is that the words chosen only describe what is real and true.

In earlier chapters, we studied how word connotations convey positive or negative feelings. Let us now consider how highly connotative words might be chosen to function as hidden persuaders. Study the following three headlines:

- Earth Day Birdcage Liner. What better occasion to honor the shameless press coverage of environmental wackies and wackos. (*American Spectator*, April 22, 2005)
- Earth Day: Sleepwalking Into an Apocalypse. (Institute for Public Policy, April 20, 2005)
- Let's Stop the "Free Trade" Nutballs. (Jim Hightower, Alternet, April 20, 2005)

Discussion Break Questions

1. Underline the words in these headlines that carry strong connotations.

2. What slant do they lend to this information?

3. What associations do you have with these words?

4. Compare the following translations of these headlines. Do they convey the same message?

- Earth Day Worthless News. Valuable only for viewing press favoritism.

- Earth Day: Are we moving unaware into world destruction?

- Let's oppose those who talk of "free trade" but mean no government protections.

5. Read the following quotations and circle the words that seem prejudicial:

   a. "Cultic America: A Tower of Babel"

   b. "Liberals love the UN because it reminds them of the form of government they support in the United States: bloated, ineffectual, anti-capitalist, and anti-American." (Mark W. Smith, *The Official Handbook of the Vast Right-Wing Conspiracy*, 2004, p. 79)

   c. "The latest draconian maneuver [in housing initiatives] comes from the mind of . . . a tantrum-prone manchild who is infamous for his fits of legislation. . . . He has had an especially bad year in pushing through special interest, pro-tenant laws. But give him credit—he's not sensible enough to know when to quit." (Ken Garcia, columnist, *San Francisco Chronicle*, November 15, 2004)

Some of the words you circled in the previous exercise may contain evaluations that you agree with, but they do require acceptance of a bias. In these quoted excerpts, no supporting reasons are provided (although, to be fair, some reasons appear in the full arguments from which they are excerpted). Within these quotations, persuasion is attempted chiefly through evaluative word choices. The task for the critical reader is to separate word choice from word meaning and thus detach from the emotional power of word connotations. Having said all this, however, one has to allow that journalists will often use highly connotative words in order to grab their readers' attention. In this age of hype and hucksterism, when ideas need to be shouted in order to be heard, even writers who know how to construct sound arguments in neutral language may feel they have to turn the volume up to be heard.

Class Discussion

Which of these arguments rely primarily on slanted words in order to be persuasive?

1. Is there anything more ridiculous in the news today than the protests against the World Trade Organization in Seattle? I doubt it. These

anti-WTO-protesters—who are a Noah's ark of flat-Earth advocates, protectionist trade unions and yuppies looking for the 1960's fix— are protesting against the wrong target with the wrong tools. (Thomas L. Friedman, *New York Times Service,* December 2, 1999)

2. Spud fans tell us that Spud Cigarettes has proved itself in the real smoking "tough spots" . . . where smoking is hardest and heaviest . . . because Spud's moist-cool, clean taste never fails. That's why so many are switching to Spud as a constant smoke. Have you discovered how Spud's mouth-happiness increases tobacco enjoyment? (Advertisement in *The Literary Digest,* May 6, 1933)

3. Wall Street money managers, investment bankers, and insurance companies are drooling over the prospect of trillions of dollars of Social Security revenue being funneled into the stocks and bonds markets and generating billions of dollars in fees, commissions and profits. *The Wall Street Journal* reported its anticipation of "the biggest bonanza in the history of the mutual fund industry." (Bed Hudnall, Business Manager, Engineers & Scientists of California, Local 20, San Francisco)

4. Government and Greed Destroy the Forest
   Look at the balance sheet. Clearing the Amazon produces hardwoods which are essential for nothing. Dams flood the forest to generate electricity to make aluminum for throw-away cans. Iron ore is dug out of the ground to be sold at throw-away prices. Diseased cattle stroll about farting their greenhouse gases into the atmosphere to pander to a particular dietary preference in the cities. Rivers are polluted with deadly mercury to produce gold that is smuggled out through Uruguay to languish in the vaults of Swiss banks. The mass of the people of the Amazon are corralled into poverty, fearing for their lives. Indigenous people are persecuted to the verge of extinction. Can it really be for this that the greatest forest on earth is being made to disappear? (David Ransom, *The New Internationalist,* May 1991)

Fallacies That Manipulate Emotions

Some fallacies manipulate by seeking intentionally to arouse such emotions as fear, anxiety and pity, insecurity, hatred, and prejudice. Once influenced by such emotions, the lack of a sound argument can be overlooked. Fallacies that manipulate emotions seek to persuade by exploiting our weaknesses instead of inviting conscious consideration and consent. They can be insidiously effective in attracting interest and clouding rational study of an issue. All of this does not mean that any

argument that arouses emotion is fallacious. Usually we are not motivated to formulate arguments unless aroused by feelings. To be sane on
many topics is to feel clear anger, indignation, or grief. However, a fallacious argument avoids or omits sound reasoning and depends primarily on arousing reactions that overwhelm clear rational thinking.
What follows are the fallacies of Emotional Appeals to Fear and Pity,
Appeal to False Authority, and Appeals to Prejudice.

Emotional Appeals to Fear and Pity

Appeals to fear are the staples of commercial advertising. The following
examples may serve as familiar reminders:

1. "What your best friends won't tell you . . ."
2. (Picture of a frantic traveler who has lost her traveler's checks.) "Next
   time be safe with our fast call-in service."
3. (Picture of man in hospital bed in a state of shock after seeing his
   bill.) "Did you think one insurance coverage plan was enough?"
4. (Picture of burglars breaking into a house.) "Are you still postponing
   that alarm system?"

Class Discussion

The use of an appeal to anger has not been considered fallacious in the
tradition of argumentation; apparently such an appeal is assumed to be
legitimate because anger usually arouses people from complacency. Listed
here are some appeals to fear, pity, and anger. Read the arguments and
decide which you think are appropriate calls for fear, anger, or pity, and
which are appeals based on exaggerations. Again, your judgments may
depend on your personal values. Defend your answers.

1. Berkeley, California has become a police state as police presence has
   increased from 12 cops to 40 to 60 on any given weekend night.
   Cops are everywhere, on foot, bicycle, motorcycle, undercover, and
   in both marked and unmarked cars. The police mobile substation, a
   menacing blue bus with smoked windows, cruises the area for added
   effect. Sinister jump squads, followed by a paddy wagon, keep tensions high by making quick arrests. (*Copwatch Report,* Fall 1992)
2. Loretta Fortuna wants out. Sickened by odors wafting from the red
   toxic pools near her home, angered by the political battleground
   she's had to maneuver, grief-stricken by two miscarriages within a
   year and perpetually worried for the health of her two small sons,

she finally had enough. Fortuna has spent the past year waging a campaign on behalf of her family and neighbors to get a leaking waste dump near her home cleaned up. But now she has decided to move elsewhere, a disheartened casualty of a frustrating battle. The Gloucester Environmental Management Services landfill . . . is one site among 1,175 toxic nightmares nationwide waiting to be cleaned up. (Robert J. Mentzinger, *Public Citizen,* May/June 1990)

3. Get out of here! The building is going to collapse!

4. "We are God in Here . . ." That's what the guards in an Argentine prison taunted Grace Guena with as they applied electrical shocks to her body while she lay handcuffed to the springs of a metal bed. Her cries were echoed by the screams of other victims and the laughter of their torturers. (Appeal letter from Amnesty International USA)

5. Smokers know they are plague victims and suspect they may be carriers. So they puff on their butts behind a closed office door, and indulge their health-nut friends by abstaining from cigarettes during the dinner hour—which without a nicotine fix, seems to stretch on for days. (Richard Corliss, *Time,* April 11, 1994)

6. Alarmed by a comet's violent collision last year with the planet Jupiter, scientists warned yesterday that speeding asteroids and comets could inflict far more damage on Earth than previously thought, perhaps even disrupting the climate and causing millions of deaths. . . . Among the ideas presented were the use of super-powerful spacecraft and well-timed nuclear explosives to pulverize potential invaders from outer space or to nudge them away from their Earth-bound orbits. . . . The meeting . . . is sponsored by the U.S. Department of Energy, NASA, and the Air Force Space Command. (*San Francisco Chronicle,* May 23, 1995)

7. The consequences of the Democratic health care plans will be ruinous, tax increases, job losses, less money in your pocket to spend the way you want to spend it. (Political advertisement, 1994)

Appeal to False Authority

Appeal to false authority is an argument whose chief or only support is a false or questionable authority. The argument is not upheld by sound reasons but by the alleged endorsements of individuals without credentials or expertise on the issue. It appeals to such insecurities as celebrity worship and fear of non-conformity.

The appeal to false authority has many variations, beginning with an appeal to a popular public figure:

- *Buzz Bonanza,* star of stage and screen, prefers Tasty Toothpaste.
- *The President of the United States* says that brushing your teeth once a week is enough.

Here Buzz Bonanza is clearly not a toothpaste expert. Yet, for those who adore him, such a discrepancy might be overlooked. Advertising psychology research has shown that if a consumer can be manipulated into equating a positive figure with a product, then the consumer will assume that owning the product will also mean owning the positive attributes of the figure. Thus, we have so many product testimonials by film stars, athletes, and even former politicians. Admittedly, this ploy is both entertaining and highly effective.

An appeal to a false authority can also refer to authorities in the form of vague entities:

- *Some people say* we don't need to brush our teeth.
- *Doctors say* you should brush your teeth every day with Florident.
- *Experts agree* you should use an electric toothbrush.
- *Inside sources* at the White House say the President doesn't like to brush his teeth.

An argument can also place false authority in tradition, popular wisdom, and the bandwagon. Here are some examples of the appeal to the authority of tradition:

- You can't be an American male unless you like beer and football.
- You have to go to law school. Every oldest child in this family for the past four generations has gone to law school.

False authority can also be claimed to reside in popular wisdom, or the infallible knowing of the masses:

- If you have any doubts about the status of American health care, just compare it with that in the other industrialized nations! *Ask anyone you know* from a foreign country where they would most like to be treated if they had a medical emergency. Ask them which country is the envy of the world when it comes to health care. (Rush Limbaugh)
- It is not fair to blame the U.S. government for not signing the international treaty to destroy all existing land mines. *Ask anyone in the world* about the U.S. record on human rights and about all it has done to alleviate human suffering.

Another variety of false authority is called the *bandwagon fallacy*. If a herd is headed in one direction, that must be the right direction. The bandwagon fallacy promises the exhilaration of joining in a march of irrepressible instinctive wisdom. It offers all the comfort of joining the crowd and coming over to the winning side. Here are some examples of bandwagon appeals:

- Don't vote for Proposition 9. The polls show it will lose 5 to 1.
- Everyone else does it; why can't I?
- Last year over 10 million people switched to Buckaroo Trucks!
- Buddy Springs! America's Beer!
- Join the Pepsi Generation!

In all these appeals to false authority, you will notice the conclusions are unsupported by reasons. What appears instead is the pressure to trust bogus authorities or to trust the wisdom of conformity. Whereas a good argument lays all its claims and proof on the table, an appeal to false authority suggests that one should not trust one's own reasoning but depend on some vague others who know better. However—and this is most important to remember—the existence of the fallacy of false authority *does not mean that a good argument should avoid using and quoting authorities*. On the contrary, authorities with relevant expertise provide excellent support for reasons and are used routinely to lend them more credibility.

> The first comprehensive study of the geographic skills of America's youngsters shows they are "getting the message that they are part of a larger world," Education Secretary Richard Riley said yesterday. "We're not at the head of the class yet, but it's a good start," said National Geographic Society President Gilbert Grosvenor in releasing the results of National Assessment of Educational Progress tests. Nearly three-quarters of the 19,000 students tested in the first national study of geographic knowledge showed at least a basic understanding of the subject, the Education Department reported. (Associated Press, October 18, 1999)

In this example you will notice that each claim is attributed to an authority. If you, as the reader, are in doubt about the qualifications of Richard Riley and Gilbert Grosvenor to offer opinions, at least you have been given enough clues for further research. However, when you decide to use authorities to support your own argument, admittedly it is not always easy to determine their suitability and reliability. So-called experts may have credentials, but you must also research their track records; furthermore, you might want to know whether other authorities agree or disagree with them. In summary, authority citation can offer impressive support for an argument, but assessing the qualifications and appropriate expertise of the authority requires experience and research.

> An **authority** is someone who has expertise in a particular subject. Authority expertise depends on the person's credentials, accomplishments, reputation for competence and reliability, and peer recognition. *A confirming quotation from an appropriate, reputable, and unbiased authority can provide excellent support for claims made in an argument.*

Class Discussion

Explain how the following statements are different kinds of appeals to authority. Which are fallacious? Which are legitimate?

1. My doctor says that I should take a nap every afternoon.
2. A ten-year study by leading scientists has found that Tuff toothpaste prevents decay in four out of five cases.
3. Buzz Bonanza, star of stage and screen, drives a Macho Motorcycle.
4. I read it in the newspapers.
5. Interviewer: "Do you feel national parks should be privatized?" Woman: "My husband says they should."
6. "Women have babies and men provide the support. If you don't like the way we're made you've got to take it up with God." (Phyllis Schlafly)"
7. For over a quarter of a century our teachers have been committed to the idea that the best way to teach students is to withhold criticisms and build self-esteem. But both Alfred Binet, the father of intelligence testing, and Sigmund Freud, the father of psychoanalysis, described the development of self-criticism, which we learn from the criticisms of others, as the essence of intelligence.
8. "One out of every five Americans experience a mental disorder in any given year, and half of all Americans have such disorders at some time in their lives but most of them never seek treatment, the surgeon general of the United States says in a comprehensive new report." (Robert Pear, *New York Times,* December 13, 1999)

Appeal to Prejudice: Personal Attack and Poisoning the Well

Prejudice is a complex feeling: a mixture of envy, fear, and resentment. A person who feels prejudice cannot maintain the openness necessary for clear reasoning. Arguments that seek to incite prejudice avoid the hard work of constructing a sound argument; the hope is that once the prejudice virus is transmitted, those infected will not even notice the argument's weaknesses. There are two basic fallacious appeals to prejudice.

The first makes a direct attack. The second "poisons the well" or contaminates a whole environment so that it will be distrusted and avoided.

■ Personal Attack

This fallacious argument is familiar when political campaigns turn negative and opponents begin to trash one another. The fallacy of personal attack occurs when arguments are not considered on their own merits, but their authors are attacked instead. They can include frontal attacks, such as abusive name-calling, or rear attacks, such as innuendo. Such arguments are fallacious because they incite prejudice and divert attention from the lack of a sound argument.

- "Richard Clark is a politically motivated historical revisionist. His attacks on our administration are scurrilous." (Condoleezza Rice *CNN. com,* May 6, 2004)
- He's another rich Republican pinhead birdbrain.
- "You're a moron. It's idiots like you who will cause this country to go up in flames. Moron, moron, moron." (Michael Savage, *The Enemy Within,* 2004)

> The **fallacy of personal attack** (also known as *ad hominem*) appears in an argument that attacks a person's character rather than addressing the other person's argument.
>
> The **poisoning the well fallacy** uses contamination rather than a frontal attack. It incites prejudice against persons or groups so that whatever they might say or do will be distrusted.

■ Poisoning the Well

This fallacy is another variety of personal attack. When any amount of poison is poured into a well, all its water becomes contaminated, so that no one dares drink from the well. Thus, when a person, idea, or cause is discredited at the outset, people could be made to feel aversion, rather than neutrality and openness. This fallacy has four variations. The first variety of poisoning the well uses a string of words with negative connotations:

- Of all the screwball, asinine, muddle-headed letters I have ever seen from this newspaper's readers, the one from Detroit advocating the legalization of drugs takes the cake.
- Every criminal, every gambler, every thug, every libertine, every girl ruiner, every home wrecker, every wife beater, every dope peddler,

every crooked politician is fighting the Ku Klux Klan. Think it over. What side are you on?

- Anticipating the deluge of enraged, frustrated letters from your core (read ultra-liberal, closed-minded) constituency, following an extremely well-crafted well-delivered acceptance speech by the president, I will provide some rational balance to the irrational liberal tirade. (Letter to the editor, *San Francisco Chronicle,* November 4, 2004)

- Next year, thousands of you will enter the bowels of academia. The track to a productive career is fraught with exposure to faculties decidedly left-leaning. (*Pittsburgh Tribune Review,* November 2, 2004)

- Whatever a right-wing Fox news pundit may have to say, believe the opposite.

Poisoning the well can also take subtler forms when it uses innuendo:

- This president, who has never worn a uniform, announced today that he would send our troops overseas.

- Senator Smith, known as the "waste-fill senator" because of the tons of propaganda he mails from his office, made a speech in favor of increasing immigration quotas before Congress today.

The second example is a fallacious argument because even if Senator Smith deserves a bad reputation for his mailings, he might be able to make a well-informed, persuasive speech on immigration quotas. If it could be shown that he bought extravagant amounts of paper from paper mill lobbyists who exploited immigrant labor, such information might make this criticism relevant. But as this argument stands, his "waste-fill" reputation is beside the point. It only serves to incite prejudice against what he might have to say.

Poisoning the well can be directed not only against individuals but also against ideas or collective groups:

- The news media has been sounding the alarm lately, loudly decrying the terrorists, tax-evaders, and assorted huddled masses poised to overrun us. These racist and alarmist stories are in sync with the message from Washington. (Kelly Gettinger, *Progressive,* August 1993)

Poisoning the well can serve to discredit and thus ward off any argument a person or group might be prepared to offer:

- You are a man. I don't want to hear what you have to say. You can't understand what women feel.

- Bought politicians and PR firms will be trying to persuade you that handing our national parks over to private corporations is good for all of us. Don't let yourself be conned.

Class Discussion

Which of the following are examples of poisoning the well?

1. Those who object to irradiated foods are picky purists whose ideas run counter to common sense.
2. *Three to Tango.* Here is a sex soufflé that falls flat. . . . This is the kind of movie that TV stars do when they're on hiatus and trying to squeeze one in. (Neve Campbell, *Rolling Stone,* November 1999)
3. Today's teenage girls are aware of the outside world, and it makes them fearful. They are a generation that knows more but does less. (Jancee Dunn, *Rolling Stone,* November 1999)
4. "Many companies charge drivers more than twice as much as other companies for identical insurance coverage . . ." That's the word from the California Department of Insurance following a new State survey on automobile insurance rates. (Ad from 20th Century Insurance)

Fallacies That Manipulate Through Distraction

Fallacies based on distraction include red herring, pointing to another wrong, straw man, and circular reasoning.

Fallacies that use the ploy of distraction can be classified in many ways, but what they all have in common is a lack of support for their arguments. All use different tricks to divert attention away from their arguments' weakness. Some, like red herring and pointing to another wrong, distract attention from the issue at hand to a different issue. The straw man fallacy falsely represents the opponent's position, pretends this depiction is accurate, and then destroys its own misrepresentation. Circular reasoning distracts through the illusion of support. Each of these fallacies can be difficult to identify because they can really succeed in distracting us.

Red Herring

> The **fallacy of red herring** does not offer reasons to support its conclusion but diverts attention to other issues that are irrelevant. The term *red herring* comes from a ruse used by prison escapees who would smear themselves with herring in order to throw the dogs off their scent.

The red herring fallacy diverts our attention from the question at hand and throws us off track into irrelevancies. Four red herring tactics can be identified.

This first example shows a typical red herring sidetracking maneuver:

- Marijuana smoking is not all that harmful. I would feel safer in a car with a driver who had smoked weed than one under the influence of liquor any day.

Here, the claim that needs to be defended is "marijuana is not all that harmful." However, instead of offering support for this claim, the writer diverts our attention into comparing the safety of drivers under the influence of marijuana versus alcohol. Thus, we become completely sidetracked as we discuss their relative effects on reflexes and perception. Meanwhile, the original claim that marijuana was not all that harmful is either forgotten or incorrectly assumed proven.

A red herring can be the most difficult of all fallacious arguments to detect because it can actually prove a claim; however, the claim proven will not be the claim that was originally presented.

- Guns are not America's major problem, or even high on the list of our problems. Cars, cancer, accidents in the kitchen all kill far more people than guns do. It is not *guns* that we should be frightened of but the effects of poverty, lack of education, a judicial system that sends criminals and psychopaths back out into the streets. Guns are not a solution, but they are not the problem, either!

In this case, it could easily be shown that guns do not cause the majority of American fatalities. Also it would not be difficult to support the claim that the problems of gun violence are tied into a complex social system. But the argument never supports the claim that "guns are not America's major problem or even high on the list of our problems."

Another red herring tactic is to make one claim and pretend to support it with another claim, without ever supporting either claim.

- I cannot understand why the environmentalists feel it is harmful to cut down the redwood forests. This work provides a good living to loggers and their families.

Here, no reasons are given as to why it is not harmful to cut down the redwoods. Nor is the meaning of the word *harmful* clarified. Instead, the writer diverts our attention to other issues by introducing another ambiguous phrase "good living to the loggers." He could then lead us into debating whether the loggers have a right to maintain their livelihood, diverting attention from the profits and responsibilities of the lumber companies. We might not even notice the writer's assumption that nothing is harmful as long as it provides an income for someone.

Finally, there is the more familiar bumper-sticker example of a fallacious red herring argument:

- Guns don't kill people. People do.

In this case, the argument does not prove the claim that guns do not kill people. Nor does it prove an implied claim that guns in themselves are not harmful. Instead it distracts attention into arguing about the nature of people. In addition, this slogan also serves as a false dilemma argument, since the issue is not a matter of either people or guns, but of both necessarily operating together to kill other people.

Class Discussion

Study the following examples of red herring arguments. For each one, determine (a) the issue and (b) the diversion.

1. TV can't be harmful to children, because it occupies their attention for hours and keeps them off the streets. (S. Morris Engel, *With Good Reason,* St. Martin's Press, 1982)
2. Those who are so ferociously involved in Mothers Against Drunk Driving would better spend their time in working with A.A. to help alcoholics.
3. Why are you always nagging at me about the way I drive?
4. Person A: I oppose school voucher programs because they undermine the public school system and give subsidies to rich families who can already afford to send their children to private schools.
   Person B: I am not going to engage in class warfare. The real issue here is opportunity.
5. When Supreme Court Justice Scalia was asked why he refused to recuse himself in a case involving his duck-hunting friend Dick Cheney, Scalia said, "If a person can be so cheaply influenced, then this country is in a bad way."
6. John Kerry: "Exporting jobs overseas causes job losses in the U.S."
   John Snow, Treasury Secretary: "Not so. The practice of moving American jobs to low-cost countries is part of trade and there can't be any doubt about the fact that trade makes the economy stronger."

Pointing to Another Wrong

> The **fallacy of pointing to another wrong** is also called two wrongs make a right. It distracts attention from a wrong-doing by claiming that similar actions went unnoticed or unpunished.

This fallacy is also called two wrongs make a right because it assumes that two wrongs cancel one another out. This weak defense can go unnoticed because it diverts attention into other issues, such as discussing whether or not the other instances are relevant or related. Pointing to another wrong can also divert attention from the issue by making attacks that would lure another to focus on self-defense. Consider these examples of pointing to another wrong, and discuss, either with a class partner or in writing, how each argument lacks reasonable support.

1. Student to instructor: "Why are you getting after me for being late to class? You never say anything to that pretty woman who comes late to class every day."

2. Motorist to police officer: "Why are you giving me a ticket for going the wrong way on a one-way street? Didn't you see that red sedan I was following doing the same thing?"

3. So what if I don't separate the cans and newspapers out from the garbage for recycling. I don't have that much time. Neither do most other people.

4. The politically correct people will tell you that Columbus brought oppression, slavery, and genocide to the peaceful Indians. But Indians committed as many atrocities against the white people as well as against one another.

5. Why do you complain about cruelty to animals in scientific experiments? Look at the way animals are cruel to one another. Have you ever seen the way lions bite into the necks of zebras, rip open their insides, then eat their hearts and entrails?

Straw Man

> The **straw man fallacy** makes a false replica of an opposing argument, then destroys it. It uses caricature, ridicule, and oversimplification by way of refutation. It can also attack and disprove an insignificant point in an argument, then claim that the whole argument has been demolished as a result.

This fallacy appears in three variations. In the first, it misrepresents and distorts the argument opposed.

- Those who are in favor of national health care want to give us army-style medicine. If the government starts running health care for us, we'll find ourselves waiting all day in barracks full of sick people, while the doctors are shuffling through piles of red tape in their offices and leaving for home by the time our turn arrives.

- When you support picketing, you are supporting a conspiracy to commit extortion through disruption of business, intimidation, and slander. I have no sympathy for strikers who always have the option of going to work for someone else if they don't like the compensation or conditions offered by their employer. I feel they have no right to force the employer to change employment policy to suit them. Why does hiring people to do a specific job, for specific pay, force the employer to practically adopt the employee, catering to him or her from the cradle to the grave? It must be stopped and the extortionists jailed for long terms.

- I am bewildered by those who support the "three strikes and you're out" law. This tough position denies all possibility for change in people. With it, we turn our backs on these people, saying they can never get better. Thus, we buy into a cycle of hate and fear in a total rejection of love and compassion, locking ourselves up in our houses of fear just like we lock up the prisoners in our prisons.

Second, the straw man fallacy can attack one trivial aspect of an idea, cause, or person and then pretend that this one aspect represents what is most essential about the whole.

- I can't respect Hindus because they wear those red spots painted on their foreheads.

- He can't stand the Germans; you know, all those "oompah pah" bands, the beer drinking, and all those thigh-slapping guys dancing in their leather shorts.

Third, a straw man argument may seek to discredit an idea on the basis of objections that are beside the point.

- Doctor: "You need to get more exercise. Why don't you walk to work?"
  Patient: "I can't walk to work—I work at home!"

- Father: "Why don't you wear your helmet when you ride your motorcycle? It's both unsafe and illegal to go without it."
  Son: "Dad, I can't do that. It's not cool."

- Boss: "What we need to get this business off the ground is for all the employees to meet together on a regular basis."
Manager: "But we don't have a meeting room large enough for all of us!"

Circular Reasoning

> The **fallacy of circular reasoning** is the assertion or repeated assertion of a conclusion without reasons being given to support it. It may imply that the conclusion is self-evident or rephrase the conclusion to sound like a reason.

The fallacy of circular reasoning creates an illusion of support by simply asserting its conclusion as though it were a reason, or by reasserting the same claim in different words. In translation, this argument says that "*A* is true because *A* is true."

- Kerosene is combustible; therefore it burns.

This fallacy also has another name: *begging the question,* which means to assume what one is supposed to prove, or to beg for acceptance rather than earning it through a sound argument. However, it may be easier to remember this fallacy by the term *circular reasoning* because that is just what it does: it goes in circles. Let's look at some examples:

- Taxing inheritances is justified because people should pay a tax on money they have been given by their families.

Here, the first half of the sentence is repeated in different words in the second half, as though the second half were a supporting conclusion.

- Running is good for your health. If you want to be healthy, you should run.

Circular reasoning can deceive by offering inference indicator words like *therefore* that suggest an inference is being drawn from the first claim. In actuality, however, no valid inference follows. Instead of having a conclusion and a reason, we have two conclusions.

- Adultery and fornication are wrong. Therefore, it follows that contraception is wrong.

Here, the gap between the first claim and the second is huge. If we agree that adultery and fornication are wrong, why is contraception also wrong? To make a good argument, we have to provide links of explanation to show that one claim follows logically from another.

Class Discussion

See if you can find the circular reasoning in these examples:

1. Movie stars are intelligent. If they weren't intelligent, they wouldn't be movie stars.
2. Concealed weapons should be discretionary. After all, people should have the right to conceal their guns if they wish.
3. To curse is immoral because it is wrong.
4. Elect Donna Brown supervisor—she is a mother and realtor.
5. The budget given to the Pentagon by Congress again exceeded military requests by a few billion dollars. Isn't it obvious that when we have the best-funded defense in the world, we will have the best defense in the world?
6. Interviewer at 1994 Miss USA Beauty Pagent: "Miss Alabama, if you could live forever, would you and why?"
   Miss Alabama: "I would not live forever because we should not live forever, because if we were supposed to live forever, then we would live forever, but we cannot live forever, which is why I would not live forever."

Chapter Summary

1. Word ambiguity uses undefined and vague words in an argument, seeking to gain an advantage by using words that could be interpreted in more than one way.
2. Misleading euphemisms are words that hide meaning by wrapping a less acceptable idea in positive or neutral connotations. The use of euphemisms is fallacious in an argument when the goal is to be evasive, to mislead, or to disarm awareness and objections.
3. Prejudicial language persuades through the use of loaded words that convey a bias while pretending to convey objective information.
4. Appeals to fear and pity seek to persuade by affecting emotions rather than through sound rational support for an argument.
5. Appeal to false authority seeks to influence others by citing phony or inappropriate authorities. This false authority may be a person, a tradition, or conventional wisdom. However, the appeal to an authentic and appropriate authority is not a fallacy; it can provide excellent support for claims.
6. Appeal to bandwagon is another example of the appeal to authority. In this case, the authority is the exhilarating momentum of the herd instinct.

7. Personal attack refutes another argument by attacking the opponent rather than addressing the argument itself. This fallacy can take the form of using abusive language or name-calling.

8. Poisoning the well seeks to prejudice others against a person, group, or idea and prevent their positions from being heard. This technique seeks to remove the neutrality necessary for listening and to implant prejudice instead.

9. The red herring is a ploy of distraction. It makes a claim, then instead of following through with support, it minimizes the issue or diverts attention into irrelevant issues.

10. The straw man is an argument that misrepresents, oversimplifies, or caricatures an opponent's position; it creates a false replica, then destroys the replica. The straw man also invalidates by attacking a minor point as though the whole argument depended upon it.

11. Pointing to another wrong is also called two wrongs make a right. It says, "Don't look at me; he did it too!"

12. Circular reasoning is the assertion or repeated assertion of a conclusion as though the conclusion were a reason. It can also pretend that no supporting reasons are needed. Circular reasoning assumes what it is supposed to prove.

Chapter Quiz

Identify the following arguments either as *NF* for *not fallacious* or as one of the types of fallacious arguments indicated for each section. In some cases, you may find that more than one fallacy applies; choose the one you consider the most appropriate. Be prepared to defend your answers.

Part I

In this section, look for arguments that are *misapplied euphemisms, bandwagon,* or *appeal to fear.*

_____ 1. It was announced today that our troops, who have been shelled for some weeks now in Lebanon, have made a *strategic transfer* to their ships offshore of that country.

_____ 2. In China, Europe, and Brazil, efforts are being made to control the population growth that adds 1 billion people to the planet every decade.

_____ 3. Africa, the birthplace of humankind, provides a disturbing clue to our future. As I fly across areas that were forests just years ago and see them becoming desert, I worry. Too many people crowd this continent, so poor they strip the land for food and wood for fuel. The subject of my life's work and our closest living relatives, the chimpanzees and gorillas are slaughtered for food or captured for the live-animal trade. Pollution of air, land, and water abounds. (Jane Goodall, National Geographic Society)

_____ 4. Five million people have already seen this movie. Shouldn't you?

_____ 5. Why do I think the president's program is sound? It is sound because the polls show that the vast majority supports it.

_____ 6. By a margin of two to one, shoppers prefer Brand X to any of the leading competitors. Reason enough to buy Brand X.

_____ 7. What if your bank fails and takes your life savings? Buy diamonds—the safe investment.

_____ 8. There is *virtually no tar* in these cigarettes.

_____ 9. It has been estimated that illegal aliens are costing taxpayers in excess of $5 billion a year. Should our senior citizens be denied full health care benefits, should our children suffer overcrowded classrooms in order to subsidize the costs of illegal aliens?

_____ 10. There are plenty of people out there on the streets waiting to get your job. If you go on strike, you may find yourself out there with them.

_____ 11. The *natural* way to relieve muscular pain is through our vitamin ointment. It *relieves* pain from burns, stiff neck, backache, swelling, and so forth.

Part II

In the following arguments, look for *straw man, poisoning the well, appeal to pity,* and *appeal to false authority.*

_____ 12. The majority of American educators, in a recent survey, agreed that longer school days, more homework, and longer school years would only penalize children and not necessarily result in better learning.

_____ 13. The President of the United States says that the problem of illiteracy can be solved only by longer school days, more homework, and longer school years.

_____ 14. No use listening to those repressive environmentalists and economic zero-growthers who don't have anything under their thick skulls. They oppose any sane domestic policies that allow timber companies to do their jobs.

_____ 15. Elijah Jones was the tenth victim of police brutality this year. Arrested for murdering his two children in a fit of insanity due to the pressures of poverty, he had hoped, on release from a mental institution, to make a new life for himself. But Sunday he was shot down mercilessly by the pigs when he ran from a police officer after robbing a liquor store.

_____ 16. Cigarettes are not addictive. I know this to be true because the chairman of the R. J. Reynolds Tobacco Company testified before Congress that tobacco is not an addictive substance.

■ Part III

In this section look for arguments that use *pointing to another wrong, red herring, prejudicial language,* and *circular reasoning.*

_____ 17. Using hidden notes on a test is not unethical; our professors wouldn't be where they are today if they hadn't done the same thing.

_____ 18. Maybe I do cheat on income tax, but so does everyone else.

_____ 19. When you support picketing, you support a conspiracy to commit extortion through disruption of business.

_____ 20. Some people would have us eliminate the use of all pesticides on fruits and vegetables. But both fruits and vegetables are essential for health and excellent sources of vitamins and minerals.

_____ 21. Why do you object to people smoking? What are you doing about the problems of smog pollution? Exhaust fumes are far more likely to give people lung cancer.

_____ 22. Capital punishment is justified for murder and rape because people should be put to death for violent and hateful acts.

_____ 23. Murder is morally wrong. Therefore it follows that abortion is wrong.

_____ 24. Senator X is trying to increase welfare benefits for single moms. Again he is trying to push one of his socialist ideas down our throats. Socialism has been proven to be no good.

_____ 25. The U.S. government has no right to accuse us Chinese of human rights violations when the United States has the highest crime rate in the world.

_____ 26. A spokesman for a chemical industrial firm, when charged and fined for disposing of toxic wastes in the lakes of Illinois, protested, "Thousands of other industries are doing the same thing."

CHAPTER 11

Inductive Reasoning and Inductive Fallacies:

How Do I Reason from Evidence?

© 1984. Reprinted courtesy of Bill Hoest and *Parade Magazine*.

"I forget . . . What are we making again?"

The kids in this cartoon are not following an architectural drawing or a definite mental plan but are working by trial and error. Creating as they go along, sometimes forgetting their original plan, their reasoning is haphazard and unsystematic.

Inductive reasoning is a method used to discover new information or to supply missing information. We could use it to guess what the kids are building. And the kids could use it to learn that nails alone will not keep the structure standing. When we use inductive reasoning, we observe, test, and check things out in some systematic fashion. Although it is an open-ended method of learning and discovering, it is not hit or miss, or trial and error, but has its own rules for arriving at the most reliable answers. This chapter serves as an introduction to the forms, methods, and rules of inductive reasoning.

DISCOVERY EXERCISES

■ Defining Key Terms

Using at least two dictionaries, write down definitions of the following terms:

1. Induction
2. Reasoning
3. Empirical
4. Scientific method
5. Inductive reasoning

Answering a Survey on Test Performance

Write your answers to the following questions in preparation for discussion. Use a mindmap or cluster if you wish. Pay attention to the way in which you must reason in order to reply.

1. Think of a time when you made a high score on a challenging test. What steps did you take to prepare yourself mentally, physically, and in actual study?
2. Think of a time when you did poorly on a challenging test. How did you prepare? What did you fail to do?
3. What conclusions can you draw on the basis of this comparison?

Now discuss the following questions in class:

1. Explain how you were reasoning in order to answer these questions. Was this inductive reasoning?
2. How was this reasoning similar to, or different from, the way you worked mentally as you worked in the first exercises describing a fruit, vegetable, or tool?

Looking at Inductive Reasoning

Induction comes from the Latin *inducere*, to lead in. In logic, induction is to reason to a conclusion about all members of a class on the basis of an examination of a few members of a class. Induction reasons from the particular to the general.

Your study of this text began with descriptive exercises that required you to use the inductive thinking process. Now is the time to step back and consider the forms and rules of inductive reasoning.

In this last discovery exercise, as well as in the descriptive work you did at the beginning of this book, you used inductive reasoning. You observed, gathered data, then drew inferences about patterns, configurations, and meanings. You recorded your findings and reported them. This method of researching from personal observation is basic to the **empirical** or **scientific method.** It was the approach, you will remember, used by Samuel Scudder. In this chapter, we are going to look more abstractly at the nature and structure of inductive reasoning. You will also review the rules and standards used to guide scientific research that has been developed over many centuries.

Induction reasons from evidence about *some* members of a class in order to draw a conclusion about *all* members of that class. We use inductive reasoning to help us out in situations where an examination of all the data would be an impossible or impractical task. Samplings and extrapolation enable us to estimate how many voters nationwide favor a particular candidate, how many needles there are in a haystack, or how many stars there are in the universe. This chapter discusses a number of the methods that have traditionally been used to learn about

Great Moments in Science

Used with permission of Mark Stivers

©1999 *Stivers*

1962: Bell Labs scientists discover that gravity does not function inside a ketchup bottle.

the whole from a study of its parts. They include sensory observation, enumeration, analogical reasoning, pattern recognition, causal reasoning, and statistical reasoning.

Reasoning from Sensory Observation

Major scientific discoveries have resulted from accidents that just happened to be given close attention by someone who was both a curious skilled observer and an inductive thinker.

> **Sensory observation** is the awareness of self and of the world through the basic senses of sight, touch, taste, smell, and hearing. Ancillary senses include a sense of time, weight, energy, pressure, motion, balance, direction, sexuality, feelings, emotions, pain, strength, weakness, solidity, lightness, darkness, color, fluidity, heat, cold, pitch, tonality, and vibration.

The ability to observe and infer will always remain the primary skills of a scientist. (Indeed, such skills have always been indispensable for human survival.) Even a scientist who uses instruments such as a computer, microscope, or X-ray machine still depends primarily on personal skills of reasoning from sensory information. Moreover, some of the most dramatic discoveries in the history of science resulted from simple observing of the right thing at the right time. The book *Serendipity: Accidental Discoveries in Science* by Roysten M. Roberts tells many stories of accidental discoveries that led to such inventions as quinine, electric batteries, synthetic dyes, rayon, nylon, and antibiotics. Here is a summary of one of these stories:

> In 1903 the French chemist, Edouard Benedictus, dropped a glass flask one day on a hard floor and broke it. However, to the astonishment of the chemist, the flask did not shatter, but still retained most of its original shape. When he examined the flask he found that it contained a film coating inside, a residue remaining from a solution of collodion that the flask had contained. He made a note of this unusual phenomenon, but thought no more of it until several weeks later when he read stories in the newspapers about people in automobile accidents who were badly hurt by flying windshield glass. It was then he remembered his experience with the glass flask, and just as quickly, he imagined that a special coating might be applied to a glass windshield to keep it from shattering. Not long thereafter, he succeeded in producing the world's first sheet of safety glass.

Class Discussion Question

Parallel stories of lucky scientific discoveries lie behind the inventions of penicillin, X-rays, Teflon, dynamite, and Post-Its. Describe how one of these discoveries, or any other you are familiar with, depended on both sensory observation and inductive reasoning.

Reasoning from Enumeration

Induction can involve a simple counting of parts in order to draw conclusions about wholes.

> **Enumerate** means (1) to count off or name one by one or (2) to determine a number from counting.

Induction uses enumeration in a range from simple counting to gathering statistics. The rules for good induction are concerned with how to draw the most likely and probable conclusions about wholes on the basis of a controlled sampling of parts.

This can of Chock Nuts contains exactly 485 peanuts.

This second can of Chock Nuts contains exactly 485 peanuts.

This third can of Chock Nuts contains exactly 485 peanuts.

(Therefore) all cans of Chock Nuts must contain exactly 485 peanuts.

You will notice that the conclusion drawn here uses the word "must," suggesting that its conclusion is a guess. It is a probability estimate, a projection, or an **extrapolation**. If you open a fourth can and find 500 peanuts, then you will know that the conclusion was incorrect because the sampling was insufficient. Therefore, you would have to revise your experiment to count more samples until a reliable average could be obtained.

Conclusions drawn from samplings can never be totally certain; at best they reflect probabilities. Yet probability estimates help out considerably in situations where all the facts cannot be known. If you have an old car that begins to have one or two major repair problems every six months, you can extrapolate a trend that may well continue until all parts are replaced. On the basis of this extrapolation, you may decide to buy a new car. However, you might wonder if that old clunker would have been the exception that held up forever.

Analogical Reasoning

Inductive reasoning also draws conclusions from making comparisons in the form of analogies.

> **Analogy** means (1) to find a correspondence of similarity between things that seem different or (2) an inference that if two things are alike in some respects, they will be alike in other respects.

Inductive reasoning can also be based on analogies, which are a form of comparisons. All of us learn from making comparisons. Even a one-year-old can get the idea that if adults can stand upright and walk, then so can he or she. Analogies are used in the teaching of all subjects in order to make the unfamiliar more understandable by comparison to the familiar. In the study of macroeconomics, a principle, such as how a government can control an economy, can be explained by comparison to the way a person can control the water level in a bathtub by judicious use of the faucet and the plug.

Analogical reasoning also serves as a mainstay of legal argumentation in countries such as Canada, England, and the United States, where the decisions depend on precedents; the rule of precedents means that similar cases must be decided in a similar manner. Thus, when an attorney argues a case, comparisons are made between the case in question and the past rulings and decisions.

Finally, in the sciences, analogical reasoning has resulted in many discoveries and inventions. Here are two famous examples:

- Ben Franklin proved by a simple experiment that materials of different colors absorb heat differently. He put squares of cloth of different colors on some banks of snow and left them in the sun. In a few hours he noticed that a black piece had sunk into the snow, the deepest, lighter-colored pieces less, and a white piece not at all. From this Franklin reasoned that dark colors absorb the sun's heat more readily than the paler ones, which reflect part of the sun's radiation. By analogous reasoning, he decided that people who live in tropical climates should wear white clothing.

- The invention of Velcro was based on a study of cockleburs. In the 1950s George de Mestral began to wonder why cockleburs would stick to his jacket when he went out for nature walks. When he put one under a microscope, he discovered that each seed bur was covered with hooks that were caught in the loops of his cloth jacket. Next he began to wonder if this pattern of hooks and loops could be put to some practical use. By analogous reasoning he came up with the concept of an alternative kind of fastener, which was eventually realized through manufacturing research.

Discovering Patterns

Inductive reasoning looks for patterns, notes their characteristics, and draws conclusions about their nature and significance.

> **Pattern** is a design or form that is perceived. A pattern can involve shapes, images, ideas, words, signs, entities, sounds, or smells that suggest some recognizable configuration or rhythm.

In the inductive process, sensory observation is used to note details and forms, to compare similarities and differences, and thus to recognize designs. This was the case in the discovery of Velcro, when a microscope revealed the pattern between seed bur hooks and fabric loops. Gradually such a discernment of pattern leads to inferences about their correspondences, trends, and tendencies as well as to explanations or conclusions about their nature and meaning. All the accumulated evidence might be called the *parts* and the generalizations the *whole*. In medicine, the name given to the whole is called the *diagnosis*.

> A child is brought to the doctor with the following symptoms: fever, cough, and eye inflammation. The doctor examines the patient and finds small red spots with white centers on the insides of her cheeks. The doctor begins to recognize a pattern of symptoms that could lead to a diagnosis of common measles. He knows that if a rash appears first on her neck and then on the rest of her body within three to five days, and if there is a diminution of the fever, then he can be sure of this diagnosis. However, the onset of other symptoms or the worsening of the patient's condition could suggest other possibilities.

Thus, the process of examining a patient and arriving at a correct diagnosis (and with that a correct treatment) requires not only considerable knowledge but also skills in discerning patterns and forming dependable hypotheses about them.

Reasoning From and About Causes

We use inductive reasoning to determine the probable causes of events.

> **Cause** comes from the Latin *causa*, meaning reason or purpose. Cause means that which produces an effect, or result, or a consequence; something that is responsible for an event; or a source of influence.

Induction is one form of reasoning that seeks to explain why certain things have occurred or might occur. Because our forebears wondered what caused our days to be divided between light and darkness, we gradually moved from the explanations of myths to the scientific explanations of astronomy and physics.

All humans show curiosity about causation because such knowledge makes life more predictable and thus more controllable. Every day newspapers supply us with facts and speculations concerning the causes of such events as natural disasters, crimes, and the rise and fall of the stock market. People want and need explanations of causality, although not all events can be satisfactorily explained. For instance, by 2005 there was still no official explanation for the cause and motives of the September 2001 anthrax attacks that occurred in the United States when letters containing anthrax bacteria were sent to several media offices and two U.S. senators, killing five people. Many theories have been advanced to explain the cause but none has been proven true.

Discussion/Writing Break Questions

1. Describe a time in your life when you needed to discover the cause of some event. (It could be something simple like a physical symptom or mechanical breakdown.)
2. List the causes that you first considered possible.
3. What steps did you take to discover the actual cause?
4. How did you know you had found the right answer?

Class Discussion

Inductive reasoning, whether using sensory observation, enumeration, analogies, pattern recognition, or guesses about causation, has its own rules or standards for producing the most reliable or probable conclusions. Study the following examples that use inductive reasoning and explain why each one is well or poorly reasoned.

1. The leaves on our maple tree turn red in October.

   Some years it is cold in October, and some years it is warm through October. No matter what the temperature, our tree always turns in October.

   October makes the leaves of maple trees turn red.

2. I always get a cold after I go swimming.

   I only get a cold when I go swimming.

   The cause of my colds is swimming.

3. The last ten times I flipped this coin, it came up tails.

   The next time I flip it, it is certain to be tails.

4. I get nervous when I drink coffee.
   I get nervous when I drink tea.
   I get nervous when I drink cola

   All drinks make me nervous.

5. Jules and Jim like the same dogs.
   Jules and Jim like the same foods.

   Jules and Jim must like the same people.

6. My lover promised to come see me at 8:00 P.M.
   I have waited until 4:00 A.M.

   He is not coming.

7. When I stopped smoking, I gained 10 pounds.

   Smoking keeps my weight down.

8. My wife and I know how beneficial fresh garlic can be to health, but we worried about the smell. Then we found a solution. We chop up pieces of garlic and put them inside a banana to share just before

going to bed. Afterward I have never noticed any garlic on the breath. Even the next morning, there is no garlic smell.

We believe we have discovered a cure for garlic breath.

9. I had a wart that was protruding and sore. I decided to try vitamin E. I applied the oil about two or three times a day, and in less than ten days the wart was gone.

This proves that vitamin E cures warts.

Reasoning with Hypotheses

Science formulates and tests hypotheses in order to explain and predict phenomena.

> **Hypothesis** comes from the Greek word *hupothesis,* meaning a supposition. A hypothesis is the name given to a trial idea, tentative explanation, or working assumption that can be used to further investigation.
>
> The **conclusion of an inductive study** generalizes to produce a universal claim based on empirical findings. This conclusion may or may not confirm the hypotheses tested. Yet such a conclusion remains probable rather than totally certain because further evidence could challenge its findings.

A preliminary conclusion derived from inductive reasoning is called a *hypothesis.* All of the "conclusions" given in the preceding examples were prematurely drawn; their sampling was insufficient to warrant their conclusions. In actuality they expressed untested hypotheses. Yet even if a hypothesis becomes confirmed through extensive testing, it may never be considered certain. The discovery of even one exception, or counterexample, challenges the truth of a hypothesis. Because inductive generalizations have these limitations, special precautions have to be taken in order to reach the most probable hypothesis. Thus, we learn the rules for gathering and examining evidence, for controlling variables, and for creating experiments that can be duplicated and thus tested by others. Moreover we have to be continually willing to modify and refine our hypotheses depending on the feedback we receive.

It takes time and testing to establish the truth of a hypothesis. Obviously Sir Isaac Newton's hypothesis that gravity explains an apple's perpendicular fall to the ground has not been improved upon. The discovery that a vaccination could prevent smallpox also proved to be true, although it took the interweaving of many hypotheses and many tests to establish its reliability. By 1979, vaccination had eradicated the disease worldwide.

The first hypothesis is not always the last; indeed, one hypothesis can lead to another and another, or can serve as an imaginative guide for further research. Here are two examples of the way in which hypotheses can function as working assumptions:

- A patient developed a high fever and complained of pains in the kidney area; the doctor first diagnosed a kidney infection (first hypothesis). However, on a second visit, an examination of the patient's mouth and throat revealed enlarged and swollen tonsils (new evidence), and it seemed more likely at this point that the fever and kidney pains were due to the infected tonsils (new hypothesis).

- In the eighteenth century, Europeans began to experiment with the nature of electricity. The similarity between lightning and electric sparks was observed, and it was conjectured that lightning was simply a big electric spark. Ben Franklin decided to test this hypothesis. Using analogous reasoning, he noticed that lightning and electric sparks were similar in color and in shape, that they traveled at about the same speed, and that both killed animals. Franklin published a proposal suggesting that a "sentry box" be built on a high tower with a man inside on an insulated platform who would draw sparks from passing clouds with a long pointed iron rod (test for a hypothesis). Before Franklin got around to trying out this experiment himself, it was conducted in France, and it was proved that clouds are electrified (confirmation of the hypothesis). Franklin then found a way to verify his hypothesis again, using his well-known kite experiment. He fixed a sharp-pointed wire to the top of a kite, then knotted a large iron key between the kite string and a length of ribbon used for insulation. When a storm cloud passed by, Franklin saw the fibers of the kite string stand on end and drew a spark from the key with his knuckle (second confirmation of the hypothesis in an experiment conducted under different conditions).

Class Discussion

Following are four examples of inductive reasoning that include hypotheses. Read and underline the hypothetical statements, and discuss whether you find adequate support for these hypotheses. What other hypotheses might better explain some of these situations? Note also whether each example uses analogies, extrapolates and predicts from patterns, speculates about cause and effect, or gathers data and statistics.

1. A study of high school students in ten major U.S. cities showed that four out of every five were not coffee drinkers. It was conjectured that this statistic could be due to TV commercials showing only older

people drinking coffee. A new advertising promotional scheme was devised to seek to change this ratio by showing teenagers enjoying coffee at athletic events, during class breaks, and on dates to see if it might change this ratio.

2. I have been wearing a wool knitted cap for the past ten years. People think it is strange, but it has kept me from having sore throats. Before I started wearing the cap, I had sore throats all the time. But since I started wearing it, I have not had any.

3. Japanese government officials and auto industry spokesmen said American drivers might be having trouble with their Japanese-made seat belts because their cars are too dirty. They reported finding animal hair in American cars, pieces of food, and soft drink drippings. In Japan, people do not drink or eat in their cars or even wear shoes. This explanation for the faulty seat belts (whose release button gradually became brittle and would not lock securely) came in response to reports that federal safety officials in the United States were planning to recall and repair defective seat belts in 9 million cars. The Japanese manufacturers said that they had received no complaints in Japan about the 4.79 million vehicles on the road with the same seat belts. (Summarized from an article in the *San Francisco Chronicle,* May 23, 1995)

4. World bicycle production increased to more than 110 million units in 1994. The trend has been rising steadily since 1970. Bikes have been found to be speedier and more efficient than cars in gridlocked U.S. cities for couriers, pizza deliverers, police, and paramedics. Developing countries, where bikes have long been popular, are also finding new uses for bikes, such as in El Salvador where they are used for trailer towing. The potential for their further growth is great. They hold promise of becoming a valuable, environmentally friendly means of transportation. (Data summarized from *Vital Signs 1995*)

Reasoning Through Statistics and Probability

Induction uses the sciences of statistics and probability to gather, organize, and interpret data and make predictions with these data.

Statistics: The mathematics of the collection, organization, and interpretation of numerical data.

Probability: In statistics, the ratio of the number of actual occurrences of a specific event to the total number of possible occurrences.

Inductive reasoning can work with statistical samplings (a form of enu-meration) and make predictions on the basis of an estimate of probabili-ties. For example, the payoffs for betting on the winners of horse races are determined by inductive reasoning. Suppose you read in the papers that today at Green Meadows racetrack the following horses will run with the odds as listed: Post Flag, 9.90 to 1; Bru Ha Ha, 3.40 to 1; Plane Fast, 6.80 to 1; En-Durance, 5.20 to 1. These odds are based on the Racing Association's estimates of each horse's chance of winning. Bettors who pick winners will be paid an amount equal to the first number in each of these odds for each dollar bet.

The field of mathematics known as statistics is a science that seeks to make accurate predictions about a whole from a sampling of its parts. Probability and statistics have yielded some basic rules for evaluating the reliability of conclusions drawn by inductive reasoning from statistical samplings. For the purposes of our introduction to the subject, there are five basic rules:

1. The *greater the size of the sample* (or number of study subjects), the greater is the probability that that sample is representative of the whole population or group it is supposed to represent.

The results of a survey of the coffee-drinking habits of students in one high school based on questioning only ten students would obviously not be as reliable as the results of a survey of the whole student body. However, samplings are made for the sake of convenience or necessity, and the same information can be extrapolated for a full population when some rules for size, margin of error, and random selection are followed. These rules are taught in the study of statistics. Yet, without knowing all these rules, you can still estimate that a survey of ten students could not speak for a whole high school, or one high school for all U.S. high schools.

2. The *more representative* the sample is of a population, the more likely it is that accurate conclusions will be drawn about the full population from the sample.

In a poll seeking a representative sampling of menopausal women in Illinois, the most representative respondents would probably be Illinois women between the ages of forty and sixty. Less likely to be representative would be women under the age of thirty. Moreover, a survey limited to women in their forties would also not be representative, nor would a survey of women in the city of Chicago only.

3. One *counterexample* can refute a generalization arrived at through inductive reasoning.

If you complain that your friend *always* comes late and is *never* reli-able, and then one day your friend arrives early, you have a counterexam-ple that refutes your generalization.

4. If statistical evidence is offered, it should be offered in *sufficient detail* to permit verification. Sources or background material about the researchers should also be cited so others can determine their reputation and independence from vested interests in the study's outcome.

In the following example, consider the vague references to "independent laboratory tests" as well as to the research data used to support the claims:

> FATOFF has been proven to cause weight loss. After years of research and expensive experimentation, an independent laboratory with expertise in biotechnology has finally uncovered a naturally occurring substance that can be taken orally in tablet form. Now it is being made available to millions of overweight men and women who are losing as much as 10 lbs. a month. It has taken over 15 years of research and over 200 medically documented studies to produce FATOFF. But there is only one catch: FATOFF is expensive to produce.

5. When polls are taken, it is important to know not only whether a *reputable organization* or agency (such as Gallup, Roper, or Harris) took the poll but also the *exact formulation* of the question.

Compare the following questions:

(*a*) Do you favor a constitutional amendment that declares, "The English language shall be the official language of the United States"?

(*b*) English is the language of the United States by custom, although not by law. In order to avoid the political upheavals over language that have torn apart Canada, Belgium, Sri Lanka (Ceylon), India, and other nations, would you favor legislation designating English the official language of the United States?

The first question might elicit quite a different response than the second.

When you hear or read about polls, be sure to see if the exact wording of the question is given so that you can analyze it for bias. Also, do not accept without question results from polls identified only vaguely as "a recent poll." If the pollster's name is given, consider whether it was an independent source or a source filtering information to represent its own political or commercial interests. You need to be able to determine whether the source was unbiased and whether the results are verifiable.

Class Discussion

The following examples offer statistical evidence. Rate the statistics given in each as *reliable* or *not reliable* and then state what rule or standard you used in making your judgment.

1. According to the Center for Academic Integrity at Duke University, three quarters of college students confess to cheating at least once.

And a *U.S. News* poll found 90 percent of college kids believe cheaters never pay the price. [*U.S. News* poll of 1,000 adults (including an oversample of 200 college students) conducted by Celinda Lake of Lake Snell Perry & Associates and Ed Goeas of the Tarrance Group. Oct. 18–23, 1999. Margin of error: plus or minus 3.5 percent.] (*U.S. News & World Report,* November 22, 1999)

2. I would guess that the average office female makes 509 visits to the lavatory to a male's 230, and spends 10.7 minutes there to a male's 2.5. What management is going to put up with this "primp time" featherbedding at equal pay? (Edgar Berman, guest columnist, *USA Today*)

3. It was May 1971 when Russell Bliss, a waste hauler, sprayed oil at Judy Piatt's stables in Moscow Mills, Mo., to help control the dust. A few days later hundreds of birds nesting in the stable's rafters fell to the ground and died. Soon, more than 20 of her cats went bald and died, as did 62 horses over the next three and a half years. Piatt herself developed headaches, chest pains and diarrhea, and one of her daughters started hemorrhaging. In 1974 the federal Centers for Disease Control in Atlanta identified the culprit as dioxin and traced it to Bliss's oil, which contained wastes from a defunct hexachlorophene plant that had paid him to dispose of it. Bliss, it turned out, had sprayed the waste-oil mixture on horse arenas, streets, parking lots and farms throughout the state, leaving what state Assistant Attorney General Edward F. Downey called "a trail of sickness and death." (*Newsweek,* March 7, 1983)

Composition Writing Application

■ *Working from Facts to Inferences to Hypotheses*

Follow these steps in this assignment:

1. Skim through books that list facts, such as *The Information Please Almanac, The Book of Lists, The People's Almanac,* and *Statistical Abstracts of the United States.*

2. Find a group of related facts on one subject and write them down.

3. Draw all the inferences you can that would explain what these facts mean. Write them down as a list of potential conclusions.

4. From these, select one conclusion that seems to you to be the most likely hypothesis to explain the facts' meaning.

5. Discuss this hypothesis and list what further facts you would need to determine whether or not it is true.

6. Make this a short essay assignment of at least two pages.
7. Title your paper with a question your hypothesis seeks to answer.
8. Make your thesis the answer to that question.

● STUDENT WRITING EXAMPLE

WHY ARE THERE FEWER INJURIES IN HOCKEY THAN IN OTHER TEAM SPORTS?
Shamma Boyarin

The Facts
Team sport injuries reported in U.S. hospitals in 1980*:
 463,000 injuries related to football
 442,900 injuries related to baseball
 421,000 injuries related to basketball
 94,200 injuries related to soccer
 36,400 injuries related to hockey

*Source: Susan Baker, *The Injury Fact Book* (Lexington, MA: Lexington Books, 1984).

Why Were Fewer Injuries Related to Hockey Reported?
Potential Conclusions or Hypothesis

1. Hockey is a less dangerous sport.
2. People who play hockey are tougher and less likely to go to the hospital with injuries.
3. Hockey is a less popular sport, so fewer people are injured.
4. Hockey is more safety conscious than other sports.

Discussion
On the basis of my knowledge of all five sports, I would say that hockey is the most dangerous. And this factor of danger leads to three practices that make hockey different from the other team sports:

1. Hockey players, even nonprofessionals, are more likely to wear protective gear.
2. The rules of hockey are designed to prevent unnecessary injuries as much as possible. Referees enforce these rules more rigorously than in other sports.
3. Because it is a very tiring game, players are allowed to rest more often. A player with a minor injury can rest more and not aggravate the injury.

Because of these precautions, I do not think that the first two hypotheses are likely. As for the third, hockey may be a less popular sport, and this may contribute to the smaller number of injuries, but I don't think this can account for its dramatic difference from the rest. I do not think that hockey is a less popular sport than soccer, which reported nearly three times as many injuries. Therefore, I select the final hypothesis as the most likely reason for fewer injuries in hockey; namely, hockey's players and officials are more safety conscious.

Supporting Argument for the Thesis

I don't know how many people injured in hockey were in fact wearing protective gear, or how many of the injuries could have been prevented by such gear, so I can't prove that protective gear prevented injuries. I also don't know how many games with injuries were official games following strict rules. After all, a player injured in a neighborhood game can step out whenever he feels like it. Also the word *related* is vague. Does this include bystanders? Is a baseball fan hit in the stands with a baseball included in "baseball related injuries"? During the 1994 football game between Atlanta and San Francisco, two players started fighting. Their teams were penalized, but they continued playing. If it had been a hockey game, both players would have been thrown out of the whole game. Since hockey has such a violent reputation, the referees are more strict with brawling players.

Finally, I can compare hockey to what I have read about injuries in football. Last year, *Sports Illustrated* ran an article on head injuries in professional football. The magazine pointed out that many injuries could be prevented by changing the rules a little as well as by putting an extra shell on players' helmets. They cited one player who said that wearing such a shell did not hinder his performance. However, the NFL has not adopted these suggestions, which seems to indicate my theory is correct: there are fewer injuries in hockey because its players and officials are more safety conscious.

Used with permission of Shamma Boyarin.

Scoring for Working from Facts to Inferences to Hypotheses

1. Minimum of two pages. *10 points*
2. Title includes question your hypothesis seeks to answer. *10 points*
3. Group of related facts listed taken from identified source. *10 points*
4. Imaginative list of (more than three) inferences that could be drawn from these facts. *20 points*
5. Further facts needed to determine reliability of hypotheses listed. *10 points*
6. Adequate support for argument defending hypothesis. *30 points*
7. No distracting errors of spelling, punctuation, sentence structure. *10 points*

Chapter Summary

1. Inductive reasoning is the process of thinking that you used in describing a fruit, vegetable, or tool in Chapter 1 when you began by not knowing the identity of the covered object.
2. The inductive method is also called the empirical or scientific method. It appeared in the reading by Samuel Scudder.
3. Induction reasons from evidence about some members of a class in order to form a conclusion about all members of that class.
4. Induction can be done through sensory observation, enumeration, analogous reasoning, causal reasoning, and pattern recognition.
5. A hypothesis is a trial idea that can be used to further investigation in an inductive study. The conclusion of an inductive study is a generalization that is probable but not certain.
6. Inductive reasoning is used as a method for obtaining information when it would be impossible to examine all the data available. This is done by taking statistical samplings or by making extrapolations.
7. The five basic rules for evaluating the reliability of hypotheses based on statistical samplings are as follows:
   a. The greater the size of the sample, the greater is its probability of being representative of the whole of a population.
   b. A sampling must be representative in order to lead to reliable results.
   c. One counterexample can refute a generalization arrived at through inductive reasoning.
   d. Statistical evidence should be offered in sufficient detail for verification.
   e. When evaluating the results of polls, it is important to examine both the polling agency and the polling question for bias.

Chapter Quiz

Rate the following statements as *true* or *false*. If you decide the statement is false, then revise the statement to make it a true one.

_____   1. Inductive reasoning is also known as the scientific method.
_____   2. You are out swimming in the ocean and you see some fish with prominent sharp teeth swimming around you. You know that some fish with sharp teeth are predatory. You take off without waiting around to see if they might harm you. Your decision is based on analogous reasoning.
_____   3. You could use inductive reasoning to put together a picture puzzle if all the pieces were available, even if there were no

box cover to show what the whole picture would look like when it was finished.

_____ 4. There is a contest to guess how many gumballs are in a jar. You can use inductive reasoning to figure this out.

_____ 5. Inductive reasoning could help you cook a new dish by carefully following instructions from a cookbook.

_____ 6. Inductive reasoning can extrapolate reliable predictions from only one or two examples of a phenomenon.

_____ 7. Counterexamples can test or refute theories or generalizations.

_____ 8. A hypothesis is a theory that can lead to new facts and discoveries, but the hypothesis itself is not a certainty.

_____ 9. Statistical evidence is always reliable regardless of the attitudes of the people who research and present the information.

Building Arguments
Induction

The first of May 1779, the troops under General John Sullivan commenced their march but did not arrive at Wyoming until the middle of June. . . .

The village was immediately set on fire, and the rich fields of corn were cut down and trodden underfoot. On the first of September, the army left the river, and struck across the wilderness. . . .

Once or twice the Indians threatened to make a stand for their homes, but soon fled in despair, and the army had its own way. The capital of the Senecas, a town consisting of sixty houses, surrounded by beautiful cornfields and orchards, was burned to the ground and the harvest destroyed.

. . . The fourth day it reached a beautiful region, then, almost wholly unknown to the white man. . . . As the weary columns slowly emerged from the dark forest and filed into this open space . . . they seemed suddenly to be transported into an Eden. The tall, ripe grass bent before the wind—cornfield on cornfield, as far as eye could reach waved in the sun—orchards that had been growing for generations, were weighted down under a profusion of fruit—cattle grazed on the banks of a river, and all was luxuriance and beauty. . . . All about were scattered a hundred and twenty-eight houses—not miserable huts huddled together, but large airy buildings, situated in the most pleasant spots, surrounded by fruit trees, and exhibiting a civilization on the part of the Indians never before witnessed.

Soon after sunrise immense columns of smoke began to rise the length and breadth of the valley, and in a short time the whole settlement was wrapped in flame, from limit to limit; and before night those one hundred and twenty-eight houses were a heap of ashes. The grain had been gathered into them, and thus both were destroyed together. The orchards were cut down, the cornfields uprooted, and the cattle butchered and left to rot on the plain. A scene of desolation took the place of the scene of beauty, and the army camped that night in a desert.

The next day, having accomplished the object of their mission, Sullivan commenced a homeward march. . . . The thanks of Congress was presented to Sullivan and his army for the manner in which they had fulfilled their arduous task. (Joel Tyler Headley, *Washington and His Generals*, 1859, an account of the 1779 tragedy in New York State when President George Washington ordered troops to secure the frontier against the Iroquois in case they should be influenced by the English to attack Americans)

Discussion Questions

1. Is this a neutral report? Is it an ironic inductive argument?
2. What words suggest where the author's sympathy lies?
3. Does the author draw a conclusion about the significance of this event or does he leave it up to the reader?

● R E A D I N G ●

The Global 2000 Study of 1975: An Interagency Forecast Prepared Under President Jimmy Carter

Predictions or forecasts are hypotheses drawn from an inductive study. In 1975 President Jimmy Carter requested an interagency study on the problem changes in the world's population, natural resources, and environment to the end of the century. The result was the Global 2000 Study, the first and only report by any national government on the economic, demographic, resource, and environmental future of the world. As you read through this excerpt from that report, take note of those predictions that have proven to be accurate and those that have not.

The world in 2000 will be different from the world today in important ways. There will be more people. For every two persons on the earth in 1975 there will be three in 2000. The number of poor will have increased. Four-fifths of the world's population will live in less developed countries. Furthermore, in terms of persons per year added to the world, population growth will be 40 percent *higher* in 2000 than in 1975.

The gap between the richest and the poorest will have increased. By every measure of material welfare the study provides—per capita GNP and consumption of food, energy, and minerals—the gap will widen. For example, the gap between the GNP per capita in the LDCs and the industrialized countries is projected to grow from about $4,000 in 1975 to about $7,900 in 2000. Great disparities within countries are also expected to continue.

There will be fewer resources to go around. While on a worldwide average there was about four-tenths of a hectare of arable land per person in 1975, there will be only about one-quarter hectare per person in 2000. By 2000 nearly 1,000 billion barrels of the world's total original petroleum resource of approximately 2,000 billion barrels will have been consumed. Over just the 1975–2000 period, the world's remaining petroleum resources per capita can be expected to decline by at least 50 percent. Over the same period world per capita water supplies will decline by 35 percent because of greater population alone; increasing competing demands will put further pressure on available water supplies. The world's per capita growing stock of wood is projected to be 47 percent lower in 2000 than in 1978.

The environment will have lost important life-supporting capabilities. By 2000, 40 percent of the forests still remaining in the LDCs in 1978 will have been razed. The atmospheric concentration of carbon dioxide will be nearly one-third higher than preindustrial levels. Soil erosion will have removed, on the average, several inches of soil from croplands all over the world. Desertification (including salinization) may have claimed a significant fraction of the world's rangeland and cropland. Over little more than two decades, 15–20 percent of the earth's total species of plants and animals will have become extinct—a loss of at least 500,000 species.

5   Prices will be higher. The price of many of the most vital resources is projected to rise in real terms—that is, over and above inflation. In order to meet projected demand, a 100 percent increase in the real price of food will be required. To keep energy demand in line with anticipated supplies, the real price of energy is assumed to rise more than 150 percent over the 1975–2000 period. Supplies of water, agricultural land, forest products, and many traditional marine fish species are projected to decline relative to growing demand at current prices, which suggests that real price rises will occur in these sectors too. Collectively, the projections suggest that resource-based inflationary pressures will continue and intensify, especially in nations that are poor in resources or are rapidly depleting their resources.

The world will be more vulnerable both to natural disaster and to disruptions from human causes. Most nations are likely to be still more dependent on foreign sources of energy in 2000 than they are today. Food production will be more vulnerable to disruptions of fossil fuel energy supplies and to weather fluctuations as cultivation expands to more marginal areas. The loss of diverse germ plasm in local strains and wild progenitors of food crops, together with the increase of monoculture, could lead to greater risks of massive crop failures. Larger numbers of people will be vulnerable to higher food prices or even famine when adverse weather occurs. The world will be more vulnerable to the disruptive effects of war. The tensions that could lead to war will have multiplied. The potential for conflict over fresh water alone is underscored by the fact that out of 200 of the world's major river basins, 148 are shared by two countries and 52 are shared by three to ten countries. Longstanding conflicts over shared rivers such as the Plata (Brazil, Argentina), Euphrates (Syria, Iraq), or Ganges (Bangladesh, India) could easily intensify.

Finally, it must be emphasized that if public policy continues generally unchanged the world will be different as a result of lost opportunities. The adverse effects of many of the trends discussed in this Study will not be fully evident until 2000 or later; yet the actions that are necessary to change the trends cannot be postponed without foreclosing important options. The opportunity to stabilize the world's population below 10 billion, for example, is slipping away; Robert McNamara, President of the World Bank, has noted that for every decade of delay in reaching replacement fertility, the world's ultimately stabilized population will be about 11 percent greater. Similar losses of opportunity accompany delayed perceptions or action in other areas. If energy policies and decisions are based on yesterday's (or even today's) oil prices, the opportunity to wisely invest scarce capital resources will be lost as a consequence of undervaluing conservation and efficiency. If agricultural research continues to focus on increasing yields through practices that are highly energy-intensive, both energy resources and the time needed to develop alternative practices will be lost.

The full effects of rising concentrations of carbon dioxide, depletion of stratospheric ozone, deterioration of soils, increasing introduction of complex persistent toxic chemicals into the environment, and massive extinction of species may not occur until well after 2000. Yet once such global environmental problems are in motion they are very difficult to reverse. In fact, few if any of the problems addressed in the Global 2000 Study are amenable to quick technological or policy fixes; rather, they are inextricably mixed with the world's most perplexing social and economic problems.

Perhaps the most troubling problems are those in which population growth and poverty lead to serious long-term declines in the productivity of renewable natural resource systems. In some areas the capacity of renewable resource systems to support human populations is already being seriously damaged by efforts of present populations to meet desperate immediate needs, and the damage threatens to become worse.

10   Examples of serious deterioration of the earth's most basic resources can already be found today in scattered places in all nations, including the industrialized countries and the better-endowed LDCs. For instance, erosion of agricultural

soil and salinization of highly productive irrigated farmland is increasingly evident in the United States, and extensive deforestation, with more or less permanent soil degradation, has occurred in Brazil, Venezuela, and Colombia. But problems related to the decline of the earth's carrying capacity are most immediate, severe, and tragic in those regions of the earth containing the poorest LDCs.

Sub-Saharan Africa faces the problem of exhaustion of its resource base in an acute form. Many causes and effects have come together there to produce excessive demands on the environment, leading to expansion of the desert. Overgrazing, fuelwood gathering, and destructive cropping practices are the principal immediate causes of a series of transitions from open woodland, to scrub, to fragile semiarid range, to worthless weeds and bare earth. Matters are made worse when people are forced by scarcity of fuelwood to burn animal dung and crop wastes. The soil, deprived of organic matter, loses fertility and the ability to hold water—and the desert expands. In Bangladesh, Pakistan, and large parts of India, efforts by growing numbers of people to meet their basic needs are damaging the very cropland, pasture, forests, and water supplies on which they must depend for a livelihood. To restore the lands and soils would require decades—if not centuries—*after* the existing pressures on the land have diminished. But the pressures are growing, not diminishing.

There are no quick or easy solutions, particularly in those regions where population pressure is already leading to a reduction of the carrying capacity of the land. In such regions a complex of social and economic factors (including very low incomes, inequitable land tenure, limited or no educational opportunities, a lack of nonagricultural jobs, and economic pressures toward higher fertility) underlies the decline in the land's carrying capacity. Furthermore, it is generally believed that social and economic conditions must improve before fertility levels will decline to replacement levels. Thus a vicious circle of causality may be at work. Environmental deterioration caused by large populations creates living conditions that make reductions in fertility difficult to achieve; all the while, continuing population growth increases further the pressures on the environment and land.

The declines in carrying capacity already being observed in scattered areas around the world point to a phenomenon that could easily be much more widespread by 2000. In fact, the best evidence now available—even allowing for the many beneficial effects of technological developments and adoptions—suggests that by 2000 the world's human population may be within only a few generations of reaching the entire planet's carrying capacity.

The Global 2000 Study does not estimate the earth's carrying capacity, but it does provide a basis for evaluating an earlier estimate published in the U.S. National Academy of Sciences' report, *Resources and Man*. In this 1969 report, the Academy concluded that a world population of 10 billion "is close to (if not above) the maximum that an *intensively managed* world might hope to support with some degree of comfort and individual choice." The Academy also concluded that even with the sacrifice of individual freedom and choice, and even with chronic near starvation for the great majority, the human population of the world is unlikely to ever exceed 30 billion.

15　　Nothing in the Global 2000 Study counters the Academy's conclusions. If anything, data gathered over the past decade suggest the Academy may have underestimated the extent of some problems, especially deforestation and the loss and deterioration of soils.

At present and projected growth rates, the world's population would rapidly approach the Academy's figures. If the fertility and mortality rates projected for 2000 were to continue unchanged into the twenty-first century, the world's population would reach 10 billion by 2030. Thus anyone with a present life expectancy of an additional 50 years could expect to see the world population reach 10 billion. This same rate of growth would produce a population of nearly 30 billion before the end of the twenty-first century.

Here it must be emphasized that, unlike most of the Global 2000 Study projections, the population projections assume extensive policy changes and developments to reduce fertility rates. Without the assumed policy changes, the projected rate of population growth would be still more rapid.

Unfortunately population growth may be slowed for reasons other than declining birth rates. As the world's populations exceed and reduce the land's carrying capacity in widening areas, the trends of the last century or two toward improved health and longer life may come to a halt. Hunger and disease may claim more lives—especially lives of babies and young children. More of those surviving infancy may be mentally and physically handicapped by childhood malnutrition.

The time for action to prevent this outcome is running out. Unless nations collectively and individually take bold and imaginative steps toward improved social and economic conditions, reduced fertility, better management of resources, and protection of the environment, the world must expect a troubled entry into the twenty-first century.

Study/Writing/Discussion Questions

Form groups to choose and study one of the following issues before reporting back to the whole class. Issues to choose from include: Population growth, growing gap between rich and poor, oil resources, life-supporting environmental capabilities, higher prices for vital resources, natural disasters. Each group might work from the following questions:

1. In your chosen area, how close did the predictions and estimates made in this report turn out to be? Explain why.

2. Have other equally serious world problems emerged unforeseen in this report?

3. In each of these areas, to what extent were the report's recommendations heeded or ignored? Why do you think this was the case?

4. What predictions might you make about developments in your area by the year 2025?

Fallacies of Inductive Reasoning

You will probably realize that this cartoon is not only satirizing the acceptance of genetically modified foods but also playing with the fallacy of questionable statistic. While studying the material in the first part of this chapter, you learned some standards for inductive reasoning that included a few examples of poor inductive reasoning. In this second section of this chaper you will study the chief fallacies of inductive reasoning; in other words, you will learn a great deal more about how inductive reasoning can go wrong. Following is a list of the fallacies that will be covered in this chapter.

Two out of three farmers approve of genetically engineered produce.

Used with permission of Mark Stivers.

1. **Hasty generalization:** A conclusion based on insufficient evidence.

2. **Either-or fallacy:** An argument that oversimplifies a situation, asserting that there are only two choices when actually there are many.

3. **Questionable statistic:** Backing up an argument with statistics that are either unknowable or unsound.

4. **Inconsistencies and contradictions:** Offering evidence that contradicts the conclusion or making claims that contradict one another.

5. **Loaded question:** Using a biased question to obtain a predetermined answer.

6. **False analogy:** Comparing two things that have some similarities but also significant differences that are ignored for the sake of the argument.

7. **False cause:** Claiming a causal connection between events without reasonable evidence to support the claim.

8. **Slippery slope:** An unwarranted claim that permitting one event to occur would lead to an inevitable and uncontrollable chain reaction.

The Hasty Generalization

> **Hasty generalization** is the fallacy of overgeneralizing, of drawing a conclusion about the whole from an insufficient sampling of its parts.

The hasty generalization is the fallacy that occurs most often in inductive reasoning. A hasty generalization is a conclusion reached prematurely without a fair and adequate study of sufficient evidence. Often it expresses stereotypes.

1. All used car salesman are crooks. One of them sold me a lemon.

2. All old people are cheap. They never give me a fair tip when I park their cars.

3. No car mechanic can be trusted. They are only out to make a buck.

4. I waited half an hour for him to get dressed. Men are really more vain than women.

5. Chinese are tall, thin, and skinny.

In all five cases, the samplings were too small to justify the conclusions drawn from them about all used car salesmen or other groups. Hasty generalizations are familiar to all of us; we tend to make them when we feel angry, or too impatient to deal with complexities.

Hasty generalizations can also result from careless interpretations of the data:

> I read recently in a survey of U.S. medical students that tuition costs, on the average, $30,000 a year. This means that only the wealthy can still make it into the medical profession.

This is a hasty generalization because it does not consider the possibility of receiving scholarships or loans. Instead only the easiest assumption is offered to account for cost payment.

How do we avoid hasty generalizations? First, by being very careful in our use of the words *all, every, everyone,* and *no.* A single exception will disqualify any generalization preceded by one of these words, which are called *quantifiers.* Test to see if what you actually mean calls for *qualifiers* such as *in this case, in some cases,* or *it appears* or *seems* or *suggests that.* A careful use of quantifiers and qualifiers can often make the difference between an accurate statement and a fallacious one. Let's see how the following generalization differs significantly from the one given previously.

> Although this survey states that the average cost of medical school tuition is $30,000 a year, it does not state how medical students manage to pay for it. Some could be wealthy, while others might qualify for scholarships or loans. All that can be said is that a student who wants to attend medical school does have to consider the cost.

Class Discussion

Which of the following statements contain hasty generalizations? Underline the generalization and then explain why its use of quantifiers or qualifiers seems careless or based on insufficient sampling.

1. Most poor black people who live in cities are anti-Semitic. That's because their landlords are Jewish.
2. Every woman in the military that I ever met was a lesbian. They are all either lesbians or about to become lesbians.
3. Because Asian students are now becoming the majority ethnic group accepted for math and science studies into West Coast graduate schools, this suggests that Asians may be either genetically gifted in abstract thinking and/or culturally encouraged in it.
4. From 1993 to 1996, network news coverage of homicide increased 721% while the national homicide rate decreased by 20%. . . . TV executives know that if they spend more time examining stories about violent crimes, more people will tune into their broadcasts. (*The Better World Handbook,* 2001, p. 32)

5. Throughout history people have preferred the slum and the sweat-shop to the even more confining poverty of the farm. She reaches back into history, quoting a North Carolina woman born in 1899. "We didn't like the farming. It was so hot from sunup to sundown. No, that was not for me. Mill work was better." (Quoted from *The Travels of a T-Shirt in the Global Economy* by Pietra Rivoli in a book review by Tom Abate, *San Francisco Chronicle*, April 3, 2005)

6. The lower economic people are not holding up their end of the deal. These people are not parenting. They are buying things for kids—$800 sneakers—for what? And won't spend $200 for *Hooked on Phonics*. (Bill Cosby on *Jim Lehrer News Hour*, July 15, 2004)

The Either-Or Fallacy, or False Dilemma

> The **either-or fallacy** or **false dilemma** is a fallacious argument that over-simplifies a situation, maintaining that there are only two choices when actually other alternatives exist.

An argument that presumes that there are only two ways of looking at a situation—or that only one of two choices can be made—when other alternatives do exist is called the either-or fallacy, or false dilemma. Sometimes these false dilemmas appear in those frustrating questions on personality assessment tests:

1. When you see a friend coming toward you on the sidewalk, do you rush forward to greet the person or do you cross to the other side of the street?

2. Do you act impulsively rather than deliberately?

3. Do you have only a few friends or a large circle of friends?

More often, false dilemmas appear in poll questions: "Are you for or against the war on drugs?" Such questions are convenient for tabulation purposes but do not allow for weighed discriminations that reflect actual opinion. You may be in favor of aggressive federal programs to prevent the import of cocaine, but not marijuana. Or you may prefer that more funding be given to programs of rehabilitation and prevention. When confronted with either-or questions, a thoughtful person is faced with another dilemma: that of refusing both choices or of compromising with an answer that plays into the questioner's assumption and bias. The usual false dilemma argument oversimplifies a complex issue; sometimes it seeks to intimidate:

- Live free or die.
- America. Love it or leave it.
- When you have a headache, all you can do is reach for aspirin.
- Either you are with me or against me.
- The Cougar convertible: you'll either own one or want one.

In each of these cases, the argument is based on a dilemma that over-simplifies the situation to fit assumptions. Sometimes, as in these slogans and commercial appeals, the false dilemma serves as an intentional ploy to negate resistance and force agreement. Here is such an example: "Mothers of young children can either have careers or stay at home. But they can't expect both to have careers and to raise happy children." This argument is based on many assumptions.

1. A father supports the family.
2. A mother (or father) has to leave home to pursue a career.
3. Parents pay attention to their children when at home.
4. Another family member or child-care worker cannot give a young child what it needs.

A false dilemma assumes that there is only one choice, whereas imagination will allow for other options.

Class Discussion

Analyze the false dilemmas just given and offer reasons for your agreement or disagreement with their designations as such.

The Questionable Statistic

> The **questionable statistic** is the fallacy of offering statistics that are unknowable, faulty, or misleading.

Inductive reasoning requires some knowledge of statistics and how statistics can be used or misused as evidence. As you learned earlier, to evaluate whether statistics are used fairly, you need to look for such things as the size of the sample, whether it was representative and random, whether a margin for error was considered, and what the margin was. These are only some of the basics involved in assessing the reliability of statistics. The fallacy of the questionable statistic refers to confusion or deception in the use of statistics, even to the point of citing figures that would be impossible to obtain.

Recall this use of statistics, quoted earlier:

> I would guess that the average office female makes 509 visits to the lava-tory to a male's 320, and spends 10.7 minutes there to a male's 2.5. What management is going to put up with this "primp time" featherbedding at equal pay?

In this case, the author is lightly mocking the use of statistics, suggesting that his estimate can be this precise because everyone knows that his claims are true. From there he jumps to a conclusion (in the form of a question) that lacks any evidence to back up his claim about either feath-erbedding or equal pay.

When statistical claims are false or deliberately misleading, they are not always easy to detect unless we have knowledge of the laws of statis-tics. A sure warning sign is *unattributed figures,* or figures given without a citation of source, purpose, and methods of calculation.

> Why isn't alcohol illegal? It has the same rate of addiction (10 percent) as cocaine.

In this case, a critical thinker would want to know how *addiction* is being defined, how this figure was derived, who conducted the study, and whether this 10 percent figure was quoted out of context.

Here is another example, also uncited, with a flashing red sign attached:

> Illegal aliens cost American citizens $5 billion a year.

First, the word *cost* is undefined; what expenses does this term cover? Second, "illegal aliens" refers to undocumented immigrants; therefore, how were they counted, on what basis was their cost to the public estimated, and by whom? Whoever made this statement should not have made this claim at all unless she could have supplied this information as well as its source. Otherwise the reader is left wondering if the 5 billion is an *unknowable statistic.*

Here is a clearer example of pure guesswork:

> If we legalize drugs, drugs would become much cheaper, at least one-fifth the cost. Then five times as many people would buy them. Then we would have five times as many addicts, and instead of 100,000

addicted babies born to addicted mothers each year, we would have a million.

The chief weakness of this argument is that it is based on the assumption that if drugs were legal, they would be less expensive. From there, the figure of "at least one-fifth the cost" seems to be drawn out of a hat. Next are repetitions of *five*, concluding with the dreadful statistic of 1 million addicted babies. The argument commits the fallacy of the unknowable statistic, not once but four times, seeking to establish as factual guesswork calculations for a hypothetical situation with too many variables and unknowns.

Sometimes it is more obvious that the statistics quoted could not have been gathered. Consider these examples:

- Two-thirds of all thefts are never detected.
- Two-thirds of all people have thoughts they would never admit to.
- Loss in federal taxes from those who barter instead of paying cash for goods is $1 billion annually.

Class Discussion

What questions would you ask about the statistics used in the following statements?

1. Only 106 of an estimated 895 cases of rape that occurred in New England last year were reported.
2. If it is elitist to say that 30 percent of the American people are dumb in the sense of uninstructed, then I'm an elitist But it's true. (William F. Buckley, Jr.)
3. It is a known fact that people use only 10 percent of their actual potential.
4. If the *Roe v. Wade* decision remains in force until the beginning of the twenty-first century, our nation will be missing more than 40 million citizens, of whom approximately 8 million would have been men of military age. (From "It's 'Life for a Life,'" quoted in "Notes from the Fringe," *Harper's*, June 1985)
5. Milk consumption is probably the number-one cause of heart disease. America's number-one killer. By the time the average American reaches the age of fifty-two, he or she will have consumed in milk and dairy products the equivalent cholesterol contained in one million slices of bacon. In 1994 the average U.S. citizen consumed 26 ounces of milk and dairy products per day. One 12-ounce glass of whole milk contains 300 calories and 16 grams of fat. Beer is taking a bad rap—protruding stomachs on overweight people should be called milk

bellies, not beer bellies. (Robert Cohen, "Milk: the Deadly Poison," *Earth Island Journal,* Winter 1997–98)

Contradictions and Inconsistencies

> **Contradictions and inconsistencies** is the fallacy of making claims or offering evidence that contradicts the conclusion.

In the Sipress cartoon on page 333, the daughter surprises her mother by pointing out her use of two contradictory claims or premises. The daughter implies that one of the claims must be false. Here's another example of reasoning from contradictory claims.

All men are equal; it is just that some are more equal than others.

The second cartoon, by Stivers on page 334, illustrates other kinds of contradictions. He shows us the incongruity between our fear of irradiated foods, yet our susceptibility to clever marketing. He also plays with the incongruity of having irradiated foods aggressively promoted, given their usual low profile.

In political life we often hear contradictions made within or between speeches or announcements. If someone wants to please as many people as possible, discrepancies often become the consequence. Here is an example of contradictions within statements:

Of course I cannot approve of hecklers disrupting my opponent's speeches. However, I would also say that in a democracy, they also have the right to be heard as much as the speaker.

In this case, the politician wanted to defend himself from any implication that he might have benefited from a tactic that prevented his opponent from being heard. He declares his disapproval while also taking the high road of defending the hecklers' right of free speech. He does not consider the rights of the audience to hear the speaker or how a democracy might function without some rules of order.

Here is an example of a contradiction expressed in a television program interview:

VETERAN: We should not send American troops to Bosnia. No American life is ever worth being shed on foreign soil.

INTERVIEWER: But didn't you fight in World War II when American soldiers died in both Europe and Asia?

VETERAN: Well, that war was fought because one man was trying to control the world. Hitler took over Europe and his allies controlled the East.

In this case, the veteran is not able to defend his claim that "No American life is ever worth being shed on foreign soil." He makes a generalization that allows for no exceptions. Then when the interviewer confronts him with the way in which his own military career contradicts this generalization, he is unable to revise his generalization accordingly. In other words, he would have to say, "You are right. No American life is ever worth being shed on foreign soil unless it would be to stop someone like Hitler."

Class Discussion

List the contradictions you find in the following examples.

1. I love mankind; it's just that I can't stand people.
2. The Nuclear Regulatory Commission has imposed strict penalties for employees at nuclear plants found to be stoned from illicit drug use on the job; but no penalties were prescribed for workers discovered to be drunk at the nuclear controls. (David Freudberg, KCBS Radio, February 16, 1990)
3. I'd like to order one Big Mac, large fries, twenty chicken nuggets, two apple pies, one chocolate sundae, and a diet Coke, please.

"HANDGUNS FOR WORLD PEACE, SIR?"

grimescartoons.com

4. Capital punishment is our society's recognition of the sanctity of human life. (Sen. Orrin Hatch, R-Utah)

5. The more killing and homicides you have, the more havoc it prevents. (Richard M. Daley, former mayor of Chicago)

The Loaded Question

> The **loaded question** is the fallacy of using a biased question in order to obtain a predetermined result.

Loaded questions occur often in polls, as discussed earlier, in order to create a bias toward a certain answer: "Do you believe pornography should be brought into every home through television?" We are all familiar with the loaded questions "Have you stopped beating your wife?" and "Are you still a heavy drinker?" In such cases, the guilt is assumed and not proven. Any reply to the question traps the respondent into either an admission of guilt or a protest that could be interpreted as a guilty defense. Loaded questions are related to the fallacy of circular reasoning (begging the question), where conclusions are asserted without evidence or premises to support them.

Class Discussion

Which of the following are loaded questions and which are not?

1. Do you feel that a school voucher program should be permitted to dismantle U.S. public schools?
2. Where did you hide the murder weapon?
3. When are you going to stop asking me so many silly questions?
4. Are you going to be good and do what I say?
5. What would you like for dinner tonight?
6. What do you think about the new brain research that says that emotional stability is more important than IQ in determining success in life?
7. Forty-three percent of U.S. grade school children are reading below grade level. Why? Is this because they are not learning phonics?
8. What will you do on the day you discover our number one brand of arthritis medication? (Ad with picture of a woman running along a beach)
9. Why do Senate Democrats hate America?

The False Analogy

The **false analogy** is the fallacy of basing an argument on a comparison of two things that may have some similarities, but also significant differences that are ignored for the sake of the argument. (The Greek word *analogos* means "according to ratio.")

As you learned earlier, an analogy is a form of reasoning in which two things are compared. A good analogy often compares some abstract principle that is difficult to understand to a concrete familiar experience in order to make the abstract principle clearer. A good or sound analogy must compare two things or ideas that have major parallels in ratio. If one uses the analogy of a pump to explain the heart, the heart does not have to physically look like a metal pump with a handle, but it should at least function on the same principles. Here is an analogy taken from physics about the nature of subatomic particles: "If you wish to understand subatomic particles, think of them as empty space that is distorted, pinched up, concentrated into point-like ripples of energy." Here the appearance is the essential parallel that permits a visualization of something invisible to us.

In a false analogy essential parallels are missing, either overlooked or willfully disregarded.

> Well, it's too bad that so many Indians had to die as America was settled by the white men. But you can't make an omelet without breaking a few eggs.

How do we decide whether an analogy is a true or a false one? A recommended technique is to first write out the equation that the analogy offers; then under two columns, headed Similarities and Differences, compare the chief characteristics of each:

Claim: There is no convincing evidence to show that cigarette smoking is harmful. Too much of anything is harmful. Too much applesauce is harmful. (cigarette manufacturer)

Equation: Too much cigarette smoking = too much applesauce.

When we see the equation, we sense that something is not right here. For a further check, make a list of the similarities and differences between each. If the differences far outweigh the similarities, you have a false analogy.

Similarities	Differences
1. Ingested into body	1. One ingested through lungs first and is not digestible
	2. One a food, other not a food
	3. One addictive, other not
	4. Both don't affect body and consciousness in same way
	5. No evidence applesauce causes cancer, but evidence that cigarette smoking does

DISCOVERY EXERCISE

■ Evaluating Analogies

Use the procedure just demonstrated to analyze the following analogies.

1. There are no grounds for the claim that the incidence of lung cancer is higher in this county because of the presence of our oil refineries.

Cancer can be caused by all kinds of things. People don't stop eating peanut butter because it causes cancer, do they? (biologist working for an oil refinery)

2. Who is the endangered species? The spotted owl or the loggers of the Northwest?

3. We welcome immigrants because our country needs them the way old soil needs new seeds.

4. Nature is cruel. It is our right to be cruel as well. (Adolf Hitler)

5. Vote for the incumbent. Don't change horses in midstream!

Class Discussion

Rate the following examples as either good analogies or false analogies and tell why.

1. If a ban on same-sex marriages violates their civil rights, then the refusal to issue a driver's license to a blind man violates his civil rights as well. After all, gay couples can not procreate any more than a blind man can safely drive a car in traffic. (Letter to the editor, *San Francisco Chronicle*, March 16, 2005)

2. People and politicians, who really . . . don't know enough about the issue of acid rain have been brainwashed by the media and environmentalists into believing that we, in Ohio, are the primary cause of the decay. The biggest killers of human life in the U.S. are automobiles, cigarettes and alcohol. Yet none of these products have been banned. Americans, and no Americans more than we in the coal fields, want to see a healthy and safe environment for all generations to come, but we just cannot accept legislation such as this without a scientific basis. (Rep. Douglas Applegate, D-Ohio, speaking against a House bill to require federally mandated emission limitations on the largest sources of sulphur dioxide)

3. If you take a piece of meat and throw it in a pack of hungry dogs, they are going to kill each other over it. If you don't have any opportunities available to you, and something that can make you easy money (selling crack cocaine) comes up, what are you going to do? (Paris, Oakland rap artist)

4. Measuring a country's health by measuring its gross domestic product is rather like measuring a person's health by how much medical care he buys. Thus, a person who just had bypass surgery and cancer radiation treatments would be considered healthy.

5. If children cannot be executed for crimes, why should we execute retarded people with the minds of children?

False Cause

> **False cause** is the fallacy of claiming a causal connection between events without reasonable and sufficient evidence to support the claim.

Inductive reasoning is used to speculate about cause or to determine cause. The criminal justice system uses inductive reasoning to gather evidence to determine guilt or innocence. Faulty reasoning about causality can result in the arrest and conviction of an innocent person or the release of a guilty person. A trial presents evidence to the jury as support for causality in a crime.

False cause is a fallacious argument that insists on a causal connection between events that cannot reasonably be connected. False cause can also be an interpretation that is oversimplistic. Sometimes false cause reasoning can be ludicrous, as shown in the little Sufi teaching stories about Nasrudin, which were designed to teach good thinking habits:

> Nasrudin was throwing handfuls of crumbs around his house.
> "What are you doing?" someone asked him.
> "Keeping the tigers away."
> "But there are no tigers in these parts."
> "That's right. Effective, isn't it?"
> "When I was in the desert," said Nasrudin one day, "I caused an entire tribe of horrible and bloodthirsty Bedouins to run."
> "However did you do it?"
> "Easy. I just ran, and they ran after me."
> Two men were quarrelling outside Nasrudin's window at dead of night. Nasrudin got up, wrapped his only blanket around himself, and ran out to try to stop the noise. When he tried to reason with the drunks, one snatched his blanket and both ran away.
> "What were they arguing about?" asked his wife when he went in.
> "It must have been the blanket. When they got that, the fight broke up."

From Idries Shah, *The Exploits of the Incomparable Mulla Nasrudin* (New York: Dutton, 1972). Reprinted with permission of The Octagon Press, Ltd., London.

Blaming the wrong target is one kind of false cause. More frequent are those false causes that vastly oversimplify a situation, such as scapegoating. The term *scapegoating* refers to the ancient practice of offering ritual sacrifices for the appeasement of some god or some person or persons. Although we may now think sacrificing maidens on altars to the gods is barbaric, scapegoating rituals still abound in our personal, political, and social lives.

Another version of false cause is known in Latin as *post hoc ergo propter hoc,* meaning "after this, therefore because of this." The post hoc fallacy reasons in a childlike way that because one event happened after another event, the second was caused by the first.

- First my cat ate a mouse, and then she had kittens. The mouse gave her the kittens.

- He committed the murder, but he couldn't help himself because he was under the influence of a sugar high after eating Twinkies.

Sometimes false cause arguments center around debates on the chicken-or-egg questions. The fictional character Nasrudin confuses us with his own confusion as he attributes his running away from the Bedouins as the cause of their running after him. Here are two contrasting chicken-or-egg arguments:

- The violence on the home screen follows the violence in our lives. (Del Reisman, president, Writers Guild of America)

- Violence on TV is definitely a cause of the growing violence in our lives. It presents violence as an appropriate way to solve interpersonal problems, to get what you want out of life, avenge slights and insults and make up for perceived injustices. (Leonard D. Eron, professor of psychology)

Finally, all the examples of causal reasoning discussed here contain a traditional Western assumption that causality is linear, that one effect must result from one cause. More recently, science has begun to use *systems thinking* to study causality in a manner that is ecological, taking the widest perspective of context, of interrelated parts and cycles. Systems thinking is concerned with the way in which the wolf's predator role is actually essential to the health of the deer. Systems thinking reveals the folly of attempting to protect the deer by killing off the wolves, which leads in turn to an overpopulation of the deer, overgrazing, and eventually mass deer starvation. When we engage in systems thinking, we avoid the fallacious reasoning that results from the assumption that causality is always single and linear.

Class Discussion

False or questionable cause is a fallacy that is often found in political arguments. Analyze the following statements. Decide if you agree or disagree that they are examples of the fallacy of false cause and state why.

1. As a white nation, we wish to survive in freedom in our own fatherland, and we demand to be governed by our own people. South Africa must retain the fatherland given us by God. (Andries P. Treurnicht,

leader, far-right conservative party, South Africa; speech reported in *The Los Angeles Times,* May 28, 1986)

2. The corruption of American youth has been caused by rock and roll music. Its rhythms and lyrics, together with the role models provided by its singers and musicians, have encouraged experimentation with drugs and promiscuity.

3. Forests are disappearing fast from the world. Loss has been caused by logging, mining, the development of energy, farming, pollution. During the 1980's 8 percent of the world's tropical forest was lost. Another 10 percent of all the world's forests may be lost by 2050. (*Atlas of the Future,* 1998)

4. Americans buy Japanese cars, cameras, and stereos because they are unpatriotic. An ad campaign appealing to their patriotism could reverse this trend.

5. State-sponsored affirmative action, bilingual education, and multi-culturalism are promoting dangerous levels of ethnic group tensions and conflicts.

The Slippery Slope

> **Slippery slope** is the fallacy of arguing, without sufficient proof, that if one event is allowed to occur, a disastrous and uncontrollable chain reaction will result. The slippery slope appeals to fear and urges agreement on the basis of a situation that contains too many variables and unknowns.

The slippery slope is another fallacy that deals with causation. In this case the claim is made that permitting one event to occur would set off an uncontrollable chain reaction. In politics this is also called the domino theory: if one country falls, so will all the rest like a line of dominoes. This argument was often given as a reason that the United States should stay in Vietnam: if Vietnam fell to the communists, China would take over the rest of Asia.

The same argument was also cited for the U.S. presence in El Salvador: if El Salvador fell to the guerrillas, so would all of Central America and Mexico, thus jeopardizing the whole Western hemisphere. Although these were predictions of a possible scenario, as arguments they were fallacious in that they urged agreement on the basis of logic for a position that contained many variables and unknowns.

Here are three examples of arguments built on the fallacy of the slippery slope:

- If you offer people unemployment insurance, they will become lazy and expect the government to support them for life.
- Sex education in the schools leads to promiscuity, unwanted pregnancies, and cheating in marriages.
- If you teach critical thinking in an Indian university, the young people would go home and question, then disobey their parents. Their families would quarrel and break up. Then they would question their bosses and everyone else. The next thing you know the whole country would fall apart. (comment made by a University of Bombay professor)

Class Discussion

Which of the following arguments are slippery slopes? Explain why.

1. I cannot support the "three strikes and you're out" law. This tough position denies all possibility of change in people. With it, we turn our backs on these people, saying they can never get better. Thus,

we buy into a cycle of hate and fear in a total rejection of love and compassion, locking ourselves up in our houses of fear just like we lock up the prisoners in our prisons. (Letter to the editor, *San Francisco Chronicle*, November 30, 1997)

2. A widely acclaimed and disturbing study out of the University of Vermont has shown a "decline in emotional aptitude among children across the board." Rich and poor, East Coast or West Coast, inner city or suburb, children today are more vulnerable than ever to anger, depression, anxiety—a massive emotional malaise. The result is that boys who can't control their emotions later commit violent crime; girls who can't control emotion don't get violent, they get pregnant. (Daniel Goleman, *Emotional Intelligence*, New York: Bantam, 1995)

3. Considering the legal union of same-sex couples would shatter the conventional definition of marriage, change the rules that govern behavior, endorse practices which are completely antithetical to the tenets of all the world's major religions, send conflicting signals about marriage and sexuality, particularly to the young, and obscure marriage's enormously consequential function—procreation and childrearing. (William Bennett, "Leave Marriage Alone," *Newsweek*, June 3, 1996)

4. We are using about two-thirds of our oil supply right now to burn in cars and airplanes and trucks. But we're producing about 40 percent of what we use in this country. And we're using 25 percent of the entire world's production of oil right now and we only have five percent of the population. So what's going to happen when a country like China, for example, comes on line and begins to rise to the level of consumerism that we have in this country? They purchased about two million cars last year; we put about 17 million on the road. And as that goes up in China we're going to see an incredible increase in world demand for oil. And when demand goes up and supply does not keep pace with it, then the prices go up. And that's what we mean by the end of cheap oil. (Bill Allen, "The End of Cheap Oil," Editorial, *National Geographic*, 2004)

Chapter Summary

1. Hasty generalization is the fallacy of basing a conclusion on insufficient evidence.

2. The either-or fallacy, or false dilemma, is an argument that oversimplifies a situation, asserting that there are only two choices when actually other alternatives exist.

3. The questionable statistic is the statistic that is either unknowable or unsound.

4. Inconsistency in evidence is the fallacy of offering evidence that contradicts the conclusion.

5. The loaded question is the use of a biased question that seeks to obtain a predetermined answer.

6. The false analogy is a comparison of two things that have some similarities but also significant differences that are ignored for the sake of the argument.

7. False cause is the fallacy of claiming a causal connection between events without reasonable evidence to support the claim.

8. The slippery slope is the fallacy of claiming without sufficient proof that permitting one event to occur would lead to a chain reaction that could not be stopped. It ignores the many variables or unknowns in the situation.

Chapter Quiz

Identify the following ten arguments in this section by name, either as *NF* for *not fallacious* or as *slippery slope, false cause, questionable statistic,* or *inconsistencies and contradictions.*

_____ 1. All riders on the buses in a Boston suburb now pay for their rides with special credit cards. All buses are equipped with electronic scanners that record account number, route, time, and date. The American public is being conditioned for the complete Big Brother totalitarian surveillance of the future.

_____ 2. The French and the German objections to importing British beef are purely a matter of their stubborn national pride. There is no reason to fear that this beef would infect any of their citizens with mad cow disease.

_____ 3. Any regulations that dampen corporate profits in the oil and coal industries will backfire because environmental preservation depends heavily on the health of the U.S. economy. The richer the United States is, the more it can help poorer countries with their pollution problems. (Public representative of a coalition of oil and gas producers)

_____ 4. Some people hesitate to have children because of the expense and trouble. The trouble of having children is entirely secondary to the blessing.

_____ 5. Legalizing marijuana would reduce the price by 50 percent.

_____ 6. The reason that I didn't stop for that light was that it was two o'clock in the morning.

_____ 7. If the baseball players start using drugs, then so will the managers, and the next thing you know all the games will be fixed and baseball will no longer be a real American sport.

_____ 8. You should never lie to your partner, although a little white lie never hurts.

_____ 9. A CIA internal investigation found no evidence linking its employees, agents or operatives with the crack cocaine epidemic in the U.S. and no connection between the agency and three men at the center of that drug trade. The findings . . . dispute allegations made by the *San Jose Mercury News* in 1996 of a CIA link to cocaine trafficking in California. The CIA released the first of two volumes of conclusions reached by agency Inspector General Frederick Hitz, who led a 17-member team that reviewed 250,000 pages of documents and conducted 365 interviews. (Associated Press release, January 30, 1998)

_____ 10. All people are equal but some deserve more privilege.

Identify the remaining ten arguments as *nonfallacious, loaded question, false analogy, hasty generalization,* or *either-or fallacy.*

_____ 11. More than any other time in history, mankind faces a crossroads. One path leads to despair and utter hopelessness. The other, to total extinction. Let us pray we have the wisdom to choose correctly. (Woody Allen, "My Speech to the Graduates" *Side Effects,* 1980)

_____ 12. Son, listen, you talk like I do, you even like the same food I do. You're gonna become a musician like me. Don't fight it!

_____ 13. Are you still getting into the movies without paying?

_____ 14. Either you stay in school or you get a job. You can't do both!

_____ 15. One of the major causes for the rapid growth of the European population in the nineteenth century was the improvement of medical knowledge.

_____ 16. When you do laundry, you should separate light clothing from dark clothing and wash each separately, because light articles streak dark ones and the dark items bleed on the light ones.

_____ 17. Is two months' salary too much to spend for something that lasts forever? (ad for diamonds)

_____ 18. I was turned down in two job interviews. I guess I just don't have what it takes.

_____ 19. Are you still fooling around with that guy?

_____ 20. Women, like rugs, need a good beating occasionally.

Advanced Optional Short Research Assignment

■ *Detecting Fallacies in an Argument*

So far, you have been examining fallacies in examples abstracted from the context in which they appear. The purpose of this assignment is to give you the opportunity to search for fallacies in an argument, to extract them, and to discuss the manner in which they affect the argument as a whole. This is a research assignment, for which you will need to find a short argument. A good source for short arguments that often contain fallacies is letters to editors. Comb newspapers and magazines for your choice, and photocopy it to accompany your analysis. Your parameters will be as follows:

1. *Topic:* Fallacies in an argument.
2. *Approach:* Critical analysis.
3. *Form:* Exposition and argumentation. Identify the fallacies involved and explain whether they affect or do not affect the soundness of the argument.
4. *Length:* Two typed pages, plus a photocopy of the argument.

CHAPTER 12

Deductive Reasoning:

How Do I Reason from Premises?

"I was a good boy, grandpa was a good boy, his father was a good boy. In fact, since the dawn of history, there have only been good boys in this family. That's why you have to be a good boy."

In this cartoon, the father uses both inductive and deductive reasoning to make his point. Yet his son looks more dismayed than convinced. If the son could defend himself, what logical error would he find in his father's reasoning? The answer to that question comes with the study of deductive reasoning, also known as logic. This chapter will explain the fundamental standards that govern deductive reasoning. It will introduce you to logic's basic vocabulary and explain how deduction and induction interplay in our thinking.

DISCOVERY EXERCISES

■ *What Is Deductive Reasoning?*

Using at least two dictionaries, look up the terms *deduction*, *deductive logic*, and *reasoning*. Then write out in your own words a definition of deductive reasoning.

■ *Evaluating Deductive Arguments*

Study the following short deductive arguments. Which of these seem to you to be based on good reasoning and which do not? Explain the basis for your decision in each case.

1. Most Americans under age thirty don't believe Social Security will be there for them when they retire. Therefore, most Americans under age thirty favor private accounts.

2. God made men to serve women. Therefore, men should obey their women.

3. People get warts from touching toads. This child has a wart on her finger. This child has touched a toad.

4. The Supreme Court's *Miranda* ruling (giving defendants the right to have a lawyer present during questioning) is wrong and only helps guilty defendants. Suspects who are innocent of a crime should be able to have a lawyer present before police questioning. But the thing is you don't have many suspects who are innocent of a crime. That's contradictory. If a person is innocent of a crime, then he is not a suspect. (Attorney General Edwin Meese, quoted in the *Oakland Tribune*, October 6, 1985)

5. If she had been the last person to leave the house, she would have locked the door. However, the door was unlocked. Therefore, she was not the last person to leave the house.

6. If the temperature goes below freezing, the orange crop will be lost. The temperature went below freezing. The orange crop will be lost.

Now write down your answers to the following questions in preparation for class discussion:

1. Which of the preceding arguments contain statements that are false?
2. In the examples with the false statements, are the inferences nevertheless reasonable?
3. Are there any that may contain true statements but seem illogical in their reasoning?
4. Are there any that contain statements that are true and seem well reasoned?
5. Can you infer any rules for deductive reasoning from what you have learned here?

About Deductive Reasoning

Deduction is taught through the study of formal logic, or the science of good reasoning.

Deduct comes from the Latin *deducere*, to lead away. In deductive reasoning we infer, or lead away, from a general principle in order to apply that principle to a specific instance.

Logic is the science of good reasoning. Both **inductive logic** and **deductive logic** are concerned with the rules for correct reasoning.

We learn *deduction* through the study of formal logic. It is called *formal* because its main concern is with creating *forms* that serve as models to demonstrate both correct and incorrect reasoning. Unlike induction, in which an inference is drawn from an accumulation of evidence, deduction is a process that reasons, in carefully worded statements, about relationships between classes, characteristics, and individuals. You will notice that these statements seem obvious, even childlike, in their simplicity:

All humans are mammals.

Jane is a human.

Jane is a mammal.

All horses are herbivorous.

This animal is a horse.

This animal is herbivorous.

All cats are night animals.

This creature is a cat.

_____

This creature is a night animal.

In these examples, the first statement is about all members of a class; here the classes were humans, horses, and cats. The second statement identifies something or someone as belonging to that class:

* Jane is a human.
* This animal is a horse.
* This creature is a cat.

At this point, the two statements lead to an inference that becomes the conclusion:

* Jane is a mammal.
* This animal is herbivorous.
* This creature is a night animal.

Here you will notice that the conclusion is inevitable. The only inference one could possibly draw from the two statements "All humans are mammals" and "Jane is a human" is that Jane is a mammal. In contrast to the inductive hypothesis, which always remains open, the deductive conclusion is unavoidable. The only objective of deductive reasoning is to draw a correct inference from a group of claims. And that inference is a final conclusion. Nevertheless, deduction often begins with a generalization that has been derived from inductive reasoning. Such is the generalization "All horses are herbivorous." This is a conclusion based on inductive observations repeatedly confirmed.

Deduction also works with generalizations not necessarily derived from inductive reasoning. For instance, it can begin with a belief:

* Horses are not humans.

Indeed, deduction starts with any statement that makes a claim. And a claim, which is an assertion about something, can be worked with logically, regardless of whether the claim is true or not. This is possible because deduction's main concern is not with sorting out evidence and searching for truth; its main concern is studying implications. The focus of deduction is on logic, or the rules of reasoning. Nevertheless, the truth of a statement is important in logic, and the objective of deductive reasoning is to arrive at conclusions that are true.

To summarize, the purpose of deductive logic is to help us reason well with the information we have already acquired. It offers us models, guidelines, and rules for correct reasoning that can lead us to draw reliable conclusions from that information. Thus, *logic,* by definition, is the science of reasoning or the science of inference.

One major barrier to understanding logic is its technical vocabulary. This vocabulary is needed to identify the components of deductive arguments and to convey its rules for correct usage. However, for the student, the task of mastering this terminology can seem formidable at first.

The Basic Vocabulary of Logic

The following are key terms needed to understand the basics of logic: *argument, reasoning, syllogism, premise* (major and minor), *conclusion, validity, soundness.* They will be defined and explained one at a time.

Argument

Arguments appear in both deductive and inductive forms. As we have seen before, deductive arguments involve one or more claims (also called *premises*) that lead to a conclusion:

> All people who flirt are showing interest in someone.
>
> She is flirting with me.
> _____
>
> **She is showing interest in me.**

Inductive arguments also establish claims through reasoning based on experiences, analogies, samples, and general evidence. Compare the following example to the preceding deductive argument:

> This woman seeks me out whenever she sees me having my lunch on the lawn. She comes over and sits next to me. She asks for a sip of my coffee.
>
> She teases me and makes me laugh a lot.
> _____
>
> **She is interested in me.**

Reasoning

Both arguments use reasoning to arrive at a conclusion. *Reasoning* draws conclusions, judgments, or inferences from facts or premises. Deductive arguments start with one or more premises, then reason to consider what conclusions must necessarily follow from them.

If I flirt back, she will encourage me further.
I will flirt back.

She will encourage me further.

Sometimes these premises appear in long chains of reasoning:

If I am nice to her, she'll think I'm flirting.
And if she thinks I'm flirting, she'll come on to me.
And if she comes on to me, I'll have to reject her.
And if I reject her, she'll be hurt.
I don't want her to be hurt.

Therefore, I won't be nice to her.

Argument is a set of claims in the form of reasons offered to support a conclusion.

Reasoning is to draw conclusions, judgments, or inferences from facts or premises.

Syllogism

Logic arranges deductive arguments in standardized forms that make the structure of the argument clearly visible for study and review. These forms are called *syllogisms*. We do not speak in syllogisms, which sound awkward and redundant, but they are useful constructs for testing the reliability of a deduction according to the rules of logic. We have already considered a number of syllogisms, beginning with:

All humans are mammals.
Jane is a human.

Jane is a mammal.

Premises *and* Conclusion

A syllogism usually contains two premises and a conclusion. The first statement is called the *major premise* and the second is called the *minor premise*.

No flirts are cross and mean. (major premise)
This man is cross and mean. (minor premise)

This man is not a flirt. (conclusion)

In deduction, the reasoning "leads away" from a generalization about a class to identify a specific member belonging to that class—or it can lead to a generalization about another class. In the preceding deductive argument, the major premise states a generalization about the class of flirts: none is cross and mean. The minor premise asserts that a specific individual does not belong to that class: *because* he is cross and mean, he *must* not be a flirt. Between the word *because* and the word *must* lie the inference and the logic. Such reasoning can be checked for reliability by outlining the argument in the strict form of the syllogism.

> **Syllogism** is a standardized form that makes the structure of a deductive argument visible. A syllogism consists of two premises and a conclusion. From the Greek *syllogismos*, a reckoning together.
>
> **Premises** are the claims made in an argument that provide the reasons for believing in the conclusion. In a syllogism, they usually appear as two statements that precede the conclusion. *Premise* comes from the Latin *praemittere*, to set in front.

Validity

The standards used for testing reliability are based on some specific rules that determine an argument's *validity* and *soundness*. Validity has to do with reasoning; and soundness, with both reasoning and truth. A deductive argument is said to be valid when the inference follows correctly from the premises:

All fathers are males.

Jose is a father.
_____

Jose is a male.

Here, because Jose is a member of the class of fathers, and all members of that class are males, it follows logically that Jose must be a male. Moreover, even if we only *assume* these premises are true, it is entirely reasonable to infer that he is a male. We do not have to ponder the matter any further.

On the other hand, invalid reasoning might proceed like this:

All fathers are males.

Jose is a male.
_____

Jose is a father.

In this argument, the first two premises do not imply this conclusion. The conclusion may be true or it may not be true. But we cannot make that determination on the basis of this line of reasoning. Even if we are certain that all fathers are males and that Jose is a male, we still cannot infer from these premises alone that Jose is a father. The conclusion could be false. Therefore, this argument is invalid.

Soundness

Standards for judging arguments refer not only to correct reasoning but also to the truth of the premises. These standards are conveyed by the use of the word *sound*. A deductive argument is sound if the premises are true and the argument is valid. A sound argument is one that uses true premises and correct reasoning to arrive at a conclusion that cannot be false. By this definition, this argument is sound because its premises are true and its reasoning is valid:

> All fathers are males.
>
> Jose is a father.
> _____
> **Jose is a male.**

However, the following argument is not sound because, although it contains true premises the reasoning is invalid, leading to a conclusion that could be false.

> All fathers are males.
>
> Jose is a male.
> _____
> **Jose is a father.**

So far, so good. Yet there are some other complexities. An argument can be valid *even though the premises are not true:*

> All men are fathers.
>
> All fathers are married.
> _____
> **All men are married.**

In this case, if all men are fathers and all fathers are married, then it would follow that all men are married. Yet common sense tells us that both the premises and the conclusion are false. Here is another such example:

> All fathers are baseball fans.
>
> All baseball fans like beer.
> _____
> **All fathers like beer.**

Thus, the logician makes a distinction between the truth or falseness of statements in an argument and the validity of the entire argument. The term *sound* is used to signify that an argument is valid and the premises are true. The rule for determining soundness is that if the premises are both true and the argument is valid, the conclusion cannot be false.

An argument can be valid even though the premises are not true.

The **rule for determining soundness** is that if the premises are both true and the argument is valid, the conclusion cannot be false.

To summarize, deductive arguments can be structured into a unit for the purposes of simplicity, clarity, and analysis according to standards for good reasoning. With this understanding of the basic vocabulary of logic, we can now consider in greater detail the unit of deductive argumentation—the syllogism.

A **valid** argument is one in which the conclusion has been correctly inferred from its premises. *Valid* comes from the Latin *valere*, to be strong.

Deductive logic is concerned with the rules for determining when an argument is valid.

A **sound** argument is one in which *the reasoning is valid and the premises are both true.* The word *sound* comes from an Old English word, *gesund*, which means healthy.

Standardized Forms in Syllogisms

Syllogisms have been discussed as a standardized form that makes the structure of a deductive argument visible. A syllogism presents claims concerning a relationship between the terms (classes or individuals) given in the premises and those in the conclusion. A standardized language, which makes these relationships clearer, has also been developed for phrasing the premises within the syllogism. Here are six examples of the standardized phrase forms used for expressing premises:

1. All _____ are _____.
2. All _____ are not _____.
3. No _____ are _____.

4. Some _____ are _____.

5. Some _____ are not ____.

6. If _____, then _____.

You will notice that in the first five forms, each of the blanks offers space for an adjective or noun phrase; in addition, each is connected by forms of the verb *to be* expressed in the present tense. This simplification allows a reduction of everyday language into verbal equations, thus making the task of argument analysis much easier. Now let's see how natural language has to be translated into this kind of standardized language for use in syllogisms. Compare the following translations:

Natural Language	Standardized Language
Ice cream always tastes sweet.	All ice cream food is sweet food.
Cats never take baths.	No cats are animals that take baths.
Some airlines have lower fares.	Some airlines are lower-fare transport.
If she is over seventy, she must be retired.	If she is a person over seventy, then she is a retired person.

DISCOVERY EXERCISE

■ *Practice in Constructing Syllogisms**

1. Rephrase each of the following sentences, if necessary, into a standard major premise. Then see if you can add a minor premise and a conclusion.

   a. All horses have exactly four legs.

   b. Everybody's got needs.

   c. Many eighteen-year-olds are college students.

   d. Lead is poisonous.

   e. If he's late, he'll be sorry.

2. Fill in the blanks in the following sentences so that all the syllogisms are valid.

   a. All horses are mammals.

   All _____ are animals.
   _____

   All horses are animals.

*For the style and method used in these exercises, I am indebted to Matthew Lipman's *Philosophical Inquiry: An Instructional Manual to Accompany Harry Stottlemeier's Discovery*, 2nd ed. Published by the Institute for the Advancement of Philosophy for Children, Upper Montclair, NJ, 1979.

b. All horses are living things.
   All living things are things that reproduce.

   All _____ are things that reproduce.

c. No sheep are creatures that sleep in beds.
   This creature is sleeping in a bed.

   Therefore, this creature is _____.

d. If today is Tuesday, this must be Belgium.
   This is _____.

   This must be _____.

3. Choose the correct answer in each of the following cases.
   a. All beers are liquids.
      It therefore follows that:
      (1) All liquids are beers.
      (2) No liquids are beers.
      (3) Neither (1) nor (2).
   b. Florida is next to Georgia.
      Georgia is next to South Carolina.
      It therefore follows that:
      (1) Florida is next to South Carolina.
      (2) South Carolina is next to Florida.
      (3) Neither (1) nor (?).
   c. Ruth is shorter than Margaret.
      Margaret is shorter than Rosie.
      It therefore follows that
      (1) Ruth is shorter than Rosie.
      (2) Margaret is shorter than Ruth.
      (3) Ruth is taller than Rosie.

What Syllogisms Do

The logician accomplishes a number of purposes by standardizing the phrasing of arguments in syllogisms. Syllogisms help us

1. Clarify the claims of the premises

2. Discover and expose any hidden premises
3. Find out if one thought follows logically from another

Each of these objectives will be discussed in turn.

What Is Said and Is It True?

Of course John is cheating on his wife. Doesn't he always come home late?

You will sense that something is wrong with this statement, but where do you begin? Here is where a syllogism helps, because a translation into a syllogism exposes an argument's structure:

All husbands who always come home late are wife cheaters.
John is a husband who always comes home late.

John is a wife cheater.

Here the syllogism reveals a stereotype or hasty generalization in a *hidden major premise*. The words *all* and *always* make the claim in this hidden premise false. We could easily point out exceptions, such as "wife cheaters" who are punctual or loyal mates who work late. But in addition, *wife cheater* is an ambiguous term. What actions constitute wife cheating? The second premise also contains the vague terms *always* and *late*, which could be exaggerations. What does *late* mean? One minute or four hours? Does this mean *late* according to one person's expectations or according to a mutual agreement? Then there is the vague term *always*. If the person accused came home early only once, the generalization would not hold. Thus, although the reasoning may be valid, the argument's use of vague terms and false generalizations makes it unsound.

Now, let's consider another example:

Our guest is Japanese. We had better cook rice rather than potatoes for dinner.

Here is the syllogism that such reasoning is based upon.

No Japanese is a potato eater.
Our guest is Japanese.

Our guest is not a potato eater.

The syllogism shows the reasoning is valid, but again the major premise, which had been hidden, is revealed as containing too broad a generalization to be true. For this reason, the conclusion is uncertain. Therefore, the argument is unsound.

Here is another example. You may have seen this claim on billboards:

Milk does a body good.

Because the billboard supplements this claim with attractive happy people, you may well conclude that you should remember to drink more milk. However, a syllogism will reveal some hidden aspects in this claim worth studying. First there is the ambiguity of the word *good*. *Good* has at least two meanings in this context: healthy and tasty. But a syllogism cannot function with words that have double meanings. In poetry, double meanings are effective. But in arguments, double meanings can be manipulative: they encourage assumptions and escape accountability. If the milk cooperative that paid for the ad were sued, its attorney could claim in court that the company was not claiming that its product was healthy, but only tasty. Nevertheless, suppose you assume that *good* means healthy in this case. You would write out the syllogism thus:

People who drink milk are people made healthy.

I am a person who drinks milk.
_____

I am made healthy.

Thus, if you assume that the premises are true, the reasoning is valid. But when you want to know whether the argument is sound, you must ask questions to test the truth of the generalization in the major premise. Are there exceptions that would challenge its universality? What if my brother is allergic to milk? What about nutritionists who say that cow's milk is good only for cows? Again, as this syllogism shows, we have a false generalization, leading to an uncertain conclusion, and therefore the whole is an unsound argument.

Is There a Hidden Premise?

A major advantage of using syllogisms is that they reveal hidden premises— as you found in the major premises of the preceding examples. Consider the following examples, which contain questionable hidden premises. Note how the form of the syllogisms requires that they be exposed.

Senator Jones is a Democrat. Expect him to tax and spend.

All Democrats are taxers and spenders. (hidden premise)
Senator Jones is a Democrat.
_____

Senator Jones is a taxer and spender.

Do I think he's sexy? Well, he drives a truck, doesn't he?

All those who drive trucks are sexy. (hidden premise)
He drives a truck.

He is sexy. (implied conclusion)

In the second example, both the major premise and the conclusion are hidden or implied. This often happens in advertising slogans:

The burgers are bigger at Burger John's!

As a syllogism, this reads as follows:

Bigger burgers are better burgers. (hidden premise)
Burger John's burgers are bigger.

Burger John's burgers are better. (hidden conclusion)

You should buy Burger John's burgers. (additional hidden conclusion)

Is the Reasoning Correct?

Here the logician is concerned with validity, or correct reasoning. The following argument is obviously valid:

She is either married or single.
She is married.

Therefore, she is not single.

The inference expressed in the conclusion automatically follows: she cannot be both married and single at the same time. Therefore if she is married, she cannot be single. The syllogism makes the validity of the reasoning transparent.

Now let's consider a more difficult example, one that appeared in a discovery exercise that opened this chapter.

Suspects who are innocent of a crime should be able to have a lawyer present before police questioning. But the thing is you don't have many suspects who are innocent of a crime . . . If a person is innocent of a crime, then he is not a suspect.

Here is a translation of that statement into a syllogism:

All innocents are not suspects.

You are a suspect.

You are not innocent.

In this case the reasoning is valid if you assume that both of the premises are true. It follows logically that if the categories of innocents and suspects are mutually exclusive, then if you belong in the category of suspects, you cannot belong in the category of innocents. However, the argument is not sound, because the major premise "All innocents are not suspects" is not true even though the minor premise "You are a suspect" might be.

Now let's take this argument a step further.

If you are a suspect, then you are questioned by the police.

You were questioned by the police.

You are a suspect.

Here, even if both the major and the minor premises were true, the conclusion could still be false. Suspects are not the only category of individuals questioned by the police. Police also question witnesses and bystanders. (Moreover, the implication of this line of reasoning is that if you are a suspect, you are guilty. But police do not make judgments about guilt or innocence; this is the function of a judge and jury.) However, simply on the basis of what is stated, the argument is invalid because the conclusion "You are a suspect" is not implied by its premises. Suspects are not necessarily always questioned by the police, and not all people questioned by the police are suspects. The illogic of the reasoning here can be recognized intuitively, but the syllogism exposes the way in which it is illogical.

Logicians have a number of rules for helping them determine whether or not an argument is valid. However, understanding these rules requires knowledge of further technical terms, which will be discussed in the next section of this chapter.

EXERCISE

■ *Reviewing the Vocabulary of Logic*

Work with a classmate to write down the definitions you can remember of the following words: *logic, reasoning, deductive* and *inductive reasoning, premise* (major and minor), *conclusion, argument, syllogism, true statement, valid argument, sound argument, hidden premise, hidden conclusion.* When you have finished, compare your definitions with those in the chapter summary on page 364. If there is a discrepancy, or if any of the definitions are still unclear to you, review the text discussion until you can explain the terms to your partner.

The Interplay of Inductive and Deductive Reasoning

Whether we are aware of it or not, our thinking moves back and forth between inductive and deductive reasoning all the time.

Inductive and deductive thinking are not isolated modes. They interweave in our minds constantly throughout the day as we confront both serious problems, such as environmental degradation, and mundane ones, such as daily transportation. Let's consider the latter for illustration purposes.

Suppose you have an apartment in the Boston suburb of Needham and commute to Boston University downtown. You have a car, but you prefer to commute by the T train. You made this decision by reasoning deductively:

All public trains are faster than car transport.

I want faster-than-car transport.
_____

I will take public trains.

Suppose this reasoning stands you in good stead for some months. However, one morning you arrive at the station to find an unusually large crowd of people waiting there. You wonder what this means. Are there fewer trains today? Has there been an accident? Will everyone be delayed? You form hypotheses through inductive reasoning. You seek to test each hypothesis by searching for more information from those waiting. But all they can tell you is that their expected train has been delayed. Therefore you reason deductively:

Delayed trains are unpredictable in schedule.

This train is delayed.
_____

This train is unpredictable in schedule.

Then you reason inductively again in order to decide whether to wait or go home and get your car. You weigh the unknown factor of when the train will arrive against the time it might take to go home, get your car, and drive through heavy traffic. You decide that although the delayed train *may* make you late, driving your car will *certainly* make you late. And so, on the basis of your estimate of time and probability, you choose to wait in the station. Because you made this decision carefully, you will not get upset if the train is delayed for yet another thirty minutes. Moreover, you can be glad you did not impulsively run home to get your car without thinking the matter through, only to feel your blood pressure go up when you found yourself stuck in traffic with the train passing you by. You made a conscious decision to take the consequences with responsibility.

In college we study deduction and induction separately both for convenience and because of their different structures and standards (see Table 12.1). But whether we are aware of it or not, in our thinking we move back and forth between the two modes all the time. Yet, taking conscious notice of how our thinking moves between deductive and inductive modes has considerable advantages; we then can purposely direct our thinking to the mode that is more appropriate. This awareness also allows us to use the different standards of the two modes to evaluate what we are doing. Thus, we have a greater probability of arriving at better decisions. And even if we are disappointed with the results of our decisions, at least we know that we made a conscious choice that we can learn from.

TABLE 12.1 Comparing Inductive and Deductive Reasoning

Inductive Reasoning	Deductive Reasoning
Specific to general (usually, not always).	General to specific (usually, not always).
Purpose is to reach a conclusion for testing and application.	Purpose is to reach a conclusion that cannot be false.
Discovers new laws.	Applies known laws to specific circumstances.
Thinking guided by theories, observation, research, and investigation.	Thinking makes inferences about the relationship of claims.
Data are collected and analyzed.	
Sudden insights and unexpected discoveries can occur.	
Tests verify measure of truth in terms of reliability, accuracy, applicability, and their ability to be replicated.	Truth of premises is assumed or determined by reasoning.
Even if the premises are true, the conclusion is only probable and could even be false. More data or major changes could call for further testing.	If the premises are true, or assumed to be true, and the reasoning valid, the conclusion cannot be false.

Composition Writing Application

■ *Writing a Deductive Argument*

Write a deductive argument within the following parameters:

1. *Topic:* Application of an aphorism, or wise saying, to life.
2. *Approach:*
   a. Explain the aphorism.
   b. Define its terms.
   c. Illustrate it.
   d. Choose to agree, disagree, or both.
3. *Form:* Exposition and argumentation—explain, justify, and persuade through logic, reasoning, and example.
4. *Length:* Concise two pages.
5. *Subject:* Choose your own aphorism or select one of the following:
   a. The most savage controversies are about those matters as to which there is no evidence either way. (Bertrand Russell)
   b. Man is a social animal who dislikes his fellow men. (Delacroix)
   c. Competition brings out the best in products and the worst in people. (David Sarnoff)
   d. Failure is when you stop trying.
   e. People get the kind of government they deserve.
   f. Prejudice is never easy unless it can pass itself off as reason. (William Hazlitt)
   g. Life was meant to be lived, and curiosity must be kept alive. One must never, for whatever reason, turn his back on life. (Eleanor Roosevelt)

Chapter Summary

1. Deductive reasoning is the process of starting with one or more statements called premises and investigating what conclusions necessarily follow from these premises.
2. Deduction is the subject of formal logic, whose main concern is with creating forms that demonstrate reasoning.
3. Logic has its own technical vocabulary. The following is a summary of the definitions of key terms:

Argument: A conclusion supported by reasons.

Claim: A true or false assertion about something.

Conclusion: The last step in a reasoning process. It is a judgment based on evidence and reasoning, an inference derived from the premises of an argument.

Hidden premise or conclusion: A premise or conclusion that is not stated but implied in an argument. When the argument is cast in a syllogism, the missing premise or conclusion is expressed.

Hypothesis: A theory, explanation, or tentative conclusion derived through inductive reasoning based on a limited view of facts or events.

Inductive reasoning: The process of noting particular facts and drawing a conclusion about them.

Logic: The science of reasoning; also called the science of inference.

Premises: Statements, evidence, or assumptions offered to support a position.

Propositions: Claims, statements, or assertions used in an argument. They can be either premises or conclusions and either true or false statements.

Reasoning: The act or process of arriving at conclusions, judgments, or inferences from facts or premises.

Sound: A sound argument is one in which all the premises are true and the reasoning is valid.

Syllogism: The formalized structure of a deductive argument, usually written, in which the conclusion is supported by two premises.

True: Corresponding to reality.

Valid: A valid argument is one in which the reasoning follows correctly from the premises to the conclusion. An argument can be valid without the premises or conclusion being true.

4. The standardized language of syllogisms allows a reduction of everyday language into verbal equations.

5. Syllogisms allow logicians to determine what is being said, to identify hidden premises, and to find out if the argument makes sense.

6. Deductive and inductive reasoning are not isolated pursuits but are mentally interwoven both in major and mundane problem solving.

7. It is possible to infer the rules of valid and invalid reasoning from the study of models.

Building Arguments
Deduction

Great Spirit, my Grandfather, you have said to me when I was still young and could hope, that in difficulty I could send a voice four times, once for each quarter of the earth, and you would hear me.

Today I send a voice for a people in despair.

To the center of the world you have taken me and showed the goodness and the beauty and the strangeness of the greening earth, the only mother, and there the spirit-shapes of things, as they should be, you have shown me, and I have seen. At the center of the sacred hoop you have said that I should make the tree to bloom.

With tears running, O Great Spirit, my Grandfather—with running eyes I must say now that the tree has never bloomed. A pitiful old man, you see me here, and I have fallen away and done nothing. Here at the center of the world, where you took me when I was young and taught me; here, old I stand and the tree is withered, my Grandfather.

Again, and maybe the last time on earth, I recall the great vision you sent me. It may be that some little root of the sacred tree still lives. Nourish it, then, that it may leaf and bloom and fill with singing birds. Hear me, not for myself but for my people; I am old. Hear me, that they may once more go back into the sacred hoop and find the good road and the shielding tree.

(Black Elk, shaman of the Oglala Sioux, 1912)

Exercise

1. Can a prayer or prophecy be a deductive argument?

2. Write out the syllogism behind the reasoning of the first statement (major premise, minor premise, and conclusion). Also write out the syllogism behind the narrator's reasoning about the sacred hoop.

3. Write a deductive argument in which you make a claim about Black Elk's prayer. Support it with premises and draw a conclusion.

Speeches of the Native Americans offered in this series were taken from Virginia Irving Armstrong, *I Have Spoken* (Athens, OH: Swallow Press/Ohio University Press, 1989).

Chapter Quiz

Rate the following statements as *true* or *false*. If you decide the statement is false, revise it in the simplest manner to make it read true.

_____ 1. A premise is a reason given to support a conclusion.

_____ 2. Syllogisms are used in logic because logicians like to make their knowledge arcane, or hidden and secret.

_____ 3. Logic is less concerned with truth than with whether one statement follows reasonably from another.

_____ 4. Reasoning occurs only in deduction—not in induction.

_____ 5. A generalization reached through induction can become a premise used in a deductive syllogism.

_____ 6. "All homeowners are taxpayers. He is a property owner. Therefore, he is a taxpayer." This is a valid argument.

_____ 7. "Bloodletting reduces fever. This patient has fever. This patient needs bloodletting." This syllogism shows valid reasoning although both premises may not be true.

_____ 8. "White-skinned people are superior to dark-skinned people. Therefore, it is the manifest destiny of white-skinned people to rule dark-skinned people." No country would ever accept such fallacious reasoning as this.

State whether the reasoning in each of the following syllogisms is correct or incorrect:

_____ 9. If the two parties agree, then there is no strike.
The two parties agree.

Therefore, there is no strike.

_____ 10. If the two parties agree, then there is no strike.
There is no strike.

Therefore, the two parties agree.

_____ 11. If the two parties agree, then there is no strike.
The two parties do not agree.

Therefore, there is a strike.

_____ 12. If the two parties agree, then there is no strike.
There is a strike.

Therefore, the two parties do not agree.

After you have decided, compare your answers to those given here. Explain why these answers are correct.

9. correct 10. incorrect 11. incorrect 12. correct

• R E A D I N G S •

The Declaration of Independence (excerpt)

Thomas Jefferson

Based on a clear line of deductive reasoning, this great historical document written in 1776 is also an enduring work of literature. Jefferson begins by stating some "self-evident truths," or axioms, which set off a revolution and formed the ideological basis for the laws of a new government. This document can be studied as a structure of reasoning in four parts. Following are the first and last parts. Notice as you read how they function as the major premise and conclusion of an argument.

When in the Course of human events, it becomes necessary for one people to dissolve the political bands which have connected them with another, and to assume among the powers of the earth, the separate and equal station to which the Laws of Nature and of Nature's God entitle them, a decent respect to the opinions of mankind requires that they should declare the causes which impel them to the separation.

We hold these truths to be self-evident, that all men are created equal, that they are endowed by their Creator with certain unalienable Rights, that among these are Life, Liberty and the pursuit of Happiness. That to secure these rights, Governments are instituted among Men, deriving their just powers from the consent of the governed. That whenever any Form of Government becomes destructive of these ends it is the Right of the People to alter or to abolish it, and to institute a new Government, laying its foundation on such principles and organizing its powers in such form, as to them shall seem most likely to effect their Safety and Happiness. Prudence, indeed, will dictate that Governments long established should not be changed for light and transient causes; and accordingly all experience has shown, that mankind are more disposed to suffer, while evils are sufferable, than to right themselves by abolishing the forms to which they are accustomed. But when a long train of abuses and usurpations, pursuing invariably the same Object evinces a design to reduce them under absolute Despotism, it is their right, it is their duty, to throw off such Government, and to provide new Guards for their future security. Such has been the patient sufferance of these Colonies; and such is now the necessity which constrains them to alter their former Systems of Government. The history of the present King of Great Britain is a history of repeated injuries and usurpations, all having in direct object the establishment of an absolute Tyranny over these States. To prove this, let Facts be submitted to a candid world . . .

We, therefore, the Representatives of the United States of America, in General Congress, Assembled, appealing to the Supreme Judge of the world for the rectitude of our intentions, do, in the Name, and by Authority of the good People of these Colonies, solemnly publish and declare, That these United Colonies are, and of Right ought to be Free and Independent States; that they are absolved from all Allegiance to the British Crown, and that all political connection between them and the State of Great Britain, is and ought to be totally dissolved; and that as Free and Independent States, they have full Power to levy War, conclude Peace, contract Alliances, establish Commerce, and to do all other Acts and Things which Independent States may of right do. And for the support of this Declaration, with a firm reliance on the protection of divine Providence, we mutually pledge to each other our Lives, our Fortunes and our sacred Honor.

● ● ●

Study/Writing/Discussion Questions

1. In the first sentence it is stated that people are entitled by "the Laws of Nature and of Nature's God" to separate and equal stations. What does this mean? Is there any evidence offered to back this claim?

2. Outline the deductive reasoning offered in the second paragraph. Which truths does Jefferson claim to be self-evident? What is the purpose of governments? From where do they derive their power?

3. How does Jefferson anticipate the argument that this kind of reasoning would allow people to overthrow governments "for light and transient causes"?

4. In the last paragraph, in the name of what authorities does he make the declaration?

5. Compare this document, and the reasoning used therein, with two of its offspring, *The Seneca Falls Declaration* written by Elizabeth Cady Stanton (1848) and the *Universal Declaration of Human Rights* (1948), which was, in large part, authored by Eleanor Roosevelt.

Letter from a Birmingham Jail (excerpt)

Martin Luther King, Jr.

This letter was written by Martin Luther King, Jr., in 1963 after his arrest at a sit-in to protest segregation of eating facilities. His actions resulted in a turning point for the civil rights movement in that, in the same year, the Supreme Court ruled that Birmingham's segregation laws were unconstitutional. Notice how in this short excerpt he draws major premises from statements made by authorities and then reasons from these premises.

I would agree with St. Augustine that "an unjust law is no law at all." . . . How does one determine whether a law is just or unjust? A just law is a man-made code that squares with the moral law or the law of God. An unjust law is a code that is out of harmony with the moral law. To put it in the terms of St. Thomas

Aquinas: an unjust law is a human law that is not rooted in eternal law and natural law. Any law that uplifts human personality is just. Any law that degrades human personality is unjust. All segregation statutes are unjust because segregation distorts the soul and damages the personality. It gives the segregator a false sense of superiority and the segregated a false sense of inferiority. Segregation, to use the terminology of the Jewish philosopher Martin Buber, substitutes an "I–it" relationship for an "I–thou" relationship and ends up relegating persons to the status of things. Hence segregation is not only politically, economically, and sociologically unsound, it is morally wrong and sinful. Paul Tillich has said that sin is separation. Is not segregation an existential expression of man's tragic separation, his awful estrangement, his terrible sinfulness? Thus it is that I can urge men to obey the 1954 decision of the Supreme Court, for it is morally right, and I can urge them to disobey segregation ordinances, for they are morally wrong.

● ● ●

Study/Writing/Discussion Questions

1. State King's argument in the form of a syllogism.
2. Why do you suppose King chose to refer to the authorities of Catholic church philosophers (St. Augustine and St. Thomas Aquinas) as well as a Jewish and a Protestant theologian (Martin Buber and Paul Tillich)?
3. Which terms does he define and why?
4. What conclusions does he draw from his premises?
5. Explain how the sound logic of his reasoning makes his argument so compelling.

Objectives Review of Part III

After you have finished Part III, you will understand:

1. Why arguments are supported claims
2. How reasons differ from conclusions
3. What questions to ask in analyzing arguments
4. Why fallacies make arguments deceptive
5. Definitions and examples of twenty informal fallacies
6. The forms and standards of inductive and deductive thinking
7. The concepts of empirical reasoning, scientific method, hypothesis, probability, and causal reasoning
8. The basic vocabulary of logic
9. The functions of the syllogism
10. The differences between deductive and inductive reasoning
11. How inductive and deductive reasoning interplay in our thinking

And you will have practice in developing these skills:

1. Identifying conclusions and separating them from reasons
2. Identifying reports and separating them from arguments
3. Articulating the question at issue
4. Analyzing arguments
5. Writing a persuasive argument under the pressure of strong feelings
6. Evaluating deductive arguments for validity and soundness
7. Identifying hidden premises
8. Applying different standards to inductive and deductive reasoning
9. Researching and preparing your take-home final

The Research Paper

Research Paper Assignments in This Text

If you have been assigned a research paper due at the end of the semester, you should begin your research by the time you finish Chapter 9 on Arguments. Instructions are provided in this appendix for two research writing assignments. Each assignment will challenge you to integrate all the critical thinking skills you have learned and apply them to writing about a controversial issue of your own choice. You may be asked to do only the first assignment, an outline analysis of two arguments, or you may be required to write a longer argumentative essay.

This section includes instructions for these two assignments together with suggestions for scheduling and researching. To give you a visual model to follow, a portion of one student writing sample also appears in this section. This sample offers an analysis of one of the three arguments on job outsourcing that appear in the Readings section at the end of Chapter 9. The complete paper written by the same student appears in the Instructor's Manual.

FIRST OPTION:
Analysis of Two Arguments Pro and Con on a Recent Controversial Issue

This assignment can also serve as a final take-home exam, because its purpose is to allow you to demonstrate all the knowledge and skills you learned while studying this book. Nevertheless you should begin to prepare for it at least a month before the end of the semester, before you finish reading the text. Indeed, having this assignment as a goal will help you understand the last three chapters even better. The skills that this assignment requires include being able to do the following:

- Isolate a recent controversial issue.
- Research to find two arguments from two different sources, if possible, representing two different viewpoints on one debate question related to that same issue.
- Identify the political or social orientation of a viewpoint.
- Select a complete argument, either in full or extracted from a larger article, in order to analyze its structure, strengths, and weaknesses according to standards learned in this text.
- Compare, evaluate, and summarize both arguments. Then choose the better argument on the basis of critical thinking standards.
- Follow instructions and communicate your findings clearly.

■ Overall Format

Follow your instructor's directions for presenting your work. You might use a simple folder to contain your take-home final research paper. The folder would contain a title page, a table of contents, four to six pages of analysis, and the photocopied arguments. The whole should come to about ten pages. Take pride in giving your work a professional appearance.

■ Research Preparation

Choose one topic of recent controversy that interests you. Stimulate your thinking by following the daily news, by browsing in the library or on the

Instructions for the Argument Analysis Assignment

This assignment is not an essay assignment but an outline analysis of two arguments. A student sample of half of this assignment appears later in this appendix. Read the instructions given below first. Then skim through the student sample to see how it serves as a visual model of the outline format you will be using. Finally, return to read the remainder of the guidelines offered here.

Outline Form Used in This Assignment

Offer your complete analysis of each argument one by one. Use the outline topic form that appears in the following, and follow through all these steps with each argument. A photocopy of each argument you selected to analyze should appear at the end of each outline.

Part I: Title Page: Write the debate question on the title page followed by your name, the date, your course number, and a short table of contents.

Part II: Headings: At the top of your first page fill in the following information:

1. **The debate question:**
2. **Title:** (of the article or argument, magazine or newspaper)
3. **Date of publication:**
4. **Form:** Argument Pro or Con (This is to test your ability to distinguish an argument from a report.)
5. **Viewpoint:** Label the viewpoint politically or socially.

Part III: Basic Structure of the Argument

6. **Conclusion:** State the argument's conclusion using your own words or short quotes.
7. **Reasons:** List all the reasons given in the argument to support this conclusion. (Do this in your own words or with short quotes.)

Part IV: Critique Questions: Review the argument according to the following items. Discuss each fully and systematically. Remember this is not just an exercise in finding flaws; you may find much in the argument to commend.

8. **Argument structure:** How is the argument structured? Briefly describe and evaluate the way it is put together without getting into too many details. Generalize about its special features and mention how the conclusion and the reasons are presented.
9. **Ambiguous or prejudicial words:** Are any central words in the argument ambiguous or prejudicial?
10. **Fallacies:** Does the argument contain any fallacies? If so, identify each fallacy and discuss each one with specific examples.
11. **Hidden assumptions:** Does the argument make any hidden assumptions? What are they and how do they affect the argument?
12. **Missing information:** Is any important information missing?
13. **Contradictory or false information:** Is any information false, irreconcilable, or contradictory?

Part V: Final Summary Comparing the Two Arguments: On a final page, summarize the two arguments. Which viewpoint do you find the more persuasive and why? Remember you are not being asked to defend your own viewpoint on this issue but only to show why you find one to be the more persuasive argument.

Internet, and by studying magazines and newspapers representing different points of view. Remember you are looking for a subject of current controversy—one that will demand more thinking than a topic that has been around long enough to accumulate a lot of familiar opinions.

Let's suppose, for instance, that you pick up a recent magazine called *Natural Health* and notice an article on the subject of irradiated foods. You might be surprised to read that Congress is considering a bill that would no longer require irradiated foods to bear prominent labels. Your curiosity might motivate you to find out more about this whole subject. You might first go onto InfoTrak or the Internet and enter "irradiated foods" in search engines such as Google or Yahoo. After reading a few recent articles on the subject, both reports and arguments, you might then try a multiple search option such as GoGettem Meta Search, which could bring up hundreds of articles to choose from. Should irradiated foods be a current hot news item, you could also go to a library to read such newspapers as *The Washington Post, The New York Times,* and *The Los Angeles Times.* You can also find online websites for these newspapers where you can search for articles written on irradiated foods during the past year; you could also use their archives for articles published in years past. After making an initial survey of the topic, you could then begin to print out a collection of the best reports and arguments for your research file. Before long you should feel reasonably informed on the topic. The test would depend on whether you know the following:

- What are the main issues or unresolved problems related to irradiated foods?
- What are the arguments pro and con on each issue?
- What are the debate questions being addressed?
- What groups, individuals, or organizations are representing each position?

Suppose the issue of the *safety* of irradiated foods is what interests you most. However, you may decide not to work with this issue, because it would involve technical opinions and speculations. You may then decide to search for pro and con arguments on the *labeling* of irradiated foods; however, as it turns out, you can only find one suitable argument. On the other hand, you have found two good pro and con arguments on the issue of the *need* for irradiated foods. At this point, you decide to select this issue for your research paper. Therefore you formulate the debate question that both of your arguments address: "Do we really need irradiated foods?" Debate questions are sometimes stated within arguments; sometimes they appear in their headings above pro and con arguments that appear on editorial pages of newspapers. They are spelled out in publications like *Speeches of the Day* or *The Congressional Digest.* Nevertheless, in most cases, you will need to study your argument selections carefully in order to recognize the debate question they are commonly addressing. Here you may need the assistance of your instructor. Before proceeding, you need confirmation that you have formulated your debate question correctly. (If you want to learn a great deal more about preparing and writing the research paper, refer to the list of handbooks on page 379.)

■ Arguments, Not Reports

A second confirmation that you will need concerns your selection of an argument rather than a report. *No matter how much work you do on this assignment, you will not succeed if you try to work with reports rather than arguments.* Reports sometimes give short quotes of pro and con arguments; however, what you need are two single coherent arguments written each by one person expressing one person's point of view. If you are unsure whether you have an argument or a report, get your instructor's opinion before beginning this assignment.

■ Length and Viewpoints of Arguments Selected

Your argument selections should be short—not more than twelve paragraphs. If you want to excerpt your argument from a longer article, photocopy the whole article and attach it to your final paper with a border

Scoring for Analysis of Two Arguments

1. Two different arguments (not reports) from two different authors addressing the same issue and taken from two different publications. *20 points*

2. Follows the format required; photocopies are attached. *10 points*

3. Conclusion and reasons correctly identified; all reasons are listed. *20 points*

4. Accurate and insightful critique that addresses:
   Analysis of argument structure
   Ambiguous and prejudicial words
   Fallacies of reasoning
   Hidden assumptions
   Missing information and/or false information
   Any other pertinent characteristics
   42 points (7 points each)

5. Final summary that compares the two and chooses the better argument. *8 points*

around the section you chose to analyze. (However, make sure the section you choose is a complete argument in itself.) Newspaper editorials and letters to the editor can also serve as short arguments. If you are working on a political topic, find two different views, such as liberal and conservative, from two different published sources. If you choose a sociological issue, such as physician-assisted suicide, find two different perspectives such as a physician's view, a minister's view, and/or a relative's view.

SECOND OPTION:
An Argumentative Research Essay

Here is an opportunity for you to express and defend your own view in depth on one current controversial issue. You can prepare by completing the previous assignment or by taking up a different issue that you have researched independently. This will be a research paper from ten to thirty pages in length, depending on your instructor's specifications.

■ *Preparation Instructions*

Prepare to write an argumentative essay by following these steps:

1. Write out fully your own viewpoint on the issue that you have researched for several weeks, either for the previous assignment or in consultation with your instructor. Write freely without self censorship for as many pages as it takes to exhaust what you have to say

2. Now shape your principal claim into a thesis, taking care to choose your key terms carefully. Use clustering as needed.

3. Leaving wide spaces between each statement, outline your support for this thesis in terms of claims and/or evidence.

4. Consult your research file and notes to see what information you have that might be pertinent to use for illustration and support. Take notes on what further research you may need to complete now and as you go along. Make notes on your outline concerning where you need supporting information or quotations. As you organize the data in your research file, remember that you will be quoting or referring to sources in the MLA style of documentation. Use a reference handbook recommended by your instructor for information about the MLA style or consult one of the reference manuals. You will need to prepare a "Works Cited" list as well as a bibliography. Therefore, as you do your research, be sure to record all the citation data you will need in order to save yourself a frantic search the night before your paper is due. You might also want to consult a handbook for more research suggestions

or review the skills of proper summarizing, quoting, and paraphrasing in order not to plagiarize your sources.

5. As you write and revise your outline, note where you need to acquire more evidence or examples and where you already have enough material to write the number of required pages.

6. Keep your outline before you as you write. Tack it up on the wall. Read and reread it to make sure that each part of the essay relates to your thesis. Revise it as needed.

■ Writing the First Draft

7. Now start to flesh out the skeleton of your outline. Introduce your subject, stating the issue in your first paragraph. Explain why this issue interests you and why it should be of interest to the reader. You might summarize some of the different positions taken on this issue. Then state your position—your thesis or principal claim. Also provide any definitions necessary to explain how you are using your terms.

8. As you write, seek to be as clear as possible. Guide your readers so that they can know exactly what you are doing at each step as you pursue your argument. Read your work aloud to friends to discover what they need to hear to understand you.

9. In the second paragraph or paragraphs give an argument to defend your principal claim, clearly stating your premises and conclusion as well as your evidence.

10. In the paragraph that follows, state any major objection or objections that others might have to your argument. You can counter these with further arguments or evidence.

11. If you think of further criticisms that might be made of your counterargument, reply to these.

12. As you continue to write your draft, decide at some point whether you can fully support your original thesis or whether you might need to modify it. If this should occur, go back to your outline and revise accordingly.

■ Final Touches

13. When you have finished your final draft, find another good listener. Notice where you are not understood or where, in explaining, you find that you need to say more in writing.

14. Rewrite your work as necessary to improve coherency and correct errors.

15. The following handbooks are recommended for guidance in research writing:

1. Lester, James D. *Writing Research Papers: A Complete Guide,* 11th edition. New York: Longman, 2005.

2. Kirszner, Laurie G., & Mandell, Stephen R., *The Wadsworth Handbook,* 7th edition. Belmont, CA: Wadsworth, 2005.

Scoring for Argumentative Essay

1. Thesis is clearly stated with all key terms defined. *10 points*
2. Support is adequate and complete in defense of the thesis. *30 points*
3. Paper shows the author is well informed on the issue selected. *20 points*
4. All citations and bibliography are correctly presented in MLA form. *10 points*
5. The argument is persuasive. *10 points*
6. Writer is able to summarize, use quotations, or paraphrase as needed. *10 points*
7. No distracting errors in spelling, mechanics, and sentence structure. *10 points*

Student Model Paper

Analysis of Two Arguments on the Issue: Is Job Outsourcing Good for America?

Claire Frey,
Vista College,
Spring Semester 2005

Table of Contents

Part 1: Argument A: Pro on the Issue

Title: 30 Little Turtles
Publication: New York Times
Date: February 29, 2004
Form: Argument
Author: Thomas L. Friedman
Viewpoint: Globalization enthusiast, *New York Times* columnist

Argument Analysis
Conclusion
Job outsourcing creates a safer and more prosperous world.

Reasons
1. Working American jobs has "transformed" the lives of these Indians by giving them "self-confidence and self-worth."
2. Indian employees have the opportunity to become consumers of U.S. goods.
3. Young women with higher paying jobs have more freedom in choosing whom they marry.

4. "There is nothing more positive than the self-confidence, dignity and optimism that comes from a society knowing it is producing wealth by tapping its own brains . . . as opposed to just tapping its own oil, let
   alone one that is so lost it can find dignity only through suicide and
   martyrdom."
5. Without American jobs, young people can become "suicide bombers in
   waiting."
6. Sending our "low-wage, low-prestige" jobs to places like India or
   Pakistan where they are considered "high-wage, high-prestige" jobs is
   inevitable in an age when our economy is so linked to the rest of the
   world.

Argument Structure

Thomas L. Friedman's argument consists of three parts. The first two paragraphs
describe a lighthearted and amusing day at an "accent neutralization" class
where students learn to replace their own Indian accents with Canadian ones.
The next four paragraphs consist of Friedman's generalization about the benefits being gained by U.S. consumers and these young Indians. Friedman
quotes students who express great pride and gratitude for their jobs helping
Americans. The last three paragraphs are devoted to Friedman's wide-ranging
implications from his day spent at the call center. The argument is concluded
with a brief summary of his argument and a reminder to Americans that job
outsourcing is not only good for our economy, but it also creates a safer world
for our own children.

Fallacies

1. Fallacy of Manipulation through Language

Friedman was very careful and deliberate with the language chosen in his
argument. When he describes the Indian students, he uses fun and positive
words to describe their enthusiasm. "Indians are so hospitable," "incredibly
enthusiastic," "transformed their lives," "self-confidence," "self-worth," "pride,"
"liberated," "independence," "dignity," and "optimism." On the other hand,
Friedman uses prejudicial language to describe what their lives could be like
without these jobs. "Suicide," "martyrdom," "no hope," "no dignity," and "suicide bombers in waiting" are all words that evoke fear and anxiety in the
American reader.

2. Fallacy of Manipulation through Emotions

This argument relies heavily on an emotional response from the reader. Friedman
seems to want readers to form their judgments on job outsourcing based on

fear, pity and prejudice rather then intellect and reason. He portrays these young Indians as good kids who are eager to serve Americans and spend their hard-earned money on American products. Friedman then paints a dismal picture of what these wholesome young people's lives would be like without American jobs. He arouses pity in his reader by implying that with these new jobs, women can somehow escape the ancient tradition of arranged marriage. This is a custom that is widely misunderstood by Americans and has little to do with the topic being argued. It is simply an emotionally charged issue that is being used to distract the reader. The example of the young Palestinian men who refer to themselves as "suicide bombers in waiting" forces the reader to feel a sense of responsibility not only for the future of these people, but also for the safety of our own country. Friedman then uses a foolproof method to convince his American audience to agree with him, fear, and what scares Americans more then a group of potential terrorists?

3. Fallacy of Manipulation through Distraction

Friedman distracts his audience with a sentimental story of his experience visiting a class in India. The name of the article "30 Little Turtles" is an example of his use of a cute and funny word exercise to show how skilled the Indians are in linguistics. The emphasis that he gives to this story distracts from the fact that he gives no attention at all to the plight of the American workers who lost these jobs or to the cumulative effect of job outsourcing on the U.S. economy. Thus this whole story becomes a red herring or a distraction from Friedman's lack of support for the broad claim made in his conclusion.

4. Fallacy of Hasty Generalization

This argument relies on several hasty generalizations that lump together people from India and the Middle East. "There is nothing more positive than the self-confidence, dignity and optimism that comes from a society knowing it is producing wealth by tapping its own brains . . . as opposed to one just tapping its own oil. Let alone one that is so lost it can find dignity only through suicide and martyrdom." There are so many things wrong with these statements. Is he referring to India? I highly doubt that Indians can only find dignity through suicide or "martyrdom." And are Indians known for tapping their own oil rather than their brains? Likewise are the Pakistanis? Here we have a confusing comment that is neither clarified nor supported with facts or research.

5. Either-Or Fallacy

The statement just discussed implies an either-or fallacy. A society either prospers by tapping its own oil or tapping its own brains. Friedman also leaves his readers with a false dilemma: either we give up American jobs or live in a world that is unsafe. This is unfounded and unfair. Friedman fails to support his claim that job outsourcing will help defeat terrorism.

6. False Analogy

One of the most disturbing mistakes that Friedman makes in his argument is the way he groups India in with Pakistan and the rest of the Middle East. For one thing, India is part of Asia, an entirely different continent. India is 83% Hindu and a Hindu government, not a Muslim one, runs India. In fact, aside from the color of their skin, there are few similarities between the majority of Indians and people from the Middle East.

Hidden Assumptions

Friedman assumes that without these jobs, Indians and possibly all other nationalities would turn to terrorism. He assumes that these highly educated people have no moral backing that might dissuade them from becoming "suicide bombers in waiting." The author also assumes that America's economy is flowing with so many jobs that shedding these "low-wage, low-prestige" jobs won't hurt our own citizens. In all these cases he is wrong.

Missing Information

One of the most heated topics related to job outsourcing is how it affects American workers. Friedman only mentions them in passing, saying that he would *never* say their jobs are less important. Yet instead of developing this claim, he devotes his essay to defending a point that few would disagree with: that job outsourcing is good for the foreign workers getting these jobs. Obviously having any job, especially a higher paying job working for an American company, is a great thing. The problem—for us in the U.S. at least—is how it affects the Americans who lose their jobs and how the continuation of this situation will affect the U.S. economy. Friedman's argument is shallow because he fails to address the full complexity of the issue.

Contradictions or False Information

Friedman's argument in favor of job outsourcing is loaded with contradictory information. Is America going to be part of this "more prosperous world" if it has to keep giving up its jobs to prevent terrorism? India alone has a population of over a billion people. Where does one draw the line? At what point will the world become "safer"? The main point that he makes in his essay, that job outsourcing will create a safer world for all, is untrue. How safe is it for America to employ the entire world when many of our own citizens can't find decent work? It is also very unlikely that a "suicide bomber in waiting" would readily hang up his dreams of destroying America to jump on the capitalist bandwagon. Friedman stresses that job outsourcing is great for geopolitics, when in fact it is the American corporations' way of taking advantage of foreign workers who are willing to work for less with no benefits. Friedman relies on his own impressions instead of providing a researched essay, and that is why his argument is not compelling.

Used with permission of Claire Frey.

Reminder to the Reader

The remainder of this student paper, with her analysis of the argument by Rory Terry and her summary conclusion, appears in the Instructor's Manual. If your instructor is willing, the whole paper can be photocopied and placed in the library for reference study.

Media Literacy:

How Can I Become Well-Informed?

On Being Well-Informed

You might call the hero of this cartoon a creative thinker. But is he a critical thinker? Like so many, he keeps his attention on day-to-day survival. There seems to be no time to ask: How did pollution get to be this bad?

Who is responsible for this problem? Can I do anything about it? Sadly for us all, he remains the proverbial poor sucker.

Ideally in a democracy, a citizen always retains sovereignty together with the power to act and make a difference. Yet acting on poor information can be worse than taking no action at all. Thus it is crucial to become an *informed* citizen. But then that raises the question of how to become well-informed. How much information is enough? How does one know if the information is reliable? Where does one begin?

Although it may take some time to find answers to these questions, the act of formulating them is a significant step forward. Many students, in particular those who must also work and support families, say that they have little time to follow the news. At most they read newspaper headlines, listen to their car radios on the way to work, catch perhaps the 6:00 TV news, or watch late evening political satire on Comedy Central. Some might give up trying altogether: "I don't believe anything I hear on the news" or "You can't do anything anyway."

We live in a world that provides us with a glut of information about a world more and more difficult to comprehend. The complex causes of the growth of air pollution provide only one example taken from hundreds of unprecedented problems that affect our planetary health and survival. At the same time that our technological resources interconnect us, we are unclear about our responsibilities to one another. Yet our planetary survival remains a collective matter.

By the time you have worked your way through this text, you will already have acquired many of the skills needed for gaining information and evaluating its reliability. As you already must know, such skills will help you academically, personally, and professionally. What now remains is this mini-chapter for those of you who want to better understand the world and participate more actively therein. These skills involve media literacy, specifically as they apply to following the daily news.

Media Literacy Skills for Assessing News Reliability

Media Literacy

Media Literacy . . . provides a framework to access, analyze, evaluate and create messages in a variety of forms — from print to video to the Internet. Media literacy builds an understanding of the role of media in society as well as essential skills of inquiry and self-expression necessary for citizens of a democracy. *Center for Media Literacy*

The idea of teaching media literacy is a relatively new one, having first made headway in public education during the 1980s. You can learn more about what this whole field has to offer through an Internet search. In this short appendix we are going to focus only on two practical issues:

1. How do we know that any piece of news information is reliable?
2. What steps might lead us most quickly to that determination?

Assessing the reliability of information begins not with the reading of **content** but with giving close initial attention to the **sources** that prepared this information. When applied to the daily print news, sources range from the newspapers themselves, such as the *Los Angeles Times* or *Boston Globe*, to the news services they employ such as Reuters and Associated Press, to individual reporters, columnists, op-ed writers, public relations releases, government releases, editorials, and to excerpts taken from other newspapers such as the *New York Times* and *Washington Post*. Thus a skilled reader always begins by looking for a source designation under the article's headline or, in an op-ed piece, by jumping to the end of the article to note the author's name and credentials. Such a habit allows a provisional assessment of the work's authenticity, its potential bias, and its accountability to standards.

Some Guiding Principles

If you want to become a well-informed reader there are five useful things to know about news information and news sources. A well-informed reader, aside from having critical thinking skills, is a person who knows how to assess news significance, assess news sources and news information for reliability, keep current on significant world events, and connect these events to past events. This is a tall order, but the time involved can be significantly reduced when one gains confidence in the skills of news discrimination, and source and information assessment. Most time loss occurs from filling the mind with junk news, with false or unreliable information, or with confusion about missing information. Thus, since most of us need to budget our time, these five guiding principles offer the attraction of avoiding such pitfalls while increasing efficiency and competence.

1. **There is no one single central reliable source of information.** Some of us may have formed the habit of reading one newspaper regularly or hearing the news on one radio station or seeing it on one television station. Yet no single source lacks limitations and biases. No one single news source can claim that it always gets the truth, even though most claim they strive for accuracy and some claim to be "fair and balanced."

2. **The most accessible sources of news information are not necessarily the most reliable.** As you will see in the discussion of the mass media that follows, your local newspaper, radio, and television stations either no longer exist or lack the independence they had in the more recent past. Today, unless you find the Internet to be your most accessible source, you are left, for the most part, with sound bite news. Even though you can see and hear more depth and range of news coverage on NPR and PBS, such stations continue to struggle to retain their independence.

3. **Reliability can best be determined by comparing multiple news sources.** People who try to be well informed make it a regular habit to read, hear, or view multiple news sources. By comparing the treatment of any one story, they are able to pick up corroborations or contradictions. They also see how different sources can offer different facts, different emphases, and different interpretations. Over time, through regular reading or viewing, the well informed might hope to discover some constants that might approach truth, especially if the topic has stimulated a lot of public debate.

4. **Obviously, you can't keep up with everything.** Election time asks us to follow a lot of issues closely. However, on an ongoing basis, you may have to choose a few issues you will have the time to follow closely. Decide how much time you can give and stick to that, even if it means allotting only one hour a week.

5. **Learning how to evaluate sources takes knowledge of their background, history, values, biases, qualifications, and reputations. It also requires knowledge of the journalistic standards that they are expected to adhere to.** This is admittedly a lot to learn. And unless you have studied journalism, you probably will not gain this knowledge in college. The purpose of the remainder of this mini-chapter is to give you a head start in that direction.

Journalism in the Role of the Fourth Estate

Fourth Estate

The fourth estate refers to the press as an unofficial balance to the three branches of government: the executive, legislative, and judicial. Ideally, the role of the press is to serve as a guardian of democracy and defender of public interest and welfare. Essential for accomplishing such purposes are a strict code of ethics together with the rights of free speech and freedom of the press.

The concept of the press in the balancing role of a Fourth Estate that defends truth and public interest goes back to mid-nineteenth century Europe. This novel idea, adopted in our country, has influenced many events in U.S. history and contributed to our health and vibrancy as a nation. There have been times when the power of this role has been clearly prominent, as in the case of the Watergate investigations that were initiated by two *Washington Post* reporters, resulting eventually in the resignation of President Nixon.

An important adjunct to the Fourth Estate role is the Journalists' Code of Ethics, a code first developed in the 1920s. It offered journalists a clearly stated code to clarify their values, help them make ethical decisions, and enable them to deserve public trust. In 1996 the Society of Professional Journalists spent some months reformulating the Code. That code is not presented here in its entirety. Three principles stated therein are: (1) to seek truth and report it; (2) act independently ("free of obligation to any interest other than the public's right to know"), and (3) "avoid conflicts of interest, real or perceived." You can read many more of their standards following. These standards have significance for us as critical readers, because it is by them that we judge news report writing. They are also standards that we might feel inspired to emulate in our writing as well.

Journalists Should:

1. Test the accuracy of information from all sources and exercise care to avoid inadvertent error. Deliberate distortion is never permissible.
2. Diligently seek out subjects of news stories to give them the opportunity to respond to allegations of wrongdoing.
3. Identify sources whenever feasible. The public is entitled to as much information as possible on sources' reliability.
4. Always question sources' motives before promising anonymity. Clarify conditions attached to any promise made in exchange for information. Keep promises.
5. Make certain that headlines, news teases and promotional material, photos, video, audio, graphics, sound bites and quotations do not misrepresent. They should not oversimplify or highlight incidents out of context.
6. Never distort the content of news photos or video. Image enhancement for technical clarity is always permissible. Label montages and photo illustrations.
7. Avoid misleading re-enactments or staged news events. If re-enactment is necessary to tell a story, label it.
8. Avoid undercover or other surreptitious methods of gathering information except when traditional open methods will not yield information vital to the public. Use of such methods should be explained as part of the story.
9. Never plagiarize.

10. Tell the story of the diversity and magnitude of the human experience boldly, even when it is unpopular to do so.
11. Examine their own cultural values and avoid imposing those values on others.
12. Avoid stereotyping by race, gender, age, religion, ethnicity, geography, sexual orientation, disability, physical appearance or social status.
13. Support the open exchange of views, even views they find repugnant.
14. Give voice to the voiceless; official and unofficial sources of information can be equally valid.
15. Distinguish between advocacy and news reporting. Analysis and commentary should be labeled and not misrepresent fact or context.
16. Distinguish news from advertising and shun hybrids that blur the lines between the two.
17. Recognize a special obligation to ensure that the public's business is conducted in that open and that government records are open to inspection.

From the Society of Professional Journalists, 3909 N. Meridian St., Indianapolis, Indiana 46208, www.spj.org. Copyright © 2005 by the Society of Professional Journalists. Reprinted by permission.

● ● ●

In the last few decades, the trend toward media consolidation has raised many new ethical challenges for reporters. In 1983, Ben Bagdigian, U.C. journalism professor and media critic, expressed alarm that the vast number of independent U.S. newspapers, book publishers, and radio and television stations had come under the control of only 50 corporations (*Media Monopoly*). Yet by the year 2005 that number was down to five mass media corporations: News Corp, NBC/General Electric, Viacom, Time Warner, and Walt Disney. These five now control the big four television networks and most cable channels in addition to having holdings in radio, publishing, movie studios, music, the Internet, sports, and theme parks.

> [In 2005] only 281 of the nation's 1,500 newspapers remain independently owned, and more than half of all U.S. markets are dominated by one newspaper . . . . The number of radio stations has plummeted by 34% since 1996 when ownership rules were gutted. That year, the largest radio owners controlled fewer than 6 stations; today, radio giant Clear Channel alone owns over 1,200. (Quotes taken from a pamphlet published by *Freepress.net*, 2005)

A number of media critics (see the attached reading list) have claimed that the quality, freedom, and diversity of journalism have suffered because of this consolidation. Some have argued that Fourth Estate purposes have little meaning in an environment where corporate values, profit motives, and vested interests predominate, where the objective is not to inform or educate the public but to entice customers into buying their own products. Moreover, they say that the corporate media tends to prefer to avoid criticism of the government in power if the criticism might affect their business association with the government.

Yet the strength and power of the journalists' professional code of ethics can be seen in a number of events that occurred in 2004–2005. These events included the use of anonymous sources, admitted fabrications by journalists, and the government's hiring of journalists to promote unpopular government programs in their columns and radio programs. In all of these cases, journalist behavior was measured against this code.

Hopefully the future will bring even more freedom of expression and more depth of information to the news media landscape. According to the Newspaper Association of America, online newspaper readership continues to rise. Should the Internet remain a forum for free speech without censorship, it may continue to allow access to a growing wide array of news sources. The present vacuum in local news could be filled by enterprising independents or by Pod casting. The approaching changeover from analog to digital television, with the opportunity for multicasting, could result in far more in-depth community and public service information.

Becoming a well-informed citizen is not easy; it does take some research effort, education, and time, but the resulting feeling of empowerment can make the effort worthwhile. What follows is a brief outline of information designed to encourage you to explore, compare, and assess multiple media sources. This exploration can be done either through class study or self-study. If you find this study to be rewarding, you might find yourself selecting a few news sources to consult on a regular basis. Gradually such a habit may lead you to feel that are able to make better informed decisions and act accordingly for the benefit of yourself and others.

Suggestions for Further Study

Some Recent Books on the Media

Alterman, Eric. *What Liberal Media?* 2003. A liberal reply to the conservative claim that the media is predominantly liberal. Good to read alongside Bernard Goldberg's book (see below).

Bagdikian, Ben. *The New Media Monopoly.* 2004 A revision of a ground-breaking book first published in the 1980s by a U.C. professor of journalism.

Coulter, Ann. *Slander: Liberal Lies About the American Right.* 2002.

Gans, Herbert J. *Democracy and the News.* 2003.

Steps for Assessing Information Reliability

What Is the Source of the Information?

Does the publication have a known bias?
Is the author of the article identified?
Are the person's credentials and affiliations provided?
What more would you like to know about this source?

Is This Information Current?

Is the date of its writing or publication given?

How Is the Information Framed?

How is it framed visually in terms of photos, page, and size selections?
How is it framed verbally in terms of headlines, lead lines, and relative
    dominance?
What information is emphasized?
Is any crucial information downplayed or omitted?

How Is the Information Organized?

Is this clearly a report, an argument, or a hybrid?
What is the ratio of facts to inferences?
Is this one person's opinion or are multiple views considered?
Are the sources used cited and identified?

How Is Language Used in This Information?

Is it mainly neutral or slanted?
Are any words ambiguous or prejudicial?

How Is Reasoning Used?

Is it logically coherent?
Is it free of contradictions?
Is it free of fallacies?

Comparison to Other Sources

Are they largely in agreement or not?
Does this comparison reveal inaccuracies?
Does this comparison reveal signs of bias?
Does the comparison reveal missing information?
Does the comparison reveal distortions due to oversimplifications?

Goldberg, Bernard. *Arrogance: Rescuing America from the Media Elite*. 2003. A conservative continues to defend his accusation of liberal bias in the U.S. media first made in an earlier book called *Bias*.

Kovach, Bill and Tom Rosenstiel. *The Elements of Journalism: What Newspeople Should Know and The Public Should Expect*. 2001. This is, in part, an appraisal of the ethics of journalism.

Mathison, David. *Be the Media*. Natural E Creative Group. 2005. ISBN 0-9760814-5-8. Education in the tools needed to create your own independent media.

McChesney, Robert W. *The Problems of the Media*. 2004. The author is a professor of journalism at the University of Illinois and author of nine books on the media and politics.

Phillips, Peter and the Project Censored. *Censored 2005: The Top 25 Censored Stories*. This annual publication involves 200 people in the collection of this material. Originating from Sonoma State University.

Solomon, Norman. *War Made Easy: How Presidents and Pundits Keep Spinning Us to Death*. 2005.

Sample Websites for Studying the News

Directories for News from International Sources

▪ *International News Archive*

The BBC News Country Profiles database with links to major media outlets.

The BBC Media Report. Compiled by the BBC World Monitoring Service, the report provides English translations of quotes from original articles from around the world.

Samples of Online Foreign News Services in English

http://news.bbc.co.uk

http://www.independent.co.uk

http://www.guardian.co.uk/wordlatest

http://arabnews.com

http://globeaned mail.com (Canadian)

Some U.S. Newspaper Sites

Some of these sites are free; some require subscriptions (which may be paid by your library). A few offer to send free daily news to your email address.

Left-Leaning Editorials	Right-Leaning Editorials
The New York Times Online	*Wall Street Journal*
The Washington Post	*Chicago Sun-Times*
Los Angeles Times	*Washington Times*
Boston Globe	*New York Post*
San Francisco Chronicle	

Some U.S. Think Tanks

Listed below are some of the more prominent U.S. think tanks. Some have reputations for being truly independent research centers seeking to influence the government and public for the common good. Others have been accused of functioning more as lobbyists for certain political, social, and economic ideas. These think tanks affect the news in that their findings are often cited in the media, their hired authors write newspaper op-ed pieces, and their "experts" appear on television programs. In the chart below their political leanings have been culled from evaluations made by InfoUSA and Wikipedia. Also consulted was a chart that appeared in the May/June 2005 edition of *Extra!* (a progressive magazine sponsored by the organization FAIR).

Centrist	Progressive	Libertarian	Conservative
Brookings Institution	Center for Public Integrity	Cato Institute	Heritage Foundation
Council on Foreign Relations	Economic Policy Institute		Hoover Institution –
Carnegie Endowment	Center on Budget and Policy Priorities		RAND
The Carter Center	Rockridge Institute		American Enterprise Institute
Worldwatch Institute			Hudson Institute
			Manhattan Institute for Policy Research

Media Critique Sites

The political orientations assigned in this chart and those that follow are self-designated.

Independent	Left Wing	Right Wing
Cjr.org (Columbia Journalism Review) Factcheck.org	Fair.org	Media Research Center
	Freepress.net (See their chart *Who Owns the Media*)	Accuracy in Media
	Medialiteracy.org	
	Mediamatters.org (David Brock)	
	Spin@prwatch.com (The Weekly Spin sent to your email address)	
	Sourcewatch	

Independent Voter Information Sites

Voter Information Services
Project Vote Smart
Politics1.com

Some Political Activism Sites

Independent	Progressive	Conservative
1. Congress.org: Issues & Action: Action Alert Search	1. Moving Ideas: The Electronic Policy Network	1. Christian Coalition
2. WWW Virtual Library: International Affairs Resources	2. Moveon.org	2. The Club for Growth
	3. Biogems	3. Concerned Women of America
	4. 20/20 Vision	4. Family Research Council
	5. True Majority	5. National Rifle Association

INDEX

CREDITS

Photo Credits

2: © David Lok/SuperStock; **13:** From *Anonymous* by Robert Flynn Johnson, Thames & Hudson, London and New York. Used with permission of Thames & Hudson Ltd.; **80:** © Anne Dowie Photography; **81:** © Anne Dowie Photography; **83:** © Eve Arnold/Magnum Photos; **89:** From *Anonymous* by Robert Flynn Johnson, Thames & Hudson, London and New York. Used with permission of Thames & Hudson Ltd.; **110:** From *Anonymous* by Robert Flynn Johnson, Thames & Hudson, London and New York. Used with permission of Thames & Hudson Ltd.; **112:** From *Anonymous* by Robert Flynn Johnson, Thames & Hudson, London and New York. Used with permission of Thames & Hudson Ltd.; **114:** From *Anonymous* by Robert Flynn Johnson, Thames & Hudson, London and New York. Used with permission of Thames & Hudson Ltd.; **117:** © Nina Winter Photography; **160:** Photo by Arthur Rothstein. Courtesy of The Library of Congress; **203:** © John Pearson Photography

Text Credits

Preface xvii: The Far Side® by Gary Larson © 1982 FarWorks, Inc. All Rights Reserved. The Far Side® and the Larson® signature are registered trademarks of FarWorks, Inc. Used with permission.

Introduction 1: Used by permission of John Grimes.

Chapter 1. 12: Used by permission of Mark Anderson. **15:** Used by permission of Clay Butler. Copyright © 1999 Clay Butler. **16:** Used by permission of Clay Butler. Copyright © 1999 Clay Butler. **17:** "Look at Your Fish" by Samuel H. Scudder. **17:** Used by permission of John Heine. **22:** My Pink Lady by Noam Manor. Used with permission of Noam Manor. **35:** "The Innocent Eye" by Dorr Bothwell from Dorr Bothwell and Marlys Mayfield, NOTAN: THE DARK LIGHT PRINCIPLE OF DESIGN, New York: Dover, 1991. Used with permission of Dorr Bothwell. **40:** "The Serpent of Paradise" by Edward Abbey. Reprinted by permission of Don Congdon Associates, Inc. Copyright © 1968 by Edward Abbey, renewed 1996 by Clarke Abbey.

Chapter 2. 44: Used by permission of Richard Guindon. **53:** Excerpt from Disturbing Peace, 1990, p.1, by Vaclav Havel. **53:** From "Through the Looking Glass" by Lewis Carroll. **55:** Barack Obama, Democratic Senator from Illinois, Dreams of My Father:

A Story of Race and Inheritance 2004, p. 11. **57, 66:** "A Tale of Murder, Insanity, and the Making of the Oxford Dictionary" from *The Professor and the Madman* by Simon Winchester, pp.xi–xiii. Copyright © 1998 by Simon Winchester. Reprinted by permission of HarperCollins Publishers Inc. **68:** "Saved" by Malcolm X from THE AUTOBI-OGRAPHY OF MALCOLM X by Malcolm X and Alex Haley. Copyright © 1964 by Alex Haley and Malcolm X. Copyright © 1965 by Alex Haley and Betty Shabazz. Reprinted by permission of Random House, Inc. **71:** "What Privacy Is and What It is Not" by Charles J. Sykes from THE END OF PRIVACY by Charles J. Sykes. Copyright © 1999 by the author and reprinted by permission of St. Martin's Press, LLC.

Chapter 3. 75: Copyright © Andy Singer. Used by permission of Andy Singer. "The Debt Explosion" by Elizabeth Warren and Amelia Warren Tyagi from THE TWO-INCOME TRAP by Elizabeth Warrend and Amelia Warren Tyagi. © 2003 by Elizabeth Warren and Amelia Warren Tyagi. Reprinted by permission of Basic Books, a member of Perseus Books, L.L.C. **99:** Excerpt from "What We Eat" by Eric Schlosser from FAST FOOD NATION by Eric Schlosser. Copyright © 2001 by Eric Schlosser. Reprinted by permission of Houghton Mifflin Company. All rights reserved.

Chapter 4. 105: Used by permission of Richard Guindon. **106:** top, Cartoon by John Heine. Used by permission of John Heine. Taken from A GOOD PLANET IS HARD TO FIND (Birmingham: Menasha Ridge Press, 1991) **106:** bottom, Cartoon by John Heine. Used by permission of John Heine. Taken from A GOOD PLANET IS HARD TO FIND (Birmingham: Menasha Ridge Press, 1991) **113:** Excerpt from Sir Arthur Conan Doyle, "The Adventure of the Speckled Band," 1892. Public domain. **123:** Doonesbury © 1985, G.B. Trudeau. Reprinted by permission of Universal Press Syndicate. All rights reserved. **125:** "Tougher Grading Better for Students." Reprinted With Permission. © 1995 San Francisco Chronicle. **130:** "Three Perceptives" from Idries Shah, THE CARAVAN OF DREAMS. New York: Penguin Books, 1972. Author and date of origin of "The Three Perspectives" unknown. Reprinted with permission of The Octagon Press Ltd, London. **132:** From Gina Berriault, "The Stone Boy," Mademoiselle, 1957. Copyright © 1957 by The Condé Nast Publications, Inc. Reprinted courtesy of Mademoiselle.

Chapter 5. 144: Used by permission of David Sipress. **145:** Used by permission of Richard Guindon. **147:** Copyright © 1997 Andrew B. Singer. Used by permission of Andrew B. Singer. **156:** Used by permission of Kirk Anderson. **168:** "Lateral and Vertical Thinking" by Edward de Bono from NEW THINK: THE USE OF LATERAL THINKING IN THE GENERATION OF NEW IDEAS by Edward de Bono Copyright © 1967 by Edward de Bono. Reprinted by permission of Basic Books, a member of Perseus Books, L.L.C. **171:** "Winterblossom Garden" by David Low. Copyright 1982 by David Low. Used with permission of David Low.

Chapter 6. 175: Used by permission of David Sipress. **187:** "Loss of Innocence" by James P. Steyer. Reprinted with the permission of Simon & Schuster Adult Publishing Group from THE OTHER PARENT by James P. Steyer. Copyright © 2002 by James P. Steyer. **189:** "A Modest Proposal" by Jonathan Swift.

Chapter 7. 195: Used by permission of David Cohen. **197:** Used by permission of David Sipress. **200:** Used by permission of John Grimes. **201, 204, 204, 205:** "Million Dollar Brutality" by Vicki Haddock. Copyright © San Francisco Chronicle. Reprinted by permission. **211:** "Prices Without Values" by Frank Ackerman and Lisa Heinzerling from PRICELESS, 2004. Copyright © 2004 PRICELESS by Frank Ackerman and Lisa Heinzerling. Reprinted by permission of The New Press. www.thenewpress.com. **213:** "Porn, Pervasive Presence: The Creepy Wallpaper of Our Lives" by William F. Buckley from 'The National Review' (Nov. 19, 2001). Copyright by National Review, Inc., 215 Lexington Ave. NY, 10016. Reprinted by permission.